This book contains ten literature surveys on important topics in Development Economics. They provide a review and synthesis of the current state of knowledge within each topic; highlight literature which has advanced understanding; and identify areas where current knowledge is lacking. Particular emphasis is given to theoretical and empirical controversies in the literature and each survey is accompanied by an extensive bibliography.

Contributors include economists from Britain, Canada, the US, and Sweden, who are already well-known and respected for their contributions to research on the topics reviewed. The surveys included cover Trade Theory and the Less Developed Countries; Trade Strategies and Industrialization in LDCs; Multinational Enterprises in LDCs; Poverty, Inequality and Development; Inflation and Stabilization Policy in LDCs; Technology Choice and Factor Proportions Problems in LDCs; The Labour Market and Human Capital in LDCs; Taxation and Development; Project Appraisal Techniques; and Agriculture and Economic Development.

The book is designed to complement development economics textbooks used in undergraduate and graduate courses in development economics and development studies. It should also provide a valuable reference source for researchers in the field, and for anyone interested in development economics.

Norman Gemmell is Lecturer in Economics at the University of Durham, specializing in development economics. He has published widely in leading academic journals on taxation issues and the role of public and service sectors in both developed and developing economies.

Surveys in Development
Economics

Surveys in Development Economics

Edited by
Norman Gemmell

Basil Blackwell

© Norman Gemmell 1987

First published 1987

Basil Blackwell Ltd
108 Cowley Road, Oxford, OX4 1JF, UK

Basil Blackwell Inc.
432 Park Avenue South, Suite 1503
New York, NY 10016, USA

British Library Cataloguing in Publication Data
Surveys in development economics.
  1. Developing countries—Economic conditions
  I. Gemmell, Norman
  330.9172'4   HC59.7
ISBN 0-631-14713-6

Library of Congress Cataloging in Publication Data
Surveys in development economics.
  Bibliography: p.
  1. Developing countries—Economic policy.
2. Developing countries—Commerce. 3. Developing
countries—Industries. 4. Economic development.
I. Gemmell, Norman.
HC59.7.S882 1987   338.9' 009172' 4   87-5164
ISBN 0-631-14713-6

Typeset in 10/11pt Plantin by DMB (Typesetting)
Abingdon, Oxfordshire.
Printed in Great Britain by TJ Press, Padstow

To Alastair and Mark

Contents

Contents

Contents

Contents

Contributors

Albert Berry is Professor of Economics at the University of Toronto, having previously taught at Yale University and worked for the Ford Foundation and the World Bank. He has published on labour markets, employment and unemployment in developing countries, with particular emphasis on Latin America. Other research interests include the economics of small-scale industry in developing countries; agriculture and the role of small farms; and income distribution and its determinants.

Arne Bigsten is Associate Professor of Economics at Gothenburg University, Sweden, and has been doing research on economic development for a number of years, particularly in East Africa. He has published on regional development, income distribution, labour markets and trade, including *Income Distribution and Development: Theory Evidence and Policy* (Heinemann, 1983) and *Education and Income Determination in Kenya* (Gower, 1984). He has also been a consultant to the UN, the World Bank and the ILO.

Henry J. Bruton has been Professor of Economics at Williams College since 1962. He taught previously at Yale University and has served as an economic consultant and visiting professor in a number of less developed countries. He has published books and articles on many aspects of economic development, including choice of technique, technical change, import substitution, and employment.

Mark Casson is Professor of Economics at the University of Reading. His recent publications include *Economic Theory of the Multinational Enterprise: Selected Papers* (with P. J. Buckley; Macmillan, 1985), *Multinationals and World Trade* (with associates; Allen and Unwin, 1986) and *The Firm and the Market: Studies on Multinational Enterprise and the Scope of the Firm* (Basil Blackwell and MIT, 1987).

Norman Gemmell is Lecturer in Economics at the University of Durham. His main research interests include the economics of taxation in developed and less developed countries, and structural change and development with special reference to middle eastern countries. He has published several articles on

Contributors

these topics and the recently published *Structural Change and Economic Development: The Role of the Service Sector* (Macmillan, 1986).

Subrata Ghatak is Senior Lecturer in Economics at the University of Leicester, having previously taught at the Universities of Guelph (Canada), Nottingham and Calcutta. He has published widely on the subject of agricultural development in poor countries including *Agriculture and Economic Development* (with K. Ingersent; Johns Hopkins and Wheatsheaf, 1984) and *Introduction to Development Economics* (Allen and Unwin, 1986). His other research interests include the role of money in economic development, technology transfer, and farm supply response in developing countries.

David Greenaway is Professor of International Economics at the University of Buckingham. He has been Visiting Professor at Lehigh University, Pennsylvania, the Graduate Institute of International Studies, Geneva, and he has been a consultant to the World Bank and UNIDO. He has published numerous articles and books on various aspects of international trade including *Economics of Intra-Industry Trade* (with C. R. Milner; Basil Blackwell, 1986) and *Current Issues in International Trade* (Macmillan, 1985).

Colin Kirkpatrick is Senior Lecturer in Economics at the University of Manchester. He has held visiting fellowships at the Institute of Development Studies, University of Sussex, the National University of Singapore, and the Research School of Pacific Studies, Australian National University. He has also acted as a consultant to various international organizations, including UNCTAD, FAO, ILO and ESCAP. He has published widely on trade and industrialization issues, including *Industrial Structure and Policy in Less Developed Countries* (with N. Lee and F. Nixson; Allen and Unwin, 1984), and *The Industrialization of Less Developed Countries* (with F. Nixson; Manchester University Press, 1983). His other research interests include international food security issues and the economies of Southeast Asia.

Chris Milner is Senior Lecturer in Economics at Loughborough University. He has been Visiting Professor at Vanderbilt University, Tennessee and a consultant to the World Bank and UNIDO. He has published books and articles on various aspects of international economics including *Economics of Intra-Industry Trade* (with D. Greenaway; Basil Blackwell, 1986) and *International Money and Political Economy* (Wheatsheaf, 1986).

Frederick Nixson is Senior Lecturer in Economics at the University of Manchester, having previously taught at Makerere University, Kampala, Uganda. He has published widely on the subject of economic development, including his recently published book *Economics of Change in Less Developed Countries* (with D. Colman; 2nd edition, Philip Allan, 1986). His main research interests include industrialization, economic integration and the role of foreign capital in the development process.

Ivy Papps is Lecturer in the Economics of the Middle East at the University of Durham, having previously taught at the University of Sussex and Chicago State University. She has published books and articles evaluating the role and performance of the public sector, and has taught cost–benefit anlaysis for many years. Her other research interests include the economics of pollution and the economics of the family.

Contributors

Robert Pearce is Senior Research Fellow in the Department of Economics at the University of Reading. He has published widely on the subject of international business, including the recently published book *The World's Largest Industrial Enterprises 1962–1983* (with J. H. Dunning; Gower, 1985). His current research interests include the industrial diversification of large firms and the decentralization of R&D by multinationals.

Preface

During the past eight years of teaching development economics to third-year undergraduates I have often lamented that many of the literature surveys available to students were either out of date or too narrowly focused to be of much assistance in a general development economics course. In addition many of these surveys occur in such diverse sources that they are often not readily accessible.

It is in an attempt to overcome these problems and provide a broad, up-to-date overview of central themes in development economics that the surveys in this book have been written. Each review seeks to highlight literature which has advanced our understanding of the relevant economic processes, as well as identifying where current knowledge is lacking or has been obscured by the existing literature. Where appropriate the surveys review both the relevant theoretical and empirical contributions, particularly empirical work which tests, or enables us to discriminate between, alternative theoretical approaches.

The book is designed to complement conventional textbooks used in final-year undergraduate or first-year graduate courses in development economics or development studies. It has generally been assumed that readers are already familiar (or can readily become familiar!) with intermediate macro- and micro-economics. Wherever possible mathematical presentation has been avoided, to make the surveys accessible to students with as wide a range of backgrounds as possible. It is hoped that, having sampled the surveys in this book, readers will not feel they have assimilated all the necessary literature on a given topic, but rather will be stimulated to pursue issues further in the primary sources. Development economics can be an exciting and challenging discipline, addressing, as it does, some of the most critical economic problems affecting millions of people.

Acknowledgments

As editor of this volume I am particularly grateful to the eleven contributors who were willing to fit into their busy research schedules a survey chapter which inevitably made heavy demands on their time. An excellent set of first drafts made my task relatively easy. I should also like to thank Sue Corbett of Blackwells for her perpetual enthusiasm for, and encouragement of, the enterprise. Much of the book was typed and retyped by Julie Bushby, Kathryn Cowton and Loraine Ord with their usual efficiency and good humour, despite my liberal offers to contributors to have alterations typed 'at this end'! The phrase 'thanks are due to my wife, without whose support . . .' appears in so many Acknowledgments that one wonders if it has become a tradition that husbands dare not dispense with! This is certainly not true here, where my thanks to Dorothy are in response to her continual interest in the book, and for the times when she put up with my editorial 'moanings'.

Finally I am grateful to Ehtisham Ahmad, Nick Stern and North-Holland publishers for permission to reproduce figure 8.3, in survey 8, from the *Journal of Public Economics* (1984); and to The Brookings Institution for permission to reproduce table 8.1, in survey 8, from Richard Goode, *Government Finance in Developing Countries*, 1984 (p. 91: table 4–2).

Norman Gemmell
Durham, September 1986

Introduction

Norman Gemmell

In the Introduction to the 1986 edition of their development economics textbook Colman and Nixson (1986, p. vi) suggest that

it is no exaggeration to state that development economics is at present going through a crisis. The recent spate of articles on the evolution and current state (and status) of development economics as a separate sub-discipline reflects the atmosphere of questioning and self-doubt amongst mainstream development economists . . . and, in part, is a reflection of both the growing influence of the neoclassical revival and the increasingly penetrating critiques of radical political economists'.

Used in its literal sense, to mean 'a turning point' or 'point of decision', the word 'crisis' is probably an appropriate term to describe the current state of development economics. The 'osmosis' of neoclassical analysis into development economics over the past decade or so represents something of a reversal of the traditional approaches to the subject which have tended to eschew 'market' analysis.

In one of the 'spate of articles' referred to above Sen (1983) suggests that 'the major strategic themes pursued ever since the beginning of the subject [were] (1) industrialization, (2) rapid capital accumulation, (3) mobilization of underemployed manpower, and (4) planning and an economically active state' (p. 746). In pursuing these issues neoclassical analysis was not thought to be very helpful, partly because some markets in LDCs were poorly developed, and partly because where they were developed and able to operate relatively freely, they were often perceived as hindering development objectives. The relative merits of the alternative approaches to economics in the context of less developed countries have been widely discussed in recent years and will not be reviewed here (but see Little, 1982, for a retrospective discussion of development theorizing). It does seem, however, that some of the justifiable criticisms of the, sometimes naive, applications of neoclassical analysis to certain problems in LDCs in recent years has led some development economists to reject neoclassical approaches *in toto*. Similarly it is clear that, in the early years of the subject, development economics (in common with other areas of economics) paid insufficient attention to the allocative role of prices and markets; so providing amunition for those whose predilections led them to reject any analysis with 'interventionist' implications.

Development economics would seem to have reached an important 'point of decision' in that, faced with apparently conflicting paradigms, the progress of future research will be advanced if development economists can identify the sources of differences in these paradigms and can establish where these differences represent genuinely inconsistent sets of assumptions or value-judgments, and where they represent differences in emphasis or differing views on the magnitude of certain important parameters. A failure to distinguish between the results of positive analysis and the role of normative considerations has bedevilled discussions of the merits of various paradigms. Thus, for example, 'neoclassical analysis' has been rejected by some because of a belief that market forces are inherently inegalitarian. Positive analyses of market forces are, however, necessary in order to identify what are their effects on certain variables which have normative importance. Whether particular markets do 'work' or are distorted in various ways (which may or may not affect their efficient operation) are important positive issues which are logically quite separate from questions concerning the *desirability* of how these markets operate. Unfortunately too many researchers, having undertaken positive analysis of some aspect of the workings of a particular economy, have jumped too readily to 'policy conclusions', without first assessing what legitimate and desirable policy objectives might be.

The surveys presented in this book are an attempt to stand back from the heat of the debate over the merits of this value-judgment or that; or the appropriateness of this or that assumption, in order to address the question: 'what have we learned in three to four decades of research on development economics?' It is hoped that, by identifying the scope, strengths and weaknesses of existing knowledge, future research and teaching of the subject will be facilitated and better directed. It is a characteristic of the social sciences that a review of the *accumulation* of empirical evidence from different sources or methodological approaches can reveal a consensus which is not apparent from the reading of individual contributions. Indeed, as a number of the surveys in this volume reveal, it is not infrequently the case that two opposing views, which are thought to stem from different theoretical positions, are shown through further research to result rather from different assumptions about the magnitude of one or more critical parameters. These differences are often, in principle, testable.

The topics of the ten surveys selected here are among those which are most important for development policy. They are grouped under five headings covering broad areas which have figured prominently in both theoretical and empirical debates within development economics. These are (i) *international* aspects of development – including trade theory and policy, and the role of multinational enterprises; (ii) *macroeconomic problems* – of income distribution and inflation; (iii) the operation of *factor markets* – for labour and technology; (iv) the role of the *public sector* – covering taxation and project appraisal; and (v) the importance of *rural development*.

In *survey 1* David Greenaway and Chris Milner examine trade theory and its relevance to LDCs' trade patterns. The literature on this subject is enormous and yet, ironically, it is not well treated, in general, in textbooks of development economics. These often address the policy debates and the role of trade in LDCs but rarely detail relevant theories for LDCs' trade or survey available evidence from tests of these theories. International economics texts, by contrast, typically cover theory and evidence in detail for developed countries, but offer only a cursory chapter or two on LDCs. The Greenaway and Milner survey therefore examines the various theories applicable to LDCs' trade at some length, outlining neoclassical, structuralist and Marxist approaches. They concentrate on positive theories of trade – labour productivity, two-factor, and specific-factor (neoclassical) models, product cycle theories, and so on – which seek to identify the source and distribution of the gains from trade among trading partners. Models of trade which have until recently been applied exclusively or mainly to developed countries – for example intra-industry trade, and product cycle, theories – are also examined in the context of LDC trade.

Testing trade theories is difficult because several share the same central predictions and their alternative assumptions may be difficult to verify. In addition it may not be possible to establish the validity of some theories conclusively because their subsidiary predictions are not all consistent with available evidence. Nevertheless, as Greenaway and Milner note, 'there are few unambiguously positive tests for each theory but there is invariably some support for the posited relationship'. This seems to apply, for example, to the more sophisticated versions of the Heckscher–Ohlin model, intra-industry trade theories and product cycle theories.

Finally, survey 1 considers the role of commercial policy and interventions in trade patterns. Various measures of protection are outlined and the merits of intervention are considered. One outcome worth stressing is that interventions – for example, in the form of tariffs – can be justified in a number of circumstances, though care must be exercised because of secondary effects. Thus an 'optimal' tariff for correcting trade distortions may not be optimal when other government objectives, such as raising tax revenues, are also considered.

Trade *policy* is the focus of *survey 2*, and here Colin Kirkpatrick discusses the relative merits of export oriented and import substituting strategies from alternative theoretical perspectives. Kirkpatrick's review clearly shows that preferences for different trade policies among the neoclassical, structuralist and radical schools result less from different theories of the causes and effects of trade on LDCs than from differences in the aspects of trade performance which they choose to emphasize. In fact, the positive aspects of each school's theoretical arguments are often *not* mutually exclusive, though they are frequently presented as such by their proponents. Thus, for example, neoclassical writers have focused on the distortionary effects resulting from the variable rates of effective protection associated with import-substitution policies in some LDCs. This is quite consistent with the analysis of the radical school that protection rates result from the interaction of domestic political and social elites with multinational corporations. Where the two schools would differ, no doubt, would be over *why* it may be desirable to remove these 'distortions' and *how* this might best be done. The conclusion of Williamson (1985), quoted by Kirkpatrick, is worth emphasizing here. He suggests that

the debate on markets, prices and macroeconomic management has been polarized between those who believe that prices do not matter and those who believe that all that is necessary to secure a correct price structure is to liberalize markets. But there is a third possible position, which is that prices are profoundly important but that markets cannot in general be trusted to set them (p. 47).

Survey 3, by Mark Casson and Robert Pearce, reviews the literature on the behaviour of multinationals in LDCs. This is an area of literature which has always been controversial, perhaps because much of the literature has a normative objective – to assess whether multinationals are beneficial for development in LDCs. In addition, as Casson and Pearce note, 'although a large amount of data has been collected on the operation of MNEs in LDCs, the interpretation of this data has proved extremely problematic'. Given the array of potential benefits and costs that MNEs bring with them to LDCs, and the complexity of their interactions with the host country, it is hardly surprising that unambiguous results of positive analysis have proved hard to obtain. For the same reason normative conclusions are likely to vary according to the emphasis placed on the various beneficial and detrimental effects identified with the MNE. One interesting conclusion to emerge from the survey is that 'several MNEs often enter an LDC industry almost simultaneously', which contrasts with the commonly held view that MNEs typically establish monopoly, or dominant market, positions for themselves at the point of entry.

Arne Bigsten, in *survey 4*, examines the critical issues of poverty and inequality in LDCs. This is an area of investigation where the methods of measurement chosen can be important for empirical outcomes, and the survey first considers these measurement problems. The failure of theories of income distribution to give unambiguous predictions concerning the effects of income inequality or redistribution on growth and vice-versa, leads to a particularly heavy reliance on empirical studies for guidance. Yet data on income distribution are notoriously poor in LDCs, and difficult to evaluate. However, after a comprehensive review of country studies of income distribution changes over time, Bigsten argues that over shorter periods of time there is no general tendency for distribution to either improve or worsen as per capita income rises. He also suggests that 'by now most countries seem to have reached a level of economic development at which the force of structural change . . . no longer affects equality so strongly'. Other factors can, however, be identified as potentially important for income distribution, and Bigsten identifies ten which *a priori* reasoning and initial empirical results suggest deserve closer attention if the determinants of inequality and poverty are to be better understood. Ultimately, however, the adoption of policies to tackle these economic and social determinants hinges on the political will to eradicate poverty, and this seems to be something over which economic advisors or even external governments are relatively powerless to change.

In their survey on inflation in LDCs, Colin Kirkpatrick and Frederick Nixson provide an interesting window onto the neoclassical versus 'traditional' debate within development economics, which in the inflation context has been labelled as 'monetarist versus structuralist'. Here it seems that improvements in empirical methodology – mainly econometric techniques – over the years has rendered many of the early results sterile. Nevertheless the debate continues over whether high inflation rates in many LDCs result primarily from excessive monetary expansion or structural rigidities, and a consensus could not yet be said to have emerged. However it is clear that some coming-together and mutual acceptance of opposing views has occurred in recent years as the force of empirical evidence has helped to refine these views and refute some arguments. In their concluding section Kirkpatrick and Nixson observe some movement towards consensus which is summed up by Seers (1981) thus: 'neither structuralist nor monetarist explanations are adequate by themselves and we need to draw on both to explain inflation. . . . In particular, monetary policy in itself will not eliminate inflationary pressures: it merely determines what its effects will be – price rises or social conflict, or some combination of the two' (p. 9).

Survey 6 concentrates on the operation of the labour market in LDCs and emphasizes the role played by education and training in that market. By surveying the 'evolution of theoretical ideas' Albert Berry identifies a number of research areas where empirical investigations have helped to refute early assumptions and reformulate others. The view that underutilization of labour is endemic in rural areas, for example, appears no longer to be valid; if indeed it ever was. Similarly, Berry suggests that the belief in the early 1970s that open urban unemployment was a large and increasing problem has been challenged in recent years. This has been associated with a simultaneous recognition that the informal sector in urban areas is not generally socially unproductive but can have an important role to play in urban employment generation. Berry's survey also identifies a number of gaps in existing knowledge which future research should aim to fill. He suggests that the development of general labour market models capable of incorporating the specific features of developed and less developed country labour markets would provide a more consistent framework of analysis. Secondly the nature of unemployment in LDCs needs more careful study if suitable analysis is to be applied. The nature of, and influences on, the so-called 'luxury unemployment' problem, for example, is not yet well understood.

Do developing countries have a choice of technology? If so, how should they choose? These are central questions addressed by Henry Bruton in *survey 7*. He suggests that they do indeed have a choice, but this is constrained in a number of ways. In particular Bruton suggests that the literature on technology choice has too often abstracted from information problems and assumed that LDCs could simply select their desired technology 'off the shelf'. He suggests that technologies are not 'given' but are 'found and learned'. Hence the acquiring of appropriate technology may take some time as techniques appropriate to a specific situation (in terms of employment effects, for example) are adapted and learned. This recent recognition that searching and learning are important for technology selection, Bruton argues, has helped to change the prevailing view that capital goods embodying technical progress should be imported. Rather it is increasingly advocated that LDCs should develop indigenous capital goods sectors which meet local needs and respond to specific, local, learning about the most appropriate technology.

The surveys in part IV are concerned with two aspects of the role of the public sector in LDCs. *Survey 8* focuses on taxation issues, reviewing the literature on the relationship between tax systems and development, and the impact of taxation on redistribution and growth. In each of these areas it seems that early misperceptions have been identified as such by subsequent research, but there are many areas where current knowledge remains inadequate as a basis for policy advice. Accumulating evidence in recent years on changes in individual countries' tax systems over time suggests that cross-sectional approximations of these changes, which are prominent in the literature, may be misleading. Similarly early views that LDC tax systems were generally regressive, but that tax policy could be used to raise an economy's growth rate, have been somewhat reversed in the past decade or so. Finally the recently applied normative analysis of 'tax reform' has provided a means of assessing the welfare effects of tax changes in LDCs. This literature is still at an early stage, but it does offer a promising way forward for investigations of the effects of tax systems on social welfare – an aspect which has been under-researched in the past.

Survey 9, by Ivy Papps, looks at techniques of project appraisal as they have been applied by governments and aid agencies to developing countries. This is an area of literature where debates have often concentrated on technical details and published results have been in diffuse and sometimes obscure sources. Perhaps as a result development economics textbooks have typically given this literature a cursory treatment, and Papps' survey therefore provides a particularly useful overview of this material. Following a brief introduction to the theoretical basis of cost–benefit analysis, the survey discusses problems identifying and measuring projects' costs and benefits. The review then concentrates on the methods of determining shadow prices and discount rates for project evaluation, of which the two most widely used and discussed are the Little–Mirrlees and UNIDO approaches. Although much discussion in the literature has concentrated on ways of measuring shadow prices in the two approaches, Papps' review suggests that 'the two sets of authors differ in the extent to which they believe that market prices will be a useful guide to shadow prices but this is really only a matter of judgement. The analytical procedures are essentially identical.' Two issues raised by the survey are worth stressing here. Firstly, the guidance offered by the alternative approaches to appraisal seems to be particularly lacking for projects where the bulk of the output is non-marketed, such as health and education projects. Yet these are prominent among government investment expenditures in LDCs. Secondly it is typically assumed that prices of inputs and outputs are unaffected by the introduction of a new project, and this poses problems when 'large' projects are being considered. The important point here is that some projects which appear small in terms of their contribution to GDP or total investment, for example, may nevertheless have significant impacts in the markets for particular inputs or outputs. Resulting price changes may need to be taken into account by appraisal exercises in these cases.

Finally, Subrata Ghatak reviews the literature on the role of agriculture in economic development in *survey 10*. In a wide-ranging review he argues that empirical evidence generally supports the view that farmers in LDCs do respond to price signals and do not react perversely to cost-reducing innovations. However farmers often operate in markets with high levels of uncertainty, and responses which appear irrational in a world of perfect information may turn out to be rational in the presence of uncertainty. This seems to have been the case with the arrival of the 'Green Revolution' in backward agriculture. Early studies suggested farmers were failing to respond to proven advantages of the new seeds which could significantly raise average crop yields. However, closer inspection has revealed the critical role played by associated inputs of fertilizer and water, the supply of which may be highly uncertain in some contexts. Thus a higher average yield is associated with a higher yield variance which can cause output to fall below critical minimum levels in some periods, so discouraging the adoption of new seed varieties.

Indeed the need to go beyond the presumption, and testing, of simple generalized relationships between, for example, farm size and productivity, or the Green Revolution and income distribution, is a recurring theme of Ghatak's survey. Rather the effects of agricultural policies or technical progress on the rural sector appear to be sensitive to a number of location-specific factors, suggesting that analysts must beware of generalizing from particular results.

REFERENCES

Colman, D. and Nixson, F. 1986. *Economics of Change in Less Developed Countries.* 2nd edition. Oxford: Philip Allan, and Totowa, NJ: Barnes and Noble.

Little, I. M. D. 1982. *Economic Development. Theory Policy and International Relations.* New York: Basic Books.

Sen, A. K. 1983. Development: Which way now? *Economic Journal*, 93, 745–62.

Seers, D. 1981. *Inflation. The Latin American Experience.* IDS Discussion Paper, DP 168.

Williamson, J. 1985. Macroeconomic strategies in South America. In E. Duran (ed.), *Latin America and the World Recession.* Cambridge: Cambridge University Press, in association with the Royal Institute of International Affairs.

PART I

International issues

1

Trade theory and the less developed countries

David Greenaway and Chris Milner

1.1 Introduction

With very few exceptions, all economies engage in international trade. The importance of international trade to a given economy can be measured relative to GNP. For instance one can measure 'openness' by the share of imports plus exports in GNP. The degree of openness varies from one economy to another. India, for example, is a relatively closed economy, with imports plus exports accounting for less than 10 per cent of GNP. By contrast, Singapore is a classic small open economy with exports plus imports accounting for in excess of 80 per cent of GNP.

The foreign trade sector provides a link between the domestic economy and the outside world. This link acts as a conduit whereby the impulses of economic activity can be transmitted from one economy to another. This conduit therefore creates a channel of interdependence between economies. Moreover, the more open the economy (in the sense defined above), the more sensitive is its welfare to economic activity elsewhere.

Over the post-war period as a whole world trade has grown faster than world output. In other words, countries have tended to become more open and more interdependent. This is no less true of less developed countries (LDCs) than developed market economies (DMEs). This being so, it is clearly important to understand the forces which stimulate international trade, and the effects of that trade on the economies concerned. It is to that end that the present survey is directed, and it is organized as follows. Section 1.2 is aimed at elaborating those theories of international trade which have been advanced to explain the trade of LDCs. The material is organized in a manner that serves to highlight not only the forces which generate trade, but also the relative gains from trade to the parties concerned. Section 1.3 evaluates the empirical literature relating to LDC trade flows. Both 'North-South' and 'South-South' trade flows are considered. In section 1.4 basic principles of the theory of commercial policy and intervention are discussed, and some attention is directed at the structure of protection in LDCs. This subject is developed further in survey 2. Finally, section 1.5 offers a summary and concluding comments.

1.2   Theories of international trade and development

1.2.1   The categorization of theory

Economists, when they discuss the role of international trade in the process of economic development, tend to adopt one of four general views. The first is a wholly optimistic view, or what Diaz-Alejandro in an earlier survey describes as 'the ultra-pro-trade-biased obiter dicta of the professional mainstream' (Diaz-Alejandro, 1975, p. 97). This establishes that the welfare of both (and by extension, all) countries which engage in trade is increased, even when trade is between developed and low-income countries. The second view is still very much part of the orthodoxy of trade theory, but is more cautious in its policy prescription. Models, embodying both traditional free trade assumptions and some market distortions, can generate results in which free trade is not necessarily the best policy available nor welfare-raising for both countries. As we shall see later, in these circumstances with the use of appropriate (even optimal) tools/instruments of government intervention, some trade can be made to be mutually beneficial. The third view is more radical and its origins more recent. The concern in this case (in its early manifestation at least) is more for empirical applicability or descriptive consistency rather than for the theoretical rigour associated with the more conservative orthodoxy. It seeks to describe the way in which differences in economic structure between countries bias the gains from trade in favour of the developed, industrialized economies and against the underdeveloped, non-industrialized economies. The fourth and final view is more recent and more dismal still. It asserts that trade and economic specialization have actually caused the polarization of the world into a developed core and an underdeveloped periphery.

Each of these types of views lends itself to the formulation of a set of policy recommendations. If trade makes all countries better off, then obviously all policy makers (including those in developing countries) should adopt liberal, open and 'outward-looking' policies in order to exploit their comparative advantage. Except in exceptional circumstances, the second view reaches similar conclusions about trade barriers. Where there are domestic market distortions the efficient operation of the market mechanism with 'correct' prices signalling the allocation of resources according to genuine comparative advantage, requires appropriate government intervention to correct for or remove the distortion at its source.

If, however, the distribution of gains from trade is biased against LDCs, policy makers should focus their efforts on changing the structures and institutions of the international economic order in a way that eliminates or reduces these biases. Finally, if trade causes underdevelopment at the periphery, those at the periphery should seek to increase barriers to trade until dependence on the core countries is eliminated.

Of course, one should not exaggerate the rigidity of this categorization of theories[1] and accompanying policy prescriptions. Optimal intervention analysis is capable, for instance, of generating fairly pessimistic conclusions about unrestricted trade, even within a neoclassical framework. Similarly structuralist and dependency theorists are sometimes seen as embracing shared policy prescriptions; certainly ones that go against the liberal orthodoxy. We can see this danger of rigid categorization also when we examine the classical theory of trade. As Myint (1958) argues, there has been a tendency to identify 'classical theory' with the comparative cost principles associated with Ricardo (see also Myint, 1977). But the 'vent for surplus' and 'productivity' doctrines of Adam Smith in the *Wealth of Nations* may be contrasted with comparative-costs theory.[2] The latter assumes that a country's resources are given and fully employed before entry into trade, and that there is a high elasticity of substitutability in production and consumption. By contrast 'vent for surplus' theory (Caves, 1965) assumes that entry into trade allows a country to bring into employment previously surplus productive capacity, which implies a lack of domestic substitutability. 'Vent for surplus' theory may be used therefore for pro- or anti-trade arguments, depending on the point of view adopted. The pro-trade argument, as used by Adam Smith, was that surplus capacity suitable for satisfying export markets allows a developing economy to acquire imports and expand domestic activity virtually 'costlessly'. The more modern anti-trade argument stemming from this 'model' is that entry into trade makes a sizeable element of productive capacity vulnerable to external disturbances, because it cannot be easily switched from export to domestic markets.

Despite these dangers of rigid categorization[3] we shall nevertheless use the four suggested views of trade and development in trade models to organize this section of the survey.

1.2.2 Models of symmetrically beneficial trade

Ricardian theory and factor productivity

Ricardian theory, in its original formulation, is based on the labour theory of value. Labour is considered to be the only means of production; value and output being determined by the labour content required in the production of each good. Given domestic factor mobility, international immobility of factors, constant unit costs in manufacturing and diminishing returns in agriculture (given a fixed supply of land) it is easy to demonstrate the comparative advantage principle of international exchange. The country with a lower ratio of the 'wage-fund' to the supply of land would have a comparative advantage in agricultural products, and hence export these in return for imports of manufactures under free trade conditions.

The development of the literature after Ricardo was directed at demonstrating that some of these conditions were not necessary, and that others could be generalized without any substantial change to the conclusion of the theory. Haberler (1936), for instance, demonstrated that the labour cost doctrine could be replaced by that of 'opportunity cost'. For the present purpose, however, we should not lose sight of two things. First, Ricardian trade theory isolates differences in technology or labour productivities as the basis for trade. This is clearly of relevance to any discussion about the composition of trade between developed and developing countries. Second, Ricardo himself constructed an implicit dynamic model of growth and trade. The gains from specialization according to comparative advantage are not simply those static welfare gains from trade but the 'gains from growth'. (For a dynamic Ricardian model of trade and growth, see Findlay, 1974 or 1984.) The Ricardo of the *Essay* (Ricardo, 1951, originally 1815) offers insights on growth and distributional issues lost in the simple/pure trade models – (for example, the redistribution from landowners to capitalists resulting from the repeal of the Corn Laws!). It is also of interest that in Findlay (1984) the secular tendency is for the terms of trade to move *in favour* of the exporter of primary products and against manufactures, contrary to the Prebisch–Singer thesis (see section 1.2.4). The model also indicates that trade reduces the rate of growth (compared with autarky) in the country exporting the agricultural product. The possibility of non-mutually beneficial trade is therefore raised in the context of Ricardian theory! It is the static principles of comparative advantage which link Ricardian trade models so directly to the Heckscher-Ohlin and specific factors models.

Neoclassical theory and factor proportions

While the Ricardian model isolates differences in the techniques of production (which would account for differences in absolute productivity between developed and developing countries) as the basis for specialization according to comparative advantage and for trade, the Heckscher–Ohlin (H–O) model focuses instead on differences between countries in their relative factor endowments and differences between commodities in the intensities with which they use these factors. Costs of production will differ therefore in general between countries (in autarky), even when each commodity is produced by the same technique in each country. On this reasoning, the capital-poor developing countries are 'recommended' by the H–O theorem to specialize in labour- or land-intensive products and export these in return for the capital-intensive products of the high-income/developed economies.[4] In its basic formulation it is supply side differences therefore that generate trade. Within this same framework, income (and therefore demand) differences between developed and developing countries could generate trade (in the absence of supply differences). Linder (1961) argues, however, that it is 'similarity of tastes' (and the resulting scope for exchanging the benefits of scale economies) which encourages trade in manufactures between industrialized countries. According to this view income and taste differences between developed and developing countries should not be a major source of growth in their two-way trade in manufactures.

The H–O model therefore provides an alternative explanation for the source and pattern of mutually beneficial trade, but one with explicit implications for internal income distribution. It is relatively easy to demonstrate the Stopler-Samuelson proposition that trade benefits the 'abundant' factor; the expectation being that labour is the abundant factor in most developing countries. This would appear to provide a basis for optimism in developing countries about the neoclassical perspective. But it must be remembered that domestic labour markets are often neither competitive nor efficient, and that trade restrictions benefit the 'scarce' factor (according to the Stopler–Samuelson proposition). The enthusiasm of many proponents of free trade regimes may well not be shared by policy makers in developing countries.

There is little doubt among academic economists that the H–O model is a rich theoretical tool capable of considerable generalization, extension and elaboration (see Ethier, 1984) especially in the form of open economy, growth models (for example Uzawa, 1961; Findlay, 1970). But in its simplest form – two goods, two factors and identical technology – its predictions are overwhelmingly rejected by the data (see section 1.3). Indeed its presentation in this form and simple predictions lead many economists to question its generality and its policy implications (Diaz-Alejandro, 1975; Bhagwati and Srinivasan, 1979). The gains from trade in this context are (comparative) static ones of specialization and exchange gained from efficient resource allocation. The H–O model can give little direct guidance in itself as to dynamic efficiencies. Such dynamic issues would seem of crucial interest in any discussion of the role of trade in development. Open economy growth models of a neoclassical vintage allow us to examine the effects of 'exogenous' parameters (such as rates of population growth and saving) on growth and trade patterns, but not to establish the effects of trade on factor accumulation and growth/development. This is an empirical issue. One can hypothesize on *a priori* grounds, for instance, that freer trade increases capital formation through increased domestic saving and capital inflows (Bhagwati, 1978), discourages complacency and improves the quality of entrepreneurship (Keesing, 1967), and enhances the possibility of scale benefits from enlarged markets (Krueger, 1978). Alternatively, one can hypothesize in Schumpeterian fashion that the 'animal spirits' of entrepreneurs are such that protected markets encourage innovation. The empirical evidence is not conclusive in either direction. This inconclusiveness, however, does not invalidate neoclassical theory or policy prescription – indeed some would aggressively defend the role of neoclassical economics in analysing dynamic processes in developing countries (Lall, 1983; see also Milner, 1987). We are in any case able to revise the basic model so as to improve its 'realism' without significantly revising general policy results.

The specific factor model

Trade theory has recently witnessed an interest in models which weaken the assumption of comprehensive intersectoral factor mobility (Jones, 1971; Neary, 1978; Samuelson, 1971). In its simplest form the model differs from the basic H–O model in only one respect: only one factor is assumed to be intersectorally mobile. Despite this, the properties and dynamic adjustment paths of the two models contrast sharply. The specific factor model, for instance, is ambiguous on the Stopler–Samuelson question of the effect of trade on real wages. The factor-price equalization theorem is also weakened in the context of specific factor models. Similarly the pattern of trade can no longer be inferred from a knowledge of factor endowments and intensities alone. Relative supply elasticities and elasticities of substitution now play a role. Conclusions about the role of factor endowments, for instance, can now only be drawn on a *ceteris paribus* basis – for instance the country with the greater endowment of the factor specific to industry *i* will, *ceteris paribus*, have a production bias towards *i*'s output, and hence will be more likely to export it. (The determinants of comparative advantage in specific factor models have been examined more fully by Amano (1977) and Dixit and Norman, 1979.)

Given the pattern of factor rewards in the move from autarky to free trade predicted by specific factor models, there are strong incentives for market forces to reduce, over time, the barriers which induce factor specificity. It may be appropriate therefore to interpret the specific factor model as the short-run equilibrium of the H–O model – over the medium term the economy's factor endowments are fixed but become perfectly mobile between sectors. Policy recommendations therefore are still neoclassical in flavour – any interventions should be aimed at the source of the distortion; in this case at the barriers which create factor specificity. This is just one of a range of modified cases for free trade, based on Paretian welfare economics and the principle of optimal intervention.

1.2.3 Orthodoxy modified or revised

Optimal intervention analysis is discussed in some depth in section 1.4. Suffice it to say at this stage that liberal welfare economics demonstrates that free trade is Pareto-optimal if markets are competitive and 'distortion'-free, and that interventions to correct for distortions are more efficacious the closer they are to the sources of the distortion. There are some instances affecting developing countries where we might wish to examine this argument in some depth. The infant-industry argument is examined in this context in section 1.4. We will focus here on some other cases.

'Immiserizing growth'

There are several striking results in which growth in an open economy could be 'immiserizing' or welfare-lowering. Bhagwati (1958) identifies the sufficiency condition for increased output turning the terms of trade against the growing country, such that the terms of trade loss more than offsets the positive production and consumption effects of trade expansion. At constant relative prices the outward movement of the production possibility frontier increases the excess supply of exportables and excess demand for importables, and this will move the terms of trade against the growing country if the country is large enough to influence its own terms of trade. An alternative type of 'immiserizing' growth was identified by Johnson (1967). In this case the terms of trade are fixed, but some trade intervention causes over-production of the importable and under-production of the exportable, in a two-sector, two-factor open economy. Johnson shows that growth under certain conditions may be welfare-reducing, if the output of the exportable (importable) is further reduced (increased) at constant relative domestic prices.

Brecher and Diaz-Alejandro (1977) show that in the Johnson case (and Brecher and Choudhri (1982a) show that in the Bhagwati case), to turn from the *possibility* of immiserization to a *necessity* the source of growth must be foreign investment. But as Bhagwati (1971) demonstrates, immiserization is due in both cases to distortions and the failure to equalize domestic and foreign rates of transformation – the presence of a trade intervention in the small economy case and the absence of an optimal tariff in the large country or terms of trade case. However applicable, or not, the conditions required for 'immiserization' may be, they do not constitute in themselves a major attack on liberal policy prescriptions for developing countries.

Recent models of intra-industry trade

The traditional models of trade thus far surveyed invariably adopt a technology which exhibits constant returns to scale, homogeneous products and, as a result, a competitive framework. Interest in the empirical phenomenon of intra-industry trade – observed two-way trade often in differentiated products within the same industry – has recently generated a large theoretical literature on models of trade in differentiated goods under imperfectly competitive conditions (Greenaway and Milner, 1986a; Kierzkowski, 1984). While intra-industry trade is predominantly observed among high-income countries, it appears to be of growing importance in the trade of developing countries, especially in their trade in manufactured goods (Balassa, 1979a).

Many of the new models provide an alternative basis to trade than initial differences in factor endowments. Again it can be mutually beneficial trade. There are the usual possible gains from exchange and specialization, but these may incorporate additional gains associated with the widening of choice via increased variety or with the reaping of dynamic benefits from scale economies permitted by enlarged markets. (The nature and extent of these gains depends crucially on the structural characteristics of the specific model used.) Although increased variety and consumer choice may not be an important consideration in many developing countries (and indeed some have suggested that it may be socially undesirable; see James and Stewart, 1981), and although relative endowments and country size factors may restrict intra-industry trade in manufactured trade of a 'North–South' nature, this ability to 'exchange' the benefits of scale may be of increasing importance in non-H–O type trade of a 'South–South' nature.

The case for the possible modification of free trade arguments has been enhanced by these recent contributions to trade theory. The proliferation of models of what are essentially 'second-best' conditions has fuelled the policy debate. More cases for intervention have been identified, and some for optimal unilateral intervention by means of a tariff even in the small country case. (For a review of the literature, see Greenaway, 1985; and Venables, 1985.) Much of the analysis is 'special case' in nature, and few general policy conclusions follow. The possibilities for 'rent snatching' or for scale benefits from import substitution are in many cases likely to be limited in most developing countries. Retaliation, also, is as ever an issue, since with retaliation tariffs are invariably welfare-lowering.

1.2.4 Models of structurally biased trade and asymmetrical development

The initial set of structural hypotheses was formulated in the 1950s and 1960s by, among others, Lewis (1954), Myrdal (1957) and Nurkse (1962). (For a review of the origins of structuralism see Arndt, 1985.) It must be seen at the outset in particular as a reaction to the neoclassical paradigm, the belief in flexible market mechanisms, and a rejection of the 'engine of growth' view of trade. It also must be viewed as a reaction to the neat theoretical elegance of neoclassical marginalism/optimization. It tended therefore to eschew the use of formal modelling. We can, however, group these contributions to the trade and development literature under various headings: terms of trade pessimism, 'two-gap' models, technology-gap models and dualistic models.

Terms of trade pessimism

The best-known exponents of the view that the gains from trade are biased against low-income countries are Prebisch (1950, 1959) and Singer (1950, 1974). They argued that the bias expresses itself through a secular decline in the terms of trade of primary producers (crudely identified as LDCs) vis-à-vis those of manufactured-good producers, resulting in a long-term transfer of income from developing to developed countries. Technological progress, which raises the productivity of primary producers' export industries, generates no benefit (where domestic consumption is insignificant) since the purchasing power in terms of importables declines. On the demand side the lower income elasticity of demand for primary products than for manufactured goods (due to Engel's law), is seen as imposing lower growth on developing than developed economies, or an inherent tendency on the part of LDCs to payments deficits, currency depreciation and terms of trade deterioration.

Labour in LDCs, also because of the additional pressure of population growth, is not able to take out productivity gains in the form of higher wages, in the face of the falling relative price of exportables. The 'Prebisch–Singer' thesis lends itself to the policy recommendation, that the protection of LDCs' manufacturing industry will raise wages in all sectors and prevent over-expansion of the primary export sector.

The secular decline is not well established empirically, (see Sapsford, 1985; Spraos, 1980). The arguments, however, that there is consistent asymmetry between developed and developing countries about how the productivity gains from technical change are diffused, are unconvincing on theoretical grounds.

The possible equilibrating forces that might arrest secular decline in the terms of trade are neglected. (For a detailed analysis and critique of the Prebisch–Singer thesis, and of the related Lewis model (Lewis, 1954, 1969), see Findlay, 1981). What remains of the thesis is an identification of a possible production distortion resulting from an 'imperfect' or partially monetarized labour market. This, as our earlier discussion of optimal intervention analysis shows, may provide a rationale for intervention (but not necessarily for a tariff) rather than a decisive critique of outward-looking trade policies.

Two-gap models

The structuralist concept of development, characterized as it is by rigidities that limit economic adjustments, seeks to emphasize the key constraints on growth in a developing country. Attempts to formalize this concept in the light of the experience of many LDCs into the 1960s – an experience of limited capital accumulation apparently constrained by limited domestic savings capabilities and foreign exchange shortages – started with relatively simple 'two-gap' models (Chenery and Bruno, 1962; Chenery and Strout, 1966; McKinnon, 1964).

In their early formulation the models tended to lack theoretical precision. Nevertheless they excited considerable academic interest and practical appeal during the 1960s and early 1970s, underpinning as they did the widely recommended and implemented import substitution policies in LDCs at that time. The theoretical formalization of the two-gap approach (see Findlay, 1971, 1973), requires the application of Harod–Domar-type assumptions to an open economy in which growth is constrained by the domestic savings rate. If there is a technologically fixed ratio of imports to output, or of imports to investment, then an economy cannot substitute domestic resources for imports as output expands.

Alternatively if an economy faces a fixed growth rate for its exports, then the economy can face a foreign exchange constraint even though domestic saving has released resources for exports. If the savings shortage is greater than the foreign exchange shortage (*ex-ante*), investment adjusts towards savings at a lower level of output (*ex post*) that is, output is *investment-constrained*. Alternatively if the relative sizes of the *ex ante* shortages are reversed (*ex-ante*), output is *trade-constrained* as the *ex-post* adjustments to saving and imports take place.

This analysis and the resulting policy prescription depends crucially, therefore, on the developing country's inability to translate increased savings into the foreign exchange necessary to sustain the required level of investment, and upon its inability to implement measures which induce import saving or export promotion (for a given level of protection and foreign assistance). The neglect of relative prices implied by these structural assumptions of low elasticities of substitution in production and consumption, plus the assumption of exogenously given growth rates for exports and some tendency to confusion of *ex-ante/ex-post* relationships, generated considerable criticism of structural models, even as they were providing the intellectual rationale for import substitution strategies during the 1960s. The export performance of some developing countries in particular of course weakened the appeal of pessimistic assumptions about export possibilities, but it does not totally negate the appeal of structuralist thinking. There is scope for modelling non-zero and non-infinite substitution possibilities, and thereby for achieving some convergence of neoclassical and structuralist thinking (see survey 2). The bulk of the structuralist literature since the 1960s, however, avoids model comparisons or synthesis, and concentrates on questioning the generality or applicability of neoclassical theorizing. Stewart (1977), for instance, addresses the issue of non-static technology and asymmetrical access to it, while Helleiner (1981a, b) examines the implications for international trade of a range of 'imperfections' in international markets.

Technology gap and product cycle theory

Although not a natural member of any of the categories used in this survey, we include 'technology gap' (Posner, 1961) and 'product cycle' (Vernon, 1966) theories of trade at this point as another strand of structuralist analysis. We might view such theory as a relation of neoclassical orthodoxy, where the patterns of dynamic comparative advantage between developed and developing countries change as factor (including technological) endowments change with the international transmission of technology. But these models again lack the formal elegance and precision of neoclassical theory. They also contrast with neoclassical theory in terms of their view of the world. Knowledge is no longer a free good which is instantaneously transmitted between countries. Scale, ignorance and uncertainty play a role in determining trade patterns.

This type of approach also presumes the existence of asymmetries between developed and developing countries in the structure of technology and likely gains from trade. (For a survey of dynamic models of technological transfer, see Pugel, 1981.)

These models focus therefore on the endogenous[5] factors which will encourage continuous product or process innovation in the developed countries, and a resulting technological lead of these countries over developing countries. Trade patterns are determined in manufactures in particular, by the vintages of products. The developed North has an advantage in producing and exporting new products, while the developing South has a comparative advantage in producing standardized or mature products and exporting them to the North. Unlike some structuralist analysis there is an identifiable basis for a developing country's comparative advantage to lie in manufactured rather than primary products. But like other structuralist analysis it offers an alternative possible source of structurally biased gains from trade, since the monopoly advantage of the North in 'new' products may permit returns not possible on standardized or 'old' products. This is a plausible but not necessarily widespread source of bias, if there are limited markets for 'new' products in the low income South. (In terms of the Linder type thesis (Linder, 1961) the dissimilarity of taste or demand conditions between developed and developing countries acts as a constraint on the exchange of products of different vintages between North and South. Although we might by similar reasoning anticipate the encouragement of South-South exchanges of different, standardized manufactures.)

Dualism and North–South models

The fact that the global economic system is characterised by asymmetries in the structures and performance of the economies in the North and in the South does not make the neoclassical explanation of the genesis of trade irrelevant; nor does it necessarily result in biased gains from trade and a rationale for inward-looking policies on the part of the South (collectively or individually). We have encountered already in this section types or aspects of 'dualism'; for example, Prebisch's views on the asymmetries in the operation of product and factor markets that may induce secular decline in the South's terms of trade. This is a representation of internal dualism which induces pessimism towards the terms of trade. There are other aspects of internal dualism which generate alternative views. Open dual-economy models (for instance, Dixit, 1969; Fei and Ranis, 1964; Paauw and Fei, 1973) are concerned with policy problems where there is a 'modern' capitalist sector (or one controlled by a planning authority), while the 'traditional' sector comprises small independent peasant producers. These models are in effect 'opening-up' the Lewis-type model of development in the presence of surplus labour (in the traditional sector) and fixed real wages. As Findlay (1984) shows, the growth rate of a small open dual economy will vary inversely with the real wage, directly with the propensity to save out of profit ('thrift') and production efficiency ('productivity'). The classical forces of thrift and productivity can induce 'export-led growth'. A single, small open economy should (in this context) 'find' its comparative advantage in some appropriate, labour-intensive activity which, with access to modern technology (perhaps via multinational corporations) and with (initially at least) low real wages, will generate high profit rates and the potential for capital accumulation.

There is of course a potential problem of composition – the export possibilities for LDCs as a whole may be constrained by external factors which are best modelled by other North–South models. There is also, however, a potential 'fallacy of decomposition' – an individual LDC should not rule out an 'outward-looking' strategy on the grounds that the terms of trade may deteriorate if all LDCs pursue the same strategy. This needs to be borne in mind when evaluating the policy implications of North–South models (for example, Chichilnisky, 1981; Krugman, 1982). Krugman, for instance, provides a model of 'uneven development' – initially higher endowments of capital in the North induce greater (external) economies in its manufacturing output and high profit rates. In classical terms this permits higher growth through further capital accumulation, and cumulative competitive advantage over the lagging South.

The basis for pessimism on the part of the South is intensified if we allow for capital mobility internationally and therefore for capital exports from the South.

1.2.5 Radical perspectives and models of trade-induced polarization

The structuralist analysis of biased or asymmetrical interdependence seeks to provide a piecemeal critique of neoclassical orthodoxy and a rationale for institutional reforms and policy interventions to influence trade relationships between developed and developing countries. More radical analyses are concerned with the fundamental relationships involved between core (developed) and peripheral (underdeveloped) countries in a global capitalist system.

Unequal exchange

In what might be described as a neo-Marxist contribution to trade theory, Emmanuel (1972) elaborates the concept of 'unequal exchange' – that is, in exchange for goods worth a day of its own labour, the South receives goods worth less than a day's labour in the North. This is clearly an idea that can be identified in other contributions such as the Prebisch–Singer thesis (see Bacha, 1978). Given international capital mobility which equalizes profit rates and an exogenous real wage rate differential, then 'unequal exchange' can only be prevented if real wages in South and North remain equal.[6] This presumably requires either a constraint on productivity growth advantage in the North or on real wage increase in the North, or a mechanism for sharing the benefits of differential productivity increase equally between workers in the North and South.

There is some ambiguity in the definition of unequal exchange being employed here by Emmanuel (see Findlay, 1984), but the concept does raise the issue of international income distribution. International distributive justice is explored by Little (1978) and Sen (1981). They do not (unsurprisingly), identify any generally acceptable theory of justice, but do identify factors which can give rise to a claim to income on moral grounds. Findlay (1982) argues, however, that simply raising wages in the South to improve the terms of trade will not help if the North's demands for the South's goods are price-elastic and employment in the South falls. He presents labour migration as the only economically viable mechanism for achieving real wage adjustments – but that is unlikely to be an acceptable Marxian policy prescription!

Marxist and dependency analysis

The Marxist policy prescription for developing countries is that only a radical break on the part of developing countries with the global capitalist system will permit genuine development.

Marxist 'universal' theory views world capitalism in terms of the 'centre' and the 'periphery', and the development process as a dialectical one. Capitalism at the centre developed on an internal dynamism of its own which is absent at the periphery – the periphery is complementary to, and dominated by, the centre (Amin, 1976). The development process therefore cannot be a gradual, steady movement towards equilibrium; it is rather a process typified by imbalances and social conflicts (Gurley, 1979).

The language and methodology of Marxist analysis is in fact unfamiliar to neoclassical orthodoxy, and often appears to lack precision and rigour (see Smith, 1980). Amin's polarization thesis for instance (Amin, 1977) is based on a quite reasonable premise that international capital mobility and labour immobility tend to induce international equality of profit rates and international inequality of wages respectively. But given productivity differentials the inference drawn is that 'value' is transferred from peripheral countries to the centre. There are clearly difficulties about the use of the value-form and about translating values into prices which undermine the Marxist proposition that there is unequal exchange because the wage differentials between centre and periphery are larger than the productivity differentials.

Nonetheless, the Marxist perspective has spawned a large literature on dependency theory,[7] in particular on the development of Latin America. Baran (1957 and 1973) and Frank (1967 and 1972) continue the central line of Marxist thought regarding the contradictory needs of 'imperialism' and of the development of the backward nations. (For a review of this work, see Little, 1982; and Palma, 1978.) Within the dependency school, different meanings are accorded to the concept of 'dependency' and different analyses are offered to explain underdevelopment resulting from the interplay between internal and external structures. 'Orthodox economists' tend, however, to be critical of the 'universality' of the approach. Lall (1975) argues, for instance, that the characteristics of the 'dependent' countries, to which underdevelopment is ascribed, are not unique to these economies. The conceptual schema is therefore defective, he argues, and runs into problems of circular reasoning – less developed countries are poor because they are dependent and the characteristics of poverty signify dependence. (These and related issues are explored in Milner, 1987.)

1.2.6 Summary

There is therefore a rich array of trade theories and models of trade and development from which we might choose, in explaining the trade and prospects for trade of developing countries among themselves (South–South trade) and with developed countries (North–South trade), as well as to analyse the effects/desirability of trade (of a particular composition and direction) for individual developing countries and for developing countries as a whole. We may select between these theories according to 'belief' and purpose. Our selection will also be influenced, however, by the empirical evidence on the trade flows of LDCs. It is to this topic that we now turn.

1.3 Empirical evidence on trade flows and LDCs

1.3.1 The changing pattern of comparative advantage

Most trade models explain the commodity pattern and direction of trade in terms of comparative advantage. Countries tend to export those goods which have the lowest relative prices under autarky. Particular models focus in turn on particular factors that determine autarkic costs and prices. Later in this section we will examine the evidence on empirical tests of particular models, firstly in the context of North–South trade[8] and subsequently in the context of South–South trade. Before doing so it may be helpful to describe the role LDCs play in world trade, and briefly to outline the main changes that have occurred in recent decades in the global pattern of comparative advantage.

The structure of world trade has in fact changed considerably over the past few decades. In aggregate the developing countries' share of world trade has remained relatively stable over the past three decades – in 1955 it was 26 per cent of world exports, while in 1985 it was 24 per cent (see Sampson, 1986). This aggregate picture, however, masks the fact that individual LDCs and groups of developing countries have fared very differently. The share of the major oil exporters, for example, has increased sharply. Similarly the group of fast-growing exporters of manufactured goods or newly industrializing countries (NICs) have doubled their share of world exports between 1970 and 1985. For the bulk of developing countries who depend upon commodity exports for the majority of their export earnings, however, their share in world exports has consistently declined from about 12 per cent in 1955 to about 6 per cent in 1985. In fact developing country manufacturing exports to the industrial countries are now more important than all non-energy commodity exports combined – clothing, engineering and textile products accounting for nearly half of these manufactured exports (see table 1.1).

This changing pattern of comparative advantage gives some empirical credence to Balassa's *stages* approach to comparative advantage (Balassa, 1979b), according to which, the structure of exports changes in line with the accumu-

Table 1.1   Product composition of LDC trade

(a) *Share of merchandise exports of LDCs to all destinations*

	Fuels, minerals and metals		Other primary products		Manufactures	
	1965	1982	1965	1982	1965	1982
Low income economies	11	20	65	30	24	50
Lower middle income economies	26	47	66	34	8	19
Upper middle income economies	41	34	38	17	20	49
High income oil exporters	98	96	1	0	1	3

Note: Low income economies are classed as those with a 1983 income per capita of $300 or less. Lower middle income economies have a per capita income in the range $401 to $1500, and upper middle income economies a per capita income in excess of $1500.

Source: World Development Report, 1985, table 10.

(b) *Product composition of South-South trade*

	Fuels, minerals and metals	Other primary products	Manufactures
1962	78	17	5
1972	76	13	11
1982	55	18	27

Source: Adapted from Newson and Wall (1985), table 3.

lation of physical and human capital. The changes are, however, restricted to a small number of developing countries. Taiwan, South Korea and Hong Kong account now for almost half the manufactured exports to developed market economies, and eight countries in total account for about 80 per cent of developing countries' exports of manufactured goods. But these exports are not only of a North–South nature. In the period 1973–83 developing country exports to other (non-oil exporting) developing countries grew more rapidly than those to developed countries. Factor productivity, factor endowments, technological or other factors may therefore be relevant in explaining the pattern of comparative advantage (and its changes) on a North–South and South–South basis. Before reviewing the empirical evidence on such possible 'sources' of comparative advantage in the context of each type of trade, we ought to comment briefly on the problems of testing trade theories.

1.3.2 Methodological problems

Given the complexities of the real world it is difficult to formulate rigorous tests of simple models. Consider for example the theory of comparative advantage; that is, countries tend to export those goods which have lowest relative costs and therefore prices under autarky. Autarkic conditions, however, are invariably not observable. The theory also predicts only the direction, and not the volume, of trade and therefore trade volumes need not be deterministically related to relative prices nor to the country characteristics which determine relative prices. Nevertheless, the temptation is to use such imperfect information. Balassa (1965), for instance, uses relative export performance as indices of 'revealed' comparative advantage[9] (much empirical work also regresses trade volumes against country characteristics, without theoretical justification).

Fortunately, however, we are not required to test the theory of comparative advantage directly in order to test our trade theories of the commodity composition of trade. These theories of trade explain comparative advantage itself in terms of other factors that *may* be observable. In the case of the Ricardian model comparative advantage is attributed entirely to inter-country differences in labour productivity; that is, relative labour costs of production. But if the labour requirements of the importable in the importing country are observable, then there must be (contrary to the simple models) incomplete specialization. We should therefore allow in our test for some factor, such as transport costs, which may account for incomplete specialization. This has tended not to be done. Indeed, for further simplicity comparisons of labour requirements (starting with MacDougall, 1951, 1952) have been restricted to two countries, and their exports to third markets (since bilateral trade between any pair of countries is relatively small).[10]

Thus we may have strong empirical verification (and in fact do have) of a valid relationship, identifiable from the Ricardian model, but do not necessarily have a valid test. Falvey (1981a) has established that other trade models are likely to predict the same relationship between labour productivities and trade as derived from the Ricardian model. Deardorff (1984) also argues that the same relationship will hold in the Heckscher–Ohlin (H–O) model, if factor abundance and relative labour productivity are positively related. In the case of the H–O theorem (which states that a country will tend to export those goods which use relatively intensively that country's relatively abundant factor), we have tended to obtain by contrast empirical rejection of the model, for a test which is also invalid.

A proper test of the (commodity version) H–O theorem would involve the relationship between factor abundance, factor intensities and trade. The classic H–O test, however, (dating from Leontief, 1953) has applied a test to a 'factor content' version of the theorem (Vanek, 1968); countries tend to export the services of their (assumed) abundant factor, embodied as factor content in the goods they trade. We must recognize the limitations of the empirical methodology employed[11] (such as the exclusion of human capital, labour skill, natural resource considerations), and the possibility that the result could be consistent with the theorem given a relaxation of specific assumptions such as balanced trade. Nevertheless the persistence of the results that contradicted the model for the 1970s and for some subsequent years (see Brecher and Choudri, 1982b) has cast much doubt over the validity of the H–O model. More recently, however, we have witnessed attempts (Harkness, 1978) to define factors more finely and to correlate factor intensities with cross-country information on factor endowments. This methodology has been rigorously applied by Leamer (1984), who finds empirical support for the H–O theorem.

Conscious therefore of the dangers of interpreting the available empirical evidence as actually testing general trade theories (such as Ricardian or neoclassical theory) or specific models (for example, neo-technology or intra-industry models) which have proliferated more recently, we will turn to the evidence relating to the trade flows of LDCs. At a minimum it will be useful in describing the determinants of trade. (For a fuller discussion of methodological problems in this area, see Bowden, 1983 and Deardorff, 1984.)

1.3.3 Empirical evidence on North–South trade

More comprehensive surveys of empirical evidence (relating to all types of trade flows) on the testing of trade theories can be found in Deardorff, 1984; Leamer,

1984; Stern, 1975; and Tharakan, 1985.[12] The aim in this section will be to summarize the results of empirical work on North–South trade.

Multiple determinants?

Thus far we have examined trade theories and their empirical testing separately. It may be that trade patterns are simultaneously influenced by several factors. This is certainly the type of conclusion reached by some empirical researchers. Hufbauer (1970), for instance sought to identify the characteristics embodied in the exports of 24 developed and developing countries for the year 1965. Rank correlation methods were used to relate export characteristics (for example capital, human capital, skill, wage differential, product differentiation, scale economy, technological characteristics) to various national attributes (factor endowment, stage of development, technological sophistication, etc.). Despite measurement limitations he identified remarkably strong correlationships and consistent ordering of country rankings. The commodity composition of developed and developing countries' exports does appear to reflect national attributes. This and other evidence (for example Leamer, 1974) suggests at least, therefore, that actual trade patterns are 'explained' by an amalgam of theories. It is an impression that is also reinforced from a review of the evidence on specific theories. There are few unambiguously positive tests for each theory, but there is invariably some support for the posited relationship.

Labour productivity

Despite the dubious nature of the indirect test for exports to a third market (referred to in section 1.3.2) invariably used to test the Ricardian model and criticized severely on theoretical grounds by Bhagwati (1964), there is a body of evidence on trade (including North–South trade) that turns out to be highly supportive of the Ricardian model. The first serious attempt to test empirically this classical theory was made by MacDougall (1951, 1952). He focused on exports by the US and UK to third markets (in 1937) and examined whether that trade could be explained in terms of the two countries' relative labour requirements. He identified a clear tendency for each country to capture a larger share of the export markets as labour requirements fell (productivity increased). A similar, significantly positive, correlation between export shares and labour productivities has been identified in subsequent studies (Balassa, 1963; MacDougall *et al.*, 1962; Stern, 1962). Although there is contradictory evidence for direct testing of bilateral flows and alternative productivity measures, (Agarwal, Askari and Corson, 1975) this was for intra-EEC trade, not North–South trade. We would anticipate, however, that productivity differences are more marked on a North–South than on a North–North basis, and that therefore Ricardian theory would potentially be more relevant in explaining some trade flows of a North–South nature.

Factor endowments

Ironically, the H–O or factor proportions theory of trade has been theoretically dominant but (apparently) empirically fragile – apparent 'paradoxes' have been identified in several studies since Leontief's classic study – for example, Baldwin, 1971; Mitchell, 1975; Stern and Maskus, 1981), These studies tend, however, to concentrate on US multilateral trade. The scope for H–O trade would appear to be greater in the specific context of North–South trade, especially where endowment differences of a natural resource, and human capital nature, are also allowed for. This appears to be borne out in several empirical studies. Bhagwati and Bharadwaj (1967) found that India's exports were relatively labour-intensive when human and physical capital were combined. Fels (1972) found that (industry) physical and human capital per employee were more highly (positively) correlated with West Germany's trade balance with LDCs than with other industrialized countries. Lowinger (1971) and Tyler (1972) concluded that Brazil's net imports of manufactures were human capital-intensive. Tharakan and Vandoorne (1979) found that natural resource requirements were significantly and negatively correlated with Belgium's export/import ratios with developing countries. Cable and Rebelo (1980) show that UK competitiveness vis-à-vis developing countries is positively related to labour skills and R&D intensity. Havrylyshyn (1985) shows that physical and human capital intensities of imports for a sample of LDCs exceed those of both domestic production and exports.[13] Finally, Hamilton and Svensson (1984) find considerable support for a formulation of the H–O theorem which looks at trade flows on a regional breakdown (globally).[14]

But these are supportive results only in so much as we have prior expectations about factor endowments in developing and industrialized countries. Leamer (1984), however, who does carefully combine (theoretically and empirically) all the components of H–O trade – factor endowments (for 11 factors), factor intensities (for 10 aggregates of manufactured goods) and the direction of trade (for 20 industrial and 40 developing countries) – does provide more comprehensive support for the H–O theory of trade.[15]

Technology gap and product cycle trade

We have already referred to two cross-country regression analyses (Hufbauer, 1970 and Leamer, 1974) which offer some support for technological theories of trade. The dynamic nature of technological progress and its close inter-relationship with human capital and skills, however, poses both conceptual and measurement problems for the testing of these types of theories, and most of the empirical work done relates predominantly to the USA. It is clear from these results that variables such as 'newness' of products or processes and specific knowledge help to explain trade flows. But this does not tell us much about these factors' significance in North–South trade. There have been some studies on the direction of US exports of manufacturing, concerned with relating per-capita income or stage of development of importing countries with the elasticity characteristics of exports (Adler, 1970) or the value (quality) variation of exports (Hufbauer and O'Neill, 1972). But these do not give empirically or theoretically robust results.

The results of other cross-country studies are also questionable. Gruber and Vernon (1970) found technological intensity to be significant only for the US. Hirsch (1974) found some co-relationship between export performance and proxies for technological intensity – but these proxies were highly co-linear with measures of country endowment of physical and human capital. That study therefore, like others (such as Hirsch, 1975; and Aquino, 1981, on the product cycle), do not convincingly 'test' for a specifically dynamic and neo-technology explanation of trade. They do, however, give some support to the view that other factors such as labour skills and technological know-how play a role, alongside traditional factor proportions, in explaining trade. They may in fact give support for a greater-than-two factor version of the H–O model.

Intra-industry trade flows

Despite the fact that there is a consensus among trade theorists and a body of evidence to support the view that much North–South trade is explainable within an extended H–O framework, there is evidence of a significant amount of trade by developing countries (especially higher–income ones) taking the form of intra-industry trade especially in the case of manufactures (see Greenaway and Milner, 1986a). Although we can model intra-industry trade (IIT) in a quasi-H–O framework where capital endowment differences determine the quality of products within industries (for example Falvey, 1981b) or in a framework which combines both factor endowment and non-H–O type factors (for example, Lawrence and Spiller, 1983), there is now a range of models which explain IIT in terms of production characteristics (such as decreasing costs) and market characteristics such as a demand for variety) rather than in terms of comparative advantage.

There is now a fairly large number of regression analyses of intra-industry trade (see Greenaway and Milner, 1986a). Most relate to the multilateral or bilateral trade flows of developed market economies. Some specifically focus on IIT for LDCs or of a North–South nature (Balassa, 1986; Havrylyshyn and Civan, 1983; Tharakan, 1984, 1986).[16] Methodological and measurement problems are particularly severe in this area given the diversity of available models of IIT and the nature of 'explanatory' variables (for example, scale economies, product differentiation, etc.), and therefore the evidence does not constitute tests of specific non-H–O theories of intra-industry trade. The studies do establish, however, that shares of IIT in total trade are systematically related (positively) to country characteristics (such as stage of development, market or country size and the degree of taste similarity between trading partners). Cross-sectional evidence on industry characteristics is more sparse, but given the support from industrial countries in their multilateral and bilateral trade of a deterministic relationship between IIT and market and production characteristics, then it is reasonable to expect that, as development takes place, the role of factor endowments becomes less significant in explaining the direction and detailed commodity composition of trade (especially of differentiated, manufactured goods). More detailed factor endowments may still be relevant, as may the traditional H–O model, for explaining comparative advantage on a broader sectoral basis (for example, between manufacturing and agricultural trade), but intra-industry trade may be viewed with some optimism by developing countries – overall relative labour abundance and capital scarcity need not necessarily constrain export capability in specific manufactures. The markets for such exports have traditionally been viewed as being in the already industrialized North, but similarity of market conditions may also be a source of South–South trade.

1.3.4 Empirical evidence on South–South Trade

The discussion of the previous section has inevitably alluded on occasions to South–South trade. It is, however, worth considering this particular orientation separately for at least two reasons. First, the 'chain of comparative advantage' approach to explaining trade suggests that the factor content of LDC trade will differ depending on whether this trade is with other LDCs (South–South) or with DMEs (North–South). Second, the policy implications of South–South trade have excited a great deal of interest and controversy. Many commentators have argued that LDCs should orient their trade policies towards the promotion of South–South trade because, *inter alia*, there are greater dynamic gains to be reaped from such trade; susceptibility to fluctuations in economic activity in DMEs would be reduced; and greater 'collective self-reliance' (Lewis, 1980) fostered. Moreover, it is claimed that trade flows are biased against the growth of South–South trade by the gearing of infrastructural services (transportation and communications) towards North–South trade (Stewart, 1976).

Details of the composition of South–South trade are provided in table 1.1b (see p. 25). It is obvious that a number of significant changes in product composition have occurred over the past 20 years or so, the most dramatic being the decline in the relative importance of fuels from 76 per cent of the total in 1962 to 52 per cent in 1982), and the increased importance of manufactures (from 5 per cent in 1962 to 27 per cent in 1982). The most dramatic growth in the latter has taken place over the past decade. Indeed, during the period 1973–82 South–South trade in manufactures grew at an annual average rate in excess of 20 per cent (faster than South–North, North–South or North-North trade). Impressive though these growth rates are, they apply to a low base, and by the early 1980s South–South trade in manufactures still only accounted for around 3 per cent of total trade in manufactures. Notwithstanding this, most commentators see the greatest potential for growth of South–South trade in trade in manufactures, and this is the aggregate which has attracted most attention.

Although manufactures have been the fastest-growing aggregate in South–South trade, the distribution of exports across LDCs has been very uneven, being dominated by the NICs. Several studies have noted this fact (see for example Havrylyshyn and Wolf, 1983; Ventura-Dias and Sorsa, 1985). Thus in 1980 over 50 per cent of all South–South trade in manufactures was accounted for by Taiwan, Singapore, Korea and Brazil. Moreover, as Newson and Wall (1985) point out, much of the growth in South–South trade is inter-NIC trade. These were the fastest-growing markets among LDCs and provided the principal opportunities for export, and import growth. The other principal source of growth of South–South trade in manufactures which is stressed by Havrylyshyn and Wolf (1983) is the expansion of exports from NICs to the capital-surplus oil exporting LDCs. The rapid growth of income per head in these economies in the late 1970s (combined with slower growth in the LDCs), encouraged a re-orientation of some export effort from DMEs to these countries. The role of market size effects in explaining the growth of South–South trade is also supported by Havrylyshyn (1985). This study stresses both the growth of income in oil exporting LDCs, and the relatively high income growth in NICs.

With regard to factor content, theory predicts that exports from more advanced LDCs to less advanced LDCs should be more capital-intensive than exports from advanced LDCs to DMEs. The little evidence which exists seems to provide support for this proposition. Using a sample of 45 LDCs for the period 1963–78, Havrylyshyn and Wolf (1983) and Havrylyshyn (1985) offer strong evidence to support the notion that South–South trade is generally more capital-intensive than South–North trade. Moreover, the evidence also seems to be consistent with the notion of a ladder or chain of comparative advantage as defined by relative factor endowments. Those countries which are higher up the ladder seem to export relatively more capital-intensive goods and import relatively less capital-intensive goods. One other interesting finding which emerges from these studies is that the factor content of trade may have been 'distorted' in some countries by commercial and industrial policy interventions. Specifically, for those countries with relatively high levels of protection for their manufacturing sectors, the capital intensity of exports appeared to be higher than the value predicted (by reference to relative factor endowments).

The final point we might make with specific reference to South–South trade relates to intra-industry trade. Several studies have been devoted to the analysis of intra-industry trade in LDCs (for example, Balassa, 1979a; Havrylyshyn and Civan, 1985). As we saw in the previous section, the consensus (from this and other work) seems to be that intra-industry trade is of increasing importance to LDCs in general and NICs in particular. Since intra-industry trade is recorded predominantly in trade in manufactures this is not surprising, and indeed the largest proportion of NIC intra-industry trade is with DMEs. Interestingly, however, NIC–NIC intra-industry trade seems to be lower than both NIC–DME and NIC–LDC intra-industry trade. In view of the fact that much of the literature on intra-industry trade associates its incidence with similarity in factor endowments this is somewhat surprising. Havrylyshyn and Alikhani (1986) explain this finding by reference to industrial diversification which, it is claimed, enhances opportunities for trade with DMEs, and the height of protective barriers in NICs compared with DMEs. Given the fact that NIC–LDC intra-industry trade is higher than NIC–NIC intra-industry trade, together with the increasing prevalence of non-tariff restrictions into DME markets, neither explanation is totally convincing.

1.3.5 Summary

There are then significant methodological difficulties in testing hypotheses relating to the direction and commodity composition of trade. Notwithstanding this, many researchers have endeavoured to generate empirical support for the trade theories relating to LDCs, both as a group and individually. Some evidence can be found to support a role for factor productivity differences both in North–South and South–South trade. The evidence on factor endowments is more controversial, but again evidence can be adduced to support (versions of) the H–O theorem (both in North–South and South–South trade). Another finding which is gaining increasing support is that intra-industry trade appears to be becoming increasingly prevalent in the trade of LDCs in general and NICs in particular. Finally, it has been noted by many commentators that trade in manufactures is the fastest-growing component in LDC trade, and by far the most rapid growth rates have been recorded by the NICs.

1.4 Commercial policy and intervention

Earlier in this survey we examined alternative theories of international trade, and their relevance for less developed countries. We also considered the nature and distribution of the gains from trade. As we saw, conventional wisdom in the form of the neoclassical paradigm suggests that the gains from trade are generally positive and mutual. These propositions have been endorsed by 'modern' trade theories which emphasize the role of technological change, and which focus on intra-industry trade. The neoclassical perspective on commercial policy is readily adduced from the basic trade theorems, viz., in the absence of distortions free trade will be the optimal policy for a small open economy. In examining theories of trade, however, we also saw that these propositions relating to the gains from trade and the optimality of free trade have not gone unchallenged. 'Structuralist' and 'Radical' commentators argue that free trade will rarely be the optimal policy for a small LDC due to the existence of various structural distortions, and that the gains from trade may be unequally distributed at the expense of LDCs. These schools of thought have been influential in fashioning trade policy in LDCs over the post-war period. The detail of these perspectives and their role in shaping trade strategies will be examined in depth in survey 2. In this section we will focus on 'positive' aspects of intervention; in other words the economic effects of various instruments of commercial policy and the criteria which can be used in deciding on their relative efficacy. Thus we will begin by reviewing various arguments for intervention which have been influential in LDCs, focusing in particular on the infant industry argument. We will then discuss the applicability of optimal intervention analysis as a basis for comparing instruments of intervention. Thirdly we will consider why tariffs and quotas are so prevalent when theory suggests that alternative, more efficient, instruments are available. Finally we will discuss the effective protection and domestic resource cost concepts and examine some of the evidence relating to the structure of protection in LDCs.

1.4.1 Arguments for intervention

In a seminal article Johnson (1965) distinguishes between 'economic', 'non-economic' and 'non-arguments' for intervention. Taking these in reverse order, 'non-arguments' refer to arguments grounded in some fallacy or misconception. The 'cheap labour' argument is a good example. Often in industrialized economies it is argued that competition from low wage economies is unfair and should be restrained. Since *relatively* low wages are invariably a reflection of *relative* factor endowments the argument is wholly fallacious. 'Non–economic' arguments refer to cases where intervention fulfils some essentially political objective. Thus the use of protectionist instruments to promote an activity which is regarded as being of 'strategic importance' would be justified by a non-economic argument. Protection of the agricultural sector often comes under this heading. 'Economic arguments' apply when some *distortion* exists which prevents the unfettered market from operating efficiently. Thus a positive production externality might result in the market provision of a commodity being less than the level which is socially optimal. Intervention to correct the distortion would be justified by an economic argument. We shall primarily focus on such economic arguments. This is not because they tend to be the arguments to which policy makers most often turn – ironically 'non-arguments' and 'non-economic arguments' tend to pervade policy discussions to a greater degree – but because these are the arguments to which the economists' tools can be most usefully applied to elucidate.

Distortions and intervention

In discussing the gains from trade we saw that in a well-functioning economy free trade is optimal (in a Paretian sense). More specifically the conditions for optimality are

$$\text{SMRT}^A_{xy} = \frac{P_x}{P_y} = \text{SMRT}^B_{xy} = \text{SMRS}^B_{xy} \tag{1.1}$$

In other words the social marginal rate of transformation, SMRT, of x into y in country A should be equal to the international terms of trade, P_x / P_y, which in turn should equal the social marginal rate of transformation in country B. Finally, the latter should be equal to the social marginal rate of substitution in consumption, SMRS. These are, of course, exacting conditions which will rarely, if ever, hold. However, they do help us to focus our attention on the reasons why they do not hold in particular circumstances. In general, two sorts of distortions could frustrate the attainment of an optimum–*exogenous* and *endogenous* distortions. The former refer to instances where structural features of the market, such as externalities, are responsible for market failure which prevents the attainment of an optimum. The latter refer to policy-induced distortions, such as taxes and subsidies, which can result in inequalities between marginal rates of substitution and transformation. Economic arguments essentially identify circumstances where endogenous distortions are used to correct exogenous distortions. Thus if an externality exists which frustrates the attainment of an optimum, it might be possible to use the tax/subsidy system to correct that distortion (see also survey 8).

Table 1.2 illustrates the kind of distortions which might exist in an economy and thereby provide an argument for intervention. The list is intended to be illustrative rather than exhaustive. It does, however, serve to indicate that distortions can in principle exist in domestic product markets, domestic factor markets or international product markets and that, moreover, they can impact upon the demand or supply side of the market. When distortions of this type exist partial market failure results and the conditions for optimality specified in equation (1.1) fail to hold. For example, a production externality in country B which is unpriced creates an inequality between $SMRT^B_{xy}$ and $SMRS^B_{xy}$. Similarly, international market power which is unexploited results in a divergence between $SMRT^B_{xy}$ and $SMRT^A_{xy}$. In both cases the equalities could be restored. In the former case an appropriate tax or subsidy could be used to encourage private producers to contract or expand their output of the commodity in question towards the socially optimal level. In the latter case an import tariff or export tax could turn the terms of trade in the home economy's favour, permitting it to benefit from its market power.

Optimal intervention

There are then a wide range of circumstances under which intervention designed to push the economy towards a social optimum may be desirable. There are also a large number of instruments which can be used for this purpose. A wide range of instruments is available through the government budget which can alter relative incentives in product and factor markets. Taxes may be aimed at changing consumption patterns (for example, sales taxes, consumption taxes, import tariffs); or production and employment patterns (for example production taxes, turnover taxes, profit taxes). Similarly, subsidies on consumption and exports, wage subsidies, and so on, may be used. In addition a variety of direct controls can be deployed, such as rationing, foreign exchange allocations, quantitative restrictions on imports or voluntary export restraints). Faced with such a wide array of instruments does it matter which is used in particular circumstances, or should the policy maker be indifferent between alternatives?

In fact it does matter which instrument is chosen for a particular purpose. This follows because intervention often has spillover effects or 'by-product distortions' (Corden, 1974). Since the number of by-product distortions may vary from one instrument to another it is possible to conceive of what Corden (1974) refers to as a 'hierarchy of policies' for each and every argument for intervention. The most efficient way of reacting to a particular distortion is to apply an instrument which minimizes the number of by-product distortions. Invariably

Table 1.2 Forms of distortions which result in market failure

Distortion	Effects
Domestic product market	
1. Consumption externality	1. Private consumption levels which exceed or fall short of socially optimal levels
2. Monopoly sellers	2. Price in excess of marginal cost leading to private production and consumption at levels which are socially sub-optimal
3. Production externality	3. Private production levels which exceed or fall short of socially optimal levels
Domestic factor markets	
1. Monopoly suppliers of labour	1. Wages in excess of marginal revenue products leading to employment below the socially optimal level
2. Interest rates in excess of social discount rates	2. Investment levels below the socially optimal level
3. Surplus labour	3. Wages in some sectors above their social opportunity cost leading to underemployment in those sectors
International product markets	
1. Market power	1. Unexploited gains from trade available to the large country

this means using an instrument which treats the distortion at its source. The central idea can be easily illustrated by reference to table 1.3 (which is based on Corden, 1974, chart 2.1). Here it is assumed that the private cost of labour exceeds its social opportunity cost in a particular sector. This could be due to minimum wage legislation which raises manufacturing wages above their social opportunity costs, or due to 'surplus labour' (Lewis, 1954). The most efficient means of removing the distortion is to treat it at source, for instance by repealing the minimum wage legislation thereby permitting wages to move towards market clearing levels, and allowing employment in manufacturing to expand. There are no by-product distortions associated with this policy change. It may, however, be regarded as politically infeasible, or indefensible on social grounds. The second-best policy would then be a wage subsidy at the cost of a by-product distortion; namely that taxes have to be raised to finance the subsidy. Unless these are lump sum taxes they will distort choices between work and leisure, or consumption and saving. Moreover, whatever the means of revenue-raising, real resources will be required for collection. A production subsidy is third-best. This follows because it involves the same by-product distortions as a wage subsidy. In addition, however it involves a further distortion – since all factors of production are being subsidized, employment will not increase by as much as with a wage subsidy. It should be clear that as we move down the list in table 1.3 the by-product distortions increase and the efficiency of the instrument used declines.

What this analysis demonstrates, then, is that even where an argument for intervention exists the form which intervention designed to correct the distortion takes is very important. Some instruments are more efficient than others at correcting a particular distortion and therefore impose fewer costs on society. This basic principle applies whether we are dealing with arguments for intervention in an industrialized economy or a less developed economy.

One point which comes through strongly in this analysis is the superiority of subsidies over tariffs and quotas. In general some kind of subsidy is a superior instrument of intervention over a tariff or a quota. The one widely accepted exception to this rule is the 'optimal tariff', that is, the use of an import tariff to exploit international market power.

1.4.2 Infant industry intervention

A wide range of arguments can be, and have been, invoked to justify intervention in the market for traded goods in LDCs. Without doubt the most influential of all the arguments advanced is the infant industry argument. This is a justification which is frequently invoked by policy makers in LDCs for introducing import tariffs and quantitative restraints. Having introduced the principle of optimal intervention it is worthwhile looking at this argument in a little detail, partly to consider its veracity, and partly to illustrate how optimal intervention analysis may be used to elucidate the problem.

The case for infant industry protection can be made by reference to one of a number of possible distortions – capital market imperfections, labour market imperfections, externalities or the existence of internal economies of scale. The case is essentially an argument for temporary protection. For instance it might be argued that an activity is potentially socially profitable but fails to come into existence because the long-run average cost curve is downward-sloping. As a result a new entrant would incur unit production costs in excess of mature foreign competitors and would be unable to gain a foothold in the domestic market. Consequently, investment in the activity does not take place. If, however, the domestic market were protected by an import tariff or an import quota which raised the prices of mature competitors toward the levels of the infant entrant, the infant would be in a position to penetrate the domestic market, and reduce unit production costs. Eventually the infant would mature, its production costs would be equivalent to those of established foreign firms and the protection could be removed.

The desire to promote manufacturing activity and industrialize has led to the belief in most LDCs that the circumstances under which infant industry protection is appropriate are widespread. It is worth probing the argument a little further. First of all we need to be more exact on the reason(s) for intervention.

The most widely held belief appears to be that economies of scale are the crucial element. In point of fact, however, economies of scale *per se* are not sufficient to provide a case for intervention. After all if the probable configuration of the cost curve is known, and if it is clear that in the medium term profits will be realized which will (after recouping initial losses), result in a rate of return at least as high as can be earned elsewhere, why will the private market fail to support the investment? Why is any kind of government intervention necessary? After all, virtually *all* manufacturing activities are subject to scale economies, yet in many countries the manufacturing sector is dominated by private enterprise. Thus, in order to make a convincing case one has to invoke the existence of other distortions.

The pedigree of the infant industry argument has ensured that a large number of possible distortions have been invoked to justify infant industry protection in different contexts. One common argument relates to the existence of some form of capital market distortion which prevents investment in an infant industry occurring. Thus as a result of incomplete information on the part of private investors, or myopia on the part of private financiers, the discount rate used in evaluating the investment may exceed the social time preference rate. Projects which are socially profitable would not appear to be privately profitable and would, as a result, remain unfinanced. One might agree that this argument has some merit. Even in circumstances where it does provide a justification for intervention, it will rarely, if ever, provide a justification for import protection. A first-best policy might be to improve information flows, or to reduce private discount rates by improving the general macroeconomic climate. A second-best policy might be an interest rate subsidy with the third-best policy being a pro-

Table 1.3 The hierarchy of policies

Distortion – private cost of labour exceeds the social opportunity cost

Instrument	*By-product distortions*
1. Remove distortions at source	None
2. Wage subsidy	Distortion from raising revenue (depending on tax used).
3. Production subsidy	(2) plus downward bias in labour intensity
4. Import tariff plus export subsidy	(3) minus distortion from raising revenue plus consumption distortion
5. Import tariff	(4) plus greater consumption distortion
6. Quantitative restriction	(5) plus potential loss of government revenue to license holders and greater administrative complexity and greater dynamic inefficiencies
7. Source specific quota/voluntary export restraint	(6) plus export of rent to foreign licence-holders and trade diversion

duction subsidy. Import protection would be inferior to all of these alternatives, although as we shall see shortly, there may still be administrative reasons for preferring protection to some form of subsidy intervention. One final point which should be made here is as follows: this argument for intervention involves reducing the welfare of present generation consumers in order to increase the welfare of future generation consumers. With intertemporal transfers of this sort going on we need to know something about social time preference rates.

Another persuasive group of arguments for intervention which have been widely discussed (for instance by Baldwin, 1969 and Johnson, 1970), deal with what might be referred to as 'first-mover disadvantages'. These refer to external effects which may impact upon initial investors in an activity (first-movers), and may be of sufficient magnitude to act as a positive disincentive to investment in the activity. Suppose, for instance, an infant industry employs a particular type of skilled labour. The initial investor in the industry must incur the investment in human capital necessary to train the labour. Having done so, however, what is to prevent a second firm entering the industry and bidding away the skilled labour from the incumbent firm? If all potential entrants perceive scope for this kind of behaviour then it may act as a brake on any one single firm acting as the first mover. Such a distortion may certainly exist and may provide an argument for intervention. Again, however, one can reasonably ask whether import protection is a first-best response. For example some form of training subsidy would undoubtedly be a more efficient means of intervention. Indeed some might go further in this particular instance and question whether *any* form of intervention is necessary at all on the grounds that a market solution is available – namely apprenticeship!

This discussion of the infant industry argument is not intended to create the impression that it is a 'non-argument' in the Johnson (1965) sense. Nor is it intended to suggest that the range of circumstances under which infant industry protection can be justified is rather narrow. Clearly the argument has had an enormous influence from a policy standpoint and deserves close scrutiny, if only because it tends to be invoked as a justification for protection more often in LDCs than any other single argument. As the recent comprehensive survey by Bell, Ross-Larson and Westphal (1984) demonstrated, however, there is no shortage of evidence of 'failed' infant industries. What the above discussion brings out is the possibility that such failures may be due to an excessive reliance on inappropriate and inefficient instruments, in particular a reliance on import quotas where some form of subsidy intervention may be more appropriate.

1.4.3 Fiscal implications of trade taxes

The proposition that some form of subsidy is invariably superior to direct trade interventions rests on a very crucial assumption; namely that the facility to levy taxes in order to finance the subsidy exists. Ideally the subsidy should be financed by non-distortionary lump-sum taxes. Such taxes are often eschewed, however, largely because of their regressive nature, in favour of second-best taxes such as income taxes or expenditure taxes. These are second-best because they distort the choice between income and leisure, or saving and consumption. Nonetheless they may be superior means of raising fiscal revenue to trade taxes.

In many LDCs, however, the option of levying widely based income taxes or expenditure taxes may not be available. For example, if income per head is relatively low any income tax which provided tax exemptions for the lowest income groups could exclude the bulk of the population. Moreover a large amount of economic activity is accounted for in informal trading and subsistence activity, thus effectively taking these outside the tax net (see Greenaway, 1980, 1984).

These are issues which are explored in some depth in survey 8. The point to note for the moment is that first- or even second-best sources of fiscal revenue may not be available to many LDCs. In these circumstances trade taxes can provide an administratively more convenient source of revenue. Import and export taxes have several characteristics which make them potentially attractive: they are levied on a range of reasonably well defined tradeable commodities and the taxable commodities may enter or exit the country through a relatively small number of frontier posts and ports. As a result the cost : yield ratio of the trade tax may be relatively low compared with alternatives. Since a revenue tariff will invariably have some protective impact one can see that this is a compelling reason why tariffs may be more widely used than subsidies. As table 1.4 indicates, the dependence of many LDCs on trade taxes can be very great indeed. (This dependence is further discussed in survey 8.) In the present context it should simply be noted that the revenue motive is a widely used second-best argument for tariff intervention.

1.4.4 The structure of protection

Section 1.4.1 discussed a set of principles which can be deployed in evaluating arguments for import protection. Section 1.4.2 focused on the most influential of all protective motives for intervention, whilst section 1.4.3 commented briefly on the revenue motive. Enough has now been said to indicate that a range of arguments can be invoked to justify intervention. It is not unusual to find that arguments are conflicting. Nor is it unusual to find that policy formulation and implementation is *ad hoc* rather than systematic. Except in cases where external

Table 1.4 Trade taxes as a percentage of government revenue for selected LDCs

Brazil	6.9	Pakistan	36.2
Singapore	8.7	Ghana	40.9
Nigeria	14.2	Sierra Leone	43.6
India	16.3	Ecuador	46.7
Peru	19.9	Chad	47.9
Thailand	26.0	Zaire	52.3
Gabon	30.2	Swaziland	53.7

Note: Data pertain to annual averages for the years 1972-77.

Source: Adapted from Greenaway (1984), table 1.

pressure is brought to bear to initiate wholesale policy rationalization, as is sometimes the case with World Bank Structural Adjustment Loans (see Greenaway and Milner, 1987b), protective structures tend to be complex. This being so, how does one evaluate the structure of protection in a particular setting?

The effective protection concept

The most widely used approach to evaluating the structure of protection is by estimating *effective protection*. The basic idea behind the effective protection concept is the recognition that the protection conferred on a given domestic producer depends not only on any tariff (or other protective instrument), which applies to his output, but also to any tariffs which apply to intermediate inputs. Rather than simply focusing on the price-raising effect of a given nominal tariff on a particular product, effective protection (EP) focuses on the impact of all protective interventions on value added in a particular production process. It can be identified as follows:

$$e_j = \frac{V_j^* - V_j}{V_j} = \frac{V_j^*}{V_j} - 1 \qquad (1.2)$$

where:

V_j^* = value added in production process j at tariff distorted prices,
V_j = value added in production process j at world prices.

Another way of writing this, assuming a single imported intermediate input, and a fixed relationship between input and output is:

$$e_j = (P_j - z_{ij}P_j) / \frac{P_j}{1+t_j} - \frac{z_{ij}P_j}{1+t_i} - 1 \qquad (1.3)$$

where:

P_j = price of the final product j at tariff distorted prices,
z_{ij} = share of imported input in the final value of j
t_j = nominal tariff on the final product j
t_i = nominal tariff on the intermediate input i.

The numerator in (1.3) refers to value added at tariff distorted prices whilst the denominator refers to value added at world prices.

The EP concept was developed by Barber (1955), Corden (1963) and Johnson (1965). It is most clearly articulated in Corden (1971). Arguably the refinement of the concept is one of the most important developments in post-war trade theory. The concept is useful for several reasons. First, it focuses on the net effect of the entire tariff structure on a given production process and summarizes the impact of the tariff structure on value added in a single, readily comprehensible statistic. This merely formalizes the fact that a tariff import competing with final on output operates like a subsidy to value added whilst a tariff on inputs operates like a tax on value added. If the net effect of the two is to yield a positive EP rate then value added in the activity can be higher than it otherwise would be in the absence on any tariff intervention. The exact relationship between e_j, t_j and t_i can be clearly identified from equation (1.3). Other things being equal a higher t_j is consistent with a higher e_j whilst a lower t_i is consistent with a higher e_j. Thus EP varies directly with the height of output tariffs but inversely with the height of input tariffs. For given values of t_j and t_i, e_j and z_{ij} vary directly. A higher z_{ij} means a lower value added in absolute terms, and therefore a greater proportionate effect of the given nominal tariffs.

A second important merit of the EP concept is that it helps us understand how relatively high levels of nominal protection may still be associated with low rates of effective protection. Moreover, it also clarifies how some activities may actually be 'disprotected' by the tariff structure. For instance a given activity may not benefit from output tariffs, but still find its inputs subject to input tariffs. In these circumstances the effective tariff would be negative; that is, value added at tariff distorted prices would actually be lower than value added at world prices. This is a situation which tends to be particularly prevalent in export-oriented activities.

There are a number of practical complications associated with the estimation of EP rates, the most serious of which relate to (1) how one treats non-tradeable inputs, (2) how one averages tariffs across product lines in cases where more than one product is produced, and (3) whether or not it is legitimate to assume that input coefficients are fixed and remain unaffected by the tariff structure. In addition, there are several methodological criticisms of the concept, the most serious of which being that EP is a partial equilibrium concept which is often used to comment on the general equilibrium impact of the tariff structure; that is, on resource allocation.[17] Notwithstanding these reservations the concept has been used very widely to comment on the structure of protection in LDCs, both in academic research and as an input into the policy reform process (Havrylyshyn and Alikhani, 1982, and World Bank, 1984, provide detailed bibliographies of studies of effective protection). This work has been summarized elsewhere, (Greenaway, 1987b). A few remarks on the principal results can, however, be made here. The literature tends to focus on the average effective protective rate, the ranking of effective rates, the range of rates, evidence of negative effective protection and evidence of negative value added. The average provides some information on the extent to which the protective structure allows domestic value added to rise above value added at world prices. For some LDCs this turns out to be very high indeed. For example the average level of effective protection in Uruguay in 1965 was 384 per cent (Krueger *et al.*, 1981); the average in Peru in 1975 was 198 per cent (World Bank, 1982); and the average for Madagascar in 1982 was 164 per cent (Greenaway and Milner, 1986b). These are all highly protected economies which have followed import substitution strategies, and as a result generated very high levels of effective protection. By contrast the average level in Korea in 1968 was − 1 per cent, and in Singapore in 1967, 9 per cent. Both are generally regarded as export promoting economies.

The ranking of a particular set of EP estimates provides an indication of the likely direction of resource pulls induced by the protective structure. Other things being equal, resources will be pulled from activities with relatively low (and negative) rates towards activities with relatively high rates. Assuming this does occur, the range of estimates provides an indication as to the potential resource misallocation associated with the protective structure. There will be a greater tendency for resource movement to be encouraged the wider the range of rates. Thus whereas the range in Singapore in 1967 was from − 1 per cent to 86 per cent (Tan and Hock, 1982), the range in India in 1968–69 was from − 21 per cent to 3354 per cent (Bhagwati and Srinivasan, 1975) and that in Burundi in 1984 was even wider at − 4 per cent to 7876 per cent (Greenaway and Milner, 1986c). Clearly potential resource misallocation associated with the tariff structure will be greater in the case of India and Burundi than in the case of Singapore.

Empirical studies have also found extensive evidence of negative EP. This seems to be especially prevalent in export-oriented industries and highlights the way in which the protective structure actually penalizes some activities. Finally, evidence of negative value added has also been reported for a number of economies. This arises when the value of inputs at world prices exceeds the value of output, also at world prices. This phenomenon can often be seen in economies with complex protective structures.

In summary, there have been a large number of studies of effective protection in LDCs. These studies provide a considerable amount of information on the structure of protection in LDCs and suggest that, in some economies at least, the tariff structure is highly protective, and potentially highly distortive. Details of some of the more readily accessible studies of effective protection are provided in table 1.5.

Domestic resource cost analysis

A concept which is closely related to effective protection is the notion of domestic resource cost (DRC). This concept has been developed in parallel with the EP concept, but can be viewed as an extension of the latter. It is an approach which has been widely used in policy evaluation in LDCs.

A detailed outline of the DRC methodology is provided by Bruno (1972) and Krueger (1972). Essentially the measure is an exercise in cost–benefit appraisal. The fundamental objective behind DRC analysis is to provide an estimate of the costs to the domestic economy of producing a unit of value added in a particular activity, where the numeraire is value at world prices. Defining the DRC ratio in this way, one can interpret it as the cost to the economy of acquiring a unit of foreign exchange through production for export, or of saving a unit of foreign exchange through the production of import substitutes. If the only reason for a divergence between domestic prices and world prices is the existence of border distortions (like tariffs and quotas), then the DRC and EP measures are identical.[18] In many LDCs, however, social opportunity costs are not reflected in marked prices as a result of product market distortions (like monopoly supply), or factor market distortions (like surplus labour). The DRC ratio estimates all domestic inputs at shadow prices rather than market prices, so that the ratio more accurately reflects social opportunity costs. The DRC ratio is defined as follows:

$$\text{DRC}_j = \frac{\sum_i V_{ij} S_i + \sum_h \sum_i d_{hj} V_{ih} S_i}{1 - \sum_i m_{ij} - \sum_f V_{fj} r_f} = \frac{\text{DC}_j}{\text{NVA}_j} \qquad (1.4)$$

where:

V_{ij} = quantity of factor of production i used in producing one unit of j;

S_i = social opportunity cost (shadow price) of factor i;

d_{hj} = quantity of intermediate non-tradeable inputs, h, used in producing a unit of j;

V_{ih} = quantity of factor of production i used in producing one unit of input h;

m_{ij} = quantity of intermediate tradeable inputs, m, used in producing a unit of j;

V_{fj} = quantity of the fth foreign-owned factor of production used in producing one unit of j.

r_f = revenues repatriated to the fth foreign-owned factor of production.

The value of unity in the denominator indicates the normalization at international prices.

This can be more compactly expressed as the ratio of domestic value added at social opportunity costs. DC_j, to international value added, NVA_j. In the event

Table 1.5 Effective protection in selected LDCs

Country	Average EP rate	Range of EPs
Brazil	63 (1967)	4→252 (1967)
Pakistan	356 (1963–4)	−6→595 (1963–4)
Korea	−1 (1968)	−15→82 (1968)
Singapore	22 (1967)	−23→708 (1967)
Uruguay	384 (1965)	17→1014 (1965)
Colombia	19 (1969)	−8→140 (1969)
India	69 (1968–9)	27→3,354 (1968–9)
Thailand	27 (1973)	−43→236 (1973)
Ivory Coast	41 (1973)	−25→278 (1973)

Note: These cases are illustrative. For a more exhaustive list see the original source.
Source: Adapted from Greenaway (1987a), table 1.

that market prices reflect social opportunity costs and the only distortions to those prices are induced by border measures, then

$$DRC_j = EP_j + 1. \tag{1.5}$$

The value of the DRC ratio is that it provides a measure of comparative costs across industries. A DRC ratio of less than unity implies that it requires less than one pound's worth of domestic resources to acquire, or save, one pound's worth of foreign exchange. A ratio in excess of unity for a given activity implies that it requires more than one pound's worth of domestic resources to earn, or save, a pound's worth of foreign exchange. As with EP analysis, one is interested in the ranking and the dispersion of DRC ratios. The ranking can provide a guide as to the (socially) most profitable uses for future investment. The dispersion of DRC ratios again provides information on the potential resource misallocation associated with exogenous, and policy-induced, market distortions.

In general the estimation of a set of DRC ratios is more complicated than an EP study. This follows in part because the data requirements are more exacting, and in part because some of the central information has to be obtained by indirect methods, as for example, with shadow prices. By definition shadow prices are not directly observable. Thus in order to estimate the shadow price of labour in manufacturing activity one has to make some judgment about the next best use of that labour. Would it have been employed in agriculture, or unemployed, or employed in the informal sector? Likewise with capital — if a given stock was not employed in activity *j*, what rate of return could it have expected in its next best use? Conventions vary with regard to shadow pricing. It is our intention simply to identify the problem rather than resolve it. The reader is encouraged to consult some of the specialist studies, such as Little and Scott (1976) (see also survey 9).

To date a range of DRC studies have been completed for a range of LDCs (see Havrylyshyn and Alikhani, 1982). The studies vary in coverage and technique. As a result they are difficult to summarize in a short space. Two observations can be made, however. First, it is not uncommon to find that the average DRC exceeds unity, and indeed, two. For example in a study of DRCs in Madagascar the average DRC turned out to be 3.70, or 2.20 if one eliminated the highest DRC. In other words, for the sample of industries covered, domestic resources per unit of value added were double their international equivalent. The other point of interest which emerges from this work is the range of DRC estimates. This is often very wide. Again to take the Madagascan case, the range here was from 0.78 to 9.35, implying that policy-induced and exogenous distortions may exert a significant impact on resource allocation.

Other indicators of protective structure

EP analysis is the most widely used approach to evaluating the structure of protection in LDCs. To an increasing extent it is being complemented with the theoretically more satisfactory but more demanding technique of DRC analysis. In addition to these widely used approaches, there are two additional techniques of more recent origin which might be briefly mentioned. These are estimates of the overall 'bias' in the trade regime, and 'true' tariffs and subsidies. Both techniques take a more aggregative perspective than EP or DRC analysis in that they attempt to summarize the implications of the protective structure for broad sectors of economic activity like importables and exportables. Bias estimation, which was pioneered by Krueger (1978), attempts to do this by reference to the extent to which domestic prices of importables and exportables diverge from those which would prevail in a situation of free trade, as follows:

$$B = \frac{\Sigma W_i (Pm_i / Qm_i)}{\Sigma W_j (Px_j / Qx_j)} \tag{1.6}$$

where P is the domestic price, Q is the world price, i is the ith import competing product, and j is the jth exportable product (at domestic and world prices). Ws are weights reflecting the importance of i and j in total value added. If the value of the bias index turns out to be unity this suggests that the overall impact of the incentive structure is neutral. If it is less than unity then incentives are biased towards production for the domestic market.

'True' tariffs (subsidies) are also generally estimated for broad sectors of activity. They aim to establish the extent to which the price of importables (exportables) increases relative to non-tradeables, as a consequence of the protective structure. The implicit assumption behind the model is that the tradeable sectors compete with non-tradeables for resources. Therefore 'true' protection provides an indication of the way in which relative incentives to invest in a particular sector are fashioned by the protective structure. The concept is developed by Sjaastad (1980) and its empirical application is discussed in Greenaway and Milner (1987b). The higher the true tariff the greater the degree of protection received by the import substituting sector (and *mutatis mutandis* for the true subsidy in the case of exportables). It is not unusual, however, to find marked divergence between nominal and true protection.

Neither of these techniques has been widely deployed, although they are useful approaches to evaluating the impact of the protective structure on relative incentives to invest in different sectors of the economy.

1.4.5 Summary

This section has addressed various aspects of the theory of commercial policy and its applicability to LDCs. We have demonstrated how the theory of optimal intervention can be used as a basis for ranking alternative instruments of intervention. One particular case for intervention, the infant industry argument, was addressed in detail and alternative bases for intervention explored. Two points in particular emerged from this analysis. First, the precise arguments for intervention may be rather more subtle than appears at first sight. Second, as and when an argument for intervention can be made, it will generally be the case that some form of direct subsidy will be a superior form of intervention to import protection. Having said this, however, we saw that tariffs may still be preferred to subsidies on the grounds that they raise fiscal revenue. Moreover, quotas will frequently be preferred to subsidies on the grounds that they more effectively ration scarce foreign exchange. Finally, it was argued that in a situation where commercial policy is used to meet multiple objectives (import protection, revenue raising and so on), the resulting protective structure may be highly complex and complicated. Several techniques are available for evaluating the structure of commercial policy, in particular effective protection analysis. Thus the latter part of this section discussed the concept of effective protection, together with the domestic resource cost concept, and two less widely used techniques, bias estimation and 'true' protection.

1.5 Concluding comments

The vast majority of LDCs are classic small open economies. Moreover, the 'openness' of most LDCs has increased over the past quarter of a century or so, and reached very high levels in some economies. Given the resultant interdependence between most LDCs and their trading partners, it is important to comprehend the forces which result in LDCs engaging in trade, the factors which determine their gains from trade, and the scope for effective use of commercial policy. This survey has been directed at these issues.

We have seen that there are a number of approaches to explaining the direction and composition of LDC trade flows, and a spectrum of views regarding the potential gains from international trade. These range from the neoclassical perspective which views international trade as providing opportunities for gains from specialization and exchange to all partners; through the structuralist perspective which argues that various inflexibilities and distortions in LDCs limit their scope for gaining from trade; to the neo-Marxist perspective which sees trade as essentially exploitative. These different views stress different bases to trade including, *inter alia*, differences in factor productivity, differences in factor endowments, technology differences and different demand patterns. Our review of the empirical evidence concluded that whilst a good deal of the evidence was conflicting, it was clear that in many cases there were multiple determinants of trade flows. Some support for most of the determinants noted above can be adduced, both in North–South trade and in South–South trade. Methodological problems contrive to ensure that this is not as conclusive as one would ideally wish.

The theory of commercial policy argues that the scope for welfare-improving trade intervention may be limited in a small open economy. Furthermore, successful intervention relies heavily on careful diagnosis of the problem and an equally careful prognosis regarding the solution. As we have seen, these principles apply to LDCs in general, and to the most celebrated argument in LDCs in particular - the infant industry argument. In practice, however, this prescription is not always followed - in part, as we discussed, for administrative reasons, in part for political reasons. The latter is beyond the scope of this survey. The application of public choice ideas has, however, persuasively demonstrated that very often an understanding of pressure group activity is the most important element in explaining the pattern of commercial policy intervention.

NOTES

1. The categorization used here emphasizes the effects/gains of trade rather than the causes of trade. Given the emphasis on the developed–less developed (North–South) relationship in the literature, it will complement subsequent discussion of commercial policy.
2. Modern characterizations of the 'vent for surplus' view set the model firmly within a framework of neoclassical optimization (e.g. Hymer and Resnick, 1969; Findlay, 1970).
3. Categorization may give the impression, for instance, that models in different categories are rivals or substitutes. This is not necessarily the case. The trade-development nexus can be simultaneously explored from the single LDC (small country) perspective and from the standpoint of the interdependence of the 'North' and 'South' as a whole.
4. It is of course possible to extend the dimensionality of the H–O model and to construct a 'chain' of comparative advantage in terms of factor intensities. There are, however, difficulties in generalizing 'chain' propositions – see Deardorff (1979) and Ethier (1984).
5. More recent attempts (e.g. Krugman, 1979) to model formally in the fashion of the product cycle approach assume exogenous rates of product innovation and given time lags between technology availability in the 'North' and 'South'.
6. Samuelson (1976), in a critique of Emmanuel's theory, points out that 'unequal exchange' is merely a tautological restatement of the fact that there is an assumed wage differential between developed and developing countries.
7. Note, however, that not all Marxists subscribe to dependency theory.
8. The discussion will concentrate on empirical tests of the causes of trade or determinants of comparative advantage. Empirical studies of models of the effects of trade, e.g. North–South models of terms of trade movements, are not covered. This literature is dealt with in survey 2.
9. See Bowen (1983) and Hillman (1980) for a critique of this approach.
10. Bhagwati (1964) provides a critique of this methodology. The results of these types of studies are, however, highly supportive of Ricardian theory. For a summary of these studies, see Bhagwati (1969).
11. This has involved either Leontief-type measurement of factor content or regressions of trade balances on factor intensities, e.g. Baldwin (1971).
12. This is distinct from the literature on short-run import and export demand functions, which seeks to identify the magnitude and time path of trade flow responses to changes in exchange rates and relative prices (see, for instance, Bahmani-Oskooee, 1986).
13. Havrylyshyn also found that exports by LDCs to other LDCs contain more physical and human capital than LDC exports to industrial countries. Similar results for individual countries have been found by Tyler (1976) for Brazil, and by Hong and Krueger (1975) for Korea.
14. The only exception to expectations was the finding for Latin America, where exports appeared to be more capital-intensive than those for most industrialized countries.

15. A linear model explains quite a large proportion of cross-sectional variance of net trade patterns. However, Leamer is careful to point out that multicollinearity and measurement errors may mean that the data do not distinguish between a number of alternative hypotheses.
16. Intra-industry trade in South–South trade is discussed later in this section.
17. Bhagwati and Srinivasan (1973) have argued that for this reason it is not legitimate to draw inferences about relative resource pulls from effective protection estimates. Strictly speaking this is true. As Corden (1971) points out, however, it is still legitimate to presume that activities with relatively high EP rates are likely to pull resources from activities with relatively low rates.
18. In fact DRC = EP + 1, as we shall see later.

REFERENCES

Adler, F. M. 1970. The relationship between the income and price elasticities of demand for United States exports. *Review of Economics and Statistics*, 52, 313–19.

Agarwal, M., Askari, H. and Corson, W. 1975. A testing of the Ricardian theory of comparative advantage. *Economia Internazionale*, 28, 341–52.

Amano, A. 1977. Specific factors, comparative advantage and international investment. *Economica*, 44, 131–44.

Amin, S. 1976. *Unequal Development*. Brighton: Harvester Press.

Amin, S. 1977. *Imperialism and Unequal Development*. New York: Monthly Review Press.

Aquino, A. 1981 Changes over time in the pattern of comparative advantage in manufactured goods: an empirical analysis of the period 1962–74. *European Economic Review*, 15, 41–62.

Arndt, H. W. 1985. The origins of structuralism. *World Development*, 13, 151–9.

Bacha, E. 1978. An interpretation of unequal exchange from Prebisch–Singer to Emmanuel. *Journal of Development Economics*, 5, 319–30.

Bahmani-Oskooee, M. 1986. Determinants of international trade flows: the case of developing countries. *Journal of Development Economics*, 20, 107–23.

Balassa, B. 1963. An empirial demonstration of classical comparative cost theory. *Review of Economics and Statistics*, 45, 231–8.

Balassa, B. 1965. Trade liberalization and 'revealed' comparative advantage. *The Manchester School*, 33, 99–123.

Balassa, B. 1979a. Intra-industry trade and the integration of developing countries in the world economy. In H. Giersch (ed.), *On the Economics of Intra-Industry Trade*, Tübingen: J. C. B. Mohr.

Balassa, B. 1979b. A stages approach to comparative advantage. In I. Adelman (ed.), *Economic Growth and Resources*. London: Macmillan.

Balassa, B. (ed.) 1982. *Development Strategies in Semi Industrialized Economies*. Baltimore: Johns Hopkins University Press.

Balassa, B. 1986. Intra-industry specialisation: a cross-country analysis. *European Economic Review*, 30, 27–42.

Baldwin, R. E. 1969. The case against infant industry protection. *Journal of Political Economy*, 77, 295–305.

Baldwin, R. E. 1971. Determinants of the commodity structure of US trade. *American Economic Review*, 61, 126–46.

Baran, P. 1957. *The Political Economy of Growth*. Mexico: F.C.E.

Baran, P. 1973. Dependence and underdevelopment in the new world and the old. In special issue of *Social and Economic Studies* (March).

Barber, C. L. 1965. Canadian tariff policy. *Canadian Journal of Economics and Political Science*, 21, 513-30.

Bell, M., Ross-Larson, B. and Westphal, L. 1984. Assessing the performance of infant industries. *Journal of Development Economics*, 16, 101-28.

Bhagwati, J. N. 1958. Immiserizing growth: a geometric note. *Review of Economic Studies*, 25, 201-5.

Bhagwati, J. N. 1964. The pure theory of international trade: a survey. *Economic Journal*, 74, 1-84.

Bhagwati, J. N. 1969. *Trade, Tariffs and Growth*. Cambridge, Mass.: MIT Press.

Bhagwati, J. N. 1971. The generalised theory of distortions and welfare. In J. N. Bhagwati, R. W. Jones, R. A. Mundell and J. Vanek, (eds), *Trade, Balance of Payments and Growth*. Amsterdam: North-Holland.

Bhagwati, J. N. 1978. *Anatomy and Consequences of Exchange Control Regimes*. Cambridge, Mass.: Ballinger, for NIER.

Bhagwati, J. N. and Bharadwaj, R. 1967. Human capital and the pattern of foreign trade: the Indian case. *Indian Economic Review*, 2, 117-42.

Bhagwati, J. N. and Srinivasan, T. N. 1973. The general equilibrium theory of effective protection and resource allocation. *Journal of International Economics*, 3, 259-81.

Bhagwati, J. N. and Srinivasan, T. N. 1975. *Foreign Trade Regimes and Economic Development: India*. New York: National Bureau of Economic Research.

Bhagwati, J. N. and Srinivasan, T. N. 1979. Trade policy and development. In R. Dornbusch and J. A. Frenkel (eds), *International Economic Policy: Theory and Evidence*. Baltimore: Johns Hopkins University Press.

Bowden, R. J. 1983. The conceptual basis of empirical studies of trade in manufactured commodities: a constructive critique. *The Manchester School*, 51, 209-34.

Bowen, H. P. 1983. On the theoretical interpretation of trade intensity and revealed comparative advantage. *Weltwirtschaftliches Archiv*, 119, 464-72.

Brecher, R. A. and Choudhri, E. U. 1982a. Immiserizing investment from abroad: the Singer-Prebisch thesis reconsidered. *Quarterly Journal of Economics*, 97, 181-90.

Brecher, R. A. and Choudhri, E. U. 1982b. The Leontief paradox continued. *Journal of Political Economy*, 90, 820-3.

Brecher, R. A. and Diaz-Alejandro, C. F. 1977. Tariffs, foreign capital and immiserizing growth. *Journal of International Economics*, 7, 317-22.

Bruno, M. 1972. Domestic resource cost and effective protection: clarification and synthesis. *Journal of Political Economy*, 80, 16-33.

Cable, V. and Rebelo, I. 1980. *Britain's pattern of specialisation in manufactured goods with developing countries and trade protection*. World Bank Staff Working Paper No. 425. Washington, DC: World Bank.

Caves, R. E. 1965. 'Vent for surplus' models of trade and growth. In R. E. Baldwin *et al.* (eds), *Trade, Growth and the Balance of Payments*. Chicago: Rand McNally.

Chenery, H. B. and Bruno, M. 1962. Development alternatives in an open economy: the case of Israel. *Economic Journal*, 72, 79-103.

Chenery, H. B. and Strout, A. 1966. Foreign assistance and economic development. *American Economic Review*, 56, 679-733.

Chichilnisky, G. 1981. Terms of trade and domestic distribution: export-led growth with abundant labour. *Journal of Development Economics*, 8, 163-92.

Corden, W. M. 1963. The tariff. In A. Hunter (ed.), *The Economics of Australian Industry*, Melbourne: Melbourne University Press.

Corden, W. M. 1971. *The Theory of Protection*. Oxford: Clarendon Press.

Corden, W. M. 1974. *Trade Policy and Economic Welfare*. Oxford: Clarendon Press.

Deardorff, A. V. 1979. Weak links in the chains of comparative advantage. *Journal of International Economics*, 9, 197-209.

Deardorff, A. V. 1984. Testing trade theories and predicting trade flows. In R. W. Jones and P. B. Kenen (eds), *Handbook of International Economics*, Vol. 1. Amsterdam: North-Holland.

Diaz-Alejandro, C. F. 1975. Trade policies and economic development. In P. B. Kenen (ed.), *International Trade and Finance: Frontiers for Research*. Cambridge: Cambridge University Press.

Dixit, A. K. 1969. Marketable surplus and dual development. *Journal of Economic Theory*, 1, 203–19.

Dixit, A. K. and Norman, V. D. 1979. 'Notes on the Ricardo-Viner model'. Mimeo.

Emmanuel, A. 1972. *Unequal Exchange: A Study of the Imperialism of Trade*. New York: Monthly Review Press.

Ethier, W. J. 1984. Higher dimensional issues in trade theory. In R. W. Jones and P. B. Kenen (eds), *Handbook of International Economics*, Vol. 1. Amsterdam: North-Holland.

Falvey, R. E. 1981a. Comparative advantage in a multi-factor world. *International Economic Review*, 22, 401–13.

Falvey, R. E. 1981b. Commercial policy and intra-industry trade. *Journal of International Economics*, 11, 495–511.

Fei, J. C. H. and Ranis, G. 1964. *Development of the Labour Surplus Economy*. New Haven: Yale University Press.

Fels, G. 1972. The choice of industry mix in the division of labour between developed and developing countries. *Weltwirtschaftliches Archiv*, 108, 71–121.

Findlay, R. 1970. *Trade and Specialisation*. Harmondsworth: Penguin.

Findlay, R. 1971. The 'foreign exchange gap' and growth in developing countries. In J. N. Bhagwati, R. W. Jones, R. A. Mundell and J. Vanek (eds), *Trade, Balance of Payments and Growth*. Amsterdam: North-Holland.

Findlay, R. 1973. *International Trade and Development Theory*. New York: Columbia University Press.

Findlay, R. 1974. Relative prices, growth and trade in a simple Ricardian system. *Economica*, 41, 1–13.

Findlay, R. 1981. Fundamental determinants of the terms of trade. In S. Grassman and E. Lundberg (eds), *The World Economic Order: Past and Prospects*. London: Macmillan.

Findlay, R. 1982. International distributive justice. *Journal of International Economics*, 13, 1–14.

Findlay, R. 1984. Growth and development in trade models. In R. W. Jones and P. B. Kenen (eds), *Handbook of International Economics*, Vol. 1. Amsterdam: North-Holland.

Frank, A. G. 1967. *Capitalism and Underdevelopment in Latin America: Historical Studies of Chile and Brazil*. New York: Monthly Review Press.

Frank, A. G. 1972. *Lumpenbourgeoisie and Lumpendevelopment: Dependence, Class and Politics in Latin America*. New York: Monthly Review Press.

Greenaway, D. 1980. Trade taxes as a source of government revenue: an international comparison. *Scottish Journal of Political Economy*, 27, 175–82.

Greenaway, D. 1984. A statistical analysis of fiscal dependence on trade taxes and economic development. *Public Finance*, 39, 70–89.

Greenaway, D. 1985. Models of trade in differentiated goods and commercial policy. In D. Greenaway (ed.), *Current Issues in International Trade*. London: Macmillan.

Greenaway, D. 1987a. Characteristics of industrialization and economic performance under alternative development strategies. Background paper to *World Development Report 1987*. Washington DC: World Bank.

Greenaway, D. (ed.) 1987b. *Economic Development and International Trade.* London: Macmillan.

Greenaway, D. and Milner, C.R. 1986a. *The Economics of Intra-Industry Trade.* Oxford: Basil Blackwell.

Greenaway, D. and Milner, C.R. 1986b. An analysis of import tariffs in Madagascar. In *Industrial Policy in Madagascar.* A report to the World Bank. London: Maxwell Stamp Associates.

Greenaway, D. and Milner, C.R. 1986c. Effective tariff analysis for Burundi. In *A Study of the Tariff System in Burundi.* A Report to the World Bank. London: Maxwell Stamp Associates.

Greenaway, D. and Milner, C.R. 1987a. 'Evaluating the process of commercial policy reform in low income LDCs'. Mimeo.

Greenaway, D. and Milner, C.R. 1987b. True protection concepts and their use in evaluating commercial policy in LDCs. *Journal of Development Studies,* 23, 39–58.

Gruber, W. H. and Vernon, R. 1970. The technology factor in a world trade matrix. In R. Vernon (ed.), *The Technology Factor in International Trade.* New York: Columbia University Press.

Gurley, J. G. 1979. Economic development: a Marxist view. In K.P. Jameson and C.K. Wilber (eds), *Directions in Economic Development.* Notre Dame: University of Notre Dame Press.

Haberler, G. 1936. *The Theory of International Trade.* London: William Hodge.

Hamilton, C. and Svensson, L.E.O. 1984. Do countries' factor endowments correspond to the factor contents in their bilateral trade flows? *Scandinavian Journal of Economics,* 86, 84–97.

Harkness, J. 1978. Factor abundance and comparative advantage. *American Economic Review,* 66, 784–800.

Havrylyshyn, O. 1985. The direction of developing country trade: empirical evidence of South–South trade. *Journal of Development Economics,* 19, 255–83.

Havrylyshyn, O. and Alikhani, A. 1982. 'An annotated bibliography of protection in developing countries'. Mimeo, Washington, DC: World Bank.

Havrylyshyn, O. and Alikhani, A. 1986. 'Changing comparative advantage among developing countries'. Paper presented to the International Economics Study Group Annual Conference, University of Sussex, UK (September).

Havrylyshyn, O. and Civan, E. 1985. Intra-industry trade among developing countries. *Journal of Development Economics,* 18, 253–72.

Havrylyshyn, O. and Wolf, M. 1983. Recent trends in trade among developing countries. *European Economic Review,* 21, 333–62.

Helleiner, G. K. 1981a. Economic theory and North–South negotiations. *World Development,* 9, 539–56.

Helleiner, G. K. 1981b. *Intra-Firm Trade and the Developing Countries.* London: Macmillan.

Hillman, A. L. 1980. Observations on the relationship between 'revealed comparative advantage' and 'comparative advantage' as indicated by pre-trade relative prices. *Weltwirtschaftliches Archiv,* 116, 315–21.

Hirsch, S. 1974. Capital or technology? Confronting the neo-factor proportions and neo-technology accounts of international trade. *Weltwirtschaftliches Archiv,* 110, 535–63.

Hirsch, S. 1975. The product cycle model of international trade – a multi-country cross-section analysis. *Oxford Bulletin of Economics and Statistics,* 37, 305–17.

Hong, W. and Krueger, A. O. (eds) 1975. *Trade and Development in Korea.* Seoul: Korea Development Institute.

Hufbauer, G. C. 1970. The impact of national characteristics and technology on the commodity composition of trade in manufactured goods. In R. Vernon (ed.), *The Technology Factor in International Trade*. New York: Columbia University Press.

Hufbauer, G. C. and O'Neill, J. P. 1972. Unit values of US machinery exports. *Journal of International Economics*, 2, 265–76.

Hymer, S. and Resnick, S. 1969. A model of agrarian economy with non-agricultural activities. *American Economic Review*, 59, 493–506.

James, J. and Stewart, F. 1981. A discussion of the welfare effects of the introduction of new products in developing countries. *Oxford Economic Papers*, 33, 81–107.

Johnson, H. G. 1965. The theory of tariff structure with special reference to world trade and development. In H. G. Johnson and P. B. Kenen (eds), *Trade and Development*. Geneva: Graduate Institute of International Studies.

Johnson, H. G. 1967. The possibility of income losses from increased efficiency or factor accumulation in the presence of tariffs. *Economic Journal*, 77, 151–4.

Johnson, H. G. 1970. A new view of the infant industry argument. In I. A. McDougall and R. H. Snape (eds), *Studies in International Economics*. Amsterdam: North-Holland.

Jones, R. W. 1971. A three-factor model in theory, trade and history. In J. N. Bhagwati, R. W. Jones, R. A. Mundell and J. Vanek (eds), *Trade, Balance of Payments and Growth*. Amsterdam: North-Holland.

Jones, R. W. and Kenen, P. B. 1984. *Handbook of International Economics*, Vol. 1. Amsterdam: North-Holland.

Keesing, D. B. 1967. Outward-looking policies and economic development. *Economic Journal*, 77, 303–20.

Kierzkowski, H. (ed.) 1984. *Monopolistic Competition and International Trade*. Oxford: Oxford University Press.

Krueger, A. O. 1972. Evaluating restrictionist trade regimes: theory and measurement. *Journal of Political Economy*, 80, 48–62.

Krueger, A. O. 1978. *Liberalisation Attempts and Consequences*. Cambridge, Mass.: Ballinger for National Bureau of Economic Research.

Krueger, A. O. , Lary, H. B., Monson, T. and Akransanee, N. 1981. *Trade and Employment in Developing Countries*. Chicago: University of Chicago Press.

Krugman, P. 1979. A model of innovation, technology transfer and the world distribution of income. *Journal of Political Economy*, 87, 253–66.

Krugman, P. 1982. Trade, accumulation and uneven development. *Journal of Development Economics*, 8, 149–61.

Lal, D. 1983. *The Poverty of 'Development Economics'*. Hobart Paperback, 16. London: Institute of Economic Affairs.

Lall, S. 1975. Is dependence a useful concept in analysing underdevelopment? *World Development*, 2, 799–810.

Lawrence, D. and Spiller, P. 1983. Product diversity, economies of scale and international trade. *Quarterly Journal of Economics*, 98, 63–83.

Leamer, E. E. 1974. The commodity composition of international trade in manufactures: an empirical analysis. *Oxford Economic Papers*, 26, 351–74.

Leamer, E. E. 1984. *Sources of International Comparative Advantage: Theory and Evidence*. Cambridge, Mass.: MIT Press.

Leontief, W. 1953. Domestic production and foreign trade: the American capital position re-examined. *Proceedings of the American Philosophical Society*, 97, 332–49.

Lewis, W. A. 1954. Economic development with unlimited supplies of labour. *Manchester School*, 21, 139–91.

Lewis, W. A. 1969. *Aspects of Tropical Trade 1883-1965*. Stockholm: Almqvist and Wiksell.

Lewis, W. A. 1980. The slowing down of the engine of growth. *American Economic Review*, 70, 555-64.

Linder, S. B. 1961. *An Essay on Trade and Transformation*. London: John Wiley and Sons.

Little, I. M. D. 1978. Distributive justice and the new international order. In P. Oppenheimer (ed.), *Issues in International Economics*. London: Oriel Press.

Little, I. M. D. 1982. *Economic Development: Theory, Policies and International Relations*. New York: Basic Books.

Little, I. M. D. and Scott, M. (eds) 1976. *Using Shadow Prices*. London: Heinemann.

Lowinger, T. C. 1971. The neo-factor proportions theory of international trade: an empirical investigation. *American Economic Review*, 61, 675-81.

MacDougall, G. D. A. 1951. British and American exports: a study suggested by the theory of comparative costs, part I. *Economic Journal*, 61, 697-724.

MacDougall, G. D. A. 1952. British and American exports: a study suggested by the theory of comparative costs, part II. *Economic Journal*, 62, 487-521.

MacDougall, G. D. A., Dowley, M., Fox, P. and Pugh, S. 1962. British and American productivity, prices and exports: an addendum. *Oxford Economic Papers*, 14, 297-304.

McKinnon, R. I. 1964. Foreign exchange constraints in economic development and efficient aid allocation. *Economic Journal*, 74, 388-409.

Milner, C. R. 1987. Trade strategies and economic development: theory and evidence. In D. Greenaway (ed.), *Economic Development and International Trade*. London: Macmillan.

Mitchell, D. J. B. 1975. Recent changes in the labour content of US international trade. *Industrial and Labour Relations Review* (April), pp. 355-69.

Myint, H. 1958. The 'classical theory' of international trade and underdeveloped countries. *Economic Journal*, 68, 317-37.

Myint, H. 1977. Adam Smith's theory of international trade in the perspective of economic development. *Economica*, 44, 231-48.

Myrdal, G. 1957. *Economic Theory and Underdeveloped Regions*. London: Duckworth.

Neary, J. P. 1978. Short-run capital specificity and the pure theory of international trade. *Economic Journal*, 88, 488-510.

Newson, M. and Wall, D. 1985. 'Policy and institutional obstacles to South-South trade in manufactures'. Mimeo. Vienna: UNIDO.

Nurkse, R. 1962. *Patterns of Trade and Development*. Oxford: Basil Blackwell.

Paauw, D. S. and Fei, J. C. H. 1973. *The Transition in Open Dualistic Economies*. New Haven: Yale University Press.

Palma, G. 1978. Dependency: a formal theory of underdevelopment or a methodology for the analysis of concrete situations of underdevelopment? *World Development*, 6, 899-901.

Posner, M. V. 1961. International trade and technical change. *Oxford Economic Papers*, 13, 323-41.

Prebisch, R. 1950. *The Economic Development of Latin America and its Principal Problems*. New York: United Nations.

Prebisch, R. 1959. Commercial policy in the underdeveloped countries. *American Economic Review*, 49, 251-73.

Pugel, T. 1981. Technology transfer and the neoclassical theory of international trade. *Research in International Business and Finance*, 2, 11-37.

Ricardo, D. 1951. *The Works and Correspondence of David Ricardo*. Edited by P. Sraffa. Cambridge: Cambridge University Press.

Sampson, G. P. 1986. 'Structural change: accommodating imports from developing countries'. Paper presented to the International Economics Study Group Annual Conference, University of Sussex, UK (September).

Samuelson, P. A. 1971. An exact Hume-Ricardo-Marshall model of international trade. *Journal of International Economics*, 1, 1–18.

Samuelson, P. A. 1976. Illogic of neo-Marxian doctrine of unequal exchange. In D. A. Belsey, E. J. Kane and P. A. Samuelson (eds), *Inflation, Trade and Taxes*. Ohio: Ohio State University Press.

Sapsford, D. 1985. The statistical debate on the net barter terms of trade: A comment and some additional information. *Economic Journal*, 95, 781–8.

Sen, A. K. 1981. Ethical issues in income distribution: national and international. In S. Grassman and E. Lundberg (eds), *The World Economic Order: Past and Prospects*. London: Macmillan.

Singer, H. W. 1950. The distribution of gains between borrowing and investing countries. *American Economic Review*, 40, 473–85.

Singer, H. W. 1974. The distribution of gains from trade and investment – revisited. *Journal of Development Studies*, 11, 376–82.

Sjaastad, L. A. 1980. Commercial policy, true tariffs and relative prices. In J. Black and B. Hindley (eds), *Current Issues in Commercial Policy and Diplomacy*. London: Macmillan.

Smith, S. 1980. The ideas of Samir Amin: theory or tautology. *Journal of Development Studies*, 17, 5–21.

Spraos, J. 1980. The statistical debate on the net barter terms of trade. *Economic Journal*, 90, 107–28.

Stern, R. M. 1962. British and American productivity and comparative costs in international trade. *Oxford Economic Papers*, 14, 275–92.

Stern, R. M. 1975. Testing trade theories. In P. B. Kenen (ed.), *International Trade and Finance: Frontiers for Research*. Cambridge: Cambridge University Press.

Stern, R. M. and Maskus, K. E. 1981. Determinants of the structure of US foreign trade, 1958–76. *Journal of International Economics*, 11, 207–24.

Stewart, F. 1976. The direction of international trade: gains and losses for the third world. In G. K. Helleiner (ed.), *A World Divided*. Cambridge: Cambridge University Press.

Stewart, F. 1977. *Technology and Underdevelopment*. London: Macmillan.

Tan, A. H. H. and Hock, O. C. 1982. 'Singapore'. In B. Balassa (ed.) *Development Strategies in Semi Industrialized Economies*. Baltimore: Johns Hopkins University Press.

Tharakan, P. K. M. 1984. Intra-industry trade between the industrial countries and the developing world. *European Economic Review*, 26, 213–27.

Tharakan, P. K. M. 1985. Empirical analyses of the commodity composition of trade. In D. Greenaway (ed.), *Current Issues in International Trade*. London: Macmillan.

Tharakan, P. K. M. 1986. The intra-industry trade of Benelux with the developing world. *Weltwirtschaftliches Archiv*, 122, 131–49.

Tharakan, P. K. M. and Vandoorne, M. 1979. Structure of Belgium's comparative advantage vis-à-vis the developing world: a tentative classification of industries. *Cahiers Économiques de Bruxelles*, pp. 213–34.

Tyler, W. G. 1972. Trade in manufactures and labour skill content: the Brazilian case. *Economia Internazionale*, 25, 314–34.

Tyler, W. 1976. *Manufactured Export Expansion and Industrialization in Brazil*. Keil Study No. 134. Tübingen: Mohr.

Uzawa, H. 1961. On a two-sector model of economic growth. *Review of Economic Studies*, 29, 40–7.

Vanek, J. 1968. The factor proportions theory: the *n*-factor case. *Kyklos*, 4, 749–56.

Venables, A. J. 1985. *International Trade, Trade and Industrial Policy, and Imperfect Competition: A Survey*. CEPR Discussion Paper No. 74. London: Centre for Economic Policy Research.

Ventura-Dias, V. and Sorsa, P. 1985. *Historical Patterns of South-South Trade*. Geneva: UNCTAD.

Vernon, R. 1966. International investment and international trade in the product cycle. *Quarterly Journal of Economics*, 80, 121–5.

World Bank. 1982. *Industrial Policy in Peru*. Mimeo. Washington, DC: World Bank.

World Bank. 1984. 'List of effective protection studies', held at the Industrial Strategy and Policy Division. Mimeo. Washington, DC: World Bank.

2
Trade policy and industrialization in LDCs
Colin Kirkpatrick

2.1 Introduction

The objective of this survey is to examine the contribution of trade policy to the industrialization process in less developed countries (LDCs). For the great majority of LDCs, industrialization is a fundamental policy objective. In such countries industrial development is considered necessary to achieve sustained economic growth, to create more employment opportunities, to provide for the basic needs of the population, and to lead to the diversification and modernization of their economies.

Within the broad parameters set by its existing stage of development, size, and resource endowments, the trade policies that a country pursues can have a significant impact on the pattern and pace of industrial development. The trade measures adopted by LDCs have differed widely, and in addition, some countries have altered their policies in important ways. These different policies have been associated in turn with significantly different trade and industrial performance, providing much evidence for analysis. Not surprisingly, the interaction between trade and industrial development has been the subject of much discussion and controversy among development economists.

The structure of this survey is as follows. Section 2.2 provides a broad overview of the progress of industrialization in LDCs during the past two decades, focusing on the growth of industrial activity and changes in its structure and composition. This section also evaluates the attempts that have been made to identify a standard pattern of industrial development. Section 2.3 identifies the main theoretical perspectives that have been used in analysing the relationship between trade policy and development, particularly of the industrial sector. The

Much of the work on this survey was undertaken while I was a visiting fellow in the Department of Economics, Research School of Pacific Studies, Australian National University. I am grateful to the School for the support and facilities provided. I am also indebted to Norman Gemmell and Philip Leeson for constructive comments on an earlier draft.

fourth section is concerned with the two major trade-related industrialization strategies adopted in LDCs – import-substituting industrialization and export-oriented industrialization. Section 2.5 contains some concluding comments.

A note on terminology is appropriate at this stage.

The term 'industrialization' is used in a variety of different ways in the economic literature, and it is necessary to clarify its meaning to avoid subsequent confusion. Industrialization will be used in this survey to refer to the growth in output of those industries which together make up the industrial sector. There is no general agreement on the types of activities to include in the industrial sector, but for present purposes it will be restricted to four major production activities – mining and quarrying; manufacturing; electricity, gas and water; and construction – with much of the discussion being focused on the manufacturing industry.[1]

'Trade policy' refers to the set of policy instruments that directly influence a country's balance of payments. These measures include tariffs, quotas, taxes and subsidies on exports and imports, as well as exchange rate policy and regulation of international capital movements. Trade policy should be conceived of as a means of pursuing the goal of industrialization and not as an end in itself. The choice and use of trade-related measures should be determined, therefore, by a country's industrialization objectives and general development goals, and implemented in conjunction with those other policy instruments that are appropriate to the attainment of these objectives.[2]

2.2 Industrialization in LDCs: an overview

This section is intended to provide an overview of the pattern of industrialization and structural change in the LDCs. We begin with a mainly statistical account of industrial development at the sectoral and industry level. This is followed by an examination of the cross-sectional evidence on the level of industrialization and the structure of international trade. Finally, we analyse the relationship between changes in industrial structure and economic growth in LDCs and in particular, evaluate the attempts that have been made to identify a standard 'pattern' of industrial development.

In making cross-country comparisons, two points should be borne in mind. The first is that the group of countries categorized as LDCs differ greatly in their economic and industrial structure; indeed these differences are often as great as those existing between groups of LDCs and developed countries (DCs). Differences in size (measured in terms of both area and population), resources, income levels, development objectives, historical experience, and social and political systems all contribute to a diversity among LDCs in their basic industrial characteristics. Second, the national data on which the comparisons are made are often imperfect (Kirkpatrick *et al.*, 1984, chapter 1). Further distortions may be created when official exchange rates are used to convert data from domestic currency to a common international value.

2.2.1   Industrial structure and growth

The post-war industrialization of LDCs has been an impressive achievement. Hughes (1980, p. 12) suggests that 'the past three decades of industrialization in developing countries have created a second industrial revolution that is transforming the world economy even more radically than did the changes that took place in Great Britain in the late eighteenth and early nineteenth centuries'. Over the period 1960–81, LDCs' industrial output grew more rapidly than GDP, resulting in a rising share of industry (and manufacturing) in GDP (table 2.1). At the same time, LDCs' manufacturing output grew faster than that of the DCs, with LDCs' share of global manufacturing activity rising from 8.1 per cent in 1963 to 11.0 per cent in 1982 (UNIDO, 1983, p. 22). The distribution of manufacturing activity between LDCs, however, is very uneven: the 10 developing countries with the largest manufacturing value added (MVA), between them accounted for 70 per cent of all LDC MVA in 1980 (UNIDO, 1983, p. 35).

Table 2.2 describes the evolution of the manufacturing sector by end-use, categorizing output into consumer non-durables, capital goods and industrial supplies or intermediates.[3] The data show that although their share has been falling, consumer non-durables continue to predominate, with capital goods accounting for less than one-third of LDC MVA in 1979.

More detailed information on the composition of LDCs' MVA is given in table 2.3. Food, beverages and tobacco (ISIC 31) was the largest industrial division in the early 1960s, but its share fell from 24 per cent in 1963 to 19 per cent in 1979. Metal products, machinery and equipment (ISIC 38) expanded

Table 2.1   Growth in LDCs' industrial sector, 1960–81

	Industry[a]				Manufacturing			
	Annual growth rate (%)		Share of GDP (%)		Annual growth rate (%)		Share of GDP (%)	
	1960–70	1970–81	1960	1981	1960–70	1970–81	1960	1981
Low income LDCs[b]	6.6	3.6	25.0	34.0	5.4	2.9	11.0	16.0
Lower middle income LDCs[c]	6.8	7.4	25.0	35.0	7.1	5.8	15.0	17.0
Upper middle income LDCs[d]	8.8	4.5	33.9	39.0	7.8	6.3	23.0	24.0

[a] Industrial sector comprises mining and quarrying, manufacturing, construction and electricity, gas and water.
[b] LDCs with per capita GNP less than $410 in 1981.
[c] LDCs with per capita GNP $410–1700 in 1981.
[d] LDCs with per capita GNP $1700–5700 in 1981.

Source: World Bank (1983, tables 2 and 3).

Table 2.2 Composition of LDCs' manufacturing output, 1963, 1973, 1979 (percentages)

Classification by end-use[a]	1963	1973	1979
Consumer non-durables	51.9	40.1	37.6
Industrial intermediates	27.3	31.5	31.2
Capital goods (including consumer durables)	20.8	28.4	31.2

[a] For the classification of ISIC codes into these categories, see UNIDO (1979), p. 172.

Source: UNIDO (1983, table III.2).

rapidly, accounting for 24 per cent of MVA in 1979. At the three-digit ISIC classification level, food, textiles and petroleum refineries were the three largest industrial branches, although their share declined from 42 per cent in 1963 to 31 per cent in 1979.

2.2.2 Trade in manufactures

The increasing importance of LDCs' industrial activity is reflected in the changes that have occurred in the structure of their merchandise trade. Between 1960 and 1981 the LDCs' share of world exports of manufactures increased from 3.9 to 9.2 per cent (UNIDO, 1983, p. 190). Table 2.4 shows that the share of manufactures in total LDC exports rose from 9.2 per cent in 1960 to 22.9 per cent in 1982: if mineral fuels and related materials are excluded, manufactures accounted for more than 50 per cent of exports in 1982.

LDCs' manufactured export trade is concentrated in a small number of countries. Three Asian economies – Hong Kong, the Republic of Korea and Singapore – together accounted for more than a third of LDC manufactured exports in 1980: the 10 largest exporters contributed almost 60 per cent of total developing countries' manufactured exports in the same year (UNIDO, 1985, table III.5).[4]

The conventional definition of manufactured exports (SITC 5–8 less 68) excludes trade in processed materials, although such activities are classified as part of the manufacturing sector (ISIC 3). Use of an alternative definition of trade in manufactures – trade in 'industrially processed goods and intermediates' – results in the inclusion of a large number of resource-based and lightly processed products. Developing countries' trade in manufactures has traditionally been dominated by exports of processed goods (mainly resource-based products), but as table 2.5 shows, this pattern has begun to change as the major LDC exporters widen their industrial base and increase the share of capital goods in total exports.

2.2.3 Patterns of industrialization

Various attempts have been made to analyse in quantitative terms the structural changes that occur during the process of industrial development, with the

Table 2.3 Structure of LDCs' manufacturing output (1975 prices) in industrial divisions and major groups, 1963, 1973, 1979 (percentages)

Major industrial group or branch	ISIC	Developing countries		
		1963	1973	1979
Food, beverages and tobacco	31	24.2	18.8	18.7
Food products	311	17.7	13.7	13.1
Beverages	313	3.1	2.7	3.3
Tobacco	314	3.4	2.4	2.3
Textiles	321	13.4	10.1	8.8
Wearing apparel, leather and footwear	322–324	5.5	3.9	3.6
Wearing apparel	322	3.4	2.5	2.3
Leather and fur products	323	0.8	0.5	0.5
Footwear	324	1.3	0.9	0.8
Wood products and furniture	33	3.9	3.2	2.9
Wood and cork products	331	2.5	2.1	2.0
Furniture and fixtures, excluding metal	332	1.3	1.1	0.9
Paper, printing and publishing	34	5.1	4.8	4.2
Paper	341	2.3	2.4	2.3
Printing and publishing	342	2.8	2.4	1.9
Chemical, petroleum, plastic products	35	20.6	24.0	23.2
Industrial chemicals	351	2.4	3.9	4.2
Other chemicals	352	4.8	5.9	6.5
Petroleum refineries	353	10.7	10.5	8.9
Miscellaneous products of petroleum and coal	354	0.3	0.5	0.5
Rubber products	355	1.6	1.9	1.9
Plastic products	356	0.8	1.4	1.3
Non-metallic mineral products	36	4.4	5.0	5.6
Pottery, china and earthenware	361	0.7	0.7	0.7
Glass	362	0.7	1.0	1.0
Other non-metallic mineral products	369	3.0	3.4	3.9
Basic metal industries	37	6.1	6.8	7.6
Iron and steel	371	4.3	4.9	5.6
Non-ferrous metals	372	1.8	1.9	2.0
Metal products, machinery and equipment	38	15.0	22.0	24.0
Metal products, excluding machinery	381	4.0	4.5	5.0
Non-electrical machinery	382	2.7	5.4	5.4
Electrical machinery	383	2.9	4.4	6.0
Transport equipment	384	5.0	7.2	7.2
Professional and scientific equipment, photographic and optical goods	385	0.3	0.4	0.4
Other manufactures	390	1.8	1.4	1.3

Note: Branch shares may not add up to group shares because of rounding. The country coverage used when deriving the structure of output for 1963 differed somewhat from that used for 1973 and 1979.

Source: UNIDO (1983, table III.7).

Table 2.4 Share of manufactures (SITC 5–8 less 68) in LDCs' total exports, 1960–82

Year	Manufactures as share of total exports (%)	Manufactures as share of total exports, excluding mineral fuels and related materials (SITC 3)
1960	9.2	12.8
1970	17.3	25.9
1975	15.1	37.0
1980	17.8	47.1
1982	22.9	53.3

Source: UNIDO (1985, table III.1).

Table 2.5 Composition of LDCs' export trade in industrially processed goods and intermediates, by end-use, 1970–79[a] (percentages)

Economic grouping	Year	End-use[b]			
		Consumer non-durable goods	Inter- mediates	Capital goods and consumer durables	Other industrially processed goods
Major exporting LDCs[c]	1970	26.7	30.8	12.6	30.0
	1979	25.4	24.2	27.3	23.1
Other LDCs[d]	1970	3.8	36.1	2.7	57.4
	1979	8.2	29.8	5.0	57.1

[a] For definitions of trade in industrially processed goods and intermediates, see UNIDO (1985), appendix I.

[b] For definition of the product groups by end-use, see UNIDO (1979), p. 172.

[c] Seven LDCs whose share in total value of exports of manufactures (SITC 5–8 less 68) from all LDCs was 2 per cent or more in 1978, i.e. Argentina, Brazil, Hong Kong, India, Malaysia, Republic of Korea, Singapore.

[d] Fifty-four LDCs for which comparable data were available for both 1970 and 1979.

Source: UNIDO (1983, table VII.6).

objective of identifying a standard 'pattern' of industrialization. The basic hypothesis is that, as per capita income rises, 'industrialisation occurs with a sufficient degree of uniformity across countries to produce consistent patterns of change in resource allocation, factor use and related phenomena' (Ballance *et al.*, 1982, p. 109).

Following the pioneering studies by Kuznets,[6] numerous empirical studies have shown that after allowing for variations in size and resource endowments of the country, there is a well-defined relationship between changes in the relative size and composition of the manufacturing sector and the level of per capita income.[7] Typically, structural change begins with a small share of manufacturing in GDP at low levels of per capita income. The rate of structural change increases rapidly over intermediate income levels. At higher income levels (that is, above $1000 per capita), the manufacturing sector's share continues to grow, but at a slower rate as the country enters the mature stage (UNIDO, 1979, pp. 44–5).[8] When the industrial sector is disaggregated, industries can be classified according to the stage of development at which they made their main contribution to development. Chenery and Taylor (1968) identified three groups of industries. 'Early' industries (for example, food, leather goods, textiles) supplied the essential demands of low income countries, utilized simple technologies, and did not increase their share of GNP above a relatively low per capita income level. 'Middle' industries (for example, non-metallic minerals, rubber products, wood products, chemicals and petroleum refining) grew rapidly as income per capita rose from very low levels, but that share grew slowly once an intermediate per capita income level was reached. 'Late' industries (clothing, printing, consumer durables with high income elasticities, paper and metal products) continued to grow faster than GNP up to the highest income levels, and they typically doubled their share of GNP in the later stages of industrialization.

Opinions differ as to the value and relevance of statistical exercises designed to identify cross-sectional patterns of industrial development. For supporters of patterns analyses,

[the results] provide insights into the manner in which resource endowment, country size and level of income bring about changes in the industrial structure and serve to indicate possible – rather than optimal – growth paths. Furthermore, information on the average structure of countries at a given income level provides a useful reference point when anticipating the industrial structure of countries that are expected to reach comparable levels in the future. (UNIDO, 1979, p. 45.)

From this perspective, Chenery and Synquin (1975, p. 135) have argued that the notion of a *dichotomy* between developed and less developed countries can be replaced by the concept of a *transition* from one state or structure of development to another.

Critics of patterns analysis point to the data limitations and definitional problems associated with cross-sectional studies of this type. Attempts to obtain a pattern from time-series data consistent with the normal cross-section pattern have been unsuccessful (Steuer and Voivodas, 1965; Jameson, 1982). The definition of industrial growth used by Chenery and others has also been criticized (summarized in Colman and Nixson, 1986, chapter 9).

With respect to the relevance of the patterns analysis to policy formulation in contemporary LDCs, critics argue that the 'normal' pattern all too often assumes a normative value or significance that it does not merit. Normal patterns are neither necessarily desirable nor even possible for all LDCs, and deviations from the normal pattern are neither good nor bad, a sign neither of success nor of failure. The pattern of development and industrialization of each individual country will be influenced by its own economic and political history, its relationship with other countries, and by changes in the external environment. Active government intervention can in turn shape and influence the nature of these relationships.

Given the complexities of the issues involved, the data limitations, and the less than complete knowledge to explain how and why economies evolve over time, the balanced assessment of Batchelor *et al.* (1980b, pp. 55–6) is worth quoting:

Belief in the futility of a search for laws of growth applicable to every corner of the world economy need not rule out the existence of identifiable groups of countries for which valid generalisations can be found and common models constructed. But the many doubts about uniform growth patterns suggest that countries must be similar in many ways before the simple model can be applied and the number of categories to which they might belong multiplies rapidly with increases in the number of criteria by which they might be classified.

2.3 Alternative theoretical perspectives

A variety of analytical perspectives can be brought to bear on the LDCs' experience of trade policy and industrialization, giving rise to differences in interpretation of the historical record and in the policy conclusions drawn. In this section we discuss the three major analytical perspectives to be found in the development literature – neoclassical, structural and radical. These different approaches are not mutually exclusive and have certain common points of reference; furthermore, there are various differences of emphasis and focus internal to each approach. But for present purposes this categorization provides a useful method of structuring this review of the trade and industrialization literature.[9]

2.3.1 The neoclassical perspective

Overview

For the neoclassical approach, with welfare economics as its theoretical core, the yardstick for economic evaluation is efficiency in the allocation of available scarce resources.

An economy is considered production efficient if the supply of any good (or service) cannot be increased without reducing the supply of some other good. One important way in which economies can make goods available is by exporting some goods in exchange for others; thus production efficiency also implies that a country has made best use of its foreign trade possibilities (World Bank, 1983, p. 42).

Using market equilibrium analysis, efficiency can be established by the pricing of inputs and outputs to reflect their relative scarcities. Neoclassical economics can thus be described as, a paradigm that tells one to investigate markets and prices, perhaps expecting them often to work well, but also to be on the watch for aberrations and ways of correcting them. Perhaps the single best touchstone is a concern for prices and their role (Little, 1982, pp. 25–6).

Inefficiencies and resource misallocations arise when markets are unable to settle at their equilibrium, market-clearing prices.

For internationally traded goods and services the efficient allocation of resources is determined according to their marginal productivities at international prices (Little and Mirrlees, 1974; Squire and van der Tak, 1975; World Bank, 1983; see survey 9). Again, this is held to be achieved through the unfettered operation of the market mechanism, with market prices serving to allocate resources efficiently according to comparative advantage.

The basic policy prescription which flows from the neoclassical analysis is the need to 'get the prices right'. To achieve these ends, two complementary policy prescriptions are invariably advocated: (1) the removal of domestic market distortions – which may be the result of either previous government intervention or other institutional factors – thereby enabling markets to operate 'freely'; (2) the 'liberalization' of international trade and exchange markets by the removal of trade and exchange controls, so allowing the economy to function as near as possible within a free trade regime (Balassa, 1982b).

Gains from trade[10]

The central proposition of neoclassical trade theory is that, given certain assumptions, free trade is superior in economic efficiency terms both to autarky and various forms of trade restriction. The superiority of free trade is demonstrated using the familiar two-commodity comparative advantage analysis.

Figure 2.1 represents the case of the small country for whom the terms of trade are given exogenously. There are two commodities, M and X, and the production possibilities curve is PP. In the closed economy situation, equilibrium is at B where the production possibilities curve and the community indifference curve are tangential to each other, and production equals consumption for both M and X. If we now introduce the possibility of international trade, with the international price ratio given by WW, the equilibrium production point moves to A, where the marginal rate of transformation (MRT) in production is equal to the MRT in international trade. Consumption possibilities are now expanded to WW, and the equilibrium consumption point resulting from the particular income distribution yielded by free trade will be, say, at C where the marginal rate of substitution in consumption (MRS) is equal to the MRT in international exchange, and the community has moved to a higher indifference curve. The essential point made by this analysis, which was originally developed by Samuelson (1939, 1962), is that there are potential gains from trade in a small country model, provided the exogenously determined world prices diverge from autarky or restricted trade prices.

It should be noted that this well-known result depends upon a number of critical assumptions. In particular, the proposition that free trade is superior to

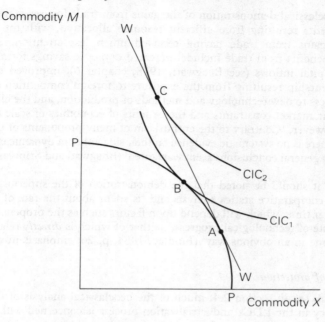

FIGURE 2.1   The gains from trade.

autarky in the small country case assumes a competitive price system which under free trade causes the economy to attain its efficient production point. Other assumptions made include the absence of increasing returns, no externalities, the feasibility of lump-sum transfers, and flexible factor prices to ensure full employment of factors of production. Furthermore, as Corden (1984, p. 72) reminds us, the comparative advantage model based on the divergence between autarky and free trade prices is only a proximate explanation of the gains from trade: 'the underlying explanation must derive from all those factors that lie behind the sources of comparative advantage, differences which give rise to the divergences between autarky and free trade prices'.

The neoclassical analysis explains the differences in comparative advantage in terms of the factor endowments of each country. The Heckscher–Ohlin theory (summarized in survey 1 and Jones and Neary, 1984, pp. 14–21) develops a two-factor (labour and capital), two-commodity model and demonstrates how each country will have a comparative advantage in, and therefore will specialize in, the production of the commodity which is relatively intensive in the use of the relatively abundant factor. If LDCs are characterized as relatively labour-abundant, their predicted comparative advantage will be in the production of labour-intensive exports. This body of analysis also rests on a number of key assumptions; notably that each country has equal access to the same production technology and that factor endowments are internationally immobile.

The neoclassical demonstration of the gains from trade focuses mainly on the static benefits resulting from efficient resource allocation, with the potential dynamic gains from trade having received much less attention. Suggested dynamic benefits from trade include increased domestic savings formation and foreign capital inflows (see Bhagwati, 1978, chapter 6), improved quality of entrepreneurship resulting from the exposure to foreign competition (Keesing, 1967), access to new technology and methods of production, and the elimination of domestic market constraints and the benefits of economies of scale (Krueger, 1978). However, 'Contrary to the enthusiasm of many proponents of liberalized regimes, there is no systematic evidence on their side either of dynamic efficiencies . . . and no general conclusions seem warranted' (Bhagwati and Srinivasan, 1979, p. 14).

Finally, it should be noted that the demonstration of the superiority of free trade is a comparative statics analysis and 'is silent about the rate of economic growth over time, which will depend upon factors such as the propensity to save and the rate of technological progress, neither of which is *directly* related to the trade regime in an obvious way' (Findlay, 1984, p. 26; emphasis in original).

Measures of protection

As we shall see in section 2.4, much of the neoclassical analysis of the role of trade policy in the LDCs' industrialization process is concerned with assessing the economic repercussions of departures from free trade.

The overall degree of protection for the economy as a whole can be estimated in a number of ways. Where quotas are widely used to restrain imports, tariff schedules will provide an inadequate guide to protection levels. It is necessary, therefore, to obtain direct price comparisons of the domestic market and import (cif) prices, and estimate the *implicit (or 'equivalent') tariff rate*.[11] A first measure of the overall level of protection is therefore given by the (weighted) average of tariff-equivalent rates of protection.

A second measure of the overall *protection 'bias'* in the economy is given by the ratio of the domestic relative price of import-competing to exportable goods to the international relative price of importables to exportables. Thus, the estimated measure of bias expresses the extent to which domestic prices diverge from those that would exist under free trade conditions.[12]

The degree of protection given to particular activities can be measured in terms of either the *effective rate of protection* (ERP) or *domestic resource cost* (DRC). The effective rate of protection is based on the notion that the potential effect of protectionist measures on resource allocation decisions will depend upon the degree of protection given to value-added, not just final outputs. The ERP is calculated by expressing value-added at domestic prices as a ratio of value-added at world (free trade) prices. The ERP assumes that the only distortions are in the tradeable sector. DRC is a more comprehensive measure of protection, since it allows for distortions in domestic factor markets. The DRC of a particular activity is estimated as the ratio of 'corrected' costs of domestic factors of production to value-added at international prices.[13]

Infant industry and optimum tariff caveats

The neoclassical analysis of the gains from trade acknowledges that departures from free trade may be justifiable in certain circumstances. The infant industry case is the oldest and best-known argument for intervention. This case for protection is based on the notion that an industry may have high costs in the early stages of its existence, but through time a decrease in costs, or positive externalities, will enable it to become competitive. The argument is therefore for temporary protection, to give the 'infant' sufficient time to 'grow up'. The infant industry argument for protection is considered in detail in Corden (1974, chapter 9) and Krueger (1984, section 1.2.1).

The second qualification to the free trade case is the optimum tariff argument. This case refers to the large country which enjoys a degree of monopoly or monopsony power in traded goods markets, enabling it to move the terms of trade in its own favour by the imposition of import tariffs and export taxes. A summary of the basic theory is given in Corden (1974) and recent extensions to the analysis are reviewed in Corden (1984, section 5).

Summary

The neoclassical trade theory emphasizes the static gains from free trade and argues that protectionist measures (with the minor exceptions of the infant industry and optimum tariff arguments) will lower the economy's level of welfare. These static gains from trade may be reinforced by various dynamic benefits. Free trade on the basis of comparative advantage will lead each country to specialize in the production of exports that are intensive in its relatively abundant factor of production. The policy implication of the neoclassical analysis is clear: greater participation in international trade and increased integration into the international economy are beneficial for the national economy.

2.3.2 The structuralist perspective

Much of the early writing on development economics in the 1950s was characterized by what became known as a structuralist approach. Influenced by the earlier work of British economists on the limitations of the market mechanism in the UK (see Arndt, 1985), structuralists sought to show that the price mechanism in LDCs did not work in accordance with the perfectly competitive model, and that neoclassical economic theory was therefore largely inapplicable in LDCs. Little (1982, p. 20) describes the structuralist economist as a person who 'sees the world as inflexible. Change is inhibited by obstacles, bottlenecks and constraints. . . . In economic terms, the supply of most things is inelastic'. The inflexibility and lack of responsiveness in the market mechanism provides a rationale for intervention to release the constraints and facilitate the process of change and growth.

Structuralists criticize the neoclassical analysis of trade and industrialization issues on a number of grounds. Prebisch (1959) and Singer (1950) argued that the long run trend in the terms of trade moved against primary products vis-à-vis manufactures, hence LDCs needed to switch from a reliance upon trade and primary exports towards domestic-market based industrialization. On similar lines, Nurkse (1962) argued that in contrast to the nineteenth century, international trade in the post-war period could no longer act as an 'engine of growth' for LDCs, and that an alternative 'engine' must be sought in domestic import-substituting industrialization. Others argued that rapid industrialization would create the need for large capital and intermediate good imports which could only be purchased from the limited export earnings if consumption good imports were restricted (Myrdal, 1956).

The notion that LDCs' industrialization efforts were constrained by a lack of foreign exchange led structuralists to view the foreign trade sector as a separate constraint on growth. This was formalized by Chenery and Strout (1966) and McKinnon (1966) in the 'two-gap' model which showed how the investment required to achieve a target growth rate could be constrained by the available foreign exchange, even when domestic savings were sufficient to meet the desired rate of economic growth. This result is obtained by assuming that the rate of growth in export earnings is exogenously given, that the import bill consists entirely of 'essential' consumption goods and investment goods, and that the import content of domestic production cannot be reduced. The two-gap model of a foreign exchange constraint was widely used in the 1960s and 1970s to estimate the foreign aid requirements of LDCs.

In the 1950s and early 1960s, structuralist thinking was in the ascendancy, and its main thrust was to demonstrate how protectionism would assist industrialization. With the resurgence of neoclassical orthodoxy in the 1960s and 1970s, the emphasis in the structuralist literature became more defensive, seeking to show why free trade will not necessarily be to the advantage of LDCs.

Much of the structuralist criticism of the pro-trade argument is directed at the static character of the neoclassical theory. It is argued that the orthodox analysis ignores the difficulties which a country may face in adapting to changes in comparative advantage over time. Adjustment to changing patterns of international demand is never frictionless, and over-specialization in a small range of exports dictated by comparative advantage may lead to problems of earnings instability and longer-run structural adjustment. The assumption that the supply of factors of production is fixed is violated by the international movement of labour and capital, and the implications of foreign capital inflows in particular for LDCs' industrial development require careful study. The assumption of a static technology with a given set of characteristics which is equally accessible to all countries obviously bears little relation to reality. Where technology is continually changing and accessibility to new technologies is imperfect, the ability to obtain and adopt the changing technology becomes an important factor in determining the relationships between trade and industrial development (Stewart, 1977).

The structure of international markets is also of concern to structuralists. Contrary to the neoclassical assumption of world prices being set by competitive market conditions with 'arms-length' transactions between independent parties, it is known that a significant proportion of world trade takes place on an intra-firm basis; that is, the buyer and seller are branches of the same transnational firm (Helleiner, 1981b). This gives rise to transactions at 'transfer', rather than open-market, prices (Lall, 1978, 1979). Other imperfections – market concentration, non-price competition, monopsony and monopoly, and product differentiation – are frequently found in international markets (Helleiner, 1979b).

Structuralists are also concerned with the distributional impact of free trade policy, both between and within countries. The orthodox gains from trade analysis does not consider how the gains are distributed between the trading partners. Structuralists argue that the imperfections in world markets systematically bias the gains from trade against the weaker bargaining partner, the LDCs. Intervention aimed at correcting these imperfections and shifting the distribution of trade gains towards the LDCs is therefore called for as, for example, in the attempts in the 1970s to introduce a 'new international economic order' by negotiated change between developed and developing countries (Cline, 1979; Kirkpatrick and Nixson, 1976, 1977). The gains to a country will also be influenced by the pattern of foreign participation in industrialization – the contribution of foreign-owned factors of production, the foreign ownership and control of marketing and distributional networks for exports, the reliance on imported technology (Kirkpatrick and Nixson, 1981).

The structuralist literature contrasts sharply with the neoclassical analysis in that it largely eschews the use of formal economic models and theory. But theoretical elegance is not necessarily correlated with either reality or the capacity to explain and predict. The danger of relying entirely upon neoclassical theory for the analysis of LDCs' trade and industrialization issues is that:

[it] accustoms the analyst to treating important elements of reality, such as oligopoly, transnational corporate intra-firm trade, or imperfect and asymmetrically available information, as mere 'wrinkles' on the 'general case'. Similarly, such difficulties of real world markets as externalities, instabilities, and 'crises' are considered as oddities. The problem is not that there is no literature on these matters (in fact there is a very vigorous one); rather, it is that habits of thought develop which generate simple, and almost subconscious and automatic, approaches to economic issues which (as the relevant theoretical literature demonstrates) are far more complex than the core model would suggest. Almost imperceptibly, prisoners of their own paradigm, students of economics risk beginning to regard all government policies as 'interventions', likely to impede the harmonious functioning of markets; and to regard the distribution of income (and power) as a matter wholly independent of market functioning, to be handled by separate policies (lump-sum transfers) which do not 'interfere' with markets (Helleiner, 1981a, p. 542).

2.3.3 The radical perspective

The structuralist perspective, which was particularly associated with economists working in the Economic Commission for Latin America (ECLA) during the 1950s, came under sustained attack for its exclusive reliance on economic analysis. As Cardoso and Faletto (1979, pp. viii–ix) put it,

In spite of their critical nature, ECLA economic theories were not based on an analysis of social process, did not call attention to imperialistic relationships among countries, and did not take into account the asymmetric relations between classes. Consequently a counter critique which cited the narrowness of the ECLA approach also spread through Latin America.

This counter-critique has been given various names – dependency, under-development, neo-Marxist, or radical. There are different emphases between these various schools, and the interested reader is referred to Colman and Nixson (1986, chapter 2), and Palma (1978) for more detailed surveys. But for present purposes it is sufficient to identify a number of common themes in this literature as it relates to trade policy and industrialization in LDCs.

The basic argument in the radical paradigm is that international trade between the 'centre' and the 'periphery' impedes the economic progress of the LDCs. This trade-induced polarization is attributed to a variety of factors. Early writers concentrated on the impact of colonial trading links, where the foreign-owned extractive or primary producing industry had few linkages with the domestic economy. In this 'enclave' type of activity, inputs were largely imported and the output was exported. Foreign control ensured that the 'surplus' earned in the enclave industries was transferred to the developed mother country (Baran, 1957; Leys, 1975, chapter 1). The ending of colonialization and the achievement of political independence left this situation of economic dependence, or neo-colonialism, substantially unaltered.

Following political independence, nationalization of foreign-owned assets was thought to be the means of ending the dependent relationship. Compulsory acquisition by the state of foreign-owned assets was wide-spread in the LDCs during the 1950s and 1960s, but it soon became clear that merely altering the ownership structure did not necessarily increase local control. In many cases the nationalized enterprise continued to rely upon foreign parties for the supply of material inputs, managerial and technical manpower, technology, and in the case of export production, access to overseas marketing and distribution networks (Kirkpatrick and Nixson, 1981).

With the spread of industrialization in the Third World, the attention of radical writers switched to the role of foreign capital in the industrialization process. Much of the industrial investment was undertaken by the transnational corporations through direct foreign investment or, in some cases, joint-ventures with local private or state interests. This reliance upon transnationals (TNCs) strengthened the LDCs' dependent relationship in a number of ways. Particular importance was attached to the question of technological dependency. It was argued that the LDC typically imported a type of technology which was inappropriate to the factor conditions prevailing in developing economies: it was often highly capital-intensive, creating few employment opportunities other than for a small, high-wage 'labour aristocracy'. Technological choice was in turn linked to product choice, and the TNC was seen as producing a range of outputs which catered only for the high-income groups' demands, inappropriate to the needs of the mass of the population. The TNCs' use of monopoly practices such as the restriction of access to new technology, transfer pricing and 'creative accounting', and their control of marketing and distribution channels for exports, were seen as additional ways in which the LDCs' dependent situation was maintained through this reliance on foreign capital. The extensive literature on the role of TNCs in the LDCs' industrial development is reviewed in Colman and Nixson (1986, chapter 10); Kirkpatrick *et al.* (1984, chapter 4), and in survey 3 of this volume.

Other writers in the dependency tradition criticized the early literature for its emphasis upon the external forces as the cause of the dependent relationship. Their argument was that dependency could only be maintained by foreign capital if it enjoyed the collaboration and cooperation of domestic interest groups. Dos Santos (1973, p. 78) suggests that

the concept of dependence itself cannot be understood without reference to the articulation of dominant interests in the hegemonic centres and in the dependent societies. 'External' domination, in a pure sense, is in principle impracticable. Domination is practicable only when it finds support among those local groups that profit from it.

This line of argument led to an examination of the class structure in LDCs and the identification of those groups – 'compradors' or 'collaboration elites' – who benefited from an association with foreign capital and the type of 'dependent' industrial development being pursued.

Radicals disagree on the possibilities of reducing the dependency of LDCs, and achieving 'independent industrialization'. For some, the establishment of a domestic technological capacity, which in turn may require a local capacity for capital goods production, is seen as a critical step towards a more independent form of industrialization. Others argue that a more autarkic form of industrial development is required. Finally, for those who see the roots of the problem in the uneven distribution of economic wealth and income in the LDCs, a removal of dependence requires nothing less than a radical transformation of the economic and political structures within the developing countries themselves.

2.4 Experience with trade policy and industrialization: import-substituting industrialization and export-oriented industrialization

A broad distinction is normally drawn between two trade-related industrialization strategies – production for the domestic market of previously imported goods (import-substituting industrialization, ISI); and the production of manufactured goods for external markets (export-oriented industrialization, EOI). In practice, most LDCs have employed elements of both strategies in their industrialization drive, while the emphasis given to each approach has altered through time. In the 1950s and 1960s, ISI dominated the industrialization strategies of the larger Latin American countries (Brazil, Argentina, Mexico) and a number of large countries in South and South-East Asia (Pakistan, India, the Philippines). In the early to mid-1960s, ISI began to be adopted in a number of more important sub-Saharan African economies (Nigeria, Kenya, Ghana, Zambia) and in the smaller Latin American and South-East Asian countries. Since the mid-1960s an increasing number of LDCs have adopted EOI strategies. The earliest adherents of this approach – Republic of Korea, Taiwan, Singapore,

Hong Kong – were joined subsequently by a number of larger semi-industrialized LDCs which shifted from the earlier ISI strategy to policies aimed at encouraging EOI.

2.4.1 Import-substituting industrialization

Origins

As noted above, ISI has exerted an undeniable attraction for the majority of LDCs. In part this lies in its common-sense appeal that, when faced with a balance of payments constraint, it appears easier to save foreign exchange through ISI than earn it by exporting manufactured goods, together with the undoubted psychological appeal of demonstrating an ability to produce something for oneself rather than to depend on imports. In many instances these motivations were reinforced by external circumstances (Hirschman, 1968). The severe decline in export earnings from primary products in the inter-war depression period and war-time shortages of imports, provided a major stimulus to ISI in Latin America.[14] Subsequently the liberalization of the post-war economy, and structural changes within the developed capitalist economies, resulted in a changed structure of capital exports to LDCs, with direct investment by the transnational corporations (TNCs) playing a major part in the post-war ISI process (Kirkpatrick and Nixson, 1983, pp. 45–55).

Experience of ISI

During the 1960s and early 1970s there was a voluminous outpouring of studies of the ISI experience. Despite its considerable achievements (in terms of growth of industrial output and structural change, for example), criticism of both the implementation and outcome of ISI was widespread, and the overwhelming consensus was that ISI had been a 'failure'. This view was shared by both neo-classicists and, as noted by Schmitz (1984), ECLA structuralists who had hitherto been among the main advocates of ISI. The main findings of this critique of ISI are reviewed in the surveys by Bruton (1970), Baer (1972), Sutcliffe (1971), Diaz-Alejandro (1975), Donges (1976) and Nixson (1982).

The neoclassical attack on ISI was initiated by the publication of the influential comparative study by Little, Scitovsky and Scott (1970). Subsequent studies by Balassa and Associates (1971) Balassa (1982a), Bhagwati (1978) and Krueger (1978) also applied the neoclassical analysis to a large number of LDCs that adopted ISI strategies.

Differences in methodology make detailed comparisons of the results difficult, but a number of generalizations can be made concerning the structure of protectionism: (1) the average levels of effective protection exceeded the nominal tariff levels; (2) there was an escalation in the level of effective protection given to different industrial activities, with lower rates on investment and intermediate goods as compared to consumption goods; (3) within each of these categories there was considerable variation in the level of effective protection given to particular activities.

The evidence on the level of effective protection in ISI-oriented LDCs was complemented by estimates of high domestic resource costs (Krueger, 1966; Pearson, 1976), and sizeable bias in the trade regimes (Bhagwati, 1978; Krueger, 1978, 1983).

This literature also documents the various economic effects of the ISI strategy: (1) aggravating income inequalities by redistributing income towards industrial sector profits; (2) encouraging the adoption of relatively capital-intensive, imported techniques of production, thereby limiting the expansion of employment in the manufacturing sector; (3) introducing a bias against the agricultural sector, with the price of manufactured goods rising relative to agricultural products in the home market; (4) discouraging exports by the maintenance of an overvalued exchange rate; and (5) causing underutilization of installed capacity in the industrial sector.

Neoclassicists have been less successful in establishing firm evidence of a causal relationship between the level of protection and the weaknesses of the ISI process. In some less sophisticated studies a 'guilt by association' procedure is adopted, and it is assumed that the observed problems of the ISI strategy will be eliminated by the 'correction' of the trade policy. Other writers have been more careful in acknowledging the problems in constructing a causal link between protection and indicators of industrial performance (Diaz-Alejandro, 1975, p. 115). First, the rankings of industries in terms of the effective protection rates can only indicate the *potential* relative incentives for domestic resources to move into protected industries: 'even if effective rates give a reasonable indication of the direction of resource pulls, they cannot on their own tell one what the responses to the pulls will be: one also needs supply elasticities' (Corden, 1975, p. 66). Furthermore, the effect of protection on resource flows is dependent on market conditions. Under monopolistic and oligopolistic market structures the excess of domestic over foreign value-added may be due to a combination of resource-allocation inefficiencies and above-normal profits: 'thus, it has not been possible to indicate the extent to which effective rates influence the allocation of resources or give rise to excess profits under noncompetitive market structures' (Balassa, 1982a, p. 19). Bhagwati and Srinivasan (1979, pp. 11–12) note that the general equilibrium repercussions of a change in trade policy on different activities cannot be forecast from a simple examination of the relative DRCs in an initial suboptimal equilibrium.

Bhagwati (1978, chapter 5) reviews a considerable body of empirical evidence on the effect of protection on capacity utilization inventory holdings, and imports of capital goods and raw materials.[15] His conclusion is worth quoting:

the notion of relating tariffs, effective or nominal, to the pattern of industrial expansion – no matter how measured – may be lacking in sufficient rationale . . . on balance therefore we are content to take the view, admittedly less ambitious, that the differential ERPs among different activities should be taken merely to indicate, *very broadly indeed*, the differential nature of the incentives that exchange control regimes tend to generate (p. 101, emphasis in original).

A final part of the neoclassical case against ISI examines the effect of the system of incentives on the growth of exports. This body of literature is summarised and evaluated in section 2.4.2.

As noted by Nixson (1982), most of the empirical findings of the neoclassicists on industrial performance during ISI would be accepted by the structuralist and radical schools. There is broad agreement that ISI has typically been associated with a highly protected, inefficient manufacturing sector, oligopolistic or monopolistic in structure, with substantial underutilization of capacity, dependent on capital-intensive technologies with low employment-creation potential. Furthermore, it is generally accepted that industrialization has been pursued at the expense of the agricultural sector, and that there has been a significant bias against the export of primary and manufactured products. The dependence upon imports has not been reduced; indeed the shift in the composition of imports towards intermediate and capital goods has increased the vulnerability to a short-fall in foreign exchange. After an initial period of growth, ISI has lost momentum, as further import substitution becomes more difficult, and the capacity to import again becomes a constraint on economic growth.

However, the structuralist–radical interpretation of the ISI experience differs fundamentally from that of the neoclassicists, and sees the sources of ISI's 'failure' in the productive structures and social class formations in LDCs. For the structuralist an important limitation of ISI as pursued in most LDCs has been its acceptance of the pattern of demand and the underlying distribution of income as given. This form of 'market-based' ISI has led to a reliance upon a variety of foreign inputs (product specification, production technology) and the production of predominantly high-income goods and services. The encouragement of direct foreign investment in the form of local subsidiaries of international firms being established behind tariff barriers led to the elimination of many local producers and created monopolistic market structures. In addition, it encouraged the adoption of imported technologies which were inappropriate to local conditions and led to reverse outflows of capital in the form of transfer pricing, royalty payments, profit and dividend remittances.

From the perspective of radical writers, the pursuit of ISI as a deliberate industrialization strategy must also be linked to the social relations and class structures that emerged with ISI. This approach offers an answer to the question of why most LDCs have pursued ISI policies, despite the considerable economic inefficiencies associated with this strategy. What is required is a recognition of the variety of ways (often conflicting) in which the TNC, domestic capital, and the state interact with one another. Ruling groups or classes have an obvious interest in securing an accommodation with foreign capital, and the TNCs in turn require and benefit from state action on their behalf (Kirkpatrick and Nixson, 1981). The interests of certain groups are therefore advanced by the pursuit of ISI, although 'national welfare' is lowered. For example, Cardoso and Faletto (1979, chapter 5) identify the various social and political forces that were important in the consolidation of the domestic market in Argentina, Mexico, Brazil and Chile, and analyse the important role of the state in the industrialisation process in those countries. They conclude that:

The distinctive features of industrialization policies in each country depended on how the roles of the state and of the industrial bourgeoisie were reconciled. The economic functions of the state were important, but so was the way in which the state, as an instrument of domination, expressed the interests of various groups (pp. 131–2).

The policy prescriptions that arise from the two interpretations of the ISI experience are very different. According to the neoclassical school, the appropriate policy recommendation is that trade restrictions should be relaxed and greater attention given to ensuring that producers face the 'correct' price signals. This should stimulate more efficient import substitution as well as encourage production for export markets by providing equal incentives to production for domestic and foreign markets (Balassa, 1982a, chapter 4; Krueger, 1983, chapter 3).

The structuralist and radical schools, in contrast, emphasize the need for significant changes in the economic structure of the economy (for example, land redistribution, increased national ownership and control). Since the 'failure' of ISI is due fundamentally to its reliance upon existing market demand, greater government intervention through centralized industrial planning is seen as essential to its successful implementation (Nixson, 1981). A planned strategy of industrial development, in which import substitution is associated with, and complementary to, policies for agricultural development and development of export opportunities, would avoid many of the problems that have emerged as a result of the largely unplanned *ad hoc* government intervention under the market-based ISI strategy. The implementation of a planned IS strategy of industrialization would require political change within the LDCs themselves, although such political change in itself is not a sufficient condition, and where such changes have occurred major economic difficulties remain and may indeed have been aggravated by the changed economic and political circumstances (Nixson, 1982; Sutcliffe, 1984).

2.4.2 Export-oriented industrialization

Origins

The apparent 'failure' of the ISI strategy strengthened the neoclassical case for the adoption by LDCs of more outward-looking, export-oriented industrialization policies. Neoclassicists argued that the implementation of an EOI strategy would generate superior results, in terms of allocative efficiency and economic growth, as compared to ISI:

export-oriented policies lead to better growth performance than policies favouring import substitution. This result is said to obtain because export-oriented policies, which provide similar incentives to sales in domestic and in foreign markets, lead to resource allocation according to comparative advantages, allow for greater capacity utilization, permit the exploitation of economies of scale, generate technological improvements in response to competition abroad, and, in labour-surplus countries, contribute to increased employment (Balassa, 1971, p. 181).

The theoretical case for EOI appeared to be confirmed by the experience of those countries which adopted EOI policies during the 1960s. This group of countries, which became known as the newly industrializing countries (NICs), achieved remarkable economic growth in manufactured exports and output, and their record provided the 'model' recommended to other LDCs for emulation by, for example, the World Bank (World Bank, 1983).[16]

The form of EOI pursued by the NICs has varied, reflecting differences in economic structure and resources, and in previous industrialization experience. For countries with substantial exports of primary products or raw materials, local processing has been an important means of increasing manufactured exports. In the larger NICs of Latin America, manufactured exports have often been based on industries established during an earlier ISI phase. In the Asian NICs, with more limited domestic markets or a lower level of IS activity, the production of manufactures intended primarily for external markets has been more significant. A further form of export manufacturing has been labour-intensive component assembly activities. This type of production resulted from the TNCs' world-wide 'sourcing' for the most economical location for various stages in their vertically integrated operations, and led to the transfer of unskilled labour-intensive activities to LDCs, where low wage costs offset the transport and communication costs incurred (Helleiner, 1973a, b; Kirkpatrick and Yamin, 1981; Nayyar, 1978; Sharpston, 1975).[17]

Experience of EOI

The export performance of the NICs has been impressive, and has undoubtedly encouraged an increasing number of LDCs to adopt outward-looking EOI policies. Trade policy, however, should not be seen as an end in itself, but rather as a means of achieving certain development objectives. The export success of some LDCs is therefore an inadequate index of the benefits of pursuing an EOI strategy.

There have been various attempts to demonstrate empirically that EOI has resulted in better growth performance than ISI. One approach has been to correlate export growth rates with GDP growth rates (Balassa, 1978, 1982a, chapter 3; Tyler, 1981). This type of exercise is of limited value since, by using export performance as an index of the degree of commitment to EOI, countries which have been unsuccessful in EOI are excluded by definition. A more useful approach is to identify the separate phases of EOI and ISI in individual countries, and compare the growth performance in the different periods (Bhagwati, 1978; Krueger, 1978, 1983). These studies suggest that countries that reduced the 'bias' against exports registered improved export performance, and an acceleration in their GDP growth rate.

Rather less attention has been given by neoclassicists to the developmental impact of export-based growth – its employment effects, the impact on income distribution, the distribution of gains between foreign and domestic interests, the implications of technology choice.

The rapid expansion of employment and the attainment of near full employment has been a feature of several of the smaller Asian NICs. But for the majority of LDCs, manufactured exports account for a small proportion of total manufacturing, and the growth of manufactured exports is unlikely to produce a significant reduction in the existing levels of unemployment and under-employment (Tyler, 1976). Krueger (1983) argues that export production is typically more labour-intensive than import-substituting production, but where allowance is made for indirect employment linkage effects the evidence is less conclusive (Lall, 1978).

EOI may increase the LDCs' dependence on imported technology and inhibit efforts to develop a domestic technological capacity (Kirkpatrick *et al.*, 1984, pp. 215–18; Stewart, 1977). Furthermore, reliance on production for export, and the general liberalization of trade, will inevitably intensify the imitative tendencies in domestic consumption patterns (Stewart, 1974). (These issues of technology and taste transfer, the interdependence between choice of product and techniques of production, and the role of the TNCs as suppliers of technology, are equally relevant in the context of ISI.)[18]

It has been argued by some neoclassicists that an EOI strategy based on labour-intensive manufactures is not only beneficial in terms of economic growth but also results in improvements in income distribution (Balassa, 1982a; Fields, 1984; Ranis, 1985b). In the smaller Asian NICs it does appear that in the early phase of EOI the rapid expansion of employment improved the interpersonal distribution of income, while at the same time constant real wages allowed the functional distribution of income to shift against labour. As labour surplus became exhausted, however, the situation appears to have been reversed (Koo, 1984; Islam and Kirkpatrick, 1986). In the larger LDCs, where export production represents a small share of total production activity, the direction of the impact of EOI on income distribution is uncertain, but almost certainly small. Given the importance of government regulation and intervention in labour markets under EOI (see below), the impact of EOI on the distribution of income cannot be predicted on *a priori* grounds, but rather it requires detailed examination of the economic structure and policies of each economy. What can be stated generally is that 'there is no short-run poverty–alleviating or distributional magic in manufacturing for export' (Helleiner, 1976, p. 216).

Even if the argument that EOI has resulted in superior economic performance in the NICs is accepted, the claim that the success of the NICs represents 'the embodiment of the neoclassical parable' (Bienefeld, 1982), and provides a model for other LDCs to follow, has been strongly contested. There are two main grounds on which the neoclassical interpretation of the NICs phenomenon can be questioned. First, it is argued that to explain the NICs' success simply in terms of 'getting the prices right' is to ignore the role of government regulation and intervention in ensuring that this condition was met. The second is to point to the specificity of the NICs' experience which limits the prospects of replicating the NIC model.

The neoclassical perspective contributes little to understanding the economic and political circumstances on which the success of the Asian NICs' EOI strategy was based (IDS, 1984; Ruggie, 1984). In particular, it fails to recognize the way in which government intervention has been used to develop and shape a country's comparative advantage, thereby establishing and maintaining its international competitive position. 'In down-playing the social, political and historical dimensions of the concept of comparative advantage, error is invited in both the attribution of causality of comparative advantage and in more narrowly prescribing the limits within which development choices can be made' (Evans and Alizadeh, 1984, p. 27). With the exception of Hong Kong, an important element in the Asian NICs' success has been the role of state planning and regulation (Sen, 1981, 1983). In the case of the Republic of Korea and Taiwan, for example, both import controls and export incentive controls have been used to pursue a strategy based on selective import substitution and export promotion, with IS being used to develop local manufacturing capacity as a basis for subsequent export activities (Kirkpatrick and Nixson, 1983, pp. 40–5; Mitchell, 1985; Wade, 1985).

The role of government regulation of markets is most clearly seen in relation to the labour market. The neoclassical discussion of labour market policy is typically presented in terms of a supply and demand wage determination process, with surplus labour conditions ensuring an elastic supply of labour at a constant real wage (Fields, 1984, p. 79; Little, 1981, pp. 33–9). In reality, with the exception of Hong Kong, 'strong' government was responsible for guaranteeing 'free' labour markets, with wages maintained at 'competitive' levels. An understanding of the basis of the NICs' success, and an assessment of the applicability of the NIC model to other LDCs, requires consideration of the way in which labour market intervention and control enabled the NICs to export profitably in world markets (Islam and Kirkpatrick, 1986).

State intervention in the NICs is in turn related to the social and class structure within these economies. In some instances the behaviour of the state can be seen as the outcome of a struggle between classes for power; in other instances the state may be able to manoeuvre relatively independently of class interests (White, 1984). An identification and explanation of these sociopolitical relationships has an important part to play in understanding the role played by the state in EOI in the NICs (Browett, 1985; Hamilton, 1983).

The second basis on which the neoclassical 'story' has been challenged is to focus attention on the distinctive features of the international economy and/or the particular characteristics of individual NICs during the period of rapid EOI. The unprecedented growth of world trade and minimal levels of protectionism during the 1960s is contrasted with the current slowdown in economic growth and heightening protectionism in the advanced countries (Cline, 1984; Kaplinsky, 1984). Adelman (1984, p. 935) predicts that 'most LDCs which are not already newly industrialized countries (NICs) with established export markets are unlikely to break into international markets for non-traditional exports in the next decade'.

A related argument suggests that the assumption that the NICs' export success can be replicated by other LDCs is subject to a fallacy of composition. Cline (1982), for example, calculates (using 1976 data) that if other LDCs had the same intensity of export production as the four Asian NICs, the share of all LDCs in the manufactured imports of the DCs would increase to 60 per cent.[19]

A further factor contributing to the rapid growth of the NICs was the ease of access to international finance. The rapid expansion of the transnational banking market, based in the 1960s on the US balance of payments deficits and in the 1970s on the oil-exporting countries' surplus, led to a massive increase in NIC borrowing, and enabled some of these economies to maintain high growth rates through 'debt-led growth' (Griffith-Jones and Rodriguez, 1984). The debt crisis and subsequent decline in DC lending of the late 1970s and early 1980s have limited the access of LDCs to the transnational private capital markets.

The increasing 'world sourcing' activities of TNCs during the 1960s, with the relocation of relatively labour-intensive processing activities in low-wage LDCs, was a further factor contributing to the growth of manufactured exports from the NICs. This process of relocation was given an added impetus by the tariff structure in several of the main DC markets which offered preferential treatment to imports incorporating domestically originating components: that is, the tariff applied only to the value–added in the assembly and manufacturing processes undertaken overseas (Finger, 1975; Helleiner, 1979a). Critics of the NIC model argue that new technologies developed in the post-1970 period are not simply an incremental advance on previous technology, but also involve changes in the organization of production (Kaplinsky, 1984). These changes in technology, particularly in electronics-based automation processes, have the effect of increasing economies of agglomeration while at the same time reducing the importance of unskilled labour costs. The diffusion of these radical electronics-based technologies may weaken the viability of the EOI strategy in LDCs (Ernst, 1985; Hoffman, 1985).

The emergence of the NICs is seen, therefore, as a response to a set of favourable international circumstances (Bienefeld, 1981, 1982). The ability of certain LDCs to respond to these opportunities for EOI is explained in terms of various internal and often unique characteristics: the island-city status of Hong Kong and Singapore, the geopolitical importance of South Korea and Taiwan to the United States, the existence of a strong, authoritarian regime in Brazil, the entrepôt trading tradition of Singapore and Hong Kong, and so on. It is argued, therefore, that the NIC model is unlikely to be replicated and is of limited relevance to other industrializing LDCs.[20]

Despite the diversity of experience in EOI, it is possible to draw a number of conclusions from the NICs' experience: (1) export success was not due to the adoption of a *laissez-faire* trade regime: considerable state intervention was involved in administering the system of economic incentives used to promote exports;[21] (2) the capacity to guarantee the necessary conditions for successful EOI required an efficient administrative system and strong government which was able to overcome political resistance to the strategy;[22] (3) the period of rapid EOI occurred when external market conditions were exceptionally favourable; (4) statistical evidence of rapid export growth is an inadequate indicator of the developmental impact of an EOI strategy.

In summary, the neoclassical 'story', in so far as it treats export growth as an end in itself, and neglects the other factors that have contributed to the economic success of the NICs, offers an incomplete account of the EOI experience and provides an inadequate 'model' for other LDCs to adopt.

2.5   Concluding comments

A first conclusion to be drawn from this survey of LDCs' industrialization experience is that the choice of trade policies has too frequently been presented in terms of the competing claims of mutually exclusive strategies. This dichotomy between ISI and EOI is misleading. If a longer time horizon is adopted, ISI and EOI can be seen as sequential phases in the industrialization process of most LDCs. In economies such as India, Pakistan and Brazil, the continuation of ISI beyond the first, 'easy' stage of consumer good import substitution led to the establishment of a domestic capital and durable consumer goods sector with significant linkages with other parts of the economy. Production was subsequently shifted to external markets, with these countries becoming major exporters of technologically advanced capital and intermediate goods. In the larger Asian NICs the period of 'easy' EOI based on unskilled labour-intensive manufacturing was superseded by a strategy of industrial 'restructuring' towards more skill- and capital-intensive activities, involving considerable import substitution in capital goods and consumer durable articles.

The issue is, therefore, much more one of the optimal sequence of ISI and EOI phases in the industrialization process than of the relative merits of EOI and ISI as alternative and competing strategies. Most observers have favoured the Asian NIC pattern of a relatively short-lived period of ISI, followed by 'early' EOI and 'secondary' ISI, arguing that it avoids many of the economic inefficiencies associated with a prolonged period of market-based ISI, while at the same time reducing unemployment and improving the distribution of income during the period of labour–intensive export-oriented industrialization (Ranis and Orrock, 1985; Ranis, 1985b). The counter-argument in favour of the Latin American pattern of extended ISI maintains that the economic inefficiencies of ISI must be set against the establishment of a balanced industrial sector, the reduction of foreign ownership and control, the creation of an indigenous technological capacity, and a more diversified pattern of manufactured exports.

A second observation is that much of the literature on LDCs' trade policies,

attributes to import substitution policies for industrialisation faults which result not from the misallocation of resources between alternatives or inefficiencies arising from such misallocation but from inefficient use of the resources allocated to the given objective of import substitution (Streeten, 1982, p. 162).

The efficient use of resources depends more on the efficiency with which they are utilized in a particular activity, rather than on their allocation between ISI or EOI. Inefficiency in export production (in the form of excessive export subsidies, for example), can occur just as readily as inefficiency in import-substituting activities. Conversely, IS production can be as efficient as EO activity (Bhagwati, 1978, p. 216). The economic performance of the industrial sector is in turn influenced by the effectiveness of the state's management of the economy.[23] Superior industrial performance has been associated with selective state intervention to achieve particular targets – for example, investment in certain large-scale industrial sectors – and the regulation of the economic environment within which the private sector operates. At the same time, policy-makers have accepted the important role of the price system in the market economy, and have used the market mechanism as an instrument for achieving clearly specified objectives. As Williamson (1985, p. 47) observes:

> the debate on markets, prices and macroeconomic management has been polarised between those who believe that prices do not matter and those who believe that all that is necessary to secure a correct price structure is to liberalise markets. But there is a third possible position, which is that prices are profoundly important but that markets cannot in general be trusted to set them.

The issue of trade policy and industrialization in LDCs has been the subject of exhaustive analytical and empirical investigation during the past two decades. Yet our understanding of the effect of different trade policies on industrial growth and economic development remains incomplete.[24] The process of industrialization is considerably more complex than has typically been allowed for in the trade–industrialization literature; and trade policy is but one among many determinants of the pattern and progress of industrial development in Third World countries.

NOTES

1. The United Nations International Standard Industrial Classification (ISIC) system uses nine major industrial divisions identified by a one-digit code: agriculture, hunting, forestry and fishing (1); mining and quarrying (2); manufacturing (3); electricity, gas and water (4); construction (5); wholesale and retail trade and restaurants and hotels (6); transport, storage and communications (7); financing, insurance, real estate and business services (8); community, social and personal services (9). Each major division is in turn divided into divisions (two-digit), divisions into major groups (three-digit) and major groups into groups (four-digit).

   International trade flows are classified using the Standard International Trade Classification (SITC), which groups merchandise exports and imports into 10 major sections, identified by a one-digit code: food and live animals chiefly for food (0); beverages and tobacco (1); crude materials, inedible, except fuels (2); mineral fuels, lubricants and related materials (3); animals and vegetable oils, fats and waxes (4); chemicals and related products (5); manufactured goods classified chiefly by material (6); machinery and transport equipment (7); miscellaneous manufactured articles (8); commodities and transactions not classified elsewhere (9).

   Since the SITC and ISIC systems are not identical, trade and industrial data cannot be directly compared with each other. For comparative purposes it is common practice to select a definition of trade in manufactures that roughly matches the range of activities commonly identified with manufacturing in the ISIC framework. For example, manufactures is normally defined as SITC sections 5–8 (in some cases SITC 68, non-ferrous metals, is excluded).

2. The term 'trade policy' is preferred, therefore, to 'trade strategy'. The same point is made by ul Haq (1973, p. 101): 'Trade should not be regarded as a pace-setter in any relevant development strategy for the developing world but merely as a derivative. The developing countries should first define a viable strategy for attacking their problems of unemployment and mass poverty. Trade policies should be geared to meeting these objectives.'

3. For a classification of SITC and ISIC codes into end-use categories, see UNIDO (1979, p. 172). An alternative classification procedure is to distinguish between 'heavy' and 'light' industry. Heavy industry is made up of the production of industrial supplies, producer goods and advanced consumer goods. Light industry consists mainly of basic consumer goods. See Hoffman (1958), UNIDO (1983, chapter III).

4. Taiwan, a major LDC exporter of manufactures, is excluded from all UN statistics.

5. The issues discussed in this section are examined in greater detail in Kirkpatrick *et al.* (1984, pp. 25–39).

6. Kuznets' work was first published under the general title of 'Quantitative aspects of the economic growth of nations', as 10 papers in various issues of *Economic Development and Cultural Change* between October 1956 and January 1967. Revised versions of the first three papers (relating to aggregate growth and to shares of production sectors in total product and labour force) have been published as Kuznets (1971). See also Kuznets (1965, 1966, 1982).

7. The earlier work is summarized in Sutcliffe (1971, chapter 2), and more recent analyses are found in Ballance and Sinclair (1983, chapters 4 and 5), Batchelor *et al.* (1980a, b), Chenery (1979), Chenery and Syrquin (1975), UNIDO (1979, chapter II).

8. The growth path exhibiting these features is described as an S-shaped (logistic) curve.

9. For similar reviews of alternative analytical perspectives, see Bienefeld and Godfrey (1982, Introduction); Little (1982, chapter 2); Smith and Toye (1979, Introduction). For a discussion of some similarities between the neoclassical and structural approaches to trade issues, see Diaz-Alejandro (1975, pp. 96–103).

10. For a more detailed review of the basic gains from trade analysis, see Corden (1984, pp. 69–77).

11. There are considerable conceptual and empirical problems in undertaking this procedure. These are discussed in Bhagwati and Srinivasan (1979). Given these difficulties, 'it is best to treat the resulting estimates of the implicit tariff structure as descriptions, in varying degrees of loose approximation' (Bhagwati and Srinivasan, 1979, p. 5).

12. For more detailed discussion of 'bias' measures, see Krueger (1984, pp. 529–30) and Bhagwati and Srinivasan (1979, pp. 6–7).

13. The effective rate of protection concept is discussed in detail in Corden (1971). The DRC measure is considered in Krueger (1984) and Pearson (1976). Both measures are discussed more fully in survey 1.

14. This view of externally enforced ISI has been questioned by some observers. See, for example, the contributions in Ingham and Simmons (1981).

15. This evidence is drawn from the individual country studies that were undertaken as part of the major National Bureau of Economic Research research project on foreign trade regimes and economic development, directed by Bhagwati and Krueger. The project's findings are reported in Krueger (1978) and Bhagwati (1978).

16. The countries classified as NICs vary. The 'core' countries are Hong Kong, Singapore, Taiwan and South Korea. Other countries normally included are Brazil, Mexico, Argentina and Colombia. In recent years a 'second tier' of NICs have emerged as exporters of manufactures – see Havrylyshyn and Alikhani (1982).

17. The different categories of LDC-manufactured exports are discussed in greater detail in Kirkpatrick and Nixson (1983, pp. 29-35).
18. For more detailed discussion of these issues, see Kirkpatrick *et al.* (1984, pp. 104-24).
19. But see the critique of Cline's study by Ranis (1985a).
20. As Browett (1985, p. 4) notes, there are dangers in extending this argument to the extreme of exceptionalism, where everything becomes a 'special case'.
21. 'Without efforts to *enable* producers to respond, getting the price and trade policies right may have no more effect than pushing on a piece of string' (Wade, 1985, p. 14; emphasis in original).
22. Sachs (1985) argues that the ability of groups favouring protectionism to maintain ISI policies explains the relatively poor economic performance of Latin American economies, as compared to East Asia.
23. After surveying the historical evidence on a century of development in 42 contemporary developing countries, Reynolds (1983, p. 976) concludes that 'my hypothesis is that the single most important explanatory variable [in economic development] is political organization and the administrative competence of government'.
24. 'When all is said and done we remain unsure as to whether and when trade is the engine, the handmaiden, the brake, or the offspring of growth' (Diaz-Alejandro, 1980, p. 300).

REFERENCES

Adelman, I. 1984. Beyond export-led growth. *World Development*, 12, 937-49.
Arndt, H. W. 1985. The origins of structuralism. *World Development*, 13, 151-9.
Baer, W. 1972. Import substitution and industrialization in Latin America: experiences and interpretations. *Latin American Research Review*, VII, 95-122.
Balassa, B. 1978. Exports and economic growth. *Journal of Development Economics*, 5, 181-9.
Balassa, B. (ed.) 1982a. *Development Strategies in Semi-Industrialized Economies*. Baltimore: Johns Hopkins University Press.
Balassa, B. 1982b. Disequilibrium analysis in developing economies: an overview. *World Development*, 10, 1027-38.
Balassa, B. and Associates 1971. *The Structure of Protection in Developing Countries*. Baltimore: Johns Hopkins University Press.
Ballance, R. and Sinclair, S. 1983. *Collapse and Survival: Industry Strategies in a Changing World*. London: Allen and Unwin.
Ballance, R., Ansari, J. A. and Singer, H. 1982. *The International Economy and Industrial Development: the Impact of Trade and Investment on the Third World*. Brighton, Sussex: Wheatsheaf Books.
Baran, P. 1957. *The Political Economy of Growth*. New York: Monthly Review Press.
Batchelor, R. A., Major, R. L. and Morgan, A. D. 1980a. *Industrialization and the Basis for Trade*. Cambridge: Cambridge University Press.
Batchelor, R. A., Major, R. L. and Morgan, A. D. 1980b. Industrialization and the basis for trade. *National Institute Economic Review*, 93, 55-8.
Bhagwati, J. N. 1978. *Anatomy and Consequences of Exchange Control Regimes*. Cambridge, Mass.: Ballinger, for the National Institute of Economic Research.
Bhagwati, J. N. and Srinivasan, T. N. 1979. Trade policy and development. In R. Dornbusch and J. A. Frenkel (eds), *International Economic Policy: Theory and Evidence*. Baltimore: Johns Hopkins University Press.

Bienefeld, M. 1981. Dependency and the newly industrializing countries (NICs): towards a reappraisal. In D. Seers (ed.), *Dependency Theory: a Critical Reassessment*. London: Francis Pinter.

Bienefeld, M. 1982. The international context for national development strategies: constraints and opportunities in a changing world. In Bienefeld and Godfrey (eds), 1982.

Bienefeld, M. and Godfrey, M. (eds) 1982. *The Struggle for Development: National Strategies in an International Context*. Chichester, Sussex: John Wiley and Sons.

Browett, J. G. 1985. The newly industrializing countries and radical theories of development. *World Development*, 13, 789–804.

Bruton, H. J. 1970. The import substitution strategy of economic development: a survey. *Pakistan Development Review*, X, 123–46.

Cardoso, F. H. and Faletto, E. 1979. *Dependency and Development in Latin America*. Berkeley and Los Angeles: University of California Press.

Chenery, H. B. 1960. Patterns of industrial growth. *American Economic Review*, 50, 624–54.

Chenery, H. B. 1979. *Structural Change and Development Policy*. Oxford: Oxford University Press, for the World Bank.

Chenery, H. B. and Strout, A. 1966. Foreign assistance and economic development. *American Economic Review*, 56, 679–733.

Chenery, H. B. and Syrquin, M. 1975. *Patterns of Development 1950–1970*. Oxford: Oxford University Press, for the World Bank.

Chenery, H. B. and Taylor, L. 1968. Development patterns: among countries and over time. *Review of Economics and Statistics*, 50, 391–416.

Cline, W. R. (ed.) 1979. *Policy Alternatives for a New International Economic Order*. New York: Praeger.

Cline, W. R. 1982. Can the East Asian model of development be generalized? *World Development*, 10, 81–90.

Cline, W. R. 1984. *Exports of Manufactures for Developing Countries: Performance and Prospects for Market Access*. Washington, DC: The Brookings Institution.

Colman, D. and Nixson, F. I. 1986. *Economics of Change in Less Developed Countries*. 2nd edn Oxford: Philip Allan.

Corden, W. M. 1971. *The Theory of Protection*. Oxford: Clarendon Press.

Corden, W. M. 1974. *Trade Policy and Economic Welfare*. Oxford: Clarendon Press.

Corden, W. M. 1975. The costs and consequences of protection: a survey of empirical work. In P. B. Kenen (ed.), *International Trade and Finance: Frontiers for Research*. Cambridge: Cambridge University Press.

Corden, W. M. 1980. Trade policies. In J. Cody, H. Hughes and D. Wall (eds), *Policies for Industrial Progress in Developing Countries*. Oxford: Oxford University Press, for the World Bank.

Corden, W. M. 1984. The normative theory of international trade. In R. W. Jones and P. B. Kenen (eds), *Handbook of International Economics*, Vol. I. Amsterdam: North-Holland.

Diaz-Alejandro, C. F. 1975. Trade policies and economic development. In P. B. Kenen (ed.), *International Trade and Finance: Frontiers for Research*. Cambridge: Cambridge University Press.

Diaz-Alejandro, C. F. 1980. Discussion on 'trade policy as an input to development'. *American Economic Review, Papers and Proceedings*, 70, 299–300.

Donges, J. B. 1976. A comparative survey of industrialization policies in fifteen semi-industrial countries. *Weltwirtschaftliches Archiv*, 112, 626–59.

dos Santos, T. 1973. The crisis of development theory and the problem of dependence in Latin America. In H. Bernstein (ed.), *Underdevelopment and Development*. Harmondsworth: Penguin.

Ernst, D. 1985. Automation and the worldwide restructuring of the electronics industry: implications for developing countries. *World Development*, 13, 333–52.

Evans, D. and Alizadeh, P. 1984. Trade, industrialization and the visible hand. *Journal of Development Studies*, 21, 22–46.

Fields, G. 1984. Employment, income distribution and economic growth in seven small open economies. *Economic Journal*, 24, 74–83.

Findlay, R. 1984. Trade and development: theory and Asian experience. *Asian Development Review*, 2, 23–42.

Finger, J. M. 1975. Tariff provisions for offshore assembly and the exports of developing countries. *Economic Journal*, 85, 365–71.

Griffith-Jones, S. and Rodriguez, E. 1984. Private international finance and industrialization of LDCs. *Journal of Development Studies*, 21, 47–74.

Hamilton, C. 1983. Capitalist industrialization in East Asia's 'Four Little Tigers', *Journal of Contemporary Asia*, 13, 35–73.

Havrylyshyn, O. and Alikhani, I. 1982. Is there a case for export optimism? An inquiry into the existence of a second generation of successful exporters. *Weltwirtschaftliches Archiv*, 118, 651–63.

Helleiner, G. K. 1973a. Manufacturing for export: multinational firms and economic development. *World Development*, 1, 13–21.

Helleiner, G. K. 1973b. Manufactured exports from less developed countries and multinational firms. *Economic Journal*, 83, 21–47.

Helleiner, G. K. 1976. Multinationals, manufactured exports and employment in less developed countries. Tripartite World Conference on Employment, Income Distribution and Social Progress and the International Division of Labour. Background Paper. Vol. II. *International Strategies for Employment*, Geneva: ILO.

Helleiner, G. K. 1979a. Intrafirm trade and the developing countries: an assessment of the data. *Journal of Development Economics*, 6, 391–406.

Helleiner, G. K. 1979b. Structural aspects of Third World trade: some trends and some prospects. *Journal of Development Studies*, 15, 70–88.

Helleiner, G. K. 1981a. The Refsnes seminar: economic theory and North–South negotiations. *World Development*, 9, 539–56.

Helleiner, G. K. 1981b. *Intra-firm Trade and the Developing Countries*. London: Macmillan.

Hirschman, A. O. 1968. The political economy of import-substituting industrialization in Latin America. *Quarterly Journal of Economics*, 82, 1–12.

Hoffman, K. 1985. Microelectronics, international competition and development strategies: the unavoidable issues. *World Development*, 13, 263–72.

Hoffman, W. G. 1958. *The Growth of Industrial Economies*. Manchester: Manchester University Press.

Hughes, H. 1980. Achievements and objectives of industrialization. In J. Cody, H. Hughes and D. Wall (eds), *Policies for Industrial Progress in Developing Countries*. Oxford: Oxford University Press, for the World Bank.

Ingham, B. and Simmons, C. (eds) 1981. The two World Wars and economic development: Editors' Introduction. *World Development*, 9, 701–6.

Institute of Development Studies (IDS) 1984. *IDS Bulletin*, 15 (Development States in East Asia).

Islam, I. and Kirkpatrick, C. 1986. Export-led development, labour market conditions and the distribution of income: the case of Singapore. *Cambridge Journal of Economics*, 10, 113–27.

Jameson, K. P. 1982. A critical examination of the patterns of development. *Journal of Development Studies*, 18, 431–46.

Jones, R. W. and Neary, J. P. 1984. The positive theory of international trade. In R. W. Jones and P. B. Kenen (eds), *Handbook of International Economics*, Vol. I. Amsterdam: North-Holland.

Kaplinsky, R. 1984. The international context for industrialization in the coming decade. *Journal of Development Studies*, 21, 75–96.

Keesing, D. B. 1967. Outward-looking policies and economic development. *Economic Journal*, 77, 303–20.

Kirkpatrick, C. and Nixson, F. 1976. UNCTAD IV and the New International Economic Order. *Three Banks Review*, 12, 30–49.

Kirkpatrick, C. and Nixson, F. 1977. The New International Economic Order: trade policy for primary products. *British Journal of International Studies*, 3, 233–58.

Kirkpatrick, C. and Nixson, F. 1981. Transnational corporations and economic development. *Journal of Modern African Studies*, 19, 367–99.

Kirkpatrick, C. and Nixson, F. (eds) 1983. *The Industrialization of Less Developed Countries*. Manchester: Manchester University Press.

Kirkpatrick, C. and Yamin, M. 1981. The determinants of export subsidiary formation by US transnationals in developing countries: an inter-industry analysis. *World Development*, 9, 373–82.

Kirkpatrick, C., Lee, N. and Nixson, F. 1984. *Industrial Structure and Policy in Less Developed Countries*. London: George Allen and Unwin.

Koo, H. 1984. The political economy of income distribution in South Korea: the impact of the state's industrialization policies. *World Development*, 12, 1029–38.

Krueger, A. O. 1966. Some economic costs of exchange control: the Turkish case. *Journal of Political Economy*, 74, 466–80.

Krueger, A. O. 1978. *Liberalization Attempts and Consequences*. Cambridge, Mass.: Ballinger, for the National Bureau of Economic Research.

Krueger, A. O. 1980. Trade policy as an input to development. *American Economic Review, Papers and Proceedings*, 70, 288–92.

Krueger, A. O. 1983. *Alternative Trade Strategies and Employment*, vol. 3: *Synthesis and Conclusions*. Chicago: Chicago University Press, for the National Bureau of Economic Research.

Krueger, A. O. 1984. Trade policies in developing countries. In R. W. Jones and P. B. Kenen (eds), *Handbook of International Economics*, Vol. I. Amsterdam: North-Holland.

Kuznets, S. 1965. *Economic Growth and Structure: Selected Essays*. New York: W. W. Norton.

Kuznets, S. 1966. *Modern Economic Growth: Rate, Structure and Spread*, New Haven and London: Yale University Press.

Kuznets, S. 1971. *Economic Growth of Nations: Total Output and Production Structure*. Cambridge, Mass.: The Belknap Press of Harvard University Press.

Kuznets, S. 1982. The pattern of shift of labour force from agriculture, 1950–70. In M. Gersovitz *et al.* (eds), *The Theory and Experience of Economic Development: Essays in Honour of Sir W. Arthur Lewis*. London: Allen and Unwin.

Lall, S. 1978. Transnationals, domestic enterprises and industrial structure in host LDCs: a survey. *Oxford Economic Papers*, 30, 217–48.

Lall, S. 1979. Transfer pricing and developing countries: some problems of investigation. *World Development*, 7, 59–71.

Lee, E. (ed.), 1981. *Export-Led Industrialization and Development*. Asian Employment Programme. Geneva: ILO.

Leys, C. 1975. *Underdevelopment in Kenya: the Political Economy of Neo-Colonialism*. London: Heinemann.

Little, I. M. D. 1981. The experience and causes of rapid labour intensive development in Korea, Taiwan Province, Hong Kong and Singapore: And the possibilities of emulation. In E. Lee (ed.), *Export-led Industrialization and Development*. Asian Employment Programme. Geneval: ILO.

Little, I. M. D. 1982. *Economic Development: Theory, Policy and International Relations*. New York: Basic Books.

Little, I. M. D. and Mirrlees, J. 1974. *Project Appraisal and Planning for Developing Countries*. London: Heinemann.

Little, I. M. D., Scitovsky, T. and Scott, M. 1970. *Industry and Trade in Some Developing Countries*. London: Oxford University Press.

McKinnon, R. I. 1966. Foreign exchange constraints in economic development and efficient aid allocation. *Economic Journal*, 76, 170–1.

Michaely, M. 1977. Exports and growth: an empirical investigation. *Journal of Development Economics*, 4, 49–54.

Mitchell, A. 1985. South Korea. *ESRC Newsletter*, 54, 15–18.

Myint, H. 1985. 'The neoclassical resurgence in development economics: its strengths and limitations.' Mimeo.

Myrdal, G. 1956. *Development and Underdevelopment*. Cairo: National Bank of Egypt.

Nayyar, D. 1978. Transnational corporations and manufactured exports from poor countries. *Economic Journal*, 88, 59–84.

Nixson, F. 1981. State intervention, economic planning and import substituting industrialization: the experience of the LDCs. *METU Studies in Development*. Special issue (Ankara, Turkey).

Nixson, F. 1982. Import-substituting industrialization and economic development: the lessons for sub-Saharan Africa. In M. Fransman (ed.), *Industry and Accumulation in Africa*. London: Heinemann.

Nurkse, R. 1962. *Patterns of Trade and Development*. Oxford: Basil Blackwell.

Palma, G. 1978. Dependency: a formal theory of underdevelopment or a methodology for the analysis of concrete situations of under-development? *World Development*, 6, 881–924.

Pearson, S. R. 1976. Net social profitability, domestic resource costs, and effective rate of protection. *Journal of Development Studies*, 12, 320–33.

Prebisch, R. 1959. Commercial policy in the underdeveloped countries. *American Economic Review, Papers and Proceedings*, 49, 251–6.

Prebisch, R. 1964. *Towards a New Trade Policy for Development*. New York: United Nations.

Ranis, G. 1985a. Can the East Asia model of development be generalized; A comment. *World Development*, 13, 543–6.

Ranis, G. 1985b. Employment, income distribution and growth in the East Asian context: a comparative study. In V. Corbo, A. O. Krueger, and F. Ossa (eds), *Export-oriented Development Strategies: the Success of Five Newly Industrializing Countries*. Boulder and London: Westview Press.

Ranis, G. and Orrock, L. 1985. Latin American and East Asian NICs: development strategies compared. In E. Duran (ed.), *Latin America and the World Recession*.

Cambridge: Cambridge University Press, in association with the Royal Institute of International Affairs.

Reynolds, L. G. 1983. The spread of economic growth to the Third World: 1850-1980. *Journal of Economic Literature*, 21, 941-80.

Ruggie, J. G. (ed.) 1984. *The Antinomies of Interdependence: National Welfare and the International Division of Labour*. Irvington, New York: Columbia University Press.

Sachs, J. D. 1985. External debt and macroeconomic performance in Latin America and East Asia. *Brookings Papers on Economic Activity*, 2, 523-73.

Samuelson, P. A. 1939. The gains from international trade. *Canadian Journal of Economics and Political Science*, 5, 195-205. Reprinted in H. S. Ellis and L. A. Metzler (eds), *Readings in the Theory of International Trade*. Philadelphia: Blakiston.

Samuelson, P. A. 1962. The gains from international trade once again. *Economic Journal*, 72, 820-9.

Schmitz, H. 1984. Industrialization strategies in less developed countries: some lessons of historical experience. *Journal of Development Studies*, 21, 1-21.

Sen, A. K. 1981. Public action and the quality of life in developing countries. *Bulletin of the Oxford University Institute of Economics and Statistics*, 43, 287-319.

Sen, A. K. 1983. Development: which way now? *Economic Journal*, 93, 745-62.

Sharpston, M. 1975. International subcontracting. *Oxford Economic Papers*, 27, 94-135.

Singer, H. W. 1950. The distribution of gains between investing and borrowing countries. *American Economic Review, Papers and Proceedings*, 40, 473-5.

Singh, A. 1979. The 'basic needs' approach to development vs. the New International Economic Order: the significance of Third World industrialization. *World Development*, 7, 585-606.

Smith, S. and Toye, J. 1979. Three stories about trade and poor economies. *Journal of Development Studies*, 15, 1-18.

Squire, L. and Van der Tak, H. 1975. *Economic Analysis of Projects*. Baltimore: Johns Hopkins University Press.

Steuer, M. D. and Voivodas, C. 1965. Import substitution and Chenery's patterns of industrial growth - a further study. *Economia Internazionale*, 18, 47-82.

Stewart, F. 1974. Trade and technology. In P. Streeten (ed.), *Trade Strategies for Development*. London: Macmillan.

Stewart, F. 1977. *Technology and Underdevelopment*. London: Macmillan.

Streeten, P. 1982. A cool look at 'outward-looking' strategies for development. *World Economy*, 5, 159-69.

Sutcliffe, R. B. 1971. *Industry and Underdevelopment*. London: Addison-Wesley.

Sutcliffe, R. B. 1984. Industry and underdevelopment re-examined. *Journal of Development Studies*, 24, 121-33.

Tyler, W. G. 1976. Manufactured exports and employment creation in developing countries: some empirical evidence. *Economic Development and Cultural Change*, 24, 121-33.

Tyler, W. G. 1981. Growth and export expansion in developing countries. *Journal of Development Economics*, 9, 121-30.

Ul Haq, M. 1973. Industrialization and trade policies in the 1970s: developing country alternatives. In P. Streeten (ed.), *Trade Strategies for Development*. London: Macmillan.

UNIDO. 1979. *World Industry Since 1960: Progress and Prospects*. New York: United Nations.

UNIDO. 1983. *Industry in a Changing World*. New York: United Nations.

UNIDO. 1985. *Industry in the 1980s: Structural Change and Interdependence*. New York: United Nations.

Wade, R. 1985. Taiwan. *ESRC Newsletter*, 54, 12–15.
White, G. 1984. Developmental states and socialist industrialization in the Third World. *Journal of Development Studies*, 21, 97–120.
Williamson, J. 1985. Macroeconomic strategies in South America. In E. Duran (ed.), *Latin America and the World Recession*. Cambridge: Cambridge University Press, in association with the Royal Institute of International Affairs.
World Bank. 1983. *World Development Report*. London: Oxford University Press, for the World Bank.

3

Multinational enterprises in LDCs

Mark Casson and Robert D. Pearce

3.1 Introduction

3.1.1 Definitions

This survey reviews the behaviour of multinational enterprises (MNEs) in less developed countries (LDCs). An MNE may be defined as an enterprise that owns and controls productive activities in more than one country. In this sense the term 'productive' is construed broadly, and refers to any activity that adds value – it therefore includes not only manufacturing, extraction and the provision of services but also marketing and R and D.

The definition of an LDC is problematic, and whatever definition is employed it is certain that there will be enormous heterogeneity. Poor agrarian LDCs such as Sudan look to MNEs to fulfil very different requirements than do relatively affluent newly industrializing countries (NICs) such as Singapore. Oil-importing countries such as Hong Kong attract very different forms of MNE activity than do oil-exporting countries in the Middle East, and so on.

The role of MNEs in LDCs has attracted considerable controversy. Writers sympathetic to the MNE emphasize its role in transferring a package of resources to the LDC. The main components of this package are said to be technology, capital and access to world markets. It is claimed that the transfer of these resources generates efficiency gains for the world economy. LDCs can therefore bargain for, or tax away, a share of these gains for themselves. Critics emphasize its role in redistributing income in favour of its own managers and shareholders. On this view, MNEs and LDCs are involved in, at best, a 'zero sum' game: the profits of the MNE are a direct loss to the host economy.

We are grateful to V. N. Balasubramanyam, Peter Buckley, John Dunning, Norman Gemmell, Colin Kirkpatrick, Fred Nixson and Louis T. Wells, Jr, for their comments on an earlier draft. Special thanks are due to Donald Lecraw for providing very detailed suggestions for improvement.

3.1.2   Some common confusions

The intensity of controversy has adversely affected the quality of the literature on the subject. While some of it has the limited objective of testing theories of the MNE using data drawn from LDCs, the bulk of it is concerned with much wider, and therefore less manageable, issues. It is normative and policy-oriented: it aims to assess whether the overall impact of MNEs on LDCs is favourable or not.

Much of this policy-oriented literature is flawed by a number of analytical confusions. The worst of these confusions are best exposed at the outset. The first arises from a failure to distinguish properly between foreign *direct* investment (FDI) and foreign *indirect* investment (FII). The essence of FDI is that the owner *controls* the foreign resources, whereas under FII the owner merely provides funds and/or carries some of the risks. Theories of FII typically explain investment flows by international differences in the cost of capital. They cannot readily be used to explain FDI because they do not address the issue of control. Specifically, they do not explain why the foreign investor prefers to hold a controlling interest in a few foreign operations rather than spread his risks more widely by holding minority stakes in a much larger number of operations.

Another error is to suppose that FDI must involve a net transfer of funds to the LDC that hosts the investment. There are two reasons why such a transfer may not take place. First, the MNE can borrow in the host economy to finance its acquisition of equity in the subsidiary. In this case, savings in the host country are tapped to finance foreign control. In some cases – such as capital-rich LDCs in the Middle East – funds are actually raised in the host country and transferred abroad to help finance the firm's operations in other markets. The second reason is that other resources may be transferred *in lieu* of funds. The most important of these is technology.

The technology factor explains why the typical MNE is so keen to control overseas operations. Technology drives a firm overseas because it has potentially global applications. Relinquishing control over the technology is dangerous to the firm because the private reward to technology is essentially a monopoly rent which can only be appropriated by collusion between those who exploit it. Control, therefore, is motivated first and foremost by the strategic problems of appropriating rents from technology, and only secondarily by access to capital. When capital transfers are involved, it is often because the reputation of the firm that owns that technology is stronger in its home country than it is abroad, or that capital is cheaper there, so that technology and capital are transferred as a bundle to the LDC.

It is therefore a mistake to argue, as many commentators have done, that the 'unbundling' of technology and capital transfer to LDCs will necessarily give LDCs greater control over imported technology. As indicated above, control is linked to the technology and not to the capital. Firms may be only too happy to accept local financing so long as they retain control over the way technology is exploited. Radical and Marxist writers have fallen most frequently into the trap of associating capital, rather than technology, with control.

The same confusion permeates the interpretation of published statistics of FDI. Commentators fail to realize that the book value of FDI reflects not only the value of funds transferred by the parent company, but also the parents' valuation of its own technology made available to its subsidiary. Even in cases where the FDI figure is large, the parent may have contributed no funds at all.

The term 'technology' is itself misleading, and here it is professional economists who have been most misled. Their emphasis on the relation between MNEs and technology is warranted only if a very broad interpretation is given to the concept of technology, so that it includes not only production engineering, but also the design, branding and advertising of the product, quality control and the management of work. This broad interpretation of the concept of technology indicates that the exploitation of technology by MNEs has major cultural implications, and it is a rather poor theory that ignores this. Unfortunately, conventional economic theory does so.

When a foreign subsidiary repatriates funds – as either capital, interest, profits or licence fees – there is a drain on the foreign currency reserves of the host country. It is, however, a common fallacy amongst non-economists to examine these remittances without considering what they are payments for. The technology and capital supplied by the parent firm constitute real resources – albeit somewhat intangible ones – and they have wide-ranging implications for the host economy. They may contribute to reducing imports, or expanding exports, or they may simply provide domestic consumers with a higher standard of living. Lower imports or higher exports improve the balance of trade and generate additional foreign exchange that helps to finance the repatriation of funds. A higher standard of living enhances the taxable capacity of the country, allowing the government to reduce its foreign borrowing and finance the repatriation of funds in that way. In the long run, at any rate, the real issue is not so much about the level of repatriated funds as about the net impact of MNE activity on the trade balance and pre-tax real income of the host economy.

The net impact of the MNE depends upon a number of factors. Many researchers have focused their attention exclusively on the effects upon the industrial structure of the host economy. They see multinational monopolies as potentially damaging to the performance of the host economy. The charge against the monopolist is that he restricts output and redistributes income in his own favour by raising price above its competitive level. Some degree of monopoly power, however, is inevitably associated with proprietary technology. Perfect competition may not be a viable alternative to monopoly in certain industries, so that the appropriate comparison is not between monopoly and competition but between a monopolistic industry or no industry at all. The monopolistic restriction of output is not, in fact, inevitable, but occurs only when the monopolist is unable to discriminate between different categories of buyer. Theory shows that strengthening the monopolist's control of the market so that he can discriminate successfully will stimulate output towards its competitive level. Monopolistic discrimination of this kind certainly occurs between markets in different countries, though whether it is viable within a market in a single country is more debatable. Finally, commentators often overlook the fact that in the long run, monopoly power is checked by the threat of potential competition. In many LDCs the protectionist stance of the government immunizes the monopolist from import competition, and the lack of profit incentives and low status afforded to indigenous entrepreneurs protects him from domestic competition. As a result, industries that are merely oligopolistic in the industrial countries tend to be monopolistic in LDCs.

To a conventional economist, the appropriate method to analyse the economic impact of MNEs is social cost–benefit analysis (SCBA). This technique rests on highly restrictive assumptions, however, many of which are particularly questionable where LDCs are concerned. Most specifically, SCBA takes a strongly individualistic view of human welfare, which contrasts with the collectivist view prevalent in many LDCs. These individualistic assumptions lead, inevitably, to policy prescriptions of a 'liberal' kind. It is probably for this reason that students of MNEs in LDCs have, with one or two notable exceptions, rejected SCBA. Unfortunately, there is no alternative technique currently available which affords the same level of logical rigour. In particular, SCBA drives a wedge between efficiency and equity considerations which, even if it is excessive, is still a considerable aid to clear thinking on policy issues. Neglect of SCBA has tended to isolate the policy analysis of MNEs from other areas of economics and has, on balance, adversely affected the quality of work in this field.

3.1.3. Plan of the survey

The rest of the survey is organized as follows. The historical background to MNE involvement in LDCs is set out in section 3.2. Section 3.3 discusses various aspects of technology transfer. The appropriateness of MNE technologies to LDCs is examined in section 3.3.1, and the alternative contractual arrangements available for its transfer are appraised in section 3.3.2. The trade effects of technology transfer are discussed in section 3.3.3.

The effects of technology transfer on industrial concentration in the host economy, and upon the development of linkages with other sectors of the economy, are reviewed in section 3.4. Particular attention is given to the growing phenomenon of export-oriented foreign investment – in particular investments attracted by abundant supplies of unskilled labour in NICs.

The country of origin of the MNE seems to materially influence its role in LDCs. Japanese firms, for example, have taken a prominent role in all forms of export-oriented investment. Their pattern of investment is superficially quite unlike that of US firms. The causes of these differences are examined in section 3.5.1. The industrialization of the more advanced LDCs has recently led to the emergence of MNEs based in these countries. These MNEs are playing an increasingly important role in the adaptation of technology from DCs, and in spreading export-oriented investment to poorer countries, as explained in section 3.5.2.

The relation between MNEs, trade and balance of payments is examined in section 3.6. Export-oriented investment leads to significant levels of intra-firm trade; this raises a number of issues which are addressed in section 3.6.1. The financing of foreign investment through international capital flows is examined in 3.6.2. Relations between MNEs and host governments are discussed in section 3.7. Section 3.7.1 considers bargaining between the host government and the MNE over the conditions of entry. The taxation of locally generated profit is considered separately in section 3.7.2. The conclusions are summarized in section 3.8.

The chief omission from this survey is discussion in detail of the impact of MNEs on industrial relations, employment creation and the personal distribution of income. The difficulties of the subject are such that it is impossible to do full justice to these issues within the scope of a general, yet brief, survey of the kind presented here. The reader may refer to Caves (1982, 1985), Enderwick (1984), Flanagan and Weber (1974) and Gunter (1978) for further details.

3.2 The history of MNE involvement in developing countries

Multinational enterprise of some kind can be traced back to the chartered trading companies of the sixteenth century, to Italian ventures in banking and merchant shipping in the fifteenth century and, before that, to the Hanseatic League. However, the origins of the modern MNE, organized as a joint stock company, lie chiefly in the nineteenth-century expansion of the European imperial powers. Businesses owned and controlled from Europe exploited new sources of materials in Africa, Asia and South America to support industrialization at home; they also established manufacturing facilities in industrialized countries, such as the US and Tsarist Russia. A little later, around the turn of the century, the trust movement in the US created some of the first very large MNEs from the merger of smaller firms with minor overseas interests (Chandler, 1977; Wilkins, 1970, 1974).

Early MNE operations were strongly oriented towards LDCs. Dunning (1983) estimates that, in 1914, 62.8 per cent of the world's stock of FDI was in LDCs – 32.7 per cent in Latin America, 20.9 per cent in Asia and 6.4 per cent in Africa. The major overseas investors were the UK (45.5 per cent), US (18.5 per cent), France (12.2 per cent) and Germany (10.5 per cent). According to Dunning (1983, p. 89), the period up to 1914 was

the heyday of the plantations, for example rubber, tea, coffee and cocoa; of cattle raising and meat processing, for example in the USA and Argentina; and of the emergence of the vertically integrated MNE in tropical fruits, sugar and tobacco. Indeed apart, perhaps, from some transnational railroad activity in Europe and Latin America, it was in the agricultural sector, more than any other, where the international hierarchial organisation first made itself felt, particularly in economies whose prosperity rested mainly on a single cash crop, the production and marketing of which was controlled by a few (and sometimes only one) foreign companies, for example Cuba (sugar), Costa Rica (bananas), Ceylon (tea) and Liberia (rubber).

Political instability and economic recession in the inter-war years discouraged the growth of FDI, although the widespread imposition of tariffs by developed countries (DCs) in the 1930s encouraged some firms to start producing overseas to protect their export markets. A notable feature of this period was the industrial and geographical redistribution of the capital stock. There was retrenchment of European railroad investments in Latin America, but quite a lot of new MNE participation in LDCs too. Dunning (1983, p. 93) mentions new oil investments in the Mexican gulf, the Dutch East Indies, and the Middle East; copper and iron ore in Africa; bauxite in Dutch and British Guyana; precious metals in South Africa and ferrous metals in South America. 'Outside the mineral sector, the growing industrial demand for rubber led both US and European manufacturers to invest in rubber plantations . . . ; whilst rising real incomes at home prompted a further flurry of activity by MNEs in sugar, tropical fruit and tobacco. There was also a sizeable expansion of public utility investments in Latin America by US firms.'

After 1945 the pattern of MNE operations changed considerably. The value of the world stock of FDI rose dramatically, but the proportion going to LDCs fell – from 65.7 per cent in 1938 to 32.3 per cent in 1960 and 27.8 per cent in 1978. One reason for this was the rising tide of nationalism in LDCs which led to expropriation and nationalization of foreign assets, especially in the mineral sector. Not only did this reduce existing investments, but it created an unfavourable political climate in which further investment in LDCs was perceived as a high-risk activity. A more important factor, however, was the growing importance of US foreign investment in the world economy. Only 27.7 per cent of the FDI stock was owned by US firms in 1938 but this percentage had risen to 49.2 in 1960. Much of this investment involved the manufacture of US-designed high-technology mass-produced goods in the UK and the European Community (EC). Later on in the 1960s, a pattern of cross-investment began to emerge, with European firms – notably West German engineering, chemical and pharmaceutical firms – establishing operations in the US to match the US investments in Europe. In the developed world, many markets became dominated by a global oligopolistic rivalry between MNEs based in different DCs competing on the novelty and the quality of their differentiated products. The role of the LDCs became essentially peripheral, at least as far as manufacturing was concerned. Foreign investors were reluctant to invest in small markets demanding relatively unsophisticated low-price products, except in response to government inducements such as tax holidays and protection against import competition.

The emergence of the new international division of labour (NIDL) in the 1970s, however, has given LDCs at the higher stages of development a new role as export platforms. MNEs have begun to relocate labour-intensive activities in LDCs as part of a global restructuring and rationalization of their operations. This process has been further stimulated by the establishment of export processing zones (EPZs) – particularly in South East Asian economies – and by the introduction of 'value-added tariffs' by the US and, more recently, by the EC.

Recent evidence on the structure of FDI shows that Japanese investment has a quite distinctive pattern compared to US and European investment. About three-quarters of US and European investment is directed towards other DCs, and their pattern for manufacturing investment is broadly similar to their pattern for investment as a whole. Compared to this, Japanese investment is biased towards LDCs, which take 53.8 per cent of total Japanese investment, about half of which goes to Asia. The bias is even more pronounced where manufacturing investment is concerned: 72.5 per cent of investment is in LDCs, and again, half of this is in Asia, with most of the rest being in Latin America, and hardly any in Africa and the Middle East.

3.3 Technology transfer

3.3.1. Appropriate technology

Although technology takes many different forms, empirical work on MNEs has focused upon production technology. Thus while the marketing methods of MNEs in LDCs have been the subject of unfavourable comment – particularly where pharmaceutical products are concerned – economists have done little research on this subject (though see James, 1983).

A major concern about the technology transferred by MNEs has been its suitability for the host economy. The product cycle theory (Vernon, 1966, 1974, 1979) suggests that techniques innovated in DCs will be attuned to an environment of high labour costs and a large group of discerning high-income consumers. The technology will be too capital-intensive, too skill-intensive and too oriented towards high product quality to be appropriate to LDCs, where the main need is for labour-intensive production of unsophisticated products. MNEs' working practices may also be geared to production in large-scale plants.

Selection and adaptation in technology transfer

Technology can adjust to LDC conditions through both *selection* and *adaptation*. Selection governs which of the technologies available in the industrialized countries are transferred to LDCs, while adaptation involves modifying these technologies when transfer is effected. The two forms of adjustment are related, since in many industries there may be a tendency to select the technologies that are most easily adapted.

A key factor governing technological selection is the nature of the product market. If the intended market is mainly the LDC domestic market – and perhaps the markets of neighbouring LDCs as well – then the decision to produce locally reflects a decision to relocate production closer to the centre of the market. Reducing transport costs and avoiding tariffs is the principal motive for such *import-substituting* investment. In manufacturing industry, transport cost savings are often largest where the finished product is bulky and delicate but the components from which it is assembled are not. Transport costs are reduced by importing kits and components from the source country and assembling them locally. Local assembly can also afford major tariff savings since in a protected market imports of components are often subjected to much lower rates of duty than finished products.

When producing only for the domestic market, demand is likely to be so small that unit costs will escalate whenever economies of scale are present. This suggests that other privileges, such as favoured treatment in government procurement, or a ban on other foreign production in the industry, may also be needed to attract the foreign investor. Such privileges are most likely in industries the government deems to be strategically important. It seems likely, therefore, that import substitution will attract mainly assembly-type manufacturing technologies which afford only modest economies of scale. The main qualification is that some strategically important industries, such as petrochemicals, are characterized by very large economies of scale.

By contrast, when producing for export to industrialized countries, the location of production decision involves a global choice between alternative locations rather than a simple dichotomous choice of whether to produce close to the market or not. Because of this, the firm has a greater opportunity to choose an LDC location on the grounds that it requires less adaptation of technology than others, and this suggests that export-oriented investments may involve less adaptation than import-substituting ones. The theory of comparative advantage suggests that the selection process for export-oriented operations will favour technologies in resource-based industries such as minerals and tropical agriculture, and in labour-intensive manufacturing industries.

There are three other reasons why export-oriented investments may involve less adaptation. The first concerns the size of the market. When producing for LDC markets only, the plant may have to be scaled down from the size normally installed in an industrialized country. The costs of redesigning the entire plant from scratch to produce an 'appropriate technology' for the LDC are likely to be prohibitive, and in any case, if this were required, the MNE would not necessarily have a cost advantage over an indigenous firm. If, however, one of the items of equipment was essentially indivisible and easily separated from the rest, it might be advantageous to dispense with it and replace it with manual labour – perhaps using working practices based on those in force in the industrialized countries before the equipment was introduced. In general it seems quite likely, therefore, that where adaptation is involved, reduction in scale and increase in labour intensity may go hand in hand.

An increase in labour intensity may cause problems, however, if capital equipment is needed to maintain fine tolerances in precision products – this is particularly important when producing components for durables that utilize interchangeable parts. Customers in industrialized countries tend to be more discerning where product quality and reliability is concerned – the opportunity cost of time wasted through breakdowns tends to be perceived by them as much greater, for a start. Thus when producing for export to industrialized countries, it seems unlikely that capital intensity will be significantly reduced because the firms' reputation for quality may be lost as a result.

When an import-substituting MNE enjoys a local monopoly, the managers of the local subsidiary are under little pressure to control costs. This could mean that they make no effort to adapt foreign technology to local conditions because of the personal cost of the effort involved. It is quite possible, however, that they might feel themselves obliged to win governmental approval by creating extra jobs, and this might even benefit the parent company in extra sales to government as well as giving local managers a quiet life. In this latter case, inertia actually leads to adaptation of sorts, though the extra jobs may not involve performing any real work at all. It is unlikely that such 'adaptation' will occur in export-oriented activities because of the more competitive (or at least oligopolistic) conditions that prevail in the markets of industrialized countries.

Theory suggests that both selection and adaptation will make the technologies transferred to LDCs more labour-intensive and less capital-intensive than the technologies most commonly used in the industrialized countries. A classic study by Reuber *et al.* (1973) and a more recent study by Lipsey, Kravis and Roldan (1982) confirm this. Reuber *et al.*'s study also confirms the hypothesis that adaptation is more prevalent in import-substituting projects. Thus of 24 export-oriented projects studied by Reuber *et al.*, only two adapted product design, four adapted production equipment and four adapted production techniques. By contrast, of 53 import-substituting projects, 18 adapted product design, 18 adapted equipment, and 23 adapted operating methods. In these cases, the need to adjust to the smaller size of the market was the predominant motivation for adaptation. Thus 18 firms reported low volume as a factor contributing to adaptation, compared with five reporting low labour costs, and four reporting lack of local skilled labour. In addition 14 firms suggested other reasons that influenced their need to adapt, these being related to 'special characteristics of demand, government regulations and standards or the quality of raw materials and components purchased locally under mandatory requirements' (p. 196).

Helfgott (1973) found that for 13 plants established by US firms in LDCs, the core technology was basically that used in DCs, though often scaled down in size. There is some suggestion of increases in labour intensity after installation of the plant due to 'overmanning, which comes about mainly through job restructuring to compensate for differences in skills and experience' (p. 244). Some adaptation to greater labour use also occurred in peripheral elements of the production process; for example, by using fewer overhead conveyances and more manual handling of parts between successive stages of production.

Morley and Smith (1977a) detect evidence of substantial adaptation by US firms operating in Brazil. Though the result was more labour-intensive production, Morley and Smith suggest that the major motivation was the need for smaller scale production. However as Lipsey, Kravis and Roldan (1982, p. 251) point out, such scale-motivated adaptation may also be seen as a response to factor price differences, since the smaller plants may only be competitive where labour costs are lower. Nevertheless Morley and Smith (1977b) suggest that the US firms did not fully explore the possibilities of adaptation in response to factor price differences, so that their substantial adaptation remained less than optimal.

International Labour Office (1972, p. 450) researchers in Kenya visited eight foreign-owned firms and concluded that all 'were using more labour-intensive methods than they would have used in their home countries'. Though in some cases this could be ascribed to the low productivity of local labour, there was also a number of cases of deliberate labour–capital substitution.

Not all researchers, however, have found convincing evidence of adaptation. Langdon (1981, pp. 55–6) found minimal evidence of *product* adaptation by 48 MNE subsidiaries in Kenya. A survey of 19 foreign firms in Nigeria reported by Biersteker (1978, p. 122) found that only five of these 'had made any adaptations to the local climate, employment conditions, raw materials, or marketing requirements'. Survey evidence compiled by Chen (1983a, pp. 115–19) suggested substantial technology adaptation by MNEs in the 'garments' and 'plastics and toys' industries in Hong Kong, but that adaptation was much less prevalent in 'textiles' and 'electronics'. Finally, production function analysis of US MNEs by Courtney and Leipziger (1975) suggested no evidence of systematic factor substitution in plant design, but some substitution in operating methods. However, the methodology underlying their results has been disputed by De Meza (1977).

Overall, these studies suggest some firms in LDCs do indeed adapt their production methods, but make few changes in either product design, or type of equipment – other than scaling down the size of plant. Other firms make no adaptation at all. Evidence presented later suggests that one reason why the basic technology tends to remain unaltered is that mechanization is crucial in achieving a uniform quality of output, and that foreign firms consider quality standards as essential in maintaining their reputation.

Comparison of imported and indigenous technology

Another method of assessing adaptation in technology transfer is to compare MNE technology not with its equivalent in the industrialized countries, but with its equivalent amongst indigenous firms. This exercise can only shed light indirectly on the issue, because in many cases no indigenous analogue of the imported technology actually exists. Even if it did exist, there can be no guarantee that this technology would represent efficient adaptation to the local environment.

The usual empirical methodology is to make a cross-section comparison of the capital intensity of MNE production and indigenous production. It is important to appreciate, however, that because MNEs are attracted selectively to LDCs, they will be more heavily represented in some sectors than in others. Thus if export-oriented manufacturing opportunities attract them they will be concentrated in labour-intensive industries, whereas if protectionism in strategic industries attracts them they may predominate in capital-intensive industries instead. It is therefore most important to control for selection factors by examining variation *within* industries rather than *between* industries when using a capital-intensive bias as a proxy for failure to adapt.

A further potential ambiguity arises because there is another quite distinct reason why MNE technology may be biased towards capital intensity. It is that MNEs and indigenous firms face different relative factor prices in the host economy. The indigenous firm, by virtue of its greater knowledge of the labour market, is likely to be able to hire labour cheaper than a foreign user of imported technology, whilst the foreign user is likely to have access to cheaper capital because of its reputation in the financial markets of the industrialized countries. Thus even if an MNE were willing and able to reduce capital intensity, it may not have the same incentive to do so as an indigenous firm. The market imperfections responsible for this may become less acute as the LDC reaches a higher stage of development. If, for example, the indigenous firm belongs to a 'group' financed by a landed aristocracy or merchant class that is diversifying into industrial development, its access to capital may be almost as easy as that of the MNE. Thus biases towards *relative* capital intensity amongst MNEs can be expected to decrease as the level of development is raised.

The importance of controlling for inter-industry differences in the selection of foreign technology is well illustrated by the International Labour Office (1972, pp. 446–52) study of Kenya which showed that across all industries the average capital intensity of foreign firms was higher than that of indigenous firms, but that this was entirely explained by the total foreign dominance of a number of very capital-intensive industries. In sectors where both foreign and indigenous enterprises operated, it was the latter that seemed to be the more capital intensive.

Even within industries, comparison is problematic because of the difficulty of finding an exact match for the foreign technology. Thus using data on US MNE affiliates for 1966, provided by the US Department of Commerce, Meller and Mizala (1982) compared the capital intensities of US subsidiaries and local firms in 13 manufacturing industries in seven Latin American countries. The conclusion drawn from this broadly based study was 'that US affiliates utilize production techniques that, in general, are much more capital intensive than those techniques employed by local manufacturing establishments of a similar size located in the same industry'. The authors admit, however, that part of the observed difference may reflect the different product specialization of US and local firms, rather than substantially different ways of producing similar items. Whatever may be the situation with regard to specialization *within* industries, Meller and Mizala suggest that their data provide no significant evidence of a tendency for US subsidiaries to be more concentrated in capital-intensive industries in Latin America.

The hypothesis that where manufacturers have a wide choice of production locations, careful selection of site reduces the need to adapt technology locally, receives considerable empirical support. Studies of export-oriented industries in Taiwan, Hong Kong, Korea and Malaysia show little systematic difference in capital intensity between foreign and indigenous firms. Riedel (1975) analysed the factor intensities of 445 foreign and domestic firms in six export-oriented manufacturing industries in Taiwan in 1973. A multivariate analysis incorporating firm characteristics such as scale of production and import-dependency indicated no significant difference in factor proportions between foreign and Taiwanese firms in any of the industries. It is worth noting, however, that when firm characteristics were not controlled for, foreign firms were significantly more labour-intensive than domestic firms in three of the six industries. This emphasizes the ever-present problem that observed differences in factor proportions may reflect characteristics other than foreignness of technology *per se*.

Chen (1983a, pp. 104–13; 1983b) analysed 369 foreign and domestic firms in Hong Kong in 1979, using two measures of capital intensity: the capital–labour ratio and value added per employee. For three of the four industries covered (textiles, plastics and toys, and electronics) foreign firms were significantly less capital-intensive than domestic firms for at least one of the measures, whilst in the fourth (garments) foreign firms were significantly more capital-intensive by both measures. Chung and Lee (1980) studied 17 matched pairs of foreign (US and Japanese) and Korean firms with respect to capital–labour and capital–output ratios. Though statistical tests suggest no *systematic* tendency for foreign firms to be either more capital- or labour-intensive, substantial differences in factor proportions were observed in many of the pairs. In a similar analysis for Malaysia, Chee (quoted in Chen, 1983a, pp. 145–50) found no statistically significant tendency for different factor intensities between foreign and local firms in 15 pairs carefully matched by size and product line. Using data at the industry level for Malaysia, Lim (1976) found no consistent tendency for either foreign or local firms to be the more capital-intensive. However the differences in average factor intensities between foreign firms and Malaysian firms were quite considerable within industries, this being especially notable in industries where, on average, foreign firms were more capital-intensive.

Willmore (1976) studied 33 pairs of foreign and local firms in Costa Rica in 1971, matched with respect to size and product mix. Three different measures for the capital–labour ratio were tested, but none provided statistically significant evidence of different factor proportions being adopted by the two groups of firms.

Two less export-oriented Asian economies provide clearer evidence of a capital-intensive bias among foreign firms. Agarwal (1976) found that in 1969 foreign firms were more capital-intensive (in terms of productive capital per employee) than local firms in 22 of 34 industries in the Indian large-scale manufacturing sector. The influences of different factor prices faced by the two groups of firms are suggested as a major contributing factor; though, in addition, Agarwal acknowledges that foreign firms 'give preference to machines also on account of their bigger reservoir of experience in capital-intensive technologies and operations whereas [local firms] are less hesitant in employing labour because they are relatively more at home in the indigenous labour market' (p. 594).

Studies for Indonesia corroborate Agarwal's view. Analysis of 22 industries in Indonesia led Balasubramanyam (1984) to conclude that foreign firms were 40 per cent more capital-intensive in their operations than local private firms, and 30 per cent more capital-intensive than public sector firms. The analysis also demonstrated that the overall greater capital intensity of foreign firms is due to their tendency to choose more capital-intensive techniques *within* industries, rather than a greater propensity to operate in inherently capital-intensive industries. Indeed it seemed that foreign firms had some tendency to be more oriented to inherently labour-intensive industries than Indonesian firms.

Wells's earlier study (1973) of plants in six light manufacturing industries in Indonesia reaches similar conclusions. Wells places particular emphasis on product market conditions; he suggests that in the absence of competitive pressures the objectives of 'engineering man' may manifest themselves in the foreign firm. These include reducing operational problems to those of managing machines rather than people; achieving high and reliable quality; and using sophisticated machinery that is attractive to the engineering 'aesthetic'. The relative capital-intensity of foreign firms in Indonesia seems, to Wells, to reflect their greater tendency to operate in environments which permit 'engineering man' to prevail over 'economic man'.

A complementary line of argument was developed by Morley and Smith (1977b) to explain the limited adaptation by US MNEs to the Brazilian production environment. Newfarmer and Marsh (1981), however, stress a wider range of factors contributing to relative capital intensity of foreign firms in Brazil, while Tyler (1978) emphasizes their higher cost of labour and lower cost of capital. Similarly in Nigeria Biersteker (1978, pp. 12–19) found a complex of factors at work: over the period 1963–72 foreign firms were more capital-intensive than local firms in the textile industry, but not in the cement and saw-milling industries.

Who makes adaptations?

There is reason to believe that despite the high cost of technological adaptation, and the possibility of managerial inertia or 'engineering man' motivation, the MNE is in a better position than anyone else to undertake adaptation, simply because of its technicians' command and understanding of the technology. The main exceptions would appear to involve consumer products for which demand is culturally specific, and products with a high content of traditional craftman-ship. In these cases environmental differences between source and host countries may be acute, and this may favour adaptation by an indigenous firm instead. The 'best of both worlds' is afforded by a collaborative venture between the MNE and an indigenous firm. Collaboration, however, is sometimes difficult to negotiate and to sustain. In this case a firm owned by resident expatriates may provide a compromise solution.

In some cases the local environment, though different from that in industrialized countries, may not be entirely specific to the host economy but similar to that in many other LDCs too. This suggests the possibility that a firm could specialize in technological adaptation to LDCs in general. Provided the technology were not too sophisticated, the exploitation of such adaptation skills might best be effected by an MNE based in an LDC.

The International Labour Office (1972) study, referred to earlier, explained the relatively low capital intensity of foreign firms within certain Kenyan industries by the fact

that foreign enterprises have more skilled supervisory staff, and that this allows them to use production techniques which use low cost unskilled labour. Local firms may be relatively deficient in technical supervision, so that they have to rely more on operative skills and machine pacing, which requires a shift to more capital intensive techniques with higher labour productivity (p. 450).

Pack's (1976) interview survey of 42 manufacturing plants in Kenya provided evidence which may be considered compatible with the ILO results; he concluded that 'it was typically a subsidiary of a foreign firm which carried out labour-intensive adaptations and was more willing to use older equipment'.

Forsyth and Solomon (1977) (see also Solomon and Forsyth, 1977) analyse the technological characteristics of three groups of firms operating in Ghana in 1970/1. In addition to subsidiaries of MNEs, 'private-owned indigenous firms' (PIFs) are distinguished from 'resident-expatriate-owned firms' (REFs), that is private firms owned by foreigners permanently resident in Ghana. With regard to factor proportions, the overall conclusion was that MNEs (and also REFs) were, on average, more capital-intensive than PIFs, though this result was not verified for all the 10 industries used in the study. There was also evidence of a tendency for PIFs to use a higher proportion of skilled labour than did either MNEs or REFs. A suggested explanation of this latter result is that the greater range of technical knowledge and experience available to MNEs makes them more effective in 'deskilling' existing technology. The fact that Forsyth and Solomon tend to find the characteristics of REFs more similar to MNEs than to PIFs is a potentially valuable and instructive result. To the extent that enterprises comparable to the REFs in Ghana exist in samples analysed by other researchers it seems likely that they would have been treated as local firms rather than MNE subsidiaries. Thus, if their characteristics conform to the result for Ghana, the outcome would have been to lessen the observed distinction between MNEs and truly indigenous firms.

Lecraw (1977, 1979) used data on 400 firms (including subsidiaries of 'traditional' MNEs; subsidiaries of firms from other LDCs; and local Thai enterprises) in 12 light-manufacturing industries in Thailand, to open new empirical perspectives on choice of techniques in LDCs. In the light of estimated production functions for each industry, and the factor prices faced by each firm, an efficient (cost-minimizing) technique for each firm was calculated and compared with that firm's actual techniques. It was found that within each industry firms from other LDCs were on average 39 per cent less capital-intensive than either subsidiaries of DC MNEs or local Thai firms; whilst there was virtually no difference in the average capital intensity of the two latter groups of firms. Lecraw's investigation revealed considerable inefficiency in selection of production technique (in the sense of deviation between cost-minimizing techniques and those actually chosen) by both DC MNEs and Thai firms, whilst firms from other LDCs were notably more efficient in this respect. In general Lecraw (1977, p. 453) summarizes this phase of his work as suggesting that the firms from other LDCs 'used technology which was appropriate to local factor cost' in Thailand, whilst the subsidiaries of traditional MNEs and local Thai firms used 'inappropriate' technology.

Lecraw (1979) proceeds to investigate the determinants of 'inefficiency' in choice of technique. Firms whose managers had experience of operations in low-wage countries tended to use more efficient technology than did firms whose managers had little such experience; this applied to both foreign and Thai firms. Also, firms managed by engineers tended to choose more appropriate technology than those managed by non-engineers. Lecraw notes that this does not necessarily imply the absence of 'engineering-man' motivation (as described by Wells), but rather that it may have been outweighed by the engineers' broader knowledge of the available technologies (as argued by Pack) and their ability to break the productive process into separate stages and calculate the cost implications of various alternative techniques at each stage.

3.3.2 Contractual arrangements for technology transfer

One of the major complaints against MNEs operating in LDCs is that the local subsidiary remains very much under the control of the parent company, and that management in the parent company is unaware of, or unsympathetic to, the problems of producing in the host economy. In the past decade many LDCs have taken active steps to weaken the amount of control exercised by the parent company, by requiring that technology be exploited through joint ventures with indigenous firms (often state-owned firms) or through licensing and industrial cooperation agreements (see for example Oman, 1984; Tomlinson, 1970). A semantic issue arises here, because if the foreign firm takes a negligible equity stake in local production, it cannot really be said to own the production in the LDC, and it may therefore cease to qualify as an MNE, according to the definition in section 3.1.1. This should not, however, deter the economist from analysing non-equity ventures, since a comparison between equity and non-equity ventures sheds important light on the nature of control.

There are strong reasons for believing that, in the absence of any constraints, a foreign firm transferring technology will prefer to hold a controlling equity stake in the LDC. This is particularly important when the technology is difficult to patent, when the product it produces is easily tradeable, and when this product has a reputable brand name that needs to be protected by quality control (Buckley and Casson, 1985, chapters 1 and 2).

Technologies that are difficult to patent need to be protected by secrecy, or at least kept uncodified in order to make them difficult to copy. This normally raises the costs of licensing the technology since potential licensees will be reluctant to pay for a technology that they cannot easily find out about, and therefore cannot be certain is reliable.

Because technology has some of the characteristics of a public good, it can be exploited simultaneously in several different plants. But if it is exploited through open competition between these plants, the monopoly rents out of which the costs of developing the technology must be reimbursed will be dissipated. It is therefore appropriate for the parent firm to organize some form of collusion in the pricing of the outputs from the different plants. One way of doing this is to bring all the plants under common ownership and control, thereby creating an MNE. Another method is to establish a cartel to which all users of the technology belong. A final method is to license the technology by an agreement which gives the patentee the right to veto the supply of licensee's products to particular markets; this allows the world market to be partitioned into non-overlapping segments, in each of which one licensee has a monopoly. Notice that, in the final case, the foreign firm retains a measure of control over the indigenous licensee even though it has no equity participation. The control is exercised not through day-to-day discretionary intervention of the kind permitted by outright ownership, but through the right to veto specific exporting decisions.

The obvious way to maintain control over the quality of a branded product is to supervise the process of production. But supervision requires access to the premises, and ownership of the premises is therefore desirable in order to guarantee this. The alternative to ownership is to subcontract production by an agreement that provides for access to the subcontractor's premises. In certain cases subcontracting may be acceptable to the proprietor of the branded product, even without such access, provided that the subcontractor can be kept economically dependent. Dependency can be secured by an agreement that the subcontractor will accept payment in arrears and will not undertake work for other firms. Once again, the alternative to outright ownership is an agreement that still reserves a measure of control to the foreign firm.

Several other restrictive agreements can be explained by the importance of quality control (Casson, 1979; UNCTAD, 1971; UNCTC, 1983a, b, c). These include the tying of purchases of key inputs, equipment and spare parts to the parent firm, and the use of expatriate personnel in key positions in the LDC affiliate.

The moral, then, is fairly clear. There is a certain logic to restrictive business practices, and most foreign firms transferring technology will continue to require them, since they are crucial not only to the profitability of their LDC operations, but to the profitability of their global operations as a whole. Outright ownership of a foreign subsidiary is a convenient way of implementing these restrictions, but government constraints on foreign ownership do not eliminate the possibility of imposing these restrictions. Foreign firms are increasingly willing to relinquish ownership for alternative arrangements that continue to give them the control they desire (Long, 1981). Some LDC governments now realize that foreign firms will never relinquish control, and have therefore tended to relax their opposition to foreign ownership – for at least with foreign ownership the exercise of control is often easier to monitor – being conspicuous rather than covert.

3.3.3 Trade effects of technology transfer

It is generally accepted that there is some tendency for MNE production to substitute for imports, though the magnitude of the effect is debatable. Appraisal is complicated by the fact that foreign production is often stimulated by protective tariffs, which simultaneously encourage the expansion of indigenous production too. It is therefore difficult to measure the extent to which MNE production substitutes for imports rather than for indigenous production. There is also the question of whether tied imports, as described in the previous section, replace inputs which would otherwise have been obtained from an indigenous source.

Whether or not MNEs promote exports depends crucially upon the type of industry. Agribusiness, for example, is normally export-oriented, and in so far as foreign technology improves agricultural productivity it is likely to stimulate exports. In the mineral sector the case is less clear. Exports may be stimulated by foreign ownership, not because of the discovery of new deposits, or the reduction of waste in extraction, but simply because a high rate of depletion is encouraged by a fear of expropriation.

Most empirical work relating to the export performance of MNEs has focused upon the manufacturing sector. The majority of studies have adopted a comparative methodology, by analysing the export performances of matched pairs of foreign and indigenous firms, or by including foreign ownership alongside other relevant independent variables – notably industry of operation – in multiple regressions with export performance as the dependent variable. No systematic difference between MNEs and indigenous firms was reported by Natke and Newfarmer (1985) for Brazil, by Morgenstern and Muller (1976) for 10 Latin American countries, and by Lim (1976) for Malaysia. Riedel's (1975) analysis of six export-oriented industries in Taiwan suggested that in only one of these industries (electronics) were foreign firms significantly more export-oriented than locals. For Mexico, Jenkins (1977) found local firms to have the better export performance in traditional and intermediate industries, though foreign subsidiaries tended to have better export performance in engineering industries. Evidence of superior exporting performance by foreign firms was found by Willmore (1976) for Costa Rica and by Lall and Mohammad (1983) for the large firm sector in India.

Though insufficient studies are available to permit the discernment of any clear patterns, there is an indication that where local firms have the technical capability to produce the product efficiently, they are able to market it competitively with MNEs. In such cases marketing expertise and market access do not seem to provide MNEs with an independent advantage. In other cases, though, differences in performance do emerge which may be compatible with De la Torre's (1974, p. 137) suggestion that 'the higher the marketing entry barrier associated with a product and the more distant or complex the market of destination, the more pronounced is the advantage of the foreign firm'. Once attention is drawn to the influence of industry and country factors, it should be recalled that the studies reviewed tend to compare performance in sectors where both MNEs and local firms operate, and exclude those relatively advanced industries, and industrially immature host countries, where MNEs may be the only viable source of exports.

When a similar type of analysis is applied to import behaviour the predominant conclusion seems to be that foreign firms tend to have a greater propensity to import than local firms. This was found for Brazilian manufacturing as a whole by Natke and Newfarmer (1985) and for the Brazilian electrical industry in particular by Newfarmer and Marsh (1981); for Mexico by Jenkins (1977); for four out of six export-oriented industries in Taiwan by Riedel (1975); and for export-oriented firms in Korea by Cohen (1973). However Willmore (1976) for Costa Rica and Lim (1976) for Malaysia, found no general difference in import propensity between local and foreign firms. Since these studies tend to exclude sectors where MNEs are the only viable producers, there may be some presumption that where local industry is not able to produce a final product in competition with an MNE it is unlikely to be able to produce inputs for that product either; so that MNE-dominated sectors of LDC industry may have a notably high propensity to import. This may be especially true of MNE-dominated export-oriented sectors; thus Riedel (1975) draws the conclusion from his study that export-oriented FDI tends to be enclavistic.

3.4 Multinationals and industrial structure

3.4.1 Impact of foreign entry on industrial concentration in the host economy

Much discussion of the effects of MNE penetration on host countries relates to possible 'spillover' or 'external' effects, that is, ways in which the MNE affects the performance of other sectors of the economy. The impact of MNEs on industrial concentration in the host economy has been particularly controversial. Attention has generally focused upon concentration in local production rather than in local sales (which include imports), even though the latter is arguably the most relevant for policy purposes.

Evidence on concentration in production is scarce and tenuous. A number of studies suggest that it is the most highly concentrated industries that are most strongly penetrated by MNEs. This result has been found for Mexico by Fajnzylber and Tarrago (quoted in Bornschier, 1980, p. 194, footnote 4) and for Guatemala by Willmore (1976). A survey by Lecraw (1983) suggests that whilst US and European MNEs operate most intensively in more concentrated industries, Japanese MNEs and MNEs from LDCs seem to operate more intensively in less concentrated (more competitive) industries.

These results, while they establish association, do not establish causation though. Lall (1979) suggests that the initial, short-run, consequence of MNE entry may be to lower concentration in the industry simply by adding to the number of enterprises operating. The reduction in concentration will be greater if, firstly, the MNEs enter by setting up 'greenfield' facilities rather than by takeover of existing locally owned plants; and, secondly, if the pioneering entry of one leading MNE in an industry induces its major competitors to follow suit. The potential importance of this second factor is emphasized by Evans (1977), who refers to the 'miniature replica' effect. In an industry dominated by a limited number of globally competing oligopolists (from several parent countries) the entry by one of them into a new market may provoke matching entry by, perhaps, a majority of its rivals, so that the LDC industry replicates the industry's global structure. Evans suggests that this effect can be observed in the relatively low levels of concentration in the pharamaceutical industry in several LDCs (for example Brazil, Argentina and Mexico). However, when there are economies of scale, the servicing of a small market by quite a large number of firms implies cost inefficiency, and in such cases the initial investor may create a barrier to the entry of rival firms.

In the long run, Lall feels, it is likely that MNE penetration will lead to higher concentration. Four main reasons can be advanced for this view. First, the

MNE's competitive strengths may force local firms out of business. This may be partly the consequence of conventional market forces which reduce the profitability of marginal suppliers and encourages them to leave the industry. It could also, however, be the result of price warfare, in which the MNE uses its privileged access to overseas capital to outlast its indigenous rivals, or systematically cross-subsidizes its local operations.

Secondly, an MNE may buy out its local rivals through acquisition. Though, for obvious reasons, there has generally been less scope for MNEs to enter by takeover in LDCs than in DCs (Vernon, 1977, p. 70), evidence for Brazil and Mexico compiled by Newfarmer and Mueller (1975) suggests a considerable increase in the use of this tactic. Newfarmer's (1979b) analysis of acquisition and mergers in the Brazilian electrical goods industry between 1960 and 1974 leads him to conclude that distortions in the 'market for firms' considerably favoured MNE affiliates as purchasers of local enterprises, with detrimental consequences for the state of competition in the industry (see also Newfarmer, 1979a, 1980).

Thirdly, the conduct of foreign firms may have an indirect effect on concentration by stimulating defensive amalgamations among local firms. Finally MNE's skills as lobbyists may allow them to bargain for themselves secure and influential positions in their industries through negotiations with the local government.

Lall presents empirical evidence on the relationship between MNE penetration and LDC market concentration using data on 46 industries in Malaysia. He infers that foreign firm presence increases industrial concentration through its influence on other variables which affect concentration, that is by raising capital intensity and minimum capital requirements, and, to a lesser degree, through increasing local advertising. But it also has an independent effect which, Lall hypothesizes, may manifest itself through (a) predatory conduct, (b) technology and marketing factors (leading to the disappearance of small or traditional producers) or (c) the gaining of special concessions.

Another study which places the relationship between MNE penetration and industrial concentration in a broad context is that of Newfarmer and Marsh (1981), which utilizes data on foreign and local firms operating in the Brazilian electrical goods industry. An index of foreign firm penetration is the dependent variable and the two independent variables found to be most strongly (and positively) related to it are industrial concentration and advertising intensity.

Neither of these two studies, however, entirely resolves the serious methodological problem of distinguishing between cause and effect where changes in industrial concentration are concerned. A tentative conclusion is that in the long run MNE activity is likely to increase industrial concentration within the host economy, particularly when that country is an LDC – even in cases where the global market outside the LDC is highly competitive (or rivalistic); but which particular mechanism is responsible for this effect is not entirely clear.

3.4.2   Backward linkages between MNEs and local firms

The term 'linkage' is used here, as defined by Lall (1980, p. 204), to refer to 'the direct relationships established by firms in complementary activities which are external to "pure" market transactions'. The linkage is a contractually agreed relationship, scheduled to persist for some time, between enterprises which remain otherwise independent of each other. As a means of achieving co-ordination of their activities it therefore falls mid-way between reliance on free markets, on the one hand, and internalization of the transactions through merger of the enterprises on the other.

Empirical assessment of the benefits to the local economy of linkages created by MNE subsidiaries has proved extremely difficult. Thus much of the research quoted on the nature and extent of linkages covers a broader range of trans-actions than those covered by the definition above.

The first issue is the extent and determinants of linkages. Reuber's survey (Reuber *et al.*, 1971, pp. 151–5) of MNE investment projects in LDCs provides the widest sample of evidence. Using data on 64 projects for 1970, Reuber identifies inter-firm linkages from information on the sources of goods and services supplied to the projects. He finds that 36.9 per cent of the value of goods and services purchased were provided by 'indigenous local firms', 8.2 per cent by 'locally based foreign subsidiaries', 43.3 per cent by the parent company and 11.4 per cent by other sources (including established suppliers to the parent company). Detailed scrutiny of the data suggests that sourcing patterns seemed to vary according to (a) the market orientation of the subsidiary (export or local), (b) the MNE's parent country, and (c) the host country.

In order to separate the more important of these influences, Reuber performed regression tests. These confirm that the share of purchases made from local firms was substantially (and statistically significantly) less for export-oriented projects, whilst the share purchased from the parent firm was significantly greater for these projects. This is interpreted as corroborating the impression 'that projects oriented towards local markets are more fully integrated into the local economy'. The results also provide statistically significant confirmation that European investors relied more heavily for supplies on indigenous firms and less heavily on their parents than did North American investors; though no significant differences were found between Japanese and North American projects. Turning to host country areas the regressions indicated less reliance on indigenous firms by projects in the Far East compared to Latin America; whilst, by contrast, projects in India showed significantly more reliance on indigenous sources and less on parent companies, compared to projects in Latin America.

Reuber's data on sources of goods and services suggested a notable increase in the use of 'indigenous local firms' between 1970 and 1972. It seems likely that in the years following the Reuber study there has been a tendency for export-oriented MNE subsidiaries in LDCs to increase their local purchases further as their operations have matured. This is certainly suggested by Lim and Pang's (1982) study of three subsidiaries of leading electronics MNEs in Singapore.

A second important issue concerns the extent to which there is a transfer of product or process know-how from the MNE to its local supplier. Such transfer could result in a general upgrading of the capability of the LDC enterprise. On the basis of a useful analytical framework, Jansson (1982) makes it clear that any presumption that such transfers would be expected as the norm in MNE–LDC enterprise links would be misguided. Thus where the motivation for sub-contracting is an existing technological complementarity of the two firms, and where the input purchased is established and standardized, there is only a limited expectation of any transfer of either process of product knowledge. However, when the MNE decides to subcontract because of its own capacity constraints, or when the component is a specialized one, transfer of both product and process know-how is likely.

A special case where quite substantial knowledge transfer from an MNE is likely is where the MNE sets up or develops its own supplier – possibly a supplier restricted to serving the MNE itself. Reuber *et al.* (1973, pp. 156–7) and Lall (1980) find evidence that some MNEs are quite active in supporting the establishment of independent local firms, though Jansson's (1982) study of Swedish subsidiaries in India suggests that they prefer to establish relationships with already operational local subcontractors (though they are sometimes prepared to be among the initial customers for small enterprises set up by their own former employees).

Turning to knowledge transfers between established enterprises, Jansson (1982, p. 116) finds in a review of 12 types of input (metals, casings, forgings, other components, etc.) bought in by Swedish MNE subsidiaries in India that there was some evidence of quality improvements for 11 of these inputs as a result of the MNE–local supplier linkage. However this quality improvement seemed to reflect the nature of the demand of the MNE rather than an upgrading of supplier potential through knowledge transfer. Thus for six of the 12 inputs there was sign of product know-how transfer, but for only two inputs was there evidence of process know-how transfer. Reuber *et al.* (1973, pp. 203–5) found that 16 out of 70 respondents in his survey of foreign projects in LDCs engaged in the training of local suppliers, this being more frequent for projects serving the local market than for export-oriented projects.

The overall impression conveyed by the data, therefore, is that while backward linkages do occur, they are by no means as frequent, or as fruitful, as the process of development would seem to require. Whether this is a consequence of biased decision making by MNEs, or a failure of local entrepreneurship, or some other factor, remains an open question.

3.4.3 The new international division of labour

The new international division of labour (NIDL) exploits the ability to separate different stages of production and locate them in different countries (Helleiner, 1973a; Moxon, 1975). Technical separability of this kind is easier in some industries than in others. If the intermediate product flowing between two adjacent stages of production is perishable, or fragile, or needs to be kept hot in order to achieve thermal economies, then spatial separation of the stages is unlikely to be successful. Given the technical feasibility of separation, however, transport costs, tariffs, and the risks of disrupted supplies may still make it economically inefficient. It is only where the benefits are high relative to the costs that separation is profitable. The principal benefit derives from comparative advantage: if different stages of production use factors of production with different intensities, the efficient use of resources encourages each stage of production to be located where its most intensively used factor is relatively most abundant.

The NIDL has been aggressively exploited both by US and Japanese firms. It is less important in Europe, though there are instances of German firms organizing textile processing in North Africa (Frobel *et al.*, 1980). The role of Japanese firms is particularly interesting because many of their skills lie in the field of production engineering. This involves redesigning products into a multi-component form suitable for mass production. Some components are best produced on capital-intensive highly automated production lines, usually located in Japan, where there are adequate supplies of skilled maintenance workers. Other components are best produced manually using a highly disciplined relatively unskilled labour force, and these are produced by low-wage workers (often women) in LDCs.

The development of NIDL has been encouraged by government policies in both DCs and LDCs. DC governments – notably the US government – have created a special tariff structure which allows goods that have been exported from the US for further processing to be re-imported subject to *ad valorem* tariffs which are levied only on the value added abroad, and not on the value inclusive of that originally added in the US (Finger, 1975; Helleiner, 1979; Moxon, 1984). Thus an item imported into the US under schedules 806.30 and 807.00 which was worth $70 when first exported and $100 when re-imported, would be charged duty on only the $30 of value added overseas.

Some LDC governments have created export processing zones (EPZs), which are particularly suited to NIDL-oriented production. An EPZ is a specially designated industrial area or estate which

1 allows all imports (including capital goods) and exports to move free of tariffs and other trade restrictions;
2 incorporates all the infrastructure, factories, ports, container handling and airport facilities that are necessary for trade; and
3 offers financial inducements such as tax holidays, concessionary rates for factory space, energy supplies, etc., and exemption from minimum wage laws and other restrictions that apply in the rest of the host economy.

Illustrations of EPZ incentive packages are given by Warr (1983, pp. 30–3; 1984, pp. 170–2). EPZs have been criticized because of the routine and unskilled nature of the employment they offer, the health and safety aspects of the working conditions, and the high proportion of women workers (Dror, 1984). It is also alleged that the EPZ is essentially an 'enclave', and provides little opportunity for the technology transferred to it to diffuse to the rest of the host economy (Wall, 1976). On the other hand, Warr's studies of Korea (Warr, 1984, p. 175) and Indonesia (Warr, 1983, pp. 34–5) suggest that if the local environment is suitably entrepreneurial, local inputs to EPZ operations can grow over time to quite significant levels.

Critics of EPZs have also suggested that the scope for the host country to obtain substantial gains is very limited. They point to the generous nature of the incentives offered by host governments and in particular to the low levels of taxation. Intense competition from LDCs for foreign investment explains, in part, why the initial inducements have to be large, but there is also the fear that the industries attracted to EPZs are essentially 'footloose' and will quit if any attempt is made to renegotiate more favourable terms later on. It is certainly true that if renegotiation is anticipated by the investor at the outset, few non-recoverable costs will be sunk in the EPZ, so that the ability to pull out with few losses can be used as a bargaining counter later on. Nevertheless, Moxon's review of the evidence for the 1970s (Moxon, 1984, pp. 194–7) suggests that the phenomenon of the 'footloose industry' is easily exaggerated.

There is a certain tendency for EPZ investments to be self-obsolescing, in the sense that if they are successful engines of development, they will raise local wage rates and render themselves uneconomic in the long run. Flamm's (1984) analysis of US offshore semi-conductor activity suggests that 'producers are reasonably sensitive to wage rates and adjust quite rapidly to what they perceive as their optimum portfolio', though 'this elasticity is small enough to guarantee that modest increases in wages will not send all investment fleeing from an export platform' (p. 246). The crucial question is how far the obsolescing low-wage-oriented investment can in due course be replaced by new investments. This will depend upon whether the wealth created by the initial investment is used to finance the education and training of the labour force. If it is, then new investment oriented towards more skilled labour will replace the old, allowing development to continue as the country 'trades up' to more sophisticated exports.

3.5 Sources of MNEs in developing countries

In any analysis of MNE operations it is important to recognize that the characteristics of both the source country in which the MNE is based and the host country in which it invests affect the outcome of an investment (Dunning, 1981). Thus the countries which have benefited most from the NIDL are the relatively high-income NICs. Governments of the more successful NICs have generally pursued an 'outward-looking' policy of encouraging exports of the products that are most profitable at existing international prices rather than an 'inward-looking' policy of protectionism; and other aspects of host government policy have been important too (Ozawa, 1979; Roemer, 1976).

So far as the source country is concerned, US firms have a reputation for exercising far tighter control over their subsidiaries than do many European firms. One reason for this may be that large US firms are more recently established in LDCs than are large European firms, which have often been trading there since colonial times. Another reason may be that US firms predominate in the high-technology sectors, where close supervision of the subsidiary is necessary in order to safeguard intellectual property and maintain quality control.

3.5.1 US and Japanese multinational operations

The high-technology emphasis of US investment has led Kojima (1973, 1978) to distinguish between a US pattern of foreign involvement and a Japanese pattern of foreign involvement. Unfortunately, Kojima's argument confuses a number of logically quite distinct issues (Buckley, 1983, 1985). He claims that US investment is anti-trade-oriented, in contrast to Japanese investment, which is trade-oriented. What he appears to have in mind here is that US investment is typically import-substituting, and therefore, in his terms, 'anti-trade'. Japanese investment (like the inter-war colonial investment of Britain and other European powers) is strongly oriented to primary products, which are exported from the LDC to the source country (see also Sekiguchi, 1979). Since the investment promotes exports, Kojima calls it 'pro-trade'.

Kojima suggests that in the manufacturing sector Japanese technology is more appropriate to LDCs than is US technology, since it relates to mass production methods in mature industries such as engineering assembly and textiles, and is therefore less 'high-tech'. He claims that Japanese technology transfer will reinforce the existing comparative advantages of LDCs, whilst US technology is strongest in industries where LDCs are comparatively disadvantaged (see also Odaka, 1985). He claims that Japanese investors can 'tutor' LDCs. A sequential development programme is advocated, in which tutoring in one industry provides experience which can be applied to other industries too.

Finally he suggests that Japanese investment involves more partnership and cooperation and less direct control, than does US investment. This relates to the fact that a high proportion of Japanese foreign involvement is effected through joint ventures and industrial collaboration agreements of the kind mentioned in section 3.3.2.

Most empirical work on Japanese investment has concentrated on the issue of whether or not it is trade-oriented relative to US investment.

Lee (1983) analysed official survey data on Japanese and US investments in Korea for 1974 and 1978. This revealed no difference in terms of factor proportions, US and Japanese firms both being equally divided between labour-intensive and capital-intensive industries. However, 83 per cent of the value added of US affiliates was in high-technology industries compared with 68 per cent for Japanese affiliates. With regard to market orientation (measured by averaged 1974 and 1978 export/sales ratios), there was little difference between US and Japanese firms in labour-intensive industries, or in those industries combining capital intensity with low technology. However a substantial difference did emerge in those industries combining capital intensity with high technology. Here Japanese firms exported 47 per cent of their sales and US firms only 9 per cent. This leads to an overall high export/sales ratio for Japanese affiliates in Korea, but not for the reasons suggested by Kojima. In an earlier study Lee (1980, pp. 28–32) had analysed new US and Japanese investments approved for entry to Korea between 1962 and 1974, on the basis of their intended market orientation. This evidence had suggested a much more distinct difference between mainly export-oriented Japanese projects and predominantly local-market-oriented US investments.

Thee (1984, pp. 97–8) suggests that 'Kojima's hypothesis cannot be said to derive strong support from the Indonesian case, where the bulk of Japanese investment has been of the import-substitution rather than the export-oriented type'. It should, however, be noted that this orientation is in response to the protection and incentive structure set up by the Indonesian government. In addition, quite a large proportion of the Japanese investment in Indonesia is in labour-intensive manufacturing sectors, which under a different trade regime, might be more export-oriented.

Hill and Johns (1985) analyse the market orientation of US and Japanese manufacturing affiliates in Asian countries for the mid-1970s. In each of the five cases (Korea, Taiwan, Indonesia, Malaysia and Singapore) for which reasonable comparisons can be made, the US firms are the more export-market-oriented. Thus in only one case for US firms (Indonesia) were exports less than 50 per cent of sales; by contrast Japanese firms only recorded one case (Taiwan) where exports exceeded 50 per cent of sales.

Direct evidence on the trade effects of Japanese investment is provided by Nakajo (1980, pp. 471–2), who analyses trade in manufactured goods between Japan and four Asian NICs in 1972 and 1975. He finds that trade with Japanese subsidiaries in these countries grew faster than total Japanese trade with them. Thus Japan's imports of manufactured products from its subsidiaries in the four Asian NICs rose from 10.7 per cent of all Japanese manufactured imports from these countries in 1972 to 27.1 per cent in 1977. Similarly Japanese exports of manufactured goods (capital equipment, components, etc.) to its subsidiaries in the four NICs was 7.9 per cent of its total manufactured exports to them in 1972 and 13.5 per cent in 1977. This is compatible with Kojima's suggestion that Japanese investment is trade-creating, though Kojima's hypothesis is not limited to trade between host countries and Japan alone. Nakajo also reviews results of a survey of 875 Japanese overseas subsidiaries in Asian countries with respect to the nature of their productive operations. Of these 875 subsidiaries, 320 (37 per cent) performed 'integrated processing from raw materials to final products'. The remaining subsidiaries all performed specialized operations, by far the most common being 'processing for final products' (that is, mainly assembly) with 319 cases (that is 37 per cent of the 875 or 58 per cent of those performing truncated operations). Thus three-quarters of the Japanese Asian subsidiaries either specialized in, or included, the completion stages of the production process. This may support the contention (for example Mason, 1980, p. 51) that a crucial advantage of early Japanese investment in Asia was marketing-skill and/or access to parents' established marketing networks.

Kojima himself has recently investigated the trade-orientation of Japanese investment (Kojima, 1985). Using data on US and Japanese investment in several Asian LDCs he concludes that Japanese investment is indeed trade-oriented, whilst US investment is not as trade-oriented as Japanese, but 'cannot be considered as anti-trade-oriented' either.

3.5.2 Multinationals from LDCs

Dunning (1981) postulates that as a country's GNP per capita rises (beyond a certain minimal level at which foreign involvement through investment becomes worthwhile) the country will move from receiving a net inflow of FDI to generating a net outflow. This turn-around may be associated with the emergence of local MNEs in a fast-growing LDC.

It is a mistake to suppose that MNEs from LDCs are fashioned in the same mould as MNEs from DCs (Agmon and Kindleberger, 1977; Kumar and McLeod, 1981). To begin with, in LDCs the 'legal shell' of incorporation with limited liability is much less important to the firm: informal ties based on the extended family are often the norm. The hiring of professional managers, and the issue of equity to the public, is less common too. The independent entrepreneur, or a 'group' of entrepreneurs, assumes greater importance in industrial organization (Leff, 1978). Many groups rely on banks which are themselves a part of the group, and are committed to financing the group on a long-term basis. MNE groups based in LDCs frequently exercise control overseas through expatriate members of the family of the leader of the group. This organizational structure seems to be particularly strong where export sales affiliates are concerned.

Wells (1983) argues that in the manufacturing sector the main skill which MNEs from LDCs transfer abroad is the ability to adapt standardized DC technology to LDC conditions. This can involve organizing the production of customized products using short production runs, keeping vintage capital equipment going through improvised repairs, working flexible hours to meet 'rush jobs', and so on. Wells's view is certainly compatible with Lecraw's evidence, reported earlier, on MNEs from LDCs producing in South East Asia and is, indeed, partly based upon it. It is also consistent with Lall's appraisal of Indian technology transferred abroad; that it has

been simplified and adapted to low income consumers (consumer goods); rendered more rugged, less automated, less specialised (capital goods); or substituted different raw materials, descaled and adapted to tropical conditions. A major part of the 'adaptation' has been simply the result of using older technologies than developed countries, but the rest has resulted from deliberate technological effort (Lall, 1986, p. 315; see also Lall, 1982; Lall and Associates, 1983).

MNEs from LDCs rely very heavily upon joint ventures, industrial collaboration agreements and 'turnkey' contracts in their overseas operations. Sometimes this is a consequence of the industry in which they operate. South Korean MNEs, for example, have achieved a dominant position in the international construction industry, where most foreign involvement is limited to the duration of the construction project and the early phase of its operation, and where local participation in the commissioning of the project, procurement of property for development, etc., is required (on Korean MNEs see Koo, 1986). More generally, joint ventures may be preferred to outright control because the MNE is unfamiliar with the local environment, and needs an indigenous partner to learn from before it can assume the risks associated with outright control. This effect will only last, however, so long as 'first time' investments predominate amongst the investments undertaken by MNEs from LDCs. It has also been noted that MNEs from LDCs tend to invest chiefly in neighbouring countries – particularly those with strong cultural and ethnic ties to the source country. This factor, too, can be expected to change as the MNEs gain experience, and as their managers become less 'ethnocentric' in their outlook.

In a questionnaire study of 25 Hong Kong-based MNEs in the garment, electronic, metal and textile product industries, Chen (1983a, chapter 8) identified the ability to manage unskilled labour-intensive manufacturing operations as a key aspect of the technology transferred abroad by the firms. The major motives of investing abroad were

1 to avoid rising labour costs in Hong Kong by transferring to cheaper labour locations such as Singapore and Taiwan;
2 to avoid quotas on Hong Kong textile exports to the UK imposed by the UK government, by switching production to other locations not covered by the quota arrangements; and
3 to diversify against the risks associated with the surrender of Hong Kong to China at the end of the century.

Chen's study suggests that the motivation of Hong Kong MNEs is somewhat similar to the motivation of Japanese manufacturing MNEs discussed earlier, in the sense that the aim is to exploit the NIDL in order to retain export markets that have been won originally as a result of skilful management of the mass production of mature products. If this interpretation is correct, then it lends support to Kojima's thesis that the Japanese technology transferred abroad is in some sense intermediate between that of the DCs and that of the LDCs, and 'shades in' to these two types of technology at each end of the spectrum. It is also compatible with Parry's view that technological adaptation by MNEs from LDCs allows them to mediate in the process of transferring the more sophisticated technologies from DCs to the poorer LDCs (Parry, 1981).

3.6 MNEs, trade and the balance of payments

3.6.1 Intra-firm trade and transfer pricing

The NIDL and the associated growth of Japanese multinational operations has led, during the past 20 years, to a significant world-wide growth of intermediate product trade. An intermediate product is any good passed on from one stage of production to another: a raw material, semi-processed good, or component ready for assembly. In a vertically integrated MNE, successive stages of production are under common control, and so an intermediate product exported from an upstream activity and imported into a downstream activity enters into international trade under the control of a single firm. This is an example of intra-firm trade. All trade between a subsidiary of an MNE and the parent company, or between different subsidiaries of the MNE, is intra-firm trade. Intra-firm trade may involve not only semi-processed products, however, but also finished goods ready for marketing by a sales affiliate, and sales of second-hand capital equipment.

Intra-firm trade is important because it means that an MNE has direct control over both the import and export of the product. A potential advantage of intra-firm trade is that it gives the LDC subsidiary immediate access to all the markets that can be reached via other subsidiaries of the company, and via the parent too. Potential disadvantages are that intra-firm trade is only indirectly affected by market forces, that it is difficult to monitor, and that it provides the firm with a mechanism for tax avoidance through transfer pricing.

Intra-firm trade has expanded rapidly over the past 20 years, in line with the growth of intermediate product trade. This appears to have been an absolute growth, though, rather than a relative one. In mining, in particular, many foreign subsidiaries have been nationalized, or made subject to local equity participation, and several raw materials that were previously traded within firms are now marketed openly by intergovernmental producer cartels (see for example Faundez and Picciotto, 1978; Moran, 1974). Nayyar (1978) estimates that between 1966 and 1974 the share of manufactured exports from developing countries controlled by foreign multinationals was fairly stable at about 15 per cent.

A number of statistical studies indicate that the importance of intra-firm trade – as measured by the proportion of the parent company's exports that are supplied to overseas subsidiaries – is greatest in high-technology industries – defined as industries where US firms have a high ratio of R and D expenditure per unit sales (Buckley and Casson, 1976, p. 22; Buckley and Pearce, 1981; Pearce, 1982). In some manufacturing industries a significant proportion of parents' exports are shipped abroad for sale without further processing. A study of the US export trade in 1977, for example, reveals that in the printing and publishing industry 83 per cent of US parents' intra-firm exports comprised almost-finished products, and in the motor industry the corresponding figure was 75 per cent (Casson and Associates 1986, pp. 34–9).

The role of finished products in intra-firm trade has been considered in detail by Lall (1978). He argues that complex durable products requiring after-sales service are marketed through sales subsidiaries, while simple non-durable products are more likely to be advertised heavily to the public and distributed through small independent retailers supplied through arm's-length trade. This is consistent with a view that intra-firm trade in finished products is stimulated by the need to control the quality of after-sales service. Lall therefore postulates that the parent's intra-firm exports will be positively associated with a dummy variable indicating the importance of after-sales servicing, and negatively associated with an index of advertising intensity. When the ratio of parent's intra-firm exports to the total sales of the foreign subsidiaries importing them is regressed upon these variables, and upon a dummy variable indicating the relevance of 'value added' tariffs, then all variables are significant at the 10 per cent level and take the expected sign.

The parent's intra-firm exports provide only indirect evidence on the dependence upon intra-firm trade of an LDC subsidiary. To begin with, they shed light only on the importance of intra-firm imports by the subsidiary, and say nothing about the structure of the subsidiary's exports. Indirect evidence on the subsidiary's exports can be obtained by studying the role of intra-firm trade in the imports of a DC. Helleiner (1981, chapter 2) has examined US imports by related parties – that is, imports originating overseas within the same ownership unit that is importing them. His study is not confined to US-owned enterprises but to any enterprise operating in the US. He finds that, in 1977, 48.4 per cent of all US imports were from related parties. The proportion increases from 23.5 per cent for primary products (excluding petroleum) to 37.6 per cent for semi-manufactures and 53.6 per cent for manufactures. This is in line with the other studies which suggest that a high proportion of intra-firm trade is accounted for by products in the final stages of processing.

The proportion of related-party imports of semi-manufactures and manu-factures tends to be lower for imports originating in LDCs as compared to DCs (17.0 per cent and 37.0 per cent, compared to 43.4 per cent and 61.1 per cent). It is slightly higher, though, where primary products are concerned (49.1 per cent, compared to 41.3 per cent). The proportion of related-party imports in petroleum was 59.4 per cent, with no significant difference between imports from LDCs and DCs. These results suggest that, using the experience of the DCs as a benchmark, the export trade of the LDCs is more notable for foreign control of minerals and raw materials than for foreign control of products at later stages of processing.

Helleiner carries out regression analysis on a sample of 100 three-digit manufactured commodity groups. He finds that research intensity has a significant positive effect on related-party imports; this corroborates the earlier results relating to parent company exports. The US wage rate has a significant positive effect too. This could reflect the use of intra-firm trade to appropriate rents from labour skills, as Helleiner argues, or it could merely reflect a cost advantage to supplying the US market from low-wage countries overseas. Plant size also has a significant positive effect. This could reflect the importance of mass-production methods in the industry, or it could be acting as a proxy for firm size, as Helleiner himself argues. Economies of scale and industrial con-centration have no significant effects.

Evidence on intra-firm trade that relates directly to subsidiaries, rather than to parent firms only, or to a mixture of both parents and subsidiaries, is difficult to obtain from official statistics. It is best obtained either from sample surveys or from industry case studies.

Lecraw's studies of MNE operations in light manufacturing industries in the ASEAN region (Lecraw, 1983, 1984, 1985) revealed the nationality of the parent company to be an important influence on levels of intra-firm trade. He found that Japanese affiliates directed 79 per cent of their exports to related units, compared to 68 per cent for US firms, 65 per cent for European firms and only 23 per cent for firms based in developing countries. A similar pattern was apparent in affiliate imports: Japanese firms obtained 84 per cent of their imports from related units, compared to 57 per cent for European firms, 53 per cent from US firms and only 37 per cent for firms based in LDCs.

A recent series of industry case studies, embracing international trade in synthetic fibres, motor vehicles, bearings, copper, tin, bananas and shipping services (Casson and Associates, 1986) suggests that three main factors promote intra-firm trade: the novelty of the product and its production methods, the difficulty of assuring quality when buying in components and materials on the open market, and the prevalence of sunk costs in the production process and distribution channel, due to the use of highly specific durable equipment. Two main factors appear to discourage intra-firm trade: the use of capital equipment which affords economies of scope, and the existence of multiple inputs and outputs in the production process. Economies of scope arise when it is cheaper to produce a variety of goods by sharing the use of the same facility than by using a separate facility for each of them. They discourage intra-firm trade because it is more difficult for the parent firm to coordinate trade flows when many different products are involved. Similar problems of managerial coordination explain why a multiplicity of inputs and outputs discourages intra-firm trade.

Transfer pricing occurs when the value of goods entering into international trade is either overstated or understated in order to misrepresent to fiscal authorities (customs, tax, exchange control authorities) the incomes generated by this trade. (The reader should be warned that some writers define transfer prices simply as internal prices, rather than as internal prices that differ from arm's-length prices, as is done here.) Transfer pricing is much easier to implement with respect to intra-firm trade than with respect to inter-firm trade.

Although transfer pricing is often claimed to be a major factor promoting intra-firm trade, there is very little reliable evidence on the issue (Lall, 1973; Natke, 1985; Plasschaert, 1985; Vaitsos, 1974b). Few of the papers in two edited volumes which address the issue (Murray, 1981; Rugman and Eden, 1985) contain much empirical detail. Lecraw's study, referred to above, found that intra-firm exports from ASEAN countries were often priced on different principles from arms's-length exports. Under-pricing of the intra-firm exports of unripened bananas is well-documented (Ellis, 1981). Investigations by the UK Inland Revenue recently led to the recovery of about £200 million in under-paid taxes by a small number of UK MNEs, on account of transfer pricing over a 7-year period.

The opportunities for transfer pricing are particularly great when intermediate products supplied by the parent to the subsidiary embody significant firm-specific know-how. The overhead costs incurred in developing the product can be imputed to the parent and then recovered by charging a very high price to the subsidiary. Since the intermediate product is specific to the firm, there is no exactly equivalent product with whose 'arms-length' price the transfer price can be compared. This makes it difficult for the customs and tax authorities to challenge the transfer prices. There is evidence that transfer pricing of this kind may be widespread in the world pharmaceutical industry. On balance it seems likely that while transfer pricing is an important aspect of corporate profitability in a number of situations, it cannot be affirmed that it is, in any sense, the dominant reason why firms undertake intra-firm trade.

3.6.2 Capital flows and the balance of payments

Analysis of the financing of MNE investments in LDCs is fraught with analytical difficulties. As Gilman (1981) notes, many authors are simply unaware of the conceptual problems involved, and jump to conclusions about the impact of MNEs on the balance of payments on the basis of published statistics which cannot readily be used for this purpose.

The statistics themselves are fraught with difficulties (see Billerbeck and Yasugi, 1979; International Monetary Fund, 1977). But for what they are worth, they suggest that capital imports into LDCs during the 1970s represented a relatively small proportion of the growth of MNE-controlled assets in these countries. For example, equity and inter-company account flows accounted for only 37 per cent of the growth of the value of the US FDI stake in manufacturing industries in LDCs between 1967 and 1979, with reinvested earnings accounting for the remainder (Whichard, 1980, table 11, pp. 24-5). Also outflows of income (dividends, interest, royalties) from direct investments in LDCs during most periods exceeded capital imports during the same period. Thus between 1967 and 1979 the outflows of income from US direct manufacturing investments in LDCs (post-tax income *minus* reinvested earnings *plus* fees and royalties) were approximately 1.6 times the value of new inflows of equity and of capital on inter-company account. The comparable ratio for all US direct investment in LDCs (including petroleum and 'other' sectors) was 4.2.

These ratios are very high relative to those for foreign investment in DCs, and are consistent with the view that foreign investors in LDCs are very quick to repatriate income from their investments. One possible explanation is that their fear of expropriation is much greater where assets located in LDCs are concerned. This would suggest that repatriation will be particularly rapid in politically sensitive industries such as petroleum, and the figures are certainly consistent with this hypothesis.

Critical observers interpret such results as showing that the operations of MNEs 'decapitalize' LDCs – that is leave them with less capital than they would have had in the absence of the MNE. A related criticism is that outflows of income damage the balance of payments of LDCs and exacerbate an existing problem of shortage of foreign exchange. Such claims are very difficult to substantiate, however (see Biersteker, 1978; Dunning, 1974; Hufbauer and Adler, 1968; Lall and Streeten, 1977). Firstly, there is a very tenuous causal relationship, in the short run, between the inflow of capital and the outflow of income, and the figures reported above cover too short a period to make any reliable inferences. Thus much of the outflow of income during a given period is likely to result from inflows in the preceding period, whilst some of the inflows are unlikely to generate substantial outflows until a later period (see UNCTAD, 1972, table 11, p. 20). More significantly, the 'decapitalization' argument makes no allowance for the value of technology transferred, and the impact of both technology transfer and purchases of plant and equipment from abroad on the competitiveness and trade performance of the LDC. Finally, the entire exercise is based on the concept of an alternative position – what would have happened in the absence of MNE involvement in the LDC. The results of extant studies show that the results are extremely sensitive to the nature of the alternative position assumed. This confirms the earlier assessment that existing data cannot be decisive on these issues.

3.7 Relations between MNEs and host governments

3.7.1 Bargaining between MNEs and host governments

Several writers (notably Streeten, 1974, pp. 265–71 and Vaitsos, 1974a, pp. 311–15) have suggested that, however technically efficient an MNE project in a LDC may be, a host country will only be sure of achieving benefits from it after a successful outcome to negotiations between its government and the foreign enterprise. Such negotiations are the crucial factor in determining the distribution of the surplus created by the project.

At the time of setting up a project the host government and the investor will negotiate over a large set of conditions, for example tax concessions, tariff protection for final product and tariff concessions on imported inputs, labour training, export targets, levels of local value added, etc. (Guisinger and Associates, 1985; Lall and Streeten, 1977, pp. 207–9; Langdon, 1981, pp. 37–40). With respect to this package of 'concessions', it is perfectly possible that at the point of entering into negotiations there will be an overlap between the minimum level of concessions which the firm will accept and the maximum level of concessions the government will offer. Any level of concessions within this overlap will be ultimately acceptable to either party. Nevertheless the firm will try to force the level of concessions as near as possible to the maximum that the government is prepared to offer, while the government will try to push the level of concessions as near as possible to the minimum acceptable to the firm.

The outcome of this bilateral negotiation will depend on many factors, including level of knowledge and bargaining experience and skill. In terms of knowledge the foreign firm will, in all probability, be in a vastly superior position. The MNE will know much more about the host economy and the government's plans for that economy than the government can find out about the activity of the whole MNE network and its future plans. Indeed, while the government may enter the negotiations with its future plans clearly set out and with little scope for manoeuvre during the negotiations, the MNE's great flexibility may mean that it has several options open to it according to how the negotiations turn out (Kapoor, 1975, pp. 287–9).

This suggests that in many cases where an LDC accepts (correctly) a project on efficiency grounds it may still have paid more for it in terms of concessions than it would have needed to were it better informed and generally in a stronger position vis-à-vis the MNE.

Researchers have recently begun to investigate empirically the deter-minants of bargaining success in MNE–host country negotiations. Needless to say, it is a major problem to devise a summary measure of the negotiation outcomes which indicates the relative success of the parties involved. The fact that most negotiations involve a wide range of issues, which may vary from negotiation to negotiation, leads to the need to either devise a suitable index of several elements, or to find a single element (common to the majority of nego-tiations) which may serve as a proxy for relative success in the wider package deal.

Fagre and Wells (1982) use as a proxy the extent of foreign ownership of sub-sidiaries (including measures which allow for the *desired* ownership patterns of MNEs and host countries) in an analysis of the influence of firm and industry characteristics on bargaining between US MNEs and Latin American host countries. A high level of foreign ownership is assumed to indicate a successful outcome for the MNE, and an unsuccessful outcome for the host government. Many influences suggested by earlier work on bargaining receive empirical support.

1 The level of technology of the MNE is important. Thus MNEs spending over 5 per cent of their sales on R and D seemed to have much greater bargaining power than those spending less. Amongst firms spending less than 5 per cent of sales on R and D there did not seem to be any systematic relationship between bargaining power and R and D intensity.
2 Product differentiation, or marketing skill (proxied by advertising expenditure as a proportion of sales), seemed to provide MNEs with bargaining strength.
3 A result that is less clearly predicted by theory is an apparent positive link between an MNE's bargaining strength and its product diversity, in terms of numbers of (three-digit SIC) products produced by the affiliate. A number of possible explanations are investigated, with none being strongly verified.
4 MNEs appear to gain bargaining power when they offer improved access to export markets. This applies both when total exports are considered, or just intra-group exports to other parts of the MNE instead.
5 Turning to industry-level influences, it is possible to confirm an intuitive expectation relating the degree of competition to bargaining power; namely, that 'a larger number of parent corporations per industry is associated with lower bargaining power for members of that industry relative to other industries' (p. 19).

Perhaps contrary to some expectations, a detailed scrutiny of their evidence led Fagre and Wells to conclude that 'the financial resources held by multinationals are not an important source of bargaining power in Latin America', and that 'a large capital investment does not appear to improve greatly the bargaining power of the firm' (p. 16).

Lecraw (1984) used the questionnaire data described earlier to analyse influences on bargaining. Measures of ownership share again served as indicators of negotiation outcome. In terms of firm characteristics, Lecraw's results support those of Fagre and Wells. Thus technological leadership, advertising intensity and export intensity all appeared to provide MNEs with bargaining strength, whilst capital intensity and capital requirements were less significant. The bargaining strength of the host countries increased with the attractiveness of the countries (as perceived by the MNE managers at the time of the investigation) and with the number of potential MNE investors. Lecraw's results also suggested that the ASEAN countries had become more successful in bargaining with MNEs over time.

Poynter (1982) analysed survey/interview information on the extent of host government intervention (that is 'government behaviour which affects the operations, policies and nature of enterprises') affecting foreign firms in Tanzania, Zambia, Indonesia and Kenya between 1970 and 1975. The most frequent forms of intervention involved withholding foreign exchange, and regulating product prices and employment practices. The intervention implemented by the government is viewed by Poynter as occurring in response to pressure by various local interest groups. To the extent that the intervention sought by the local interest groups aims to increase benefits to parts of the local economy, such intervention can be seen as an agent of income redistribution (Philip, 1976). The assumption is that such intervention will be less, the greater is the MNE subsidiary's bargaining power. Poynter found that the MNE subsidiaries retained high bargaining power where influential host nation groups believed in the continued importance of the foreign relationship to local operations. In particular four firm characteristics were found to have some association with the extent of intervention:

1 the subsidiary's managerial and operational complexity;
2 the volume of exports;
3 the extent of corporate control over the sourcing of production inputs and sales to associated firms; and
4 the proportion of foreigners in managerial and technical positions.

Poynter considers these factors to influence 'the economic attractiveness of intervention'. Firms were also found to be more vulnerable to intervention the larger they were (especially in terms of employment) and the more strategically important to the host economy was their industry of operation. The influence of these factors Poynter considers to be more politically motivated.

The analysis of bargaining has, to date, concentrated on the negotiations relating to the initial entry decision. However there is growing interest (Kapoor, 1975, pp. 328–33; Stoever, 1979) in the increasing tendency for established agreements to be subjected to renegotiation. The background to such renegotiations, it has been suggested, is a systematically changing balance of bargaining power as a project matures. The MNE's advantages may diminish as local abilities increase in various facets of the firm's operations. Similarly, the host country may stand to gain once the MNE has sunk large costs in the location, especially if the subsidiary plays a distinctive role in the MNE's global strategy which could not be replicated elsewhere in the short term (or with comparable efficiency). This 'obsolescing-bargain' has been most commonly perceived in resource-based industries, but may be of increasing relevance in manufacturing industries too.

3.7.2 Taxation

If MNE operations increase the local economy's productive potential, this should result in an increase in the government's tax revenue. There has, however, been a tendency for many LDCs to forgo much of this potential, by offering substantial tax concessions to foreign enterprises as an investment incentive. This is now widely believed to be a rather dubious policy. Though a large number of foreign investments in LDCs have qualified for tax holiday periods, tax reductions, or allowance for accelerated depreciation as part of investment incentives schemes, evidence tends to suggest that such inducements (whilst welcomed by the foreign firms) do not substantially influence investment decisions. If this is indeed so, the LDCs may have relinquished valuable tax revenue unnecessarily.

Reuber *et al.*'s survey evidence (1973, p. 127) suggested that MNEs embarking on export-oriented projects in LDCs found tax concessions of more relevance than did those with projects oriented to local markets (where tariff protection was considered a more important inducement). Studies such as Agoda (1978) and Root and Ahmed (1978), which have included fiscal incentives alongside other factors in empirical analyses of the determinants of foreign investment in LDCs, have tended to find them insignificant. In an interesting analysis of this type, Lim (1983) found that foreign investment flows into 27 LDCs in the period 1965–73 were negatively (and statistically significantly) related to the generosity of fiscal incentives, when the countries' resource strength, level of economic development and growth rate were controlled for. One interpretation could be that tax incentives actually discourage investment because 'fiscal hypergenerosity was seen by potential foreign investors as a danger signal (a disincentive) and not as a lure (an incentive)'. An alternative explanation is the existence of an 'illusory compensating effect', in which those LDCs believing themselves weak in other factors conducive to foreign investment (for example mineral resources; a proven growth performance) were offering very high tax concessions in an (unsuccessful) attempt to counteract these weaknesses.

Despite this evidence, many LDCs have persisted in the belief that tax concessions could be vital at the margin. Because of this, individual LDCs have been reluctant to unilaterally reduce them, even though the evidence suggests that all governments would benefit from a mutually agreed de-escalation of inducements. Thus it is often suggested 'that the developing countries have a great deal to gain by supporting a multilateral convention that would limit tax incentives to foreign investors' (Root and Ahmed, 1978, pp. 88–90).

3.8 Conclusions

Although a large amount of data has been collected on the operations of MNEs in LDCs, the interpretation of this data has proved extremely problematic. Many of the issues raised in political debate over MNEs cannot adequately be analysed given the present state of development of the theory. Certain statistical associations, and broad tendencies, can, however, be discerned.

1　US MNEs producing for the local market predominate in 'high-technology' industries of the kind which are often protected in LDCs. These industries also tend to exhibit capital-intensive production, and relatively high levels of industrial concentration in both the source country and the LDC. By contrast, firms producing for export tend to operate in labour-intensive manufacturing industries or in the resource sector.

2　MNEs in high-technology industries produce on a smaller scale in LDCs than they do in the source country because of the relatively small size of the protected market, and this smaller scale is associated with the use of more labour-intensive methods.

3　The basic design of plant and equipment is not significantly altered when technology is transferred by MNEs to LDCs. Firms producing for export are less prone to adapt technology than are firms producing only for the domestic market, mainly because of the need to maintain product quality.

4　MNE production in LDCs is not so labour-intensive as indigenous production in the same industries, though the effect is small. Firms controlled by resident expatriates and MNEs from LDCs seem to adjust better to local conditions than either indigenous firms or MNEs from DCs.

5　Japanese MNEs operate predominantly in resource-based industries, and in some industries exploiting the NIDL. A relatively high proportion of Japanese FDI is located in South East Asia.

6　Japanese MNEs make greater use of joint ventures than do US and European firms.

7　MNEs based in LDCs are still in the early stages of expansion and certain aspects of their behaviour – reliance on collaborative arrangements with indigenous firms, and a propensity to invest in neighbouring countries – reflect this. In the manufacturing sector, their main skill lies in adapting DC technologies to the need for short production runs, use of vintage equipment, etc., which arises in poorer LDCs.

8　Licensing has become a more common mode of technology transfer during the past decade, partly as a result of host government restrictions on foreign ownership. The factors governing the attitudes of MNEs to licensing include the patentability of the technology and the importance of quality control.

9　Complexity of the technology, and the absence of close substitutes for it, assist the MNE in bargaining with the host government for a substantial equity stake in local production.

10　Quality control over intermediate products, and the need for integrated and highly specific investment in upstream and downstream activities, are major factors promoting intra-firm trade.

11　There is little evidence of superior export performance by MNEs compared to indigenous firms in LDCs. MNEs, however, tend to import more than indigenous firms in the same industry.

12　Several MNEs often enter an LDC industry almost simultaneously. In the short run this may promote local competition, but it is likely that in the long run one or two MNEs will assume a dominant position in the industry.

13 Backward linkages between MNEs and local suppliers do not occur frequently, and when they do occur are not a major channel of technology transfer. Use of indigenous suppliers is more common in firms producing for the dometic market than in firms producing mainly for export, probably because quality control is less important in the former case.

14 Tax concessions are less important in attracting FDI to LDCs than many host governments seem to believe.

It should be emphasized that these conclusions are only provisional, and may well need to be revised in the light of future research.

REFERENCES

Agarwal, J. 1976. Factor proportions in foreign and domestic firms in Indian manufacturing. *Economic Journal*, 86, 589–94.

Agmon, T. and Kindleberger C. P. (eds) 1977. *Multinationals from Small Countries*. Cambridge, Mass.: MIT Press.

Agoda, O. 1978. The determinants of US private manufacturing investments in Africa. *Journal of International Business Studies*, 9, 95–107.

Balasubramanyam, V. N. 1984. Factor proportions and productive efficiency of foreign owned firms in the Indonesian manufacturing sector. *Bulletin of Indonesian Economic Studies*, 20, 70–94.

Biersteker, T. J. 1978. *Distortion or Development? Contending Perspectives on the Multinational Corporation*. Cambridge, Mass.: MIT Press.

Billerbeck, K. and Yasugi Y. 1979. *Private Direct Foreign Investment in Developing Countries*. World Bank Staff Working Paper No.348. Washington, DC: World Bank.

Bornschier, V. 1980. Multinational corporations and economic growth: a cross-national test of the decapitalization thesis. *Journal of Development Economics*, 7, 191–210.

Buckley, P. J. 1983. Macroeconomic versus international business approach to direct foreign investment: a comment on Professor Kojima's interpretation. *Hitotsubashi Journal of Economics*, 24, 97–100.

Buckley, P. J. 1985. The economic analysis of the multinational enterprise: Reading versus Japan. *Hitotsubashi Journal of Economics* ,26, 117–24.

Buckley, P. J. and Casson, M. C. 1976. *The Future of the Multinational Enterprise*, London: Macmillan.

Buckley, P. J. and Casson, M. C. 1985. *Economic Theory of the Multinational Enterprise: Selected Papers*. London: Macmillan.

Buckley, P. J. and Pearce, R. D. 1981. Market servicing by multinational manufacturing firms: exporting versus foreign production. *Managerial and Decision Economics*, 2, 229–46.

Casson, M. C. 1979. *Alternatives to the Multinational Enterprise*. London: Macmillan.

Casson, M. C. and Associates. 1986. *Multinationals and World Trade: Vertical Integration and the Division of Labour in World Industries*. London: Allen and Unwin.

Caves, R. E. 1982. *Multinational Enterprise and Economic Analysis*. Cambridge: Cambridge University Press.

Caves, R. E. 1985. Income and Labour Relations. In T. H. Moran (ed.), *Multinational Corporations: The Political Economy of Foreign Direct Investment*. Lexington, Mass.: Lexington Books, pp. 173–98.

Chandler, A. D. (Jr.). 1977. *The Visible Hand: The Managerial Revolution in American Business*. Cambridge, Mass.: Belknap Press of Harvard University.

Chen, E. K. Y. 1983a. *Multinational Corporations, Technology and Employment*. London: Macmillan.

Chen, E. K. Y. 1983b. Factor proportions of foreign and local firms in developing countries: a theoretical and empirical note. *Journal of Development Economics*, 12, 267-74.

Chung, B. S. and Lee, C. H. 1980. The choice of production techniques by foreign and local firms in Korea. *Economic Development and Cultural Change*, 29, 135-40.

Cohen, B. I. 1973. Comparative behaviour of foreign and domestic export firms in a developing economy. *Review of Economics and Statistics*, 55, 190-7.

Courtney, W. A. and Leipziger, D. M. 1975. Multinational corporations in LDCs: the choice of technology. *Oxford Bulletin of Economics and Statistics*, 37, 297-304.

De la Torre, J. 1974. Foreign investment and export dependency. *Economic Development and Cultural Change*, 23, 135-50.

De Meza, D. E. 1977. Multinational corporations in LDCs: a comment. *Oxford Bulletin of Economics and Statistics*, 39, 237-44.

Dror, D. M. 1984. Aspects of labour law and relations in selected export processing zones. *International Labour Review*, 123, 705-23.

Dunning, J. H. 1974. Multinational enterprises and trade flows of less developed countries. *World Development*, 2, 131-8.

Dunning, J. H. 1981. *International Production and the Multinational Enterprise*. London: Allen and Unwin.

Dunning, J. H. 1983. Changes in the level and structure of international production: the last one hundred years. In M. C. Casson (ed.), *The Growth of International Business*. London: Allen and Unwin, pp. 84-139.

Ellis, F. 1981. Export valuation and intra-firm transfer in the banana export industry in Central America. In R. Murray (ed.), *Multinationals Beyond the Market*. Brighton: Harvester, pp. 61-76.

Enderwick, P. 1984. *Multinational Business and Labour*. Beckenham, Kent: Croom Helm.

Evans, P. B. 1977. Direct investment and industrial concentration. *Journal of Development Studies*, 13, 373-85.

Fagre, N. and Wells, L.T. (Jr.). 1982. Bargaining power of multinationals and host governments. *Journal of International Business Studies*, 13, 9-23.

Faundez, J. and Picciotto, S. (eds) 1978. *The Nationalization of Multinationals in Peripheral Economies*. London: Macmillan.

Finger, J. M. 1975. Tariff provisions for offshore assembly and the exports of developing countries. *Economic Journal*, 85, 365-71.

Flamm, K. 1984. The volatility of offshore investment. *Journal of Development Economics*, 16, 231-48.

Flanagan, R. J. and Weber, A. R. 1974. *Bargaining Without Boundaries: The Multinational Corporation and International Labour Relations*. Chicago: University of Chicago Press.

Forsyth, D. J. C. and Solomon, R. F. 1977. Choice of technology and nationality of ownership in manufacturing in a developing country. *Oxford Economic Papers*, 29, 258-82.

Frobel, F., Heinrichs, J. and Kreye, O. 1980. *The New International Division of Labour*. Cambridge: Cambridge University Press.

Gilman, M. 1981. *The Financing of Foreign Direct Investment*. London: Frances Pinter.

Guisinger, S. E. and Associates. 1985. *Investment Incentives and Performance Requirements*. New York: Praeger.

Gunter, H. 1978. *Transnational Industrial Relations*. London: Macmillan.

Helfgott, R. B. 1973. Multinational corporations and manpower utilization in developing nations. *Journal of Developing Areas*, 7, 235–46.

Helleiner, G. K. 1973a. Manufactured exports from less developed countries and multinational firms. *Economic Journal*, 83, 21–47.

Helleiner, G. K. 1973b. Manufacturing for export, multinational firms and economic development. *World Development*, 1, 13–21.

Helleiner, G. K. 1979. Intra-firm trade and the developing countries. *Journal of Development Economics*, 6, 391–406.

Helleiner, G. K. 1981. *Intra-firm Trade and the Developing Countries*. London: Macmillan.

Hill, H. and Johns, B. 1985. The role of direct foreign investment in developing East Asian countries. *Weltwirtschaftliches Archiv*, 121, 355–81.

Hirschmann, A. O. 1969. How to divest in Latin America and why. *Essays in International Finance*, No. 76. Princeton, N J: Princeton University.

Hufbauer, G. C. and Adler, F. M. 1968. *Overseas Manufacturing Investment and the Balance of Payments*. Washington, DC: US Treasury Dept., Tax Policy Research Study No. 1.

International Labour Office. 1972. *Employment Incomes and Equality. A Strategy for Increasing Productive Employment in Kenya*. Geneva: ILO.

International Monetary Fund. 1977. *Balance of Payments Manual*, 4th edn. Washington, DC: IMF.

James, J. 1983 *Consumer Choice in the Third World*. London: Macmillan.

Jansson, H. 1982. *Interfirm Linkages in a Developing Economy. The Case of Swedish Firms in India*. Acta Universitatis Upsaliensis. Studia Oeconomiae Negotiorum 14, Upsala.

Jenkins, R. 1977. The export performance of multinational corporations in Mexican industry. *Journal of Development Studies*, 15, 89–107.

Kapoor, A. 1975. *Planning for International Business Negotiations*. Cambridge, Mass.: Ballinger.

Kojima, K. 1973. A macroeconomic approach to foreign direct investment. *Hitotsubashi Journal of Economics*, 14, 1–21.

Kojima, K. 1978. *Direct Foreign Investment - A Japanese Model of Multinational Business Operations*. London: Croom Helm.

Kojima, K. 1985. Japanese and American direct investment in Asia: a comparative analysis. *Hitotsubashi Journal of Economics*, 26, 1–36.

Koo, B-Y. 1986. Korea. In J. H. Dunning (ed.), *Multinational Enterprises, Economic Stucture and International Competitiveness*. Chichester: John Wiley, for IRM, pp. 281–307.

Kumar, K. and McLeod, M. G. (eds). 1981. *Multinationals from Third World Countries*. Lexington, Mass.: Lexington Books.

Lall, S. 1973. Transfer-pricing by multinational manufacturing firms. *Oxford Bulletin of Economics and Statistics*, 35, 173–93.

Lall, S. 1978. The pattern of intra-firm exports by US multinationals. *Oxford Bulletin of Economics and Statistics*, 40, 209–22.

Lall, S. 1979. Multinationals and market structure in an open developing economy: the case of Malaysia. *Weltwirtschaftliches Archiv*, 115, 325–48.

Lall, S. 1980. Vertical interfirm linkages in LDCs: an empirical study. *Oxford Bulletin of Economics and Statistics*, 42, 203–26.

Lall, S. 1982. *Developing Countries as Exporters of Technology*. London: Macmillan.

Lall, S. 1986. India. In J. H. Dunning (ed.), *Multinational Enterprises, Economic Structure and International Competitiveness*. Chichester: John Wiley, for IRM, pp 309–35.

Lall, S. and Associates. 1983. *The New Multinationals: The Spread of Third World Enterprises*. Chichester: John Wiley, for IRM.

Lall, S. and Mohammad, S. 1983. Foreign ownership and export performance in the large corporate sector of India. *Journal of Development Studies*, 20, 56–67.

Lall, S. and Streeten, P. 1977. *Foreign Investment, Transnationals and Developing Countries*. London: Macmillan.

Langdon, S. 1981. *Multinational Corporations in the Political Economy of Kenya*. London: Macmillan.

Lecraw, D. J. 1977. Direct investment by firms from LDCs. *Oxford Economic Papers*, 29, 442–57.

Lecraw, D. J. 1979. Choice of technology in low-wage countries: a non-neoclassical approach. *Quarterly Journal of Economics*, 93, 631–54.

Lecraw, D. J. 1983. Performance of transnational corporations in less developed countries. *Journal of International Business Studies*, 14, 15–33.

Lecraw, D. J. 1984. Bargaining power, ownership, and profitability of transnational corporations in developing countries. *Journal of International Business Studies*, 15, 27–43.

Lecraw, D. J. 1985. Some evidence on transfer pricing by multinational corporations. In A. M. Rugman and L. Eden (eds), *Multinationals and Transfer Pricing*, London: Croom Helm, pp. 223–40.

Lee, C. H. 1980. United States and Japanese direct investment in Korea: a comparative study. *Hitotsubashi Journal of Economics*, 20, 26–41.

Lee, C. H. 1983. International production of the United States and Japan in Korean manufacturing industries: a comparative study. *Weltwirtschaftliches Archiv*, 119, 744–53.

Leff, N. H. 1978. Industrial organisation and entrepreneurship in the developing countries: the economic groups. *Economic Development and Cultural Change*, 26, 661–75.

Lim, D. 1976. Capital utilization of local and foreign establishments in Malaysian manufacturing. *Review of Economics and Statistics*, 58, 209–17.

Lim, D. 1983. Fiscal incentives and direct foreign investment in less developed countries. *Journal of Development Studies*, 19, 207–12.

Lim, L. Y. C. and Pang, E. F. 1982. Vertical linkages and multinational enterprises in developing countries. *World Development*, 10, 585–95.

Lipsey, R. E., Kravis, I. B. and Roldan, R. A. 1982. Do multinational firms adapt factor proportions to relative factor prices? In A. O. Krueger (ed.), *Trade and Employment in Developing Countries*, vol 2. Chicago: University of Chicago Press, pp. 215–55.

Long, F. 1981. *Restrictive Business Practices, Transnational Corporations and Development. A Survey*. Boston: Martinus Nijhoff.

Mason, R. H. 1973. Some observations on the choice of technology by multinational firms in developing countries. *Review of Economics and Statistics*, 55, 349–55.

Mason, R. H. 1980. A comment of Professor Kojima's 'Japanese type versus American type of technology transfer'. *Hitotsubashi Journal of Economics*, 20, 42–52.

Meller, P. and Mizala, A. 1982. US multinationals and Latin American manufacturing employment absorption. *World Development*, 10, 115–26.

Moran, T. H. 1974. *Multinational Corporations and the Politics of Dependence: Copper in Chile*. Princeton, NJ: Princeton University Press.

Morgenstern, R. D. and Muller, R. E. 1976. Multinational versus local corporations in LDCs: an economic analysis of export performance in Latin America. *Southern Economic Journal*, 42, 399–406.

Morley, S. A. and Smith G. W. 1977a. The choice of technology: multinational firms in Brasil. *Economic Development and Cultural Change*, 25, 239–64.

Morley, S. A. and Smith, G. W. 1977b. Limited search and the technology choices of multinational firms in Brasil. *Quarterly Journal of Economics*, 91, 263–88.

Moxon, R. W. 1975. The motivation for investment in offshore plants: the case of the US electronics industry. *Journal of International Business Studies*, 6, 51–65.

Moxon, R. W. 1984. Export platform foreign investments in the Asia-Pacific region. In R. W. Moxon, T. W. Roehl, and J. F. Truitt (eds), *Research in International Business and Finance*, vol. 4: *International Business Strategies in the Asia-Pacific Region: Environmental Changes and Corporate Responses Part A*. Greenwich; Conn.: JAI Press, pp. 153–203.

Murray, R. (ed.). 1981. *Multinationals Beyond the Market: Intra-firm Trade and the Control of Transfer Pricing*. Brighton: Harvester Press.

Nakajo, S. 1980. Japanese direct investment in Asian newly industrializing countries and intra-firm division of labour. *The Developing Economies*, 18, 463–83.

Natke, P. A. 1985. A comparison of import pricing by foreign and domestic firms in Brasil. In A. M. Rugman and L. Eden (eds), *Multinationals and Transfer Pricing*. London: Croom Helm, pp. 212–22.

Natke, P. A. and Newfarmer, R. 1985. Transnational corporations, trade propensities and transfer pricing. In UNCTC. *Transnational Corporations and International Trade: Selected Issues: A Technical Paper*. New York: United Nations, pp. 16–43.

Nayyar, D. 1978. Transnational corporations and manufactured exports from poor countries. *Economic Journal*, 88, 59–84.

Newfarmer, R. S. 1979a. Oligopolistic tactics to control markets and the growth of TNCs in Brasil's electrical industry. *Journal of Development Studies*, 15, 108–40.

Newfarmer, R. S. 1979b. TNC takeovers in Brasil: the uneven distribution of benefits in the market for firms. *World Development*, 7, 25–43.

Newfarmer, R. S. 1980. *Transnational Conglomerates and the Economics of Dependent Development: A Case Study of the International Electrical Oligopoly and Brasil's Electrical Industry*. Greenwich, Conn.: JAI Press.

Newfarmer, R. S. and Marsh, L. C. 1981. Foreign ownership, market structure and industrial performance. *Journal of Development Economics*, 8, 47–75.

Newfarmer, R. S. and Mueller, W. 1975. *Multinational Corporations in Brazil and Mexico: Structural Sources of Economic and Non-Economic Power*. Report to the Sub-committee on Multinational Corporations of the Committee on Foreign Relations, US Senate. Washington, DC: US Government Printing Office.

Odaka, K. 1985. Is the division of labour limited by the extent of the market? A study of automobile parts production in East and Southeast Asia. In K. Ohkawa and G. Ranis (eds), *Japan and the Developing Countries*. Oxford: Basil Blackwell, pp. 389–425.

Oman, C. 1984. *New Forms of International Investment in Developing Countries*. Paris: OECD.

Ozawa, T. 1979. International investment and industrial structure: new theoretical implications from the Japanese experience. *Oxford Economic Papers*, 31, 72–92.

Pack, H. 1976. The substitution of labour for capital in Kenyan manufacturing. *Economic Journal*, 86, 45–58.

Parry, T. G. 1981. The multinational enterprise and two-stage technology transfer to developing nations. In R. G. Hawkins and A. J. Prasad, (eds), *Research in International Business and Finance*, vol. 2: *Technology Transfer and Economic Development*. Greenwich, Conn.: JAI Press, pp. 175–92.

Pearce, R. D. 1982. Overseas production and exporting performance: an empirical note.

University of Reading Discussion Papers in International Investment and Business Studies, No. 64.

Philip, G. 1976. The limitations of bargaining theory: a case study of the international petroleum company in Peru. *World Development*, 4, 231-9.

Plasschaert, S. R. F. 1985. Transfer pricing problems in developing countries. In A. M. Rugman and L. Eden (eds), *Multinationals and Transfer Pricing*. London: Croom Helm, pp. 247-66.

Poynter, T. A. 1982. Government intervention in less developed countries: the experience of multinational companies. *Journal of International Business Studies*, 13, 9-25.

Reuber, G. L. with Crookell, H., Emerson, M. and Gallais-Hamonno, G. 1973, *Private Foreign Investment in Development*. Oxford: Clarendon Press.

Reidel, J. 1975. The nature and determinants of export-oriented direct foreign investment in a developing country: a case study of Taiwan. *Weltwirtschaftliches Archiv*, 111, 505-28.

Roemer, J. E. 1976. Japanese direct foreign investment in manufactures: some comparisons with the US pattern. *Quarterly Review of Economics and Business*, 16, 91-111.

Root, F. R. and Ahmed, A. A. 1978. The influence of policy instruments on manufacturing direct foreign investment in developing countries. *Journal of International Business Studies*, 9, 81-93.

Rugman, A. M. and Eden, L. (eds). 1985. *Multinationals and Transfer Pricing*. London: Croom Helm.

Sekiguchi, S. 1979. *Japanese Direct Foreign Investment*. London: Macmillan.

Solomon, R. F. and Forsyth, D. J. 1977. Substitution of labour for capital in the foreign sector: some further evidence. *Economic Journal*, 87, 283-9.

Stoever, W. A. 1979. Renegotiations: the cutting edge of relations between MNCs and LDCs. *Colombia Journal of World Business*, 14, 5-14.

Streeten, P. 1974. The theory of development policy. In J. H. Dunning (ed.), *Economic Analysis and the Multinational Enterprise*. London: Allen and Unwin, pp. 252-79.

Thee, K. W. 1984. Japanese direct investment in Indonesian manufacturing. *Bulletin of Indonesian Economic Studies*, 20, 90-106.

Tomlinson, J. W. C. 1970. *The Joint Venture Process in International Business: India and Pakistan*. Cambridge, Mass.: MIT Press.

Tyler, W. G. 1978. Technical efficiency and ownership characteristics of manufacturing firms in a developing country: a Brazilian study. *Weltwirtschaftliches Archiv*, 114, 360-78.

UNCTAD. 1971. *Restrictive Business Practices - Interim Report by the UNCTAD Secretariat*. New York: United Nations.

UNCTAD. 1972. *Restrictive Business Practices: The Operations of Multinational United States Enterprises in Developing Countries. Their Role in Trade and Development. A Study by Raymond Vernon*. New York: United Nations.

UNCTC. 1983a. *Transnational Corporations in World Development: Third Survey*. New York: United Nations Centre on Transnational Corporations.

UNCTC. 1983b. *Management Contracts in Developing Countries: an Analysis of Their Substantive Provisions*. New York: United Nations Centre on Transnational Corporations.

UNCTC. 1983c. *Main Features and Trends in Petroleum and Mining Agreements*. New York: United Nations Centre on Transnational Corporations.

Vaitsos, C. V. 1974a. Income distribution and welfare considerations. In J. H. Dunning (ed.). *Economic Analysis and the Multinational Enterprise*. London: Allen and Unwin, pp. 300-41.

Vaitsos, C. V. 1974b. *Intercountry Income Distribution and Transnational Enterprises.* Oxford: Clarendon Press.

Vernon, R. 1966. International investment and international trade in the product cycle. *Quarterly Journal of Economics.* 80, 190–207.

Vernon, R. 1974. The location of economic activity. In J. H. Dunning (ed.), *Economic Analysis and the Multinational Enterprise.* London: Allen and Unwin.

Vernon, R. 1977. *Storm Over the Multinationals.* London: Macmillan.

Vernon, R. 1979. The product cycle hypothesis in a new international environment. *Oxford Bulletin of Economics and Statistics,* 41, 255–67.

Wall, D. 1976. Export processing zones. *Journal of World Trade Law,* 10, 478–89.

Warr, P. G. 1983. The Jakarta export processing zone: Benefits and costs. *Bulletin of Indonesian Economic Studies,* 19, 28–49.

Warr, P. G. 1984. Korea's Masan free export zone: benefits and costs. *The Developing Economies,* 22, 169–85.

Wells, L. T. (Jr.). 1973. Economic man and engineering man: choice of technology in a low-wage country. *Public Policy,* 21, 319–42.

Wells, L. T. (Jr.). 1983. *Third World Multinationals: the Rise of Foreign Investment from Developing Countries.* Cambridge, Mass.: MIT Press.

Whichard, O. G. 1980. US direct investment abroad in 1979. *Survey of Current Business,* 60(8), 16–37.

Wilkins, M. 1970. *The Emergence of Multinational Enterprise: American Business Abroad from the Colonial Era to 1914.* Cambridge Mass.: Harvard University Press.

Wilkins, M. 1974. *The Maturing of Multinational Enterprise.* Cambridge, Mass.: Harvard University Press.

Willmore, L. 1976. Direct foreign investment in Central American manufacturing. *World Development,* 4, 499–517.

PART II

Macroeconomic problems

4

Poverty, inequality and development

Arne Bigsten

4.1 Introduction

The purpose of this survey is to give an overview of the current state of knowledge with regard to the relationships between income distribution, poverty, and development in LDCs.

The outline of the survey is as follows. In section 4.2 we discuss general problems with regard to the evaluation of changes in income distribution, poverty, and per capita incomes. We also discuss problems of measuring income, poverty, and inequality in LDCs. In section 4.3 we present some theories of income distribution that are relevant to the LDCs. In section 4.4 we review the sprawling empirical literature on income distribution and poverty in LDCs. The coverage of the field must of necessity be incomplete, but it should be sufficiently broad to ensure identification of the major factors. In section 4.5 we discuss the impact of development strategies and economic policy on income distribution and poverty. Finally, in section 4.6, we provide some concluding remarks.

4.2 Evaluation and measurement

In this section we shall discuss problems that are encountered when analysing income distribution and poverty in LDCs. The first one concerns the evaluation of the results of empirical computations. The second concerns the methods of obtaining reasonable and reliable results for an evaluation, and the third concerns the choice of indices of inequality and poverty.

4.2.1 Evaluation

A much-quoted definition of economic development is attributed to Meier (1976, p. 6), who defines it as 'the process whereby the real per capita income of a country increases over a long period of time – subject to the stipulation that the number below an 'absolute poverty line' does not increase, and that the distribution of income does not become more unequal'. The three aspects mentioned are obviously of great importance to the welfare of the population, even if the views about their relative importance may differ. Various ways of weighing these aspects against each other will be discussed in this section.

The group of countries referred to as LDCs is obviously a most heterogeneous group, and some are gradually being absorbed into the group of developed economies. In this section, however, we consider a dual economy in which a low-productivity sector coexists with a more advanced sector. The evaluation of the welfare effects of growth in such an economy is an intricate affair. Different criteria may yield contradictory results. Fields (1979a, b) points to three alternative approaches to the measurement of the effects of growth on economic welfare:

The first one is the relative income approach in which some inequality index (I) is inserted as one argument in a social welfare function where the other argument is per capita income (y). This gives us the social welfare function

$$W = f(y, I) \tag{4.1}$$

The second alternative is the absolute income approach. In this income distribution is analysed directly, but lower weight is given to income accruing to the wealthier, and higher weights to that of the poorer individuals. When individuals are ordered from the poorest to the richest the social welfare function becomes

$$W = g(Y_1, Y_2, \ldots, Y_n) \quad g_i > g_j, i < j \tag{4.2}$$

The extreme version of this approach would be to maximize the income of the poorest individual, which would be similar to what has been suggested by Rawls (1971).

$$W = g(Y_1) \quad g_1 > 0 \tag{4.3}$$

The third alternative, the absolute poverty approach, focuses on the extent of poverty. The social welfare function incorporating a measure of the extent of poverty (P) only can be written

$$W = h(P) \quad h < 0 \tag{4.4}$$

Both the relative and the absolute approaches may be of interest. However, the analysis of a dual economy requires particular caution. Following Fields we assume that the income levels in the modern and traditional sectors are y^m and y^t, and that there is a poverty line which lies between these two levels and which is constant over time. The labour force shares of the respective sectors are f^m and f^t. Growth in national per capita income in this economy implies changes in y^m, y^t, f^m, and f^t. (It should be noted that intra-sectoral income differences are disregarded here. If we were to allow for these there would also be poor people in the modern sector and our results would be less clear-cut, as is shown by Anand and Kanbur, 1985.)

Let us now define a general welfare function as

$$W = W(y, I, P) \tag{4.5}$$

which says that welfare is some function of per capita income y, relative inequality I, and absolute poverty P. Assume that the total labour force is L. Total income Y then is equal to the sum of modern sector income Y^m and traditional sector income Y^t, which can also be written as

$$Y = Y^m + Y^t = (y^m f^m)L + (y^t f^t)L \tag{4.6}$$

Dividing through by L gives

$$y = (y^m f^m) + (y^t f^t) \tag{4.7}$$

which shows that total average income is equal to the weighted sum of the income levels in the two sectors.

Obviously the degree of inequality must be some function of the four variables mentioned above. Thus

$$I = I(y^m, f^m, y^t, f^t) \tag{4.8}$$

Furthermore, the poverty index must be some function like

$$P = P(y^t, f^t) \tag{4.9}$$

Substituting (4.7–4.9) into (4.5) yields

$$W = W\{ y^m f^m + y^t f^t, I(y^m, f^m, y^t, f^t), P(y^t, f^t) \} \tag{4.10}$$

With this formulation of the welfare function of a dual economy it is obvious that the following conditions should hold

$$\partial W/\partial y > 0; \quad \partial W/\partial I < 0; \quad \partial W/\partial P < 0.$$

The first of these three conditions, $\partial W/\partial y > 0$, says that, all other things given, an increase in per capita incomes increases welfare. The second condition, $\partial W/\partial I < 0$, states that, all other things given, a more equal distribution provides higher welfare than a less equal one. The third condition, $\partial W/\partial P < 0$, states that, all other things given, a decrease in absolute poverty represents an increase in welfare.

The growth of a dual economy is equal to the weighted sum of the growth of its two sectors. The growth of sectoral output in turn is due to two effects:

1 an enlargement (or contraction) effect which reflects the percentage change in the labour force within the sector;
2 an enrichment effect, due to the change in the income level within the sector.

A typical pattern of change in a dual economy is growth of the modern sector share of the labour force (f^m) combined with increasing income levels (y^m, y^t) in both sectors. To evaluate how different groups benefit from growth one may take the first difference of (4.7) and decompose the change in per capita income as follows:

$$\Delta y = \underbrace{\{(f_2^m - f_1^m)(y_1^m - y_1^t)\}}_{\alpha} + \underbrace{\{(y_2^m - y_1^m) f_1^m\}}_{\beta}$$

$$+ \underbrace{\{(y_2^m - y_1^m)(f_2^m - f_1^m)\}}_{\gamma} + \underbrace{\{(y_2^t - y_1^t) f_2^t\}}_{\delta} \qquad (4.11)$$

α = modern sector enlargement effect,
β = modern sector enrichment effect,
γ = interaction between modern sector enlargement and enrichment effects,
δ = traditional sector enrichment effect.

Obviously, the effects in (4.11) need not be positive. Note that we calculate the effects net of the growth required to absorb the growing population at the initial income levels and labour allocation.

Per capita income growth may thus be due either to the modern sector enlargement effect, or to enrichment effects. The welfare evaluation of growth will be affected by the relative valuation of different types of effects.

The poor may benefit by being drawn into the modern sector, or by receiving a higher income within the traditional sector. Our general welfare function is affected as follows:

$$\frac{\partial W}{\partial \alpha} > 0; \quad \frac{\partial W}{\partial \beta} \lessgtr 0; \quad \frac{\partial W}{\partial \delta} > 0.$$

The ambiguous sign for $\partial W/\partial \beta$ is due to the fact that this type of growth may lead to higher inequality. Some kind of weighting procedure is required, if a definite conclusion about the overall welfare effect is to be obtained.

It is obvious that inequality will follow an inverted-U pattern over time in this economic setting. When $f^m = 0$, I will also be zero; when $f^m = 1$, we once again have $I = 0$. Between these two extreme points $I > 0$ if $y^m \neq y^t$. This effect was pointed out by Kuznets in 1955, although he also assumed intra-group inequality (see also Knight, 1976).

When evaluating modern sector enlargement growth, different criteria yield different results. The absolute income approach, or absolute poverty approach, suggests that it is a welfare improvement. The Rawlsian type of criterion is not affected at all. The relative inequality approach may rate it as a deterioration as long as the inequality index increases, but after the turning point it will definitely be rated as an improvement. This last-mentioned conclusion suggests that one should avoid postulating that *any* change which leads to greater inequality implies a deterioration in welfare, since that would imply that most of the types of economic change that are feasible in a very poor country would be rated as negative. This is hardly justified. Thus, for an observer who wants to draw a welfare conclusion, some kind of trade-off between growth, distribution and poverty seems necessary. Obviously, we need some form of social welfare function.

4.2.2 Empirical measurement

In a study of income distribution it is necessary to choose an income concept which is both theoretically acceptable and practically applicable. The ideal measure (Hicks, 1939) would be what is sometimes referred to as the claims concept. According to this income is equal to the amount a person, or a family, could have spent during a certain period while maintaining the value of his (or its) wealth intact. Thus, to measure this information about the value of consumption plus the change over the period concerned in the value of assets owned would suffice. In theory this should be equal to the sum of earnings, capital gains, the value of fringe benefits and production for home consumption as well as imputed rent. It is, however, difficult to apply in practical analyses. The major problem lies in measuring the changes in wealth due to revaluations of the capital stock.

In practice, therefore, it is necessary to use some measure of current income, of which there are at least four different possibilities: (1) gross income, (2) income net of taxes, to which transfers may be added to give (3) disposable income. Finally, an allocation of public goods consumption by household (or individual) might be attempted to get (4) disposable income adjusted for public goods consumption. The latter is not easy to compute, but some attempts have been made to illustrate how the distribution of public consumption affects the distribution of economic resources (see, for example, Foxley *et al.*, 1979; Meerman, 1979).

As an alternative to the measurement of income distribution the distribution of consumption might be measured, thus disregarding net savings. It might be argued that the consumption distribution is the relevant factor to observe in a welfare evaluation, but the use of the actual distribution of consumption implies a departure from the concept of income as a measure of consumption *capacity*, which we have adopted here.

Once some income concept has been decided upon the appropriate income units must also be chosen. Since the household normally is the unit within which consumption is shared, the household should, ideally, be used as the income unit. One should then preferably adjust for household size and calculate per capita household income, or, better still, adjust also for household composition and calculate household income per adult equivalent. In the latter case each child is given a weight which is some fraction of the weight of an adult. If it is not possible to use household units due to the lack of data, the analysis has to be confined to inter-personal income distribution.

Apart from the inter-personal, or inter-family income distribution the distribution of income may also be considered in other dimensions, such as the distribution by income source, by socio-economic groups, by occupational classification, or by industry. Although the inter-personal or inter-household distribution is the most important one from a welfare point of view, the other classifications may be more important from a policy point of view, since the impact of policies often must be analysed in terms of their effects on these kinds of classification.

Another problem in the analysis of income distribution is associated with the choice of time period. Normally, an individual has a certain life-cycle of income;

it might therefore be argued that it is the distribution of life-time incomes that should be measured to get a correct measure of inter-personal inequality. Certainly, inequality will be reduced if life-time incomes are used instead of, say, annual incomes, but the possibilities for such an analysis in an LDC are small.

A problem with the estimation of income distribution and poverty is that the price level tends to be higher in urban than in rural areas, which means that relative urban incomes tend to be overestimated, while urban poverty is underestimated (see, for example, Thomas, 1980). Another problem is that to be able to measure changes in poverty the changes in absolute income must be measured. This means that the rate of inflation must be measured, and that is difficult to do accurately in many countries. In countries whose price system is in disarray, and where black markets are important, one cannot be very sure about what actually is being measured. Rationing through queues may also exist, but it is not clear how this should be brought into the analysis. Queuing for hours every day obviously represents a welfare cost. Lastly, it is far from clear how differences in consumption bundles should be treated. Should, for example, the money which an urban worker has to spend on bus fares really be included when his standard of living is being compared to that of a rural farmer who does not have to spend anything on travel.

An important, although frequently ignored, point is that when comparing data on income distribution from two different points in time, they show changes in the shares of income accruing to groups which remain fixed in relative size but vary in composition. The longer the time between the two 'snap-shots', the more the composition of the deciles has changed. In addition, there are often large movements in and out of the group comprising the 'poor'.

Most empirical studies of income distribution and poverty in LDCs base their analyses on household budget surveys. The scope for non-sampling errors in the data collection is vast, to which should be added the possibility of sampling errors, given that sample surveys are expensive to conduct and that, as a result, the sample size is not very large. It is therefore vital to try to identify and assess possible imperfections, so that the direction and degree of bias in the results may be established. If the quality of data cannot be ascertained *a priori*, one should at least check internal consistency. The problems of measurement are particularly difficult for items such as fringe benefits, entrepreneurial income, property income (imputed rent for owner-occupied housing, etc.) and transfers. Consistency checks and quality controls should therefore be made on national accounts, employment and earnings surveys, etc., whenever possible. This is, however, not the place for an extensive discussion of survey design and survey evaluation. The reader is referred to standard textbooks on the subject, such as Cochran (1977) and Kisch (1965).

4.2.3 Indices of inequality and poverty

In recent years there has been an extensive discussion in the literature about the desired properties of inequality and poverty measures. It is not possible to review this vast literature here; instead the reader is referred to other sources, such as Bigsten (1983), Cowell (1977, 1980, 1985) and Sen (1973). Here we have to confine ourselves to a brief description of a few inequality and poverty indices which have proved to be useful.

To discuss inequality measurement we introduce the Lorenz curve (see figure 4.1). This plots cumulative percentage of persons or households against cumulative percentage of income. This means that if every individual has the same income the curve coincides with the diagonal and there is no inequality. The further away from the diagonal, the higher the inequality. If we compare curves A and B we see that B in all its length lies inside A. This is sometimes called Lorenz domination, and from very general assumptions it can be shown that it is reasonable to consider inequality to be higher in case A than in case B. The criterion of Lorenz domination says that a transfer from a richer person to a poorer one that does not change the ranking of persons always reduces the inequality measure, which obviously is an attractive feature, but the Lorenz criterion is unfortunately not complete. It does not, for example, allow a ranking of the distributions illustrated by curves A and C in figure 4.1. In order to facilitate comparisons between distributions with crossing Lorenz curves, some cardinal measure is usually introduced. The measure that is used most often, and the one which corresponds directly to the Lorenz curve, is the Gini coefficient, which for distribution A is equal to the ratio between the shaded area and the triangle DEF. Other measures that are easy to use and which also satisfy

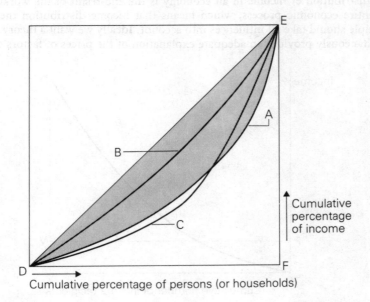

FIGURE 4.1 The Lorenz curve

reasonable axioms, are the coefficient of variation and the Theil index. Formulas for these indices are given in, for example, Bigsten (1983).

When it comes to poverty measurement the first step is to define a poverty line which makes it possible to decide who is poor. Once this line has been established a decision must be made about what measure of poverty to use. The easiest and probably most common one is, of course, the proportion of the population that lies below the poverty line. It has one drawback, however, and that is that the same weight is given to a person or a household which is 1 per cent below the poverty line as to another which is 75 per cent below the line. This may be taken into account by computing the poverty gap, which is equal to the shaded area in figure 4.2. The poverty gap measures the total sum of money needed to bring everybody who is below the poverty line up to the line. To put this into perspective, it must be related to some relevant magnitude such as the total income of the economy or total government expenditures.

Sen (1974, 1976) has developed a useful index of poverty which takes both the number in poverty and the size of each individual's poverty gap into account. Examples of empirical applications are Bigsten (1986) and van Ginneken (1980b). Foster *et al.* (1984) present a useful discussion of decomposable poverty measures.

4.3 General theories of income distribution

The distribution of income in an economy is the end-result of the workings of the entire economic process, which means that income distribution theory in principle should take all influences into account. Ideally we want a theory which simultaneously provides an adequate explanation of the prices of factors of pro-

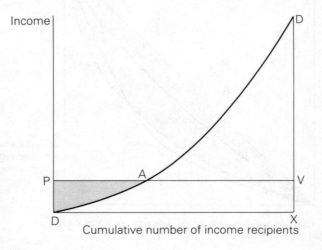

FIGURE 4.2 The poverty gap

duction, functional shares, and the size distribution of income. In practice, however, we have to be content with more or less partial models giving a part of the story. In the following we shall provide a brief review of some important theories of interest to LDCs. (For reviews of income distribution theory, see Bigsten, 1983; Bronfenbrenner, 1971; Johnson, 1973; Reder, 1969; Sahota, 1978).

For the classical economists from Adam Smith to Ricardo and Marx the question of how the product was divided among wages, rent, and profit was central, and there are those who work more or less faithfully within these traditions. The classical idea of a subsistence wage was revived by Lewis in 1954 when he formulated his dual-economy model, which since then has been a cornerstone of development economics.

From about 1870 the marginalist revolution changed in the main-stream economists' view of the problem of income distribution. According to standard marginalist theory all factors are assumed to be paid according to the value of their marginal product. The prices of factors of production are assumed to be determined at the same time as the prices of goods by the market process. In this model the demand for factors is derived from the demand for products, while the supply of labour is assumed to be determined by a process of maximization, where a person allocates his time between work and leisure in such a way that marginal utilities are equalized. Factor shares are determined by the prices paid to factors and the income of an individual is determined by the amount of factors he owns and the prices they fetch. Factors which influence the change of income distribution over time in this system may be, for example, changes in relative factor quantities, the elasticity of substitution, changes in the demand for products, and the character of technical change.

Alternatives to this model have been proposed by Kalecki (1950) and Kaldor (1956). In Kalecki's model monopoly analysis is used to determine the sizes of functional shares (wages, profits). Kalecki assumes that firms set prices according to a mark-up rule, and that the mark-up is higher the more monopolistic the market. The lower the degree of monopoly power, the greater the share of wages.

Kaldor and other neo-Keynesians make the basic assumption that the level of investment is exogenously determined, and that workers and capitalists have different propensities to save. For savings to equal investments, total income has to be distributed between workers and capitalists in a certain proportion. In this model the change in functional income distribution is therefore the equilibrating mechanism, while in a neoclassical model this is not the case. In the latter model savings determine the size of investments, while an increase in investments in a neo-Keynesian model must lead to an increase in the profit share, since the propensity to save out of profits is higher than the propensity to save out of wages. From this it follows that changes in income distribution depend on the growth rate of the economy.

A wide range of theories have been proposed to explain the size distribution of income. The oldest idea in the field is, of course, that incomes are distributed according to ability. Since ability was assumed to be normally distributed it came as a surprise that income is not normally distributed, but rather lognormally. This was first pointed out by Pareto (1897). Various more or less mechanical, stochastic theories have been proposed to explain this (for example, Champernowne, 1953; Gibrat, 1931), but they tend to give little economic insight or help to policy-makers. Pigou's (1932) suggestions that the skewed distribution is due to the fact that wealth is inherited, and that there exist non-competing groups and lack of mobility among groups, are perhaps more relevant.

A major attempt at explaining income distribution is due to the human capital school (Becker, 1964; Mincer, 1958, 1974). According to this school individuals are optimizing agents, who decide to invest in themselves in the form of, for example, education on the basis of expected present value of future incomes in different occupations. The alternative that maximizes this value is chosen. According to this approach differences in annual income are due to the fact that people with longer education have to have higher annual incomes in order to earn the same discounted life-time income, (see survey 6).

Bliss and Stern (1978) have presented a theory according to which in a poor country it may be in the employer's interest to pay a worker above the market-clearing wage, if this is necessary to make it possible for the worker to get sufficient nutrition. The employer then should increase wages such that the value of the increase in the worker's efficiency is equal to the extra wage paid. It may thus pay for an employer to invest in the human capital of the worker.

The human capital theory certainly contains some important insights, but certain factors are disregarded, and these factors are important in LDCs. One problem is that the freedom of choice is usually more limited in LDCs than in developed countries. Fewer people can get the education to which they aspire. Capital markets are less developed, which makes it more difficult to borrow money for an education. Opportunities to borrow are not equally distributed, nor is information. Educational investments therefore differ considerably across people. Another type of critique which can be levelled against the theory is that it is mainly concerned with the supply side of the market, while the demand side is disregarded. The argument here is that there exist a certain number of job openings with different incomes attached to them determined primarily by the productivity of the job, but maybe also by status considerations, tradition or other factors. What the educational system does, according to this view, is rather to screen or sort people across jobs. If you are successful in the educational system you end up at the top of the queue, even if you have not acquired any human capital that is useful in the job you get. If you are not successful in the educational system, you end up further back in the queue and may have to take an unqualified job with only a minimum wage attached to it. The point is that the wage is not determined by how much human capital is acquired, but by what type of job is obtained and how well paid that job is (see, for example, Arrow, 1973; Bowles and Gintis, 1975; Cain, 1976; Doeringer and Piore, 1971; Stiglitz, 1975). This view of the labour market differs strongly from the traditional neoclassical view, according to which the labour market functions smoothly and equilibrates wages of people with identical skills. The alternative model is often denoted the 'job-competition' model to indicate that workers compete for positions, while the neoclassical model is called the 'wage-competition' model.

None of these views are plausible in their extreme form. One needs to take both the supply side and the demand side into account. There are some examples of extensions of the human capital model which take both the supply side and the demand side into account; for example Blinder (1974) and Tinbergen (1970, 1975). Tinbergen introduces heterogeneity both on the demand and the supply side, and this is certainly a trait which is attractive if one wants to perform an analysis of an LDC. The problem is, however, that it is difficult to perform the analysis outlined by Tinbergen empirically, which means that one in practice is stuck with more traditional supply and demand theory.

The theories we have discussed so far have mostly been concerned with the distribution of earnings, but income from property is a large share of national income, which should not be neglected. There are two main ways in which wealth can be acquired. One is through inheritance, the other is through savings. In a long-run analysis of how income distribution changes these factors are certainly crucial and should be taken into account. They do present some empirical problems, however, since good data on the distribution of capital income in LDCs are very scarce.

In this section we have only been able to touch upon some of the interesting theories which are available, and which can be useful ingredients in an analysis of income distribution in LDCs. Different theories may be appropriate in different contexts and one cannot say *a priori* that there is one theory which is generally superior to all the others.

Whenever an analysis is to be done, there are nevertheless three problems that must be faced. First, what determines ownership and supply of factors of production? Second, what determines demand for factor services? Third, how is supply equated with demand? To answer these old economic questions we have to dig in our tool kit and try to piece together a model which fits the actual case we are analysing.

In an analysis of income distribution in an LDC it is important to take the structural characteristics of the economy into account. Sectoral and regional differences are much larger in these economies than in industrialized countries, and the set of constraints within which choices are made may be different from that of a developed country. The first step of a full analysis would therefore be to explain income distribution by sectors and by factors. The distribution can subsequently be mapped into a distribution by individuals and households. Here the distribution of both human and material capital is important, and both human capital theory and theories regarding savings and inheritance are of great importance. So far, we have found no comprehensive theory of income distribution for LDCs, or for industrialized countries for that matter, but attempts to explain income distribution should try to incorporate factors relating both to the individual and the social and economic structure.

4.4   Empirical studies

In this section we shall attempt to provide a concise summary of what we have
learnt so far from empirical studies concerning income distribution and poverty
in LDCs, and particularly about their evolution over time. The literature is vast,
and there is no room here for a detailed presentation or critique of individual
studies. The coverage will therefore have to be selective, but our aim is to make
it broad enough to make it possible to identify the major determinants of changes
in income distribution and poverty.

4.4.1   The time pattern of inequality

The first attempts to derive empirical propositions about the evolution of
inequality over time were based on cross-section evidence. The pioneer was
Kuznets (1955, 1963), who advanced the hypothesis of the 'inverted-U', according to which inequality first increases and then decreases with rising per capita
incomes. This pattern is due to the fact that growth in early stages of development tends to be concentrated in the modern sector of the economy which, at
that time, is small in terms of employment. There are several reasons for the increase in the Gini coefficient following from such a pattern of structural change.
Inequality may rise because the gap between the modern and traditional sectors
increases; it may also rise because inequality within the expanding modern sector
is greater than inequality within the traditional sector. Finally, even if the gap
between the average incomes in the two sectors were to remain the same and the
inequality within both sectors remains the same the Gini coefficient may
increase when the small modern sector starts to expand at the expense of the
traditional sector. This is a purely compositional effect; one should therefore be
cautious of drawing welfare conclusions directly from changes in the Gini coefficient.

Kuznets' seminal contribution was followed by a string of other studies,
such as Adelman and Morris (1971, 1973), Ahluwalia (1976a,b), Chenery and
Syrquin (1975), Kravis (1960), Lydall (1977), Oshima (1962), Paukert (1973),
and Swamy (1967). Since these studies are cross-sectional their results should be
interpreted with caution, but they tend to support the hypothesis that there is a
tendency towards increasing inequality in the early stages of development,
followed by a period of declining inequality after a certain income level has been
reached. (See also Ahluwalia *et al.*, 1979; Braulke, 1983; Cline, 1975; Lecaillon
et al., 1983; Nugent, 1983; Robinson, 1976; Smith, 1980.) It should be pointed
out, however, that what is predicted is the long-run pattern of change, while
there is ample evidence that the relationship does not hold in the short run. On
the contrary, short-term setbacks in the growth of per capita incomes often lead
to increasing inequality.

An important conclusion that Ahluwalia (1976b) draws from his material is
that it takes a long time before the poorest 20 per cent experience any increase in
their relative income share. Although this does not necessarily mean that their
absolute income declines, it does suggest that they will experience only modest

real income gains, if any, for a long period of time. In many cases absolute poverty may actually have increased, which has certainly been the case since the mid-1970s in many LDCs. It should be pointed out that income distribution is the link between per capita income levels and the extent of poverty. The reason for the increases in poverty in recent years, however, is usually not increasing inequality but falling per capita incomes. In a policy aimed at reducing poverty, one should nevertheless consider the need for both growth and equality.

Before we leave the cross-country studies it should be pointed out that even if an inverted-U relationship does exist, the level of per capita income explains only a small part of the variation in inequality. There is a very large, unexplained, inter-country variation of about 80 per cent, which is due to other factors. In order to increase our understanding, we must proceeed to country studies, in which the causes of this can be investigated in a historical context. (For a critique of the cross-section analyses see Anand and Kanbur, 1984; Saith, 1983). In this context it should, however, be pointed out that country studies normally cover only limited periods of time, which means that the long-term pattern of change will tend to be blurred by the effects of short-term fluctuations.

Latin American countries

Of the Latin American nations, Brazil is the most thoroughly studied. The period of the sixties and the seventies has been extensively discussed by, for example Ahluwalia *et al.* (1980), Bacha and Taylor (1978), Camargo (1983), Denslow and Tyler (1984), Fields (1977, 1980), Fishlow (1972, 1980), and Morley (1982). The conclusion of this discussion seems to be that, although inequality in Brazil increased most of the time and the share of the poorest decreased, their absolute income level increased. In the case of Columbia the development from the thirties to the sixties has been analysed by Berry and Urrutia (1976). They find that inequality peaked during the fifties, and that there is some consistency with the Kuznets hypothesis. The extent of poverty does not, therefore, seem to have increased during this period (see also Fields, 1979c; Fields and Schultz, 1980; Urrutia, 1976). Among the other countries in Latin America, Cuba (MacEwan, 1981) and Puerto Rico (Mann, 1985) seem to have managed to decrease inequality, while the evidence for countries such as Mexico (van Ginneken, 1980a, 1984), Costa Rica (Gonzales-Vega and Cespedes, 1983), Peru, Argentina, Chile, and Venezuela (Foxley, 1976) suggests that there was little systematic change in inequality in these countries during the sixties and early seventies. Nor is there evidence of a widespread deterioration of the absolute income of the poor over this period. Since the mid-seventies, however, the political and economic crises in Latin America have certainly changed the picture for the worse (see, for example, Figueroa, 1984).

It may be pointed out that countries which perform badly with regard to poverty eradication relative to their per capita income level (for example Brazil, Mexico, and Peru) also have a high degree of overall inequality. Thus, even if an uneven income distribution does not automatically imply a high incidence of poverty relative to the country's income level, there is a strong correlation between the two (Sen, 1980). Poverty eradication and income equalization therefore often go hand in hand.

Asian countries

For Asia the most extensive studies cover India. The evidence about the development of both income distribution and poverty is mixed (see, for example, Ahluwalia, 1978; Dandekar and Rath, 1971; Griffin and Ghose, 1979; ILO, 1977; Khan and Lee, 1984; Mathur, 1985; Minhas, 1970; Nayyar, 1979; Rajaraman, 1975; Saith, 1981). Ahluwalia found that rural poverty declined from the mid-fifties to 1960/1, increased again until 1967/8, and then decreased until 1973/4. As a whole, it is difficult to find any significant trend over the period. Ahluwalia concludes that the 'Green Revolution' has been associated with reductions in the incidence of poverty. However, this has been questioned by Saith (1981). In his comparison of the two stands Mathur comes out in favour of Ahluwalia's position.

In Asia rural poverty generally seemed to increase between the early sixties and the early seventies, with some exceptions such as Sri Lanka (see Berry, 1978; Fields, 1984; Guisinger and Hicks, 1978; Khan and Lee, 1984; King and Weldon, 1977; Lee, 1977). Since then the picture has changed somewhat and poverty has been reduced in several countries, such as India and Thailand, while other countries such as Nepal, Bangladesh, and Sri Lanka may have experienced a further increase (see the papers in Khan and Lee, 1984). The most densely populated and poor areas of Asia seem to have gone through the least favourable development in terms of poverty in recent years.

When it comes to changes in inequality the picture is mixed. For Pakistan the evidence does not suggest any clear trend (Guisinger and Hicks, 1978). In Bangladesh inequality was reduced in the sixties, while it increased again in the seventies (Osmani, 1982; Osmani and Rahman, 1983). Inequality in Malaysia increased from the fifties to the seventies (Lee, 1977; Snodgrass, 1980), while it decreased in Sri Lanka (Fields, 1984; Lee, 1977) (see also Berry, 1978; Fields, 1980; King and Weldon, 1977).

There are, however, a few countries which have done exceptionally well in terms of growth, and there is evidence that in several cases it has been possible to achieve rapid growth without a deterioration in income distribution. Both Hong Kong and Taiwan have experienced improving income distribution (Chinn, 1977; Chow and Papanek, 1981; Fei *et al.*, 1978, 1980; Hsia and Chau, 1978a). South Korea managed to sustain a very rapid rate of growth in the sixties while preserving a relatively even distribution of income (Adelman and Robinson, 1978), although there is some evidence of increasing inequality in the seventies (Koo, 1984; Szal, 1984). The rapid expansion of employment and gross income in South Korea and Taiwan has nevertheless contributed to a very significant reduction of poverty (Sen, 1980).

Until the recent period of reform the distribution of income in China was probably even by Asian standards (Perkins, 1980). Since then inequality has probably increased, but considering the rapid increase in agricultural output poverty must also be assumed to have decreased considerably.

African countries

For Africa there is little to be found in terms of consistent long-term analyses of what has happened to income distribution and poverty. Bigsten (1986), however, has attempted to estimate income distribution change in Kenya between 1914 and 1976, using the same method throughout. It is found that inequality increased until about 1950, fluctuated until about 1971, then declined. Poverty was found to have decreased until about 1964, while it remained approximately constant between 1964 and 1976. This study thus gives support to the inverted-U hypothesis, with increasing inequality in early stages of development. Studies of Zambia (van der Hoeven, 1977), Nigeria (Collier, 1981), Tanzania (Bukuku, 1983), and Malawi (Christiansen and Kydd, 1983) also tend to support the hypothesis. Per capita incomes in many African countries have fallen since the mid-seventies, and unless there have been significant improvements in income distribution, there must have been a large increase in the incidence of poverty over this period.

The conclusion from this review of country studies is that, over shorter periods of time, we are unable to predict the change in income distribution on the basis of our knowledge of per capita income changes. The evidence nevertheless seems to support the Kuznets hypothesis, although by now most countries seem to have reached a level of economic development at which the force of structural change identified by Kuznets no longer affects equality so strongly. This further underlines the necessity of going further in the search for determinants of income distribution and poverty.

4.4.2 Determinants of income distribution and poverty

As has been pointed out earlier in this survey, practically all economic factors contribute in one way or another to the determination of income distribution and thus also to poverty.

To be able to present the evidence that has been gathered in empirical studies we have grouped it under ten headings. In this section we present the evidence relating to the characteristics of the economy, while evidence relating to economic policy is discussed in section 4.5. The headings are as follows:

Institutional determinants:
  1. Type of economic system

Determinants of functional income distribution:
  2. Factor proportions
  3. Technology

Determinants relating to both functional and size distribution:
  4. Sectoral structure

  5. Regional structure
  6. Factor markets
  7. Commodity markets

Determinants of size distribution:
  8. Ownership of assets
  9. Possession of human capital
 10. Social stratification

Our ultimate aim is to explain the size distribution of income. The factors listed here are all important to this end, but they are somewhat different in character. The first factor is the type of economic system, and this is the basic framework within which all the other factors work. The other factors are grouped according to how they affect size destribution. First we have a few factors which can be said to influence primarily the functional income distribution. They therefore exert an indirect influence on the size distribution, since the ownership of factors is not evenly distributed. The third group contains factors which influence size distribution both directly and indirectly via the functional distribution. Finally, in the last group we find the factors which mainly affect size distribution directly, that is distribute factor incomes over households or individuals.

Type of economic system

The type of institutional and legal framework within which economic activities take place is, of course, a fundamental determinant of income distribution. We may point out that the concept of entitlements introduced by Sen (1981) can be used to characterize an economic system. In a market economy entitlements may be based on trade, organization of production, own work, inheritance, and transfers, while entitlement based on the organization of production would not be valid in a socialist economy. Although we cannot go too deeply into this issue here, we conclude that the system of entitlements is a very important determinant of income distribution and poverty.

LDCs are difficult to classify, but most of them could probably be called mixed capitalist economies. The mix of private and public activities, however, varies greatly. In general income distribution would be expected to be more uneven in an economy with a dominant private sector than in one with state-owned enterprises, since capital incomes in the latter are appropriated by the government to a much greater extent. As far as can be judged from the sparse data on income distribution in socialist LDCs (for example, Lardy, 1978 on China; MacEwan, 1981 on Cuba) the income distribution in these seems to be more even than in more capitalist economies. That is, we seem to observe that the level of inequality is lower, although we really cannot say much about differences in the pattern of change over time. Whether or not a socialist orientation is good for poverty eradication is difficult to say. In the short run it probably is, since an even income distribution tends to go with low levels of poverty. In the long run, however, one has to consider the impact of the choice of economic system on the growth of per capita incomes. Some socialist countries have been successful in this respect, while others have failed. It is therefore difficult to draw any clear-cut conclusion about this.

Factor proportions

A rapid growth of the labour force tends to keep wages down, while land rents and capital incomes increase, and vice-versa. Since the factor proportions of an economy do change very slowly, they exert a stabilizing influence on the income distribution. It is noted in several studies that the surest way of bringing up wages is to make labour more scarce. On the basis of the experiences of Taiwan, Ranis (1978) draws the conclusion that 'the only sure method of achieving a sustained improvement in equity lies in hastening the advent of commercialization, that is, the end of the labour surplus condition' (p. 407) (see also van de Walle, 1985).

Technology

Apart from changes in factor quantities, the change in the demand for factors and yields of these is affected by the pattern of technological change. A much-discussed aspect of this is the 'Green Revolution' (see Griffin, 1974 and survey 10 in this volume), which on the whole does not seem to have affected income distribution as much as was thought initially. It appears to have contributed to increased inequality in those cases where it has taken the form of increased mechanization which has decreased labour absorption (see, for example, Arief, 1983; Lipton, 1978). Where the Green Revolution has taken a form that has increased the demand for labour it has contributed to a widespread improvement in incomes and a reduced incidence of poverty without necessarily leading to an increase in inequality (Ahluwalia, 1978; Tuckman, 1976). The case of hybrid maize in Kenya is a case in point (Gerhardt, 1975).

A general problem with regard to technological development is that a large part of all technological research and development takes place in the industrialized countries and is adjusted to the relative factor prices existing there. This means that they are generally too capital-intensive for LDCs. They underutilize labour which, in turn, leads to a more concentrated distribution of labour incomes than would have resulted from a more labour-intensive technique (see Baer, 1976; Bhalla, 1975; Fransman, 1985; Sen, 1975; Stewart, 1974, 1978; Tokman, 1975; Wehr, 1977).

Sectoral structure

Changes in sectoral structure have already been shown to form a central determinant of changes in income distribution and poverty when there are large differences between sectors in productivity. We have also concluded that this factor weighs the most in the very early stages of development, which is where we find the majority of sub-Saharan African countries today. There is ample evidence of the fact that growth based on the extraction of minerals and oil tends to yield a skewed distribution of income (see, for example, Anand, 1977; Arief, 1983; Lee, 1977). A process of growth which is based on the sectors in which the majority of the labour force is engaged generates less·inequality, and consequently does more to reduce poverty. This means that growth based on a thriving smallholder agriculture tends to be beneficial to income distribution, while agricultural growth based on estate agriculture is less beneficial to equality as in, for example, Malawi (Christiansen and Kydd, 1983). However, growth based on estate agriculture may still be better than growth based primarily on a small industrial sector because of the higher labour intensity in agriculture generally.

The effect of industrialization on income distribution is uncertain (see, for example, Bruton, 1977; Hsia and Chau, 1978a,b; Morawetz, 1974). As we pointed out above, the immediate impact on income distribution may be negative, but even that is uncertain. It depends to a large extent on the form of industrialization pursued. If it is of the import substitution variety behind high tariffs, there is quite extensive evidence of the fact that the impact on income distribution tends to be negative, but this will be further discussed in the following section.

Indonesia is a case in which growth is based on capital-intensive industry and oil extraction plus a pattern of agricultural development which tends to save on labour (Arief, 1983). This kind of development implies that the demand for unskilled labour is held down, and this means that inequality almost certainly increases.

Regional structure

Apart from sectoral productivity differences, LDCs display large inter-regional or urban–rural differences. Williamson (1965) did a cross-section analysis of regional inequality similar to Kuznets' study of inter-personal inequality, and found a similar pattern. This has consequences for the inter-personal income distribution, since imbalances between regions in terms of access to income opportunities and rewards represent a fairly permanent structural feature which is not easily changed. The basic reason for spatial concentration is economies of scale which, for a given level of production, lead to a concentration of production in one or a few plants. The location of these plants is then influenced by the location of the sellers of inputs and the location of the buyers of the output. These factors together with other agglomeration economies breed concentration to one or a few regions. Because of these strong economic forces regional integration of a country is a process which takes a long time. To speed it up there is a need for investments in infrastructure and a regional policy (see Bigsten, 1980; Lardy, 1978).

Large economic differences exist between urban and rural areas. Lipton (1977) argues that there is an urban bias in development and that the most important class conflict in LDCs is between urban and rural classes. Collier and Lal (1984), however, show that in Kenya it is the access of smallholder families to urban employment which makes it possible for them to finance innovations and increase their incomes. Migration to the urban areas may therefore reduce the gap between income levels in the urban and rural areas both by the generation of remittances and by the reduction of population pressure in the rural areas (see, for example, Bacha and Taylor, 1978; Berry and Urrutia, 1976; Bigsten, 1980).

The rural areas that have shown a pattern of positive economic development are those in which the rural infrastructure is well developed, and where non-agricultural economic activities flourish alongside agriculture. In these areas it is possible for smallholder households to supplement their incomes by non-farm earnings and thus achieve a reasonable total income (Chinn, 1979, p. 299; Fei *et al.*, 1978, p. 34; Young *et al.*, 1979). Improved economic integration and reduced regional income inequalities thus contribute to the equalization of household incomes.

Factor markets

Let us start by considering the labour market. There are two competing paradigms with regard to wage determination: the traditional wage competition model and the job competition model. The latter implies a high degree of rigidity in relative wages, and if wages are slow to change in the face of the increasing supply of skilled labour the distribution of labour income will be slow to change. In other words high wages are only brought down slowly by competition, and inequalities remain large.

The job competition perspective gained popularity in the sixties when it was used to explain the situation with increasing supply of skilled labour and increasing unemployment (as in the Harris–Todaro model). In recent years, however, evidence has accumulated which suggests that the labour markets are actually relatively flexible (Bigsten, 1984; see also survey 6).

There is widespread agreement that the most efficient way to increase the wages of unskilled labour is to make it more scarce; that is to increase demand for unskilled labour, as has been done in Hong Kong (Hsia and Chau, 1978a, pp. 14–17), Pakistan (Guisinger and Hicks, 1978, p. 121), or India (Nugent and Walther, 1982). Countries such as Taiwan, which have managed to end their labour surplus condition, have tended to experience improvements in the income distribution. To get to the commercialization point as soon as possible is thus of fundamental importance for sustained, long-run improvements in income distribution. High growth should thus be considered to be central to the goal of long-run equalization. This may imply the existence of a conflict between what is good for equity in the short run and what is good for equity in the long run.

Of course, there are imperfections in labour markets in LDCs such as trade unions or government wage-setting. Few studies have analysed the effects of trade unions, or the use of legal minimum wages on the overall distribution of income. Unions may be expected to raise the income of their members at the expense of the rest of the community – that is employers and non-union workers. Minimum wages have a similar effect of raising wages and reducing employment. The effect on the overall income distribution, however, is uncertain.

There are also examples of government activities aimed at holding back wages. Bacha and Taylor (1978) argue that the official wage squeeze in Brazil in the 1960s contributed to the increase in inequality.

Income inequality and poverty may be aggravated by malfunctioning factor markets. An interesting example of this is shown in Collier's (1983) analysis of smallholder factor markets in Kenya. These are attenuated so that little labour is sold, tenancy is almost completely absent, and access to credit is restricted to a minority of smallholders. This leads to an inefficient allocation of resources, where the big losers are those smallholders with atypical factor proportions. It is most unfortunate that it is almost impossible for those smallholders who have little land relative to labour to lease land or sell their labour in the rural areas. These smallholders are thus poor because they have little land and earn low returns on their abundant resource, labour. In this situation the urban labour market offers a way out. By migrating to towns and working in the wage labour market the abundant factor is put to use, generating incomes which finance the consumption of smallholder families and also contribute to capital formation and innovations in the smallholdings. Thus rural-urban migration and remittances function as surrogates for functioning rural labour, land, and credit markets.

This is just one example of the complexities of rural markets in LDCs. Since these are not yet fully understood, and since most of the poor are to be found in the rural areas, this is a field in need of further research (Lipton, 1983b).

The conclusion from the above seems to be that, if a positive effect on income distribution is desired, it is necessary to pursue a policy which increases the demand for unskilled labour, and makes it easy for poor people to sell their labour. In this way market forces will support the policy of equalization.

Commodity markets

Changes in relative prices affect income distribution and poverty very strongly (see, for example, Murty, 1985). Commodity prices are determined by the interaction of supply and demand in markets that may be more or less perfect. A number of studies have shown that one of the most crucial factors in determining the income distribution and the extent of poverty is the rural–urban terms of trade (see Adelman and Robinson, 1978). These terms of trade may, in turn, be influenced by policy, as will be shown in the following section.

This complex issue will be discussed from the perspective of the entitlements approach, presented in Sen's already classic book on poverty and famine (1981). Extremes of poverty or famine do not only depend on low average incomes, but may also appear in vulnerable entitlement systems. The famines discussed by Sen were caused by sudden failures in the entitlement system. In many instances there was no aggregate food shortage, but the market mechanism destroyed the entitlements of certain groups. The entitlement failures may be due to declines in ownership (for example cattle dying), but may also be caused by declines in exchange entitlements, that is the terms at which someone can exchange his commodity bundle for the one he wishes to acquire (for example, food). To understand famines one should therefore concentrate on entitlements rather than aggregate food availability.

The Bengali famine of 1943 was not caused by aggregate food shortage, but was due to war-time inflation with rapidly increasing rice prices. The smallholders who produced their own food were not much affected, but the landless workers lost two-thirds of their purchasing power in a very short period. It thus became impossible for large groups to buy food in spite of the fact that there was no general food shortage. It should be noted that inflation, even today, tends to increase rural poverty in India (Mathur, 1985).

Another example given by Sen is the 1972–4 famine in Ethiopia, where many farmers experienced crop failures and cattle death. To get cash to buy food on the market, they tried to sell part of their assets, such as land and cattle, but since many tried to do this at the same time the prices of the assets fell drastically. It was therefore impossible to get enough cash to buy food. The farmers no longer had any legal means through which they could acquire enough food. This is another example of a relative price shift which causes extreme poverty and famine.

The point in Sen's analysis is thus that we must look at entitlements and patterns of ownership to understand poverty and income distribution. It is of utmost importance to understand how the markets work.

Ownership of assets

As we have already pointed out, the amount of land and capital available to the economy relative to the amount of labour available is a vital determinant of the functional income distribution. The distribution of capital and land among households is, in turn, a crucial determinant of the size distribution of land rent and capital income.

Particularly in the poorest LDCs the distribution of land is a major determinant of the distribution of income and of the incidence of poverty (Quan and Koo, 1985). The countries that have managed to combine growth with a relatively equitable income distribution, such as Taiwan, South Korea, and Costa Rica, have often been characterized by an equal distribution of land (Francks, 1979; Gonzales-Vega and Cespedes, 1983; Lee, 1979; Rao, 1978). This had made it possible for large segments of the rural inhabitants to share in the increased agricultural incomes. On the other hand, countries with an uneven distribution of land tend to have an uneven distribution of income, and also often a high incidence of poverty. Increasing landlessness is one of the major causes of increased poverty in the LDCs (Griffin, 1981; Griffin and Khan, 1978; ILO, 1977; Khan and Lee, 1984; Osmani, 1982; Osmani and Rahman, 1983).

It should also be pointed out that when we come to land reforms we do not normally face the classical conflict between growth and distribution, since small farms are at least as efficient as large farms in their resource use (Cline, 1972; Lipton, 1977; Singh, 1979, p. 19; Yotopoulos and Nugent, 1976; see also survey 10 in this volume). However, even if land reforms do not imply any aggregate economic sacrifice it is one of the most difficult types of reform to carry out. Landowners are a very strong political force in most LDCs.

The distribution of capital is often even more unequal than that of land. How this changes over time depends on the savings rates of different socio-economic groups, unless there is redistribution through taxation or confiscation. Since the rich save more than the poor, there may be a tendency for the distribution of capital to become more uneven over time. Of course, the banking system tends to reinforce the unequal distribution of capital, since those who are better off normally have better access to bank lending. The accumulation of government capital is, in some countries, a countervailing factor.

Possession of human capital

A parallel to the distribution of asset ownership is the distribution of human capital over the labour force. The more even this is, the more even is the distribution of labour incomes, *ceteris paribus*. When only a minority has access to education it may reap very large rewards, but when larger segments of the population gain access to higher education these rewards are brought down by competition, if the labour markets are flexible (see survey 6). The latter has been in doubt, but the evidence now seems to suggest that there is considerable flexibility. Bigsten (1984), in a study of Kenya, shows that the rates of return on educational investments have gone down in the face of a rapidly increasing supply of skilled labour. During the seventies market forces seem to have become increasingly important in the labour market in Kenya. In such a situation educational policy may be an efficient policy for equitable growth.

Social stratification

There may be many causes of social stratification apart from the purely economic ones (see, for example, Baster, 1970; Baster and Scott, 1969; Myrdal, 1968; Nafzinger, 1977). Ethnic affiliation is, for example, often an important factor, exemplified, for instance, by the enormous racial income gaps in Kenya (Bigsten, 1986). Another example is the Chinese in South East Asian countries such as Malaysia, where a policy aimed at helping the underprivileged Malays may have reduced their disadvantage as a group, but instead increased inequalities within the group. This may be inevitable, however, since once opportunities are opened up for an underprivileged group there are always some who seize them, while others are unable to do so. Inequalities among black Kenyans, for example, have increased significantly since independence.

When stratification is pronounced, for one reason or another, privileges tend to stay with the favoured group(s) which, of course, has a great effect on the size distribution of income. A rigid social structure may even be an impediment to growth. Opportunities are not open to large segments of the population, or they may not even be known to them. The children of the rich therefore tend to get a better education, have assets bequeathed to them, and start out with a better network of social contacts. Inequality is thus transferred from generation to generation and, when this is the case, political power is often distributed in the same manner. The result is that, in reality, it is most difficult to pursue a policy aimed at equity.

4.5 Economic policy and inequality

According to the inverted-U hypothesis an even income distribution requires rapid growth in the long run so that the phase of declining inequality is reached as soon as possible. However, a policy which maximizes growth may be bad for equity and poverty eradication in the short run, and there may thus be a policy conflict.

As has already been pointed out, the inverted-U hypothesis is very far from being an iron law, and income inequality is to a great extent due to factors unrelated to the level of per capita income. The hypothesis nevertheless contains an important element of truth, namely that income distribution changes in the very long run to a considerable degree are determined by the course of structural change. Factors which determine structural change are, for example: (1) income elasticities, (2) price elasticities, (3) productivity growth and technical change, (4) increases in factor availability, and (5) development policy and strategy.

What is the scope for policy here? The elasticities have more or less the same character as technical coefficients, and policy-makers thus have to accept them as more or less given. Technical progress and changes in factor availability may to some extent be influenced by policy-makers, but even here there are definite limits to what can be achieved. However, even when strong structural forces push the economy along the inverted-U trajectory, there is considerable scope for movements away from this central course. It is therefore far from futile to discuss income distribution policies.

4.5.1 Equity oriented development strategies

During the fifties and the early sixties the general view among economists was that, if growth was rapid, poverty and inequality would eventually be alleviated by the natural course of change. There is some basis for this belief, but two caveats have to be made: first, the long run may be a very long time from now, and it may not be morally acceptable to wait for generations before doing anything to help the poorest segments of the population. Second, even if there are forces working towards equity in the long run, everything should not be left entirely to them. The degree of inequality and poverty along the development path can be affected by policy measures. We therefore conclude that there is scope for policy.

During the sixties it became increasingly clear that the LDCs were characterized by a high degree of inequality and poverty, and the seventies were therefore characterized by a search for development strategies, of which income equalization and poverty alleviation were integral parts.

A landmark in this discussion is the book *Redistribution with Growth*, by Chenery *et al.*, published in 1974. It argued that policy should be aimed at certain target groups of the poor. The groups that were identified were small farmers, landless, urban unemployed and the working poor (see also Cutler, 1984; Haaland and Keddeman, 1984). For the rural poor the most important factors were identified as access to land, knowledge and credit; policies should thus aim at giving the poor better access to these things. With regard to the urban poor there is a wider spectrum of factors to choose from, since this group interacts in a more complex way with the rest of the economy. The authors advocate a production strategy and a transfer strategy. The former should be aimed at increasing employment opportunities and increasing the productivity in existing jobs, for example through correction of biases in factor prices and support of small-scale producers. The transfer strategy includes giving the poor better access to public goods and housing. The authors appreciated that in a typical LDC large-scale income transfers are highly unlikely, both for political and administrative reasons, and it is therefore argued that development policy should be devised in such a way that it enables the end-user of the income to earn it directly. The structure of growth should thus be such that the incomes earned by the target groups grow.

A more direct approach to poverty eradication was suggested by the ILO in 1976, when it proposed the *basic needs strategy*, the aim of which was to raise the standard of living of the poor directly (see also Hopkins and van der Hoeven, 1983). The basic needs mentioned were private goods such as food, shelter, and clothes; and certain public goods such as health services, education, water, and transport. The success of the development policy should be measured against the levels on these indicators.

The main ingredients in the basic needs strategy were as follows:

1 productive employment for the poor;
2 increased investments in traditional agriculture and the informal sector, and the elimination of obstacles for the development of these sectors;
3 access to basic services for the entire population;
4 reduced differences between households in their access to basic goods and services;
5 increased exports to finance imports to meet basic needs without too much dependence on aid;
6 creation of institutions that would make it possible for the poor majority to take an active part in the development efforts.

The main point in the strategy outlined by the ILO was thus that there should be a direct effort at improving the lot of the poorest without waiting for the 'trickle-down' process to do the job. Among the policy measures discussed in relation to the basic needs strategy were changes in relative prices, direct transfers of resources to the poor for consumption and investment, and redistribution of the stock of assets and land in favour of the poor. The strategy thus emphasized both the need for a change of the structure of growth and change in the pattern of ownership. These kinds of policies have now been tried in various countries, and even where they have functioned best they seem to have affected poor people, but not the poorest of the poor (Lipton, 1983a). The effects trickle *up* rather than down.

When it comes to poverty alleviation we may consider the categorization of policies proposed by Selowsky (1981). The first type includes *elimination of distortions* that inhibit trickle-down. Their goal should be to increase the employment content of growth. The second type concerns investment policies aimed at *increasing the human and physical capital endowments* of the poor. The third type is pure basic needs policies aimed at *improving the health status, literacy,* etc., of the poor. The content of these policies will be further discussed in the following section.

4.5.2 Equity-oriented policies

Ideally the impact of policies on income distribution and poverty should be analysed within the framework of a general equilibrium model, in which indirect effects may also be taken into account. Among models that do this are Adelman and Robinson (1978), Anker and Knowles (1983), Rodgers *et al.* (1978), and Taylor *et al.* (1980). To these should be added the analyses based on social accounting matrices. They are more restricted, but still capture some of the interdependencies. See, for example, Chander *et al.* (1980), Defourny and Thorbecke (1984), Hayden and Round (1982), Pyatt and Roe (1977), Pyatt and Round (1977, 1979), and Round (1984).

In the models of Adelman and Robinson and Rodgers *et al.* the size distribution of income is very stable, but depending on how the policy package is designed the relative position of different groups may be changed. To be able to change income distribution significantly, concerted efforts are required using a package of mutually supporting policies.

Adelman and Robinson identify two potentially useful strategies for equitable growth: one is *export-led, labour- and skill-intensive growth.* Important preconditions for such a strategy are (1) that a large proportion of the labour force consists of well-educated and skilled workers, and (2) that there is some way of controlling the development of the agricultural terms of trade (vis-à-vis the rest of the economy). The second strategy emphasizes *rural development.* The preconditions here are that there is (1) a relatively equitable distribution of land, and (2) control of the agricultural terms of trade. Other models also show the crucial importance of urban–rural links for income distribution, mainly urban–rural terms of trade and migration.

Agricultural policies

For most LDCs the majority of the poor are to be found in the rural areas. What is happening to agriculture is therefore of vital importance to poverty and income distribution. As has already been pointed out, the gap between agriculture and the rest of the economy is one of the most important determinants of the degree of inequality. Policies which improve the relative position of agriculture will therefore almost always increase equity and reduce poverty. Policies may either enhance agricultural productivity or improve the agricultural terms of trade. There is a long and well-known list of policies aimed at improving agricultural productivity, including a functioning infrastructure, education, supply of inputs, efficient marketing channels, and a reasonable system of prices. On the latter point we note that the import substitution policy pursued by practically all LDCs, in reality is a tax on non-protected sectors.

What the final outcome of such policies will be depends on how the rest of the economy adjusts. Model experiments have shown that if a country manages to increase agricultural output strongly, while simultaneously having difficulties exporting its commodities, farmers are liable to lose what gains they make in quantity through falling terms of trade. International competitiveness is therefore also important in the context of income distribution.

Apart from policies primarily affecting the position of agriculture relative to the rest of the economy, there are also policies which primarily change the distribution within the agricultural sector. The distribution of land-ownership is the most important determinant of income distribution within the agricultural sector (Nguyen and Martinez-Salvidar, 1979). There are examples, however, of policies aimed at equalization within the rural sector, such as the villageization programme in Tanzania, which has turned out to have so negative consequences on productivity that poverty has increased. When it comes to agriculture there is overwhelming evidence that the goal of efficiency is achieved mainly through decentralized decision-making and thus price incentives. Since efficiency is a necessary goal, one should try to bring about an equitable income distribution and poverty reductions through land reforms without collectivization, and through a fair allocation of complementary resources.

Industrial and trade policies

The basis for industrialization policy in practically all LDCs has been the import substitution policy, although some Asian countries have moved towards export promotion in recent years. It has been extensively analysed and innumerable studies may be quoted, of which the major ones probably are those of Bhagwati (1978), Krueger (1978), and Little *et al.* (1970). This policy shifts the terms of trade against agriculture, and since the majority of the poor are to be found in the rural areas this contributes to inequality and poverty. The policy has implied a bias in favour of capital over labour, and it has also included an investment policy giving priority to industry and urban activities over agriculture. Bhagwati (1973a) noted that 'the exchange rate regime has made mockery of income distributional objectives by creating profits and privileges'.

An example of a successful break with this policy is South Korea. The two main policy changes which were initiated in the sixties were an interest rate reform, which meant a doubling of interest rates, and a 50 per cent devaluation. These two changes led to a rapid increase in exports and non-farm employment. The export-oriented development strategy based on production according to comparative advantage led to a more labour-intensive production pattern. This is further proof of the argument advanced earlier that if an improvement for the poor is to be brought about one should pursue a policy leading to increased demand for unskilled and semi-skilled labour.

Prices and incomes policy

Price policy can take many different forms, but basically it affects domestic terms of trade (that is, the relative sectoral prices). The prices of export crops may be held down through export taxes, which means that export producers earn less. This, in turn, tends to reduce production of the affected crops and both the reduced price and reduced quantities reduce rural incomes. This normally affects income distribution negatively.

Several governments also control prices of essential consumer goods, for example food (see Mellor, 1978). This hurts the producers of these products, and in the case of food, once again the farmers. Normally one would expect them to be poorer than the urban workers who are protected by the controls. In controlled systems of this nature it seems to be easier for urban, industrial producers to be allowed to charge higher prices than it is for farmers to get permission to raise their prices. This is another example of the urban bias which permeates policy-making in LDCs.

Many governments pursue some form of incomes policy, at the same time as they try to raise low wages through minimum-wage legislation. It is doubtful, however, whether this leads to any significant change in the overall income distribution.

Fiscal policy

If we first consider the general economic policy pursued by the government, we note that policies which contribute to increasing unemployment tend to affect income distribution negatively. The incidence of unemployment is normally regressive. On the other hand a very expansionary policy leading to rapid inflation normally transfers money to property-owners from the rest of the community, which tends to make income distribution worse. Taxation policy in poor countries seems to have a limited impact on income distribution (see survey 8). A progressive tax structure may, in principle, contribute to the equalization of the income distribution, but in practice it seems to be difficult to implement such a structure even though it exists on paper. In many countries it is more important to improve the methods of collecting taxes than to devise new tax schedules. The income side of the budget is normally dominated by indirect taxes, which tend to be regressive. In the more developed LDCs with a broader tax base there should be some scope for equalizing taxes, but there is little evidence of this.

It seems as if the expenditure side offers more hope for policy-makers aiming at equity (see, for example, Foxley *et al.*, 1979; Meerman, 1979). Direct transfers of money play an insignificant role in LDCs, but government service provision contributes to equalization, if services are distributed free of charge or at subsidized rates, and if most people really have access to them.

One example of such a service that has expanded rapidly throughout the LDCs is education. The growth of this sector may be one of the more important egalitarian reforms in the past few decades. This does not mean, however, that education is evenly distributed. There is ample evidence that family background determines how far you proceed in the educational system, and that privileged regions tend to have a more developed school system than the backward ones. This, however, is not something which is specific to LDCs, and the situation has improved tremendously during recent decades. Access to education may thus be seen as an egalitarian reform. It is also clear that educational level is an important determinant of a person's income level, but that does not prove that a country with more education has a more even distribution of income than one with less education. (See Bhagwati, 1973b; Bigsten, 1984; Carnoy *et al.*, 1979; Fields, 1975; Fishlow, 1972; Harbison, 1977; Hinchliffe, 1975; Hoerr, 1973; Jallade, 1976; Lal, 1976; Psacharopoulos, 1977; Ram, 1984; Rodgers, 1978.) An increasing educational level should, however, contribute to higher productivity and thereby to poverty eradication. It seems plausible to assume that an increased supply of skilled labour tends to reduce skilled–unskilled wage differentials, and thereby to reduce the wage dispersion which, in turn, would probably contribute to overall equality. One may also assume that education may facilitate a development strategy which is labour-intensive. This would tend to generate an improving income distribution.

All types of policies seem to suffer from one common problem: they have difficulties in reaching the ultra-poor. Maybe entirely new measures to reach them are needed; for example measures to increase their nutritional status as suggested by Lipton (1983a).

4.6 Concluding remarks

We started this survey by arguing that economic welfare is some function of per capita income, poverty, and income distribution, and that welfare maximization requires some trade-off among these goals. Measures that contribute to some goal may often have costs in terms of some other goal, but we also find policies that affect all goals positively.

It should be pointed out that, if the need for efficiency and growth is neglected, one may eventually have to give up noble, egalitarian policies. The consequence of inefficiency and economic decline for poverty eradication is naturally even more disastrous.

There is scope for income distribution and poverty-oriented policies. The fact that a potential exists does not, however, guarantee that such a policy will be realized. The classes benefiting from the existing structure of policies may find it in their interest to resist policy changes, and since the majority in most LDCs have few chances of making their voice heard, the elite may have its way.

An active policy aimed at income equalization and poverty eradication must thus have a political commitment. There must also be a correspondence between ends and means; that is, the policies must be feasible. Good intentions are not enough. Experience shows that solutions requiring a lot of detailed, central administration are bound to fail. Planning and administration cannot be substitutes for incentives to economic agents.

For egalitarian reforms to be successful there must be political will and power in support of them. Yet equity is not the only aim of a government, but it has to balance this aim against others, for example efficiency and long-term growth. Once this trade-off has been decided upon, congruence between ends and means must be ensured, and in this context due regard must be given to the administrative, economic and social constraints that exist in the particular economy.

REFERENCES

Adelman, I. and Morris, C. T. 1971. 'An anatomy of income distribution in developing nations – a summary of findings'. Mimeo.

Adelman, I. and Morris, C. T. 1973. *Economic Growth and Social Equity in Developing Countries*. Stanford: Stanford University Press.

Adelman, I. and Robinson, S. 1978. *Income Distribution Policy in Developing Countries. A Case Study of Korea*. Oxford: Oxford University Press.

Ahluwalia, M. S. 1976a. Income distribution and development: some stylized facts. *American Economic Review. Papers and Proceedings*, 66, 128–35.

Ahluwalia, M. S. 1976b. Inequality, poverty, and development. *Journal of Development Economics*, 3, 307–42.

Ahluwalia, M. S. 1978. Rural poverty and agricultural performance in India. *Journal of Development Studies*, 14, 298–323.

Ahluwalia, M. S., Carter, N. G. and Chenery, H. B. 1979. Growth and poverty in developing countries. *Journal of Development Economics*, 16, 299–341.

Ahluwalia, M. S., Duloy, J. H., Pyatt, G. and Srinivasan, T. 1980. Comment to Who benefits from economic development. *American Economic Review*, 70, 242–5.

Anand, S. 1977. Aspects of poverty in Malaysia. *Review of Income and Wealth*, 23, 1–16.

Anand, S. and Kanbur, S. M. R. 1984. Inequality and development: a reconsideration. In H.-P. Nissen (ed.), *Towards Income Distribution Policies*. Tilburg: European Association of Development Research and Training Institutes, Book Series 3.

Anand, S. and Kanbur, S. M. R. 1985. Poverty under the Kuznets process. *Economic Journal*, 95, 42–50.

Anker, R. and Knowles, J. 1983. *Population Growth, Employment and Economic Demographic Interactions in Kenya: Bachue-Kenya*. Aldershot: Gower.

Arief, S. 1983. *Income Distribution in Indonesia*. New York: UN.

Arrow, K. J. 1973. Higher education as a filter. *Journal of Public Economics*, 2, 193–216.

Bacha, E. L. and Taylor, L. 1978. Brazilian income distribution in the 1960s: facts, models, results and the controversy. *Journal of Development Studies*, 14, 271–97.

Baer, W. 1976. Technology, employment and development: empirical findings. *World Development*, 4, 121–30.

Baster, N. 1970. *Distribution of Income and Economic Growth*. Geneva: United Nations Research Institute for Social Development.

Baster, N. and Scott, W. 1969. *Levels of Living and Economic Growth, A Comparative Study of Six Countries 1950–1965*. Geneva: United Nations Research Institute for Social Development.

Becker, G. 1964. *Human Capital*. New York: National Bureau of Economic Research.

Berry, A. 1978. Income and consumption distribution trends in the Philippines, 1950–1970. *Review of Income and Wealth*, 24, 313–31.

Berry, A. and Urrutia, M. 1976. *Income Distribution in Colombia*. New Haven: Yale University Press.

Bhagwati, J. N. 1973a. *India in the International Economy*. Lal Bahadur Shastri Memorial Lectures. Hyderabad: Institute of Public Enterprise.

Bhagwati, J. N. 1973b. Education, class structure and income inequality. *World Development*, 1, 21-36.

Bhagwati, J. N. 1978. *Foreign Trade Regimes and Economic Development: Anatomy and Consequences of Exchange Control Regimes*. Cambridge, Mass.: Ballinger.

Bhalla, A. S. (ed.) 1975. *Technology and Employment in Industry*. Geneva: ILO.

Bigsten, A. 1980. *Regional Inequality and Development. A Case Study of Kenya*. Farnborough: Gower.

Bigsten, A. 1983. *Income Distribution and Development. Theory, Evidence and Policy*. London: Heinemann.

Bigsten, A. 1984. *Education and Income Determination in Kenya*. Aldershot: Gower.

Bigsten, A. 1986. Welfare and economic growth in Kenya, 1914-1976. *World Development*, 14, 1151-60.

Blinder, A. S. 1974. *Toward an Economic Theory of Income Distribution*. Cambridge, Mass.: MIT press.

Bliss, C. and Stern, N. 1978. Productivity, wages, and nutrition, Parts I-II. *Journal of Development Economics*, 4, 331-98.

Bowles, S. and Gintis, H. 1975. The problem with human capital theory – a Marxian critique. *American Economic Review, Papers and Proceedings*, 65, 74-82.

Braulke, M. 1983. A Note on Kuznets' 'U'. *Review of Economics and Statistics*, 65, 135-9.

Bronfenbrenner, M. 1971. *Income Distribution Theory*. Chicago: Aldine Atherton.

Bruton, H. J. 1977. Industrialization policy and income distribution. In C. R. Frank Jr and R. C. Webb (eds), *Income Distribution and Growth in Less Developed Countries*. Washington, DC: The Brookings Institution.

Bukuku, E. 1983. *Income Distribution in Tanzania*. New York: UN.

Cain, C. G. 1976. The challenge of segmented labour market theories to orthodox theory: a survey. *Journal of Economic Literature*, 14, 1215-57.

Camargo, J. M. 1983. *Income Distribution in Brazil*. New York: UN.

Carnoy, M., Lobo, J., Toledo, A. and Velloso, J. 1979. *Can Educational Policy Equalize Income Distribution in Latin America?* Harmondsworth: Saxon House.

Champernowne, D. G. 1953. A model of income distribution. *Economic Journal*, 63, 318-51.

Chander, R., Gnasegarah, S., Pyatt, G. and Round, J. I. 1980. Social accounts and the distribution of income. The Malaysian economy in 1970. *Review of Income and Wealth*, 26, 67-85.

Chenery, H. B. and Syrquin, M. 1975. *Patterns of Development*. London: Oxford University Press.

Chenery, H. B., Ahluwalia, M. S., Bell, C. L. G., Duloy, J. H. and Jolly, R. 1974. *Redistribution with Growth*. London: Oxford University Press.

Chinn, D. L. 1977. Distributional equality and economic growth: the case of Taiwan. *Economic Development and Cultural Change*, 26, 65-79.

Chinn, D. L. 1979. Rural poverty and the structure of farm household income in developing countries: evidence from Taiwan. *Economic Development and Cultural Change*, 27, 283-301.

Chow, S. C. and Papanek, G. F. 1981. Laissez-faire, growth and equity – Hong Kong. *Economic Journal*, 91, 466-85.

Christiansen, R. E. and Kydd, J. G. 1983. *Income Distribution in Malawi*. New York: UN.

Cline, W. R. 1972. Interrelationships between agricultural strategy and rural income distribution. *Food Research Institute Studies*, 11, 139-57.

Cline, W. R. 1975. Distribution and development: a survey of literature. *Journal of Development Economics*, 1, 359-400.

Cochran, W. G. 1977. *Sampling Techniques*, 3rd edn. New York: Wiley.

Collier, P. 1981. *Oil and Inequality in Rural Nigeria*. ILO, WEP-Working Paper, Geneva: ILO.

Collier, P. 1983. Malfunctioning of African rural factor markets: theory and a Kenyan example. *Oxford Bulletin of Economics and Statistics*, 45, 141-72.

Collier, P. and Lal, D. 1984. Why poor people get rich: Kenya 1960-69. *World Development*, 12, 1007-18.

Cowell, F. A. 1977. *Measuring Inequality*. Oxford: Philip Allan.

Cowell, F. A. 1980. On the structure of additive inequality measures. *Review of Economic Studies*, 47, 521-31.

Cowell, F. A. 1985. Multilevel decomposition of Theil's index of inequality. *Review of Income and Wealth*, 31, 201-5.

Cutler, P. 1984. The measurement of poverty: a review of attempts to quantify the poor, with special reference to India. *World Development*, 12, 1119-30.

Dandekar, V. M. and Rath, N. 1971. *Poverty in India*. Bombay: Indian School of Political Economy.

Defourny, J. and Thorbecke, E. 1984. Structural path analysis and multiplier decomposition within a social accounting matrix framework. *Economic Journal*, 94, 111-36.

Denslow, D. and Tyler, W. 1984. Perspectives on poverty and income inequality in Brazil. *World Development*, 12, 1019-28.

Doeringer, P. B. and Piore, M. J. 1971. *International Labour Markets and Manpower Analysis*. Lexington, Mass.: D.C. Heath.

Fei, J. C. H., Ranis, G. and Kuo, S. W. Y. 1978. Growth and the family distribution of income by factor components. *Quarterly Journal of Economics*, 92, 17-53.

Fei, J. C. H., Ranis, G. and Kuo, S. W. Y. 1980. *Growth with Equity. The Taiwan Case*. New York: Oxford University Press.

Fields, G. S. 1975. Higher education and income distribution in a less developed country. *Oxford Economic Papers*, 27, 906-25.

Fields, G. S. 1977. Who benefits from economic development? - a re-examination of Brazilian growth in the 1960s. *American Economic Review*, 67, 570-82.

Fields, G. S. 1979a. A welfare economic approach to growth and distribution in the dual economy. *Quarterly Journal of Economics*, 93, 325-53.

Fields, G. S. 1979b. Decomposing LDC inequality. *Oxford Economic Papers*, 31, 437-59.

Fields, G. S. 1979c. Income inequality in urban Colombia: a decomposition analysis. *Review of Income and Wealth*, 25, 327-41.

Fields, G. S. 1980. Reply to comments to Who benefits from economic development? *American Economic Review*, 70, 257-62.

Fields, G. S. 1984. Employment, income distribution and economic growth in seven small economies. *Economic Journal*, 94, 74-83.

Fields, G. S. and Schultz, T. P. 1980. Regional inequality and other sources of income variation in Colombia. *Economic Development and Cultural Change*, 28, 447-67.

Figueroa, A. 1984. Crisis and income distribution in Peru, 1975-1980. In H-P. Nissen (ed.), *Towards Income Distribution Policies*. Tilburg: European Association of Development Research and Training Institutes, Book Series 3.

Fishlow, A. 1972. Brazilian size distribution of income. *American Economic Review, Papers and Proceedings*, 62, 391-402.

Fishlow, A. 1980. Comment to Who benefits from economic development? *American Economic Review*, 70, 250-6.

Foster, J., Greer, J. and Thorbecke, E. 1984. A class of decomposable poverty measures, *Econometrica*, 52, 761-6.

Foxley, A. (ed.) 1976. *Income Distribution in Latin America.* Cambridge: Cambridge University Press.

Foxley, A., Aninat, E. and Arellano, J. P. 1979. *Redistributive Effects of Government Programmes.* Oxford: Pergamon Press.

Francks, P. 1979. The development of new techniques in agriculture: the case of mechanization of irrigation in the Saga plain area of Japan. *World Development,* 7, 531-9.

Frank, C. R. Jr and Webb, R. C. (eds). 1977. *Income Distribution and Growth in the Less-Developed Countries.* Washington, DC: The Brookings Institution.

Fransman, M. 1985. Conceptualizing technical change in the Third World in the 1980's: an interpretative survey. *Journal of Development Studies,* 21, 572-652.

Gerhardt, J. 1975. 'The diffusion of hybrid maize in Western Kenya'. Princeton University, Ph.D. thesis.

Gibrat, R. 1931. *Les Inégalités Economiques.* Paris: Recueil Sirey.

Gonzales-Vega, C. and Cespedes, V. H. 1983. *Growth and Equity: Changes in Income Distribution in Costa Rica.* New York: UN.

Griffin, K. 1974. *The Political Economy of Agrarian Change. An Essay on the Green Revolution.* London: Macmillan

Griffin, K. 1981. *Land Concentration and Rural Poverty,* 2nd edn. London: Macmillan.

Griffin, K. and Ghose, A. K. 1979. Growth and impoverishment in the rural areas of Asia. *World Development,* 7, 361-83.

Griffin, K. and Khan, A. R. 1978. Poverty in the Third World: ugly facts and fancy models. *World Development,* 6, 295-304.

Guisinger, S. and Hicks, N. L. 1978. Long-term trends in income distribution in Pakistan. *World Development,* 6, 1271-80.

Haaland, G. and Keddeman, W. 1984. Poverty analysis: the case of rural Somalia. *Economic Development and Cultural Change,* 32, 843-60.

Harbison, F. H. 1977. The education-income connection. In C. R. Frank Jr. and R. C. Webb (eds), *Income Distribution and Growth in the Less-Developed Countries.* Washington, DC: The Brookings Institution.

Hayden, C. and Round, J. I. 1982. Developments in social accounting methods as applied to the analysis of income distribution and employment issues. *World Development,* 10, 451-65.

Hicks, J. 1939. *Value and Capital.* Oxford: Oxford University Press.

Hinchliffe, K. 1975. Education, individual earnings and earnings distribution, In F. Stewart (ed.), *Employment, Income Distribution and Development.* London: Frank Cass.

Hoerr, O. D. 1973. Education, income and equity in Malaysia. *Economic Development and Cultural Change,* 21, 247-73.

Hopkins, M. and van der Hoeven, R. 1983. *Basic Needs and Development Planning.* Aldershot: Gower.

Hsia, R. and Chau, L. 1978a. *Industrialization, Employment and Income Distribution. A Case Study of Hong-Kong.* London: Croom Helm.

Hsia, R. and Chau, L. 1978b. Industrialization and income distribution in Hong-Kong. *International Labour Review,* 117, 465-79.

ILO, 1976. *Employment, Growth, and Basic Needs.* Geneva: ILO.

ILO, 1977. *Poverty and Landlessness in Rural Asia.* WEP Study. Geneva: ILO.

Jallade, J.-P. 1976. Education finance and income distribution. *World Development,* 4, 435-43.

Johnson, H. G. 1973. *The Theory of Income Distribution.* London: Gray-Mills.

Kaldor, N. 1956. Alternative theories of income distribution. *Review of Economic Studies,* 23, 94-100.

Kalecki, M. 1950. The distribution of the national income. In American Economic Association, *Readings in the Theory of Income Distribution*. London: Allen and Unwin.

Khan, A. R. and Lee, E. (eds). 1984. *Poverty in Rural Asia*. Bangkok: ILO.

King, D. Y. and Weldon, P. D. 1977. Income distribution and levels of living in Java, 1963-1970. *Economic Development and Cultural Change*, 25, 699-711.

Kish, L. 1965. *Survey Sampling*. New York: Wiley.

Knight, J. B. 1976. Explaining income distribution in less developed countries: a framework and an agenda. *Oxford Bulletin of Economics and Statistics*, 38, 161-77.

Koo, H. 1984. The political economy of income distribution in South Korea: the impact of the State's industrialization policies. *World Development*, 12, 1029-37.

Kravis, B. 1960. International differences in the distribution of income. *Review of Economics and Statistics*, 42, 408-16.

Krueger, A. O. 1978. *Liberalization Attempts and Consequences*. Cambridge, Mass.: Ballinger.

Kuznets, S. 1955. Economic growth and income inequality. *American Economic Review*, 45, 1-28.

Kuznets, S. 1963. Quantitative aspects of the economic growth of nations. VIII: Distribution of income by size. *Economic Development and Cultural Change*, 11, 1-80.

Lal, D. 1976. Distribution and development: a review article. *World Development*, 4, 725-38.

Lardy, N. R. 1978. *Economic Growth and Distribution in China*. New York and London: Cambridge University Press.

Lecaillon, J., Paukert, F., Morrison, C. and Germidis, C. 1983. *Income Distribution and Economic Development: an Analytical Survey*. Geneva: ILO.

Lee, E. 1977. Development and income distribution: a case study of Sri Lanka and Malaysia. *World Development* 5, 279-89.

Lee, E. 1979. Egalitarian peasant farming and rural development: the case of South Korea. *World Development*, 7, 493-517.

Lewis, W. A. 1954. Economic development with unlimited supplies of labour. *Manchester School of Economic and Social Studies*, 22, 139-91.

Lipton, M. 1977. *Why Poor People Stay Poor. Urban Bias in World Development*. London: Temple Smith.

Lipton, M. 1978. Inter-farm, interregional and farm–non-farm income distribution: the impact of the new varieties. *World Development*, 6, 319-37.

Lipton, M. 1983a. *Poverty, Undernutrition and Hunger*. World Bank Staff Working Paper No. 597. Washington, DC: World Bank.

Lipton, M. 1983b. *Labour and Poverty*. World Bank Staff Working Paper No. 616. Washington, DC: World Bank.

Little, I. M. D., Scitovsky, T. and Scott, M. 1970. *Industry and Trade in Some Developing Countries*. London: Oxford University Press.

Loehr, W. and Powelson, J. P. (eds). 1977. *Economic Development, Poverty and Income Distribution*. Boulder, Col.: Westview Press.

Lydall, H. 1977. *Income Distribution During the Process of Development*. WEP Working Paper. Income Distribution and Employment Programme. Geneva: ILO.

MacEwan, A. 1981. *Revolution and Economic Development in Cuba*. London: Macmillan.

Mann, A. J. 1985. Economic development, income distribution, and real income levels: Puerto Rico, 1953-1977. *Economic Development and Cultural Change*, 33, 485-502.

Mathur, S. C. 1985. Rural poverty and agricultural performance in India. *Journal of Development Studies*, 21, 422-39.

Meerman, J. 1979. *Public Expenditure in Malaysia. Who Benefits and Why*. New York: Oxford University Press.

Meier, G. M. 1976. *Leading Issues in Economic Development*, 3rd edn. New York: Oxford University Press.

Mellor, J. C. 1978. Food price policy and income distribution in low income countries. *Economic Development and Cultural Change*, 27, 1–26.

Mincer, J. 1958. Investment in human capital and personal income distribution. *Journal of Political Economy*, 66, 291–302.

Mincer, J. 1974. *Schooling, Experience, and Earnings*. New York: National Bureau of Economic Research.

Minhas, B. 1970. Rural poverty, land distribution and development strategy: facts. *Indian Economic Review*, 3, 97–128.

Morawetz, D. 1974. Employment implications of industrialization in developing countries: a survey. *Economic Journal*, 84, 491–552.

Morley, S. A. 1982. *Labour Markets and Inequitable Growth: the Case of Authoritarian Capitalism in Brazil*. Cambridge: Cambridge University Press.

Murty, G. V. S. N. 1985. Prices and inequalities in a developing economy: the Case of India. *Journal of Development Studies*, 21, 533–47.

Myrdal, G. 1968. *Asian Drama*. New York: Pantheon.

Nafzinger, E. W. 1977. Entrepreneurship, social mobility, and income redistribution in south India. *American Economic Review, Papers and Proceedings*, 67, 76–80.

Nayyar, R. 1979. Rural poverty in Bihar 1961–62 to 1970–71. *Journal of Development Studies*, 15, 194–201.

Nguyen, D. T. and Martinez-Saldivar, M. L. M. 1979. The effects of land reform on agricultural production, employment and income distribution: a statistical study of Mexican states, 1959–69. *Economic Journal*, 89, 624–35.

Nissen, H.-P. 1984. *Towards Income Distribution Policies*. Tilburg: European Association of Development Research and Training Institutes, Book Series 3.

Nugent, J. B. 1983. An alternative source of measurement error as an explanation for the inverted-U hypothesis. *Economic Development and Cultural Change*, 31, 385–404.

Nugent, J. B. and Walther, R. J. 1982. Short run changes in rural income inequality: a decomposition analysis. *Journal of Development Studies*, 18, 239–69.

Oshima, H. 1962. The international comparison of size distribution of family income with special reference to Asia. *Review of Economics and Statistics*, 44, 439–45.

Osmani, S. R. 1982. *Economic Inequality and Group Welfare: a Theory of Comparison with Application to Bangladesh*. Oxford: Clarendon Press.

Osmani, S. R. and Rahman, A. 1983. *Income Distribution in Bangladesh*. New York: UN.

Pareto, V. 1897. *Cours d'Économie Politique*. Lausanne: Rouge.

Paukert, F. 1973. Income distribution at different levels of development: a survey of evidence. *International Labour Review*, 108, 97–125.

Perkins, D. H. 1980. The central features of China's economic development. In R. F. Dernberger (ed.), *China's Development Experience in Comparative Perspective*. Cambridge, Mass.: Harvard University Press.

Pigou, A. C. 1932. *The Economics of Welfare*, 4th edn. London: Macmillan.

Psacharopoulos, G. 1977. Schooling, experience and earnings: the case of an LDC. *Journal of Development Economics*, 4, 39–48.

Pyatt, G. and Roe, A. 1977. *Social Accounting for Development Planning with Special Reference to Sri Lanka*. Cambridge: Cambridge University Press.

Pyatt, G. and Round, J. I. 1977. Social accounting matrices for development planning. *Review of Income and Wealth*, 23, 339–64.

Pyatt, G. and Round, J. I. 1979. Accounting and fixed price multipliers in a social accounting matrix framework. *Economic Journal*, 89, 850–73.

Quan, N. T. and Koo, A. Y. C. 1985. Concentration of land holdings: an explanation of Kuznets' conjecture. *Journal of Development Economics*, 18, 101-17.

Rajaraman, I. 1975. Poverty, inequality, and economic growth: rural Punjab 1960/61-1970/71. *Journal of Development Studies*, 11, 278-90.

Ram, R. 1984. Population increase, economic growth, educational inequality, and income distribution. *Journal of Development Economics*, 14, 419-28.

Ranis, G. 1978. Equity with growth in Taiwan: How 'special' is the 'special case'? *World Development*, 6, 397-409.

Rao, D. G. 1978. Economic growth and equity in the Republic of Korea. *World Development*, 6, 383-96.

Rawls, J. 1971. *A Theory of Justice*. Cambridge, Mass.: Harvard University Press.

Reder, M. W. 1969. A partial survey of the theory of income size distribution. In L. Soltow (ed.), *Six Papers on the Size Distribution of Income and Wealth*. New York: Columbia University Press.

Robinson, S. 1976. A note on the inverted-U hypothesis relating income inequality and economic development. *American Economic Review, Papers and Proceedings*, 66, 122-27.

Rodgers, G. B. 1978. *An Analysis of Education, Employment and Income Distribution Using an Economic-Demographic Model of the Philippines*. WEP-Working Paper, Population and Employment Programme. Geneva: ILO.

Rodgers, G. B., Hopkins, M. J. D. and Wery, R. 1978. *Population, Employment and Inequality: Bachue-Philippines*. Westmead: Saxon House.

Round, J. I. 1984. Income distribution within a social accounting matrix: a review of some experience in Malaysia and other LDCs. In H.-P. Nissen (ed.), *Towards Income Distribution Policies*. Tilburg: European Association of Development Research and Training Institutes, Book Series 3.

Sahota, G. S. 1978. Theories of personal income distribution: a survey. *Journal of Economic Literature*, 16, 1-55.

Saith, A. 1981. Production, prices and poverty in rural India. *Journal of Development Studies*, 17, 196-213.

Saith, A. 1983. Development and distribution: a critique of the cross country U-hypothesis. *Journal of Development Economics*, 13, 367-82.

Santiago, C. E. and Thorbecke, E. 1984. Regional and technological dualism: a dual–dual development framework applied to Puerto Rico. *Journal of Development Studies*, 20, 271-89.

Selowsky, M. 1981. Income distribution, basic needs and trade-offs with growth: the case of semi-industrialised Latin American countries. *World Development* 9, 73-92.

Sen, A. K. 1973. *On Economic Inequality*. Oxford: Clarendon Press.

Sen, A. K. 1974. Poverty, inequality, and unemployment: some conceptual issues in measurement. In T. N. Srinivasan and P. K. Bardhan (eds), *Poverty and Income Distribution in India*. Calcutta: Statistical Publishing Society.

Sen, A. K. 1975. *Employment, Technology and Development*. Oxford: Clarendon Press.

Sen, A. K. 1976. Poverty: an ordinal approach to measurement. *Econometrica*, 44, 219-31.

Sen, A. K. 1980. *Levels of Poverty: Policy and Change*. World Bank Staff Working Paper No. 401. Washington, DC: World Bank.

Sen, A. K. 1981. *Poverty and Famines: an Essay on Entitlements and Deprivation*. Oxford: Clarendon Press.

Shalit, H. 1985. Calculating the Gini index of inequality for individual data. *Oxford Bulletin of Economics and Statistics*, 47, 185-9.

Singh, J. 1979. *Small Farmers and the Landless in South Asia.* World Bank Staff Working Papers No. 320. Washington, DC: World Bank.

Smith, C. L. 1980. Community wealth concentration: comparisons in general evolution and development. *Economic Development and Cultural Change,* 28, 801–18.

Snodgrass, D. R. 1980. *Inequality and Economic Development in Malaysia.* Kuala Lumpur: Oxford University Press.

Soltow, L. (ed.). 1969. *Six Papers on the Size Distribution of Wealth and Income.* National Bureau of Economic Research. New York: Columbia University Press.

Srinivasan, T. N. and Bardhan, P. K. (eds). 1974. *Poverty and Income Distribution in India.* Calcutta: Statistical Publishing Society.

Stewart, F. 1974. Technology and employment in LDCs. *World Development,* 2, 17–46.

Stewart, F. (ed.). 1975. *Employment, Income Distribution, and Development.* London: Frank Cass.

Stewart, F. 1978. Inequality, technology and payments systems. *World Development,* 6, 275–93.

Stiglitz, J. E. 1975. The theory of 'screening', education, and the distribution of income. *American Economic Review,* 65, 283–300.

Swamy, S. 1967. Structural change and the distribution of income by size: the case of India. *Review of Income and Wealth,* series B, 155–70.

Szal, R. 1984. Trends in income distribution in South Korea and their relationship to policy and planning. In H.-P. Nissen (ed.), *Towards Income Distribution Policies.* Tilburg: European Association of Development Research and Training Institutes, Book Series 3.

Taylor, L., Bacha, E. L., Cardoso, E. A. and Lysy, F. J. 1980. *Models of Growth and Distribution for Brazil.* New York: Oxford University Press.

Thomas, V. 1980. Spatial differences in poverty: the case of Peru. *Journal of Development Economics,* 12, 85–98.

Tinbergen, J. 1970. A positive and normative theory of income distribution. *Review of Income and Wealth,* 16, 221–34.

Tinbergen, J. 1975. *Income Distribution. Analysis and Policy.* Amsterdam: North-Holland.

Tokman, V. E. 1975. Income distribution, technology and employment in developing countries: an application to Ecuador. *Journal of Development Economics,* 2, 49–80.

Tuckman, B. H. 1976. The Green Revolution and the distribution of agricultural income in Mexico. *World Development,* 4, 17–24.

Urrutia, M. 1976. Income distribution in Colombia. *International Labour Review,* 113, 205–16.

van der Hoeven, R. 1977. *Zambia's Income Distribution During the Early Seventies.* WEP-Working Paper. Income Distribution and Employment Programme. Geneva: ILO.

van Ginneken, W. 1980a. *Socio-Economic Groups and Income Distribution in Mexico.* London: Croom Helm.

van Ginneken, W. 1980b. Some methods of poverty analysis: an application to Iranian data. *World Development,* 8, 639–46.

van Ginneken, W. 1984. Socio-economic groups and income distribution in Mexico. In H.-P. Nissen (ed.), *Towards Income Distribution Policies.* Tilburg: European Association of Development Research and Training Institutes, Book Series 3.

van de Walle, D. 1985. Population growth and poverty: another look at the Indian time series data. *Journal of Development Studies,* 21, 429–39.

Wehr, P. 1977. Intermediate technology and income distribution in developing nations. In W. Loehr and J. P. Powelson (eds), *Economic Development, Poverty and Income Distribution.* Boulder, Col.: Westview Press.

Williamson, J. G. 1965. Regional inequality and the process of national development: a description of patterns. *Economic Development and Cultural Change*, 13, 1–84.

Yotopoulos, P. A. and Nugent, J. B. 1976. *Economics of Development: Empirical Investigations*. New York: Harper and Row.

Young, F. W., Freebaim, D. K. and Snipper, R. 1979. The structural context of rural poverty in Mexico: a cross-state comparison. *Economic Development and Cultural Change*, 27, 669–86.

5

Inflation and stabilization policy in LDCs

Colin Kirkpatrick and Frederick Nixson

5.1 Introduction

This survey is concerned with the inflation experience of less developed countries (LDCs). Inflation is 'a process of continuously rising prices, or equivalently, of a continuously falling value of money' (Laidler and Parkin, 1975, p. 741). This definition of course refers to the symptoms of inflation but says nothing about the causes or effects of inflation. It implies that a rise in the price of individual commodities is not inflationary if offset by falls in other prices. In addition, a once-and-for-all increase in the general price level is not inflationary unless it is accompanied by responses which produce a series of price increases continuing over time (Killick, 1981b, chapter 7). A sustained rise in the general price level means that a given sum of money will buy a smaller quantity of goods: hence the alternative characterization of inflation as a continuous decline in the purchasing power of money.

Although inflation has traditionally been seen as an economic phenomenon, there is now greater awareness that the study of its causes and consequences cannot be confined to economic analysis alone: 'it pervades the political and social structures of society and may become embedded in those structures' (Hirsch and Goldthorpe, 1978, p. 1). *A fortiori*, the analysis of inflation in LDCs cannot be divorced from the more general problem of underdevelopment. Any attempt to avoid the discussion of social, political and institutional factors will merely obscure the real issues involved, and will quite illegitimately reduce a complex economic and socio-political problem to a 'straightforward' technical one. As Hirschman (1981, p. 177) has argued:

It has long been obvious that the roots of inflation . . . lie deep in the social and political structure in general, and in social and political conflict and conflict management in particular . . . it would be difficult to find an economist who would not agree that

Thanks are due to Philip Leeson for comments on an earlier version.

'underlying' social and political forces play a decisive role in causing both inflation and the success or failure of anti-inflationary policies.

The remainder of the survey is structured as follows. Section 5.2 considers the record of inflation in LDCs. Section 5.3 reviews the literature on the causes of inflation in LDCs, concentrating on the structuralist–monetarist debate. The relationship between the balance of payments and inflation in the context of the developing economy is discussed in section 5.4. The consequences of inflation provide the focus for section 5.5. The penultimate section reviews the recent controversy concerning the role of the International Monetary Fund in LDCs. The final section provides a summary and concluding comments.

5.2 The record of inflation in LDCs

Table 5.1 presents data on the record of inflation for both developed and less developed countries from the mid-1960s onwards.

The first point to note is that LDCs are clearly more prone to inflation than are developed, industrial economies. Over the period 1967–76 the weighted average rate of inflation of the LDCs was approximately twice that of the developed economies. From 1977 onwards the LDC rate was approximately three times as great as that of the developed economies, and in the 1980s the gap widened even further. As the IMF (1984, p. 12) noted, in the LDCs, unlike in the developed economies, inflation has not shown uniform signs of decelerating in recent years, although the estimated and projected rates for 1985 and 1986 are lower than the rates of inflation experienced in previous years. A second point relates to the varied experience of LDCs with respect to inflation. The weighted average figures in table 5.1 show that the western hemisphere LDCs typically experienced rates of inflation far above those of other LDCs. Asian LDCs in particular appear to have been remarkably successful in containing inflationary pressures. The variation in individual country inflation rates explains the differences between the weighted average and median rates of inflation recorded in table 5.1. The weighted average figures are, according to the International Monetary Fund (IMF, 1984, p. 12) 'dominated by the poor performance of a few large countries', and they thus tend to overstate the rise in inflation for the majority of LDCs. An examination of line three of table 5.1 clearly shows that for developing countries the median inflation rate is significantly less than the weighted average rate. The median inflation rate peaked in 1980, declined to 10 per cent in 1983 and is estimated to have fallen further since then. The weighted average rate also reached a peak in 1980, declined marginally in the subsequent two years, but rose quite substantially in 1983 and 1984. This disparity is attributed by the IMF to the 'quite atypical' inflationary experience of five countries – Argentina, Bolivia, Brazil, Israel and Peru – for which the composite rate of inflation accelerated from about 100 per cent in 1981–2 to almost 260 per cent in 1984 (IMF, 1984, p. 71).[1]

An additional feature of inflation in LDCs deserves mention. Fluctuations around the inflationary trend have tended to be greater in LDCs than in

Table 5.1 Inflation, 1967–86[a] (percentages)

	Average 1967–76[b]	1977	1978	1979	1980	1981	1982	1983	1984	1985[e]	1986[e]
Industrial countries[c]	6.7	7.5	7.6	8.0	9.2	8.7	7.2	4.9	4.1	3.9	3.7
Developing countries[d]	13.8	24.8	18.8	21.5	27.3	26.1	24.7	33.0	37.7	34.8	22.6
Median inflation rates	7.8	11.3	9.8	11.5	14.5	13.3	10.7	9.8	10.0	9.3	8.0
By region[d]											
Africa	8.5	18.8	16.9	16.7	16.6	21.4	13.4	19.0	17.8	16.1	12.7
Asia	9.4	7.8	4.0	8.0	13.1	10.6	6.2	6.6	6.9	5.5	5.4
Europe	9.0	15.1	19.8	25.9	37.9	24.0	23.8	23.2	28.0	22.4	19.0
Middle East	8.7	18.0	12.8	11.1	17.4	15.6	12.7	12.7	16.5	17.3	15.1
Western hemisphere	24.5	49.9	41.9	46.5	54.0	58.6	65.5	100.5	119.8	113.7	59.7
By analytical criteria[d]											
Fuel exporters	9.7	18.1	12.5	11.8	15.9	16.4	18.0	25.5	20.1	15.3	12.1
Non-fuel exporters	16.2	28.0	21.4	25.7	32.2	30.6	28.0	36.9	47.1	45.0	27.9
Market borrowers	18.7	32.6	28.2	31.8	36.3	38.7	38.5	55.5	65.7	60.3	35.0
Official borrowers	9.7	17.3	13.7	19.5	22.3	28.4	17.2	21.9	15.8	13.8	13.4

[a] As measured by changes in GNP deflators for industrial countries and changes in consumer prices for developing countries.

[b] Compound annual rates of change.

[c] Averages of percentage changes in GNP deflators for individual countries weighted by the average US dollar value of their respective GNPs over the preceding 3 years.

[d] Except where otherwise noted, percentage changes of geometric averages of indices of consumer prices for individual countries weighted by the average US dollar value of their respective GNPs over the preceding 3 years. Estimates exclude China prior to 1978.

[e] Figures for 1985 are estimates; figures for 1986 are projections.

Source: IMF (1985, table 7, p. 212).

developed economies, with few LDCs experiencing steady inflation. Table 5.2 shows that, over the period 1960–81, price variability was more than three times higher in LDCs than in industrialized countries. There are sizeable regional differences, however, with Latin America having the highest level of price instability.

Finally, there appears to be a positive relationship between the level and variability of inflation in LDCs. The variation in the strength of the relationship across regions is small, but there is some evidence to suggest that the sensitivity of the variability of inflation to its level is greater in higher inflation regimes (Ram, 1985, table 2).[2]

To summarize, although relatively few LDCs have experienced hyper-inflation, most have, since the mid-1960s, had higher and more variable rates of inflation than those recorded in the developed industrialized economies.[3] The causes, consequences and control of inflation thus remain important issues for most LDCs.

5.3 The causes of inflation in LDCs: the early structuralist–monetarist debate[4]

The debate over the causes of inflation in LDCs arose in the mid-1950s when, as a result of chronic inflation and balance of payments problems, a number of major Latin American economies sought the assistance of the International Monetary Fund. The analysis and recommendations of the 1954 Klein–Saks Mission to Chile were challenged by the 'structuralist' school, centred around the Economic Commission for Latin America. This debate over the analysis of inflation in turn led to the emergence of the more general structuralist approach to the problems of underdevelopment (see survey 2, section 2.3.2 for a summary of the structuralist approach).[5]

Table 5.2 Variability in inflation rates, 1960–81[a] (percentages)

Region	1960–81
Industrial Countries	3.9
Developing Countries	10.3
Africa	7.6
East Asia[b]	5.6
South Asia	9.2
Latin America	12.6

[a] Variation is measured as the standard deviation of the annual inflation rate in the country during the period.
[b] Excluding Indonesia.

Source: Ram (1985, Appendix).

The structuralist approach was juxtaposed with the orthodox 'monetarist' approach of the IMF. Each represented a distinctive approach to the problem of inflation in particular, and to economic development in general. In addition, the two groups were usually distinguished by differences in political ideology, structuralists being 'of the left' and monetarists 'of the right' (Felix, 1961).[6] Seers (1964, p. 89) delineated the two approaches in the following way:

it is . . . not just a technical issue in economic theory. At the heart of the controversy . . . are two different ways of looking at economic development, in fact two completely different attitudes toward the nature of social change, two different sets of value judgements about the purpose of economic activity and the ends of economic policy, and two incompatible views on what is politically possible.

5.3.1 The structuralist view

The structuralists argued that inflation was inevitable in an economy that was attempting to grow rapidly in the presence of structural bottlenecks or constraints, defined by Thorp (1971, p. 185) as 'certain fundamental facets of the economic, institutional and socio-political structure of the country which in one way or another inhibit expansion'. The fundamental changes in the socio-economic structure that were required by economic development could not be brought about by the price mechanism operating within very imperfect market structures characterized by limited resource mobility, and thus shortages and disequilibria appeared.

The structuralist analysis was concerned with the identification and analysis of these alleged bottlenecks (the basic or structural inflationary pressures, to use Sunkel's (1960) terminology).[7] The key bottlenecks were generally taken to be (1) the inelastic supply of foodstuffs, (2) the foreign exchange constraint and (3) the government budget constraint.

With respect to the agricultural sector bottleneck, it was argued that urbanization and rising incomes led to a rapidly increasing demand for foodstuffs which could not be met by the agricultural sector. The supply response was poor because of the structural constraints within the sector – the domination either by large non-capitalistic *latifundia* which were not profit-maximizers, or by *minifundia* operating almost at a subsistence level and hardly integrated into the market economy.[8] The inelastic supply constituted a structural inflationary factor. As Sunkel noted with respect to Chile:

the stagnation of global agricultural production cannot be attributed to market demand and/or price conditions, but must be due to factors inherent in the institutional and economic structure of the main part of the agricultural sector itself (Sunkel, 1960, p. 115).

The second major bottleneck, the foreign exchange constraint, arose because the rate of growth of foreign exchange receipts was not sufficient to meet rapidly rising import demands generated by accelerated development efforts, rapid population growth and the industrialization effort which took place in an environment of technological limitations, structural imbalances and imperfect factor mobility. Import shortages and rising import prices triggered off cumulative price rises; balance of payments difficulties eventually forced countries to devalue their currencies and this in turn added to domestic inflationary pressures, especially when the price elasticity of demand for imports was very low.

The third bottleneck, identified by some structuralist writers but not others, was the lack of internal financial resources (the fiscal constraint). Development efforts increased the scope of necessary government involvement in the economy (especially in the provision of social and physical infrastructure facilities), but government revenue rarely expanded sufficiently rapidly to meet the growth of expenditure. Tax structures were regressive and tax-collecting bureaucracies were sometimes 'antiquated, inefficient and . . . corrupt' (Baer, 1967, p. 10). The insufficiency of revenue was usually overcome by recourse to deficit financing, which had inflationary consequences.

For the various structural constraints to give rise to price increases, which in turn led to a rapid and continuous increase in the price level, there had to exist an effective transmission or propagation mechanism which permitted the manifestation of the various inflationary pressures. If various classes or groups in society did not attempt to maintain their relative positions in the face of price increases, the chances of an inflationary spiral being generated would be reduced, and the increase in prices would lead to a redistribution of income. In Chile, Sunkel (1960) argued that the propagation mechanism resulted from the inability of the political system to resolve two major struggles of economic interests; namely, the distribution of income between different social classes and the distribution of productive resources between the public and the private sectors of the economy. The propagation mechanism was thus seen as:

the ability of the different economic sectors and social groups continually to readjust their real income or expenditure: the wage-earning group through readjustment of salaries, wages and other benefits; private enterprise through price increases, and the public sector through an increase in nominal fiscal expenditure (Sunkel, 1960, p. 111).

One of the major components of the propagation mechanism was the budget deficit which was closely related to domestic credit expansion since public expenditure was not easily reduced and revenue not easily increased. The public sector deficit thus represented 'the existence of a number of structural problems which preclude the realisation of a balanced-budget policy' (Sunkel, 1960, p. 122). To the structuralist, the increase in the supply of money was a permissive factor which allowed the inflationary spiral to manifest itself and become cumulative – it was a symptom of the structural rigidities which give rise to the inflationary pressures, rather than the cause of inflation itself.

5.3.2 The monetarist view[9]

Monetarists saw inflation as a purely monetary phenomenon, originating in and sustained by expansionary monetary and fiscal policies (government deficit spending, expansionist credit policies and expansionary exchange operations of central banks). The control of inflation required as a necessary and sufficient condition the control of the money supply such that it grew at a rate consistent with the growth of demand for money at stable prices. Specifically, the rate of inflation would be reduced, and concomitant distortions in the economy eliminated, via the curbing of excess demand through monetary and fiscal policies, the control of wage increases and the elimination of over-valued exchange rates.

The monetary model is based on a stable demand function for real money balances. Such balances are demanded for transactions and precautionary purposes, and their level is hypothesized to be a function of the level of real income and the opportunity cost of holding money instead of alternative assets which could satisfy at least the precautionary motive. It is further argued that the money supply is exogenous and can be controlled by the monetary authorities (Ayre, 1982, p. 68). In this model, inflation is the result of the supply of money expanding more rapidly than the demand for money. The empirical evidence from LDCs suggests that the demand function for money is stable, although expected price changes rather than interest rates tend to be of greater significance than in developed economies. Nevertheless, some measure of income remains the main determinant of real money holdings (Ghatak, 1981, p. 33).

Monetarists did not deny the existence of constraints but they argued that they were not structural or autonomous in nature. They resulted from the price and exchange rate distortions which were generated by the inflation itself and government attempts to reduce the rate of price increase. For example, they argued that the alleged structural inelasticity of food supplies in fact resulted from the all-too-frequent administrative control of food prices, the result of attempts by governments to protect urban consumers and avoid growing pressures for wage increases. This interference in the operation of market forces had a disincentive effect on food producers, but it was a distortion induced by administrative controls and was not inherent in the structure of land ownership. High prices for some items were necessary to induce an adequate supply, but within the context of the overall control of the money supply and the re-allocation of resources through the market mechanism, high prices for such items were offset by low prices for others, and hence inflationary pressures were not generated. Monetarists further argued that the slow growth of exports was policy, rather than structurally, induced. Exchange rates were typically over-valued and development efforts 'inward-looking'.

Monetarists thus admitted the existence of constraints but reversed the causal relationship. The bottlenecks in the economy that retarded growth would be eliminated when inflation was brought under control. The majority of monetarists recognized the 'social priority of development', but argued that stable and sustained growth could only be achieved in an environment of monetary stability (Campos, 1967). Structuralists, on the other hand, were often accused of favouring inflation as a means of accelerating growth, but in general this was not the case. They were concerned with the problem of making stability compatible with development, but argued that price stability could only be achieved through economic growth, which was a long-run process. Short-run stabilization policies, although effective in reducing the rate of inflation, imposed heavy social and economic costs and retarded the processes of structural changes necessary for longer-term growth and development. In effect, structuralists preferred inflation to stagnation, it being regarded as the lesser of two evils.

5.3.3   Empirical evidence

Structuralism

An important investigation of one aspect of the structuralist analysis was carried out by Edel (1969) in his study of the alleged food supply bottlenecks in eight Latin American countries. He tested the propositions that (1) food supply lagged behind the required rate of growth, and (2) that this agricultural lag was associated with inflation, balance of payments difficulties and stagnation. The adequacy of food supply was defined as that rate of autonomous growth of production (resulting from the adoption of new techniques, increases in the labour force and area of production, etc.) sufficient to satisfy demand without any change in relative prices.

Edel found that in Mexico, Brazil and Venezuela, supply outpaced or at least approximately equalled food requirements. Taking into account price changes, five countries with inadequate growth rates (Chile, Colombia, Peru, Uruguay and Argentina) had increasing relative prices, and thus inadequate growth could not have been a function of price deterioration. He did not find a perfect relationship between food supply and inflation but the evidence justified the conclusion that

the direction of the relationship is the one indicated by the structuralist theory that less adequate food production means more inflation, as well as relative rises in the food prices, more food imports, and slower growth in other sectors of the economy (Edel 1969, pp. 135–6).

Furthermore, the degree of price control on foodstuffs did not appear to be related systematically to agricultural performance for the countries studied, whereas there was evidence that land tenure and low productivity were related to one another.[10]

In this study of Brazil, Kahil (1973) analysed four alleged structural constraints. These were the agricultural sector bottleneck, the inadequate mobility of capital, the external sector bottleneck and the effects of rapid urbanization (increased private and public demand for goods and services and increased costs of supplying food to the urban areas). He argued that structural weaknesses did not play a significant role in the evolution of the price level over the period studied (1946–64). The aggravation of these structural weaknesses was more an effect than a cause of inflation. Price rises were caused by large and growing public deficits, a too rapid expansion of bank credit in the early period and unnecessarily large and increasingly frequent increases in legal minimum wages at a later stage. These factors interacted in such a way that it was impossible to distinguish cause from effect, and thus the basic causes of inflation appeared to have become mere parts of the structuralist propagation mechanism.

Kahil qualified his monetarist conclusion by arguing that the factors ultimately responsible for inflation were political rather than economic. The two major policy aims of the 1950s were rapid industrialization and the winning of the allegiance of the urban masses, at the same time serving the interests of other politically important groups (big industrialists, bankers, etc.). Inflation was thus the outcome of the attempt by the state to promote growth and development and grant privileges (albeit temporary and illusory) to mutually antagonistic groups or classes. We discuss the implications of these conclusions below.

Argy (1970) attempted to assess the contribution of structural elements to inflation using data for 22 countries for the period 1958–65. He constructed a variety of indices to test four structural hypotheses – the demand-shift hypothesis (shifts in the composition of demand, as distinct from generalized excess demand, cause upward shifts of the price level), the export instability hypothesis (fluctuations in the export earnings will tend to create a long-term upward movement in the price level), the agricultural bottleneck hypothesis and the foreign exchange bottleneck (both discussed above). Two additional variables were included in some of the regressions – the government deficit rate and the rates of change in the money supply.

Argy concluded that the results for the structuralist variables were poor (except for the fact that there was a slight tendency for countries where food prices had risen most relative to the cost of living to have higher rates of inflation), but that the monetary variables performed well – 'In every case the addition of a monetary variable to structuralist variables improved substantially the results' (Argy, 1970, p. 83).

Argy's study clearly showed (as the author himself admitted) the difficulties involved in testing the structuralist position. It is very difficult to specify correctly and construct indicators which adequately encompass the essence of the alleged structuralist constraints. For example, to test the foreign exchange bottleneck, Argy used (1) the average annual percentage change in the terms of trade and (2) the average import ratio (imports over gross domestic production). But neither of these measures indicate the *capacity* to import, and are thus not a satisfactory test of the (*ex-ante*) balance of payments constraint. There is also likely to be significant multicollinearity between the independent variables used in the regression analysis.

Monetarism

Harberger's (1963) influential study of Chile covered the period 1939–58, during which inflation was almost continuous and the cost of living index rose over eight-fold. Within the monetarist framework, Harberger regressed the annual rate of price change in the cost of living index upon the percentage change in the money supply during the same year and the preceding one, and the percentage change in real income in that year. Expected changes in the cost of holding idle balances were allowed for by introducing past changes in the rate of inflation as an additional independent variable. Wage changes were also included in the regression equation.

The results of the analysis supported the monetarist interpretation, with each of the monetary variables statistically significant and the inclusion of the wages variable failing to increase the overall explanatory power of the monetary variables.

Vogel (1974) extended the Harberger model to 16 Latin American countries for the period 1950–69. The dependent variable was the consumer price index and the independent variables were money supply (currency plus demand deposits), real income and past changes in the rate of inflation (as a proxy for the expected cost of holding real balances). On the basis of his results, Vogel concluded that:

the most important result of the present study . . . is that a purely monetarist model, with no structuralist variables, reveals little heterogeneity among Latin American countries, in spite of their extreme diversity. The substantial differences in rates of inflation among these countries cannot under the present model be attributed to structural differences, but must rather be attributed primarily to differences in the behaviour of the money supply (Vogel, 1974, p. 113).

In reviewing other work on inflation in Latin America, Vogel noted that very different conclusions about the monetarist–structuralist controversy had been reached from essentially similar findings. He suggested that further work was needed on the determination of the money supply, and that structural variables could be added to the model. Even if a purely monetarist model could adequately explain the causes of inflation, stabilization policies might have to be more than purely monetarist in character, given that rates of inflation took up to 2 years to adjust to changes in the money supply, and that this might be a longer period of austerity than could be tolerated politically by the majority of Latin American regimes.[11]

Monetarists can be criticized for treating high correlation between the monetary variables and the inflation rate as evidence of causation, and failing to offer an explanation of the underlying causal relationships that exist between structural constraints, monetary expansion and inflation. Equally, structuralist writers can be criticized on the grounds that they devoted insufficient attention to the nature of the propagation mechanism in general, and the expansion of the money supply in particular (which is necessary, other things being equal, for the manifestation of spiralling price rises). Structuralist assertions that increases in the money supply are merely permissive may tend to obscure the wider socio-economic framework within which this policy option is chosen by, or forced upon, the government. Both structuralists and monetarists accepted the proposition that changes in the money supply occur in response to political factors, but the basic question remains as to whether these changes permit, or are the actual cause of, the inflationary process.

5.3.4 Integrating the monetarist and structuralist approaches

Dissatisfaction with the sharp dictotomy between monetarist and structuralist models encouraged attempts to develop models that would integrate elements of both approaches.

Wachter (1976) develops a reformulated structuralist model in which it is assumed food prices are more flexible than non-food prices. If prices rise in agriculture, even if there is no excess aggregate demand, inflation results in the short run, because prices in non-agricultural sectors do not fall by an equivalent amount. Once inflation becomes anticipated, and expectations are validated by monetary and fiscal policy, an on-going inflation is possible at the equilibrium-expected rate (Wachter, 1976, p. 136). This inflation rate cannot persist, however, without changes in government policy, specifically an increase in the rate of monetary expansion – 'for the higher inflation rate to be maintained, money must respond; but it is quite possible that the money supply is passive and does respond to higher prices' (p. 136).

The monetarist (Harberger) and reformulated structuralist models were tested by Wachter with data from Argentina, Chile, Brazil and Mexico. She concludes that:

The empirical results . . . support a broad model of inflation. The findings of significant coefficients with the anticipated signs for the demand-pull and expectational variables in the Harberger and Phillips-curve equations are consistent with the Latin American monetarist argument that excessive aggregate demand is responsible for inflation. However, the reformulated structuralist model is also substantially supported by the finding . . . of a significant and positive coefficient for the rate of change in the relative price of food (Wachter, 1976, p. 137).

Wachter also tested for the existence of a passive money supply in a two-way regression between prices and money and concludes that, at least for Brazil, Chile and Mexico, the 'structuralist hypothesis of a passive money supply cannot be rejected' (p. 137). For Argentina, the results indicated that structural imbalances had an impact on the inflation rate in the short run, but that in the longer run, because the monetary authorities refused to accommodate structural inflation, the existence of structural constraints did not result in a permanently higher rate of inflation.

Bhalla's (1981) approach was to combine the basic Harberger monetarist model with structuralist variables (relative food prices changes and import price changes) to form a 'hybrid reduced-form model'. The model is applied to annual time-series data for 29 developing countries covering the period 1956–75. The results indicate that the structural variables are important. The money supply variables are significant in both the Harberger model and the hybrid model, but 'for all of the countries the explanatory power of the monetarist model is con-siderably increased with the introduction of food supply bottlenecks and import price changes' (p. 85).[12]

The major problem of so-called 'hybrid' models of inflation is that they are not adequate tests of structuralist hypotheses. To adapt a monetarist model merely by the addition of a number of proxy variables for structural factors will almost certainly increase the overall statistical 'fit' of the equation. The problem remains, however, of identifying and measuring structural constraints, relating them to the process of growth and change occurring in LDCs, especially with respect to industrialization, and then constructing a genuinely structuralist model of inflation.

A third example of an attempt to integrate the monetarist and structuralist model is found in the analysis of the fiscal constraint bottleneck by Aghevli and Khan (1978). In this model the fiscal deficit performs the dual role of both the original force and the propagating mechanism in the inflationary process. Having accepted that government deficits perform a major destabilizing role, the deficit in turn is explained by the fundamental difference in the behaviour of government expenditure and revenue during an inflationary process:

Even if governments fully recognise the need to restrain expenditures during periods of inflation, they find it difficult to reduce their commitments in real terms. On the other hand, in contrast to the situation in most developed countries, where nominal revenues often more than keep pace with price increases, in developing countries they lag substantially behind. The contrast arises both because of low nominal income elasticities of tax systems and long lags in tax collection in developing countries (p. 391).

An initial inflationary shock will lead to an expansion of the budget deficit, which in turn leads to an expansion of the money supply. Inflation-induced fiscal deficits, explained in terms of the structural constraints on the fiscal system, thus become one of the dynamic forces sustaining inflation in LDCs. The Aghevli and Khan model is monetarist in the sense that the expansion of the money supply leads to inflation, but, in contrast to the Harberger-type models, the money supply is no longer exogenous, the fiscal constraint constituting a crucial link in the inflationary process.[13]

The Aghevli and Khan model can be criticized, however, from a structuralist perspective for presenting a somewhat superficial and mechanical explanation of the budget deficit, and of failing to identify the more fundamental determinants of government expenditure and revenue in LDCs.[14]

5.4   Inflation and the balance of payments

5.4.1   The monetary approach to the balance of payments

The persistence of high rates of inflation in many Latin American economies during the 1950s was linked to increasing balance of payments (BOP) difficulties, and precipitated the adoption of stabilization programmes designed to correct these macroeconomic disequilibria. Once the limits on the temporary financing of balance of payments deficits by running down reserves or borrowing had been exhausted, countries found it necessary to approach the International Monetary Fund (IMF), whose principal function is to assist member countries experiencing serious BOP disequilibria. The means by which the IMF provides support is to assure a member that it can borrow foreign exchange during a specified period of time, and up to a specified amount, provided the member adheres to the terms of the borrowing. The conditions that the Fund attaches to its loans require the borrowing country to adopt various economic measures, designed to correct the BOP problem and reduce inflation to an acceptable level.[15]

The policy recommendations of the IMF reflected an underlying 'view' of the causes of the LDCs' macro-disequilibria. The economic theory that formed the basis for the Fund's programmes was the monetary theory of the balance of payments. The model developed by Polak (1957), at that time deputy director of the Fund's research department, established the basic conclusions of the monetary approach to the balance of payments (MABOP), and became the basis for the operations of the IMF's country programmes.

The MABOP extends the quantity theory approach to the open economy, and emphasizes the role of the balance of payments in achieving an equilibrium between the demand and supply of money. The nominal demand for money is a stable function of nominal income. Real income is assumed to be fixed at the full capacity level of output, so that changes in nominal income involve changes in prices rather than output. In the open economy the supply of money consists of the sum of domestic credit creation and international reserves. A disequilibrium between the demand and supply of money is removed by some combination of changes in prices, domestic credit creation, and/or international reserves.

The Polak version of the MABOP concentrates on the relationship between changes in reserves and changes in domestic credit creation. A number of assumptions are made in order to highlight the adjustment process. In addition to assuming a fixed exchange rate and international capital immobility, the level of exports is taken to be determined exogenously. Starting from an initial situation of monetary equilibrium, an expansion in the rate of domestic credit creation has the immediate effect of creating excess cash balances. Individuals reduce their surplus cash holdings by increased expenditure, which in the Polak model is made entirely on imports. The current account deteriorates, reserves decline, and provided the authorities do not 'sterilize' the effect of the change in reserves on total money supply by means of a compensating change in domestic credit creation, the disequilibrium is removed by a fall in the supply of money until monetary equilibrium is restored.

The policy implication of Polak's model is that BOP difficulties are caused by excess domestic credit creation: deficit countries should therefore limit their rate of domestic credit creation to a level consistent with a satisfactory BOP outcome. By emphasizing the link between external balance and changes in the supply of money, Polak's model directs attention away from the role of changes in the demand for money, prices and nominal income, in the adjustment process. The implication is that excessive domestic credit creation is completely offset by changes in reserves, so that the impact on prices and output is negligible.

In the 1960s an alternative version of the MABOP was developed, which gave more attention to the role of price changes in the adjustment process.[16] A distinction is drawn between internationally traded and non-traded goods. With the initial monetary equilibrium disturbed by an increase in domestic credit creation, part of the increased demand is for domestically produced goods. Since, however, the economy is assumed to be operating at or near to its full capacity output level, the result is a rise in the price of non-traded goods. This in turn diverts productive resources from the traded to the non-traded sector, reducing the supply of exports, and worsening the current account. At the same time, the increase in non-traded goods prices may lead to a rise in wages, with further upward pressure on the general price level. The policy requirement is the same as in the Polak model: to reduce the current account deficit and rate of inflation it is necessary to lower the rate of domestic credit creation (or abandon a fixed exchange rate policy).

A third variant of the MABOP, known as 'global monetarism' (Whitman, 1975), offers the most direct relation between the domestic inflation rate and the balance of payments. From a global monetarist perspective it is argued that all countries are 'co-participants in a common process of world inflation' (Harberger, 1978). The world economy had become highly integrated, and the fixed exchange rate regimes, which existed up till the early 1970s, 'operated as the international equivalent of a common (domestic) currency, linking the monetary forces operating in the various countries of the world in the same way that the possession of a common currency brings about a convergence of inflationary trends in the different regions of a nation-state' (Burton, 1982, p. 23). The world inflation rate is determined by the rate of growth of the world money supply, and for a small open economy, with a fixed exchange rate system, the domestic rate of inflation is given exogenously by the world rate of inflation. In Harberger's (1978) words,

the cause of inflation in Costa Rica or Iran or the Philippines cannot be very different from that of the 'world inflation' so long as they maintain a fixed exchange rate with the major currencies, and so long as they do not introduce dramatic new interferences with the movement of goods and services (p.154).

5.4.2 The structuralist response

The MABOP has two major implications for inflation analysis: first, the excessive domestic inflation and BOP difficulties are due essentially to domestic macro-mismanagement; and second, the process of correcting these macro-disequilibria has no effect on the level of real output in the economy. Both these propositions of the monetary approach to inflation in the open economy have been challenged by structuralists.

BOP disequilibrium and inflation

As we saw in section 5.3.1, the early structuralist literature emphasized the role of the foreign exchange bottleneck in creating BOP difficulties and inflationary pressures. The growth in export earnings was thought to be insufficient to meet the rapidly increasing import needs associated with development, with the availability of foreign exchange acting as the effective constraint on growth. Shortfalls in 'essential' imports in turn had a deleterious effect on the level of domestic economic activity and output.

Recent research into the causes of LDCs' BOP disequilibria provides support for the structuralist argument. Dell and Lawrence's (1980) detailed study of the ways in which LDCs adjusted to the oil crisis of 1974–5 found that the majority had been forced to compress 'developmental' imports below the level normally required at current levels of activity. Killick (1984) suggests that this experience continued into the early 1980s. By 1981 the import volume of low-income LDCs was only 6 per cent above the 1973 level, implying a substantial per capita reduction.

The study by Khan and Knight (1983) used a sample of 32 non-oil LDCs during the period 1973–81 to examine the relative importance of external and domestic factors in current account movements. Three factors are classified as external – the deterioration in the terms of trade, the slowdown in economic activity in the industrial countries, and the increase in real interest rates in international credit markets. Domestic factors are proxied by increasing fiscal deficits and appreciation of real effective exchange rates.[17] The results provide empirical confirmation for the view that both external and internal factors were at play in affecting the current account outcome; nevertheless, the most important explanatory variable was the terms of trade.

External influences on the BOP can translate into domestic inflationary pressure in a number of different ways.

In the early 1970s the LDCs were faced with a series of external 'shocks': 'unprecedented global inflation in 1973 and 1974, including the quadrupling of oil prices in 1974, was followed in 1974 and 1975 by the most severe world recession since the Great Depression of the 1930s' (Cline and Associates, 1981, p. 1). Previously rapid inflation had been confined to a relatively small number of LDCs (Brazil, Argentina and Chile in particular), but it became a general problem for all LDCs in 1973 and 1974. Attention thus began to be focused on the importance of 'imported inflation' in the inflationary process in LDCs, and an attempt was made to identify the channels through which, or the mechanisms by which, such 'external shocks' manifested themselves within the LDCs. The principal channels were:

1 the rise in the price of imported commodities (especially such important items as foodstuffs, oil and capital goods);
2 the rise in the price of imported services, including international lending, with increases in interest rates being a significant element in imported inflation;
3 the increase in international borrowing and the consequent capital inflows into LDCs, leading to increases in the domestic money supply;
4 rises in export prices, not offset by rises in import prices, leading to an accumulation of foreign exchange reserves and an increase in domestic money supply;
5 forced reduction in imports which caused prices to go up nationally because of supply restrictions;
6 'forced' import-substituting industrialization (ISI) or export promotion (EOI) resulting from a deteriorating current account which could not be externally financed, which raised average costs in the affected sectors and added indirectly to inflationary pressures (Griffith-Jones and Harvey, 1985, pp. 10–11).

Bhalla (1981) attempted an empirical investigation of the importance of external inflationary pressures and concluded that the monetary channel was one of the major mechanisms for the transmission of inflation during the period 1972–5:

External factors seem to have been to a larger extent responsible for the monetary acceleration than were domestic factors. External reserves increased (for most countries) at an unusual rate in 1972 and these increases were systematically related to money supply changes (Bhalla, 1981, p. 69).

Bhalla argued that the behaviour of import prices was also of crucial importance, accounting for well over half of domestic inflation in 30 LDCs studied for the period 1973–4, and were largely responsible for the fall in inflation in 1975 (p. 94):

The monetarist model of inflation in the thirty developing countries examined . . . indicates that the money changes had a strong and systematic effect on the price level. Structural factors – food bottlenecks and particularly changes in import prices – were also significant. The inflation boom seems indeed to have been imported (p. 95).

Killick (1981a) takes a different view, arguing that 'it is difficult to believe that rising import prices could directly explain more than a modest part of LDC inflation' (p. 10). The important point to note, however, is that whatever the relative importance of the external 'shock', its ultimate impact on the inflationary process in the LDC must in part depend on the specific structural features of the individual LDC. The susceptibility of LDCs to imported inflationary pressures depends, *inter alia*, on economic size, level and characteristics of development, degree of industrialization, structure of trade and 'openness' of economy, availability of technical skills and infrastructure, etc. In addition, Griffith-Jones and Harvey (1985, p. 337) argue;

whatever the mechanisms for transmitting external factors into higher rates of internal inflation, the consequence was frequently that those higher rates were then built into the domestic economy . . . a domestic inflationary process which was started or accelerated by external forces became so institutionalised that it could only be reversed with great difficulty.

Inflationary pressures can also increase as a result of the policies adopted by a country in response to exogenous adverse movements in the balance of payments. If import controls and quotas are used to restrict the level of imports, the result will be excess demand and domestic shortages with an increase in the domestic market price of imported items. Where domestic substitutes are available their prices will tend to increase in line with those of imported commodities. The increase in prices may lead to demands for increased money wages, and by means of an accommodating increase in domestic credit creation, inflation occurs.

A persistent balance of payments disequilibrium may lead to devaluation of the nominal exchange rate. The immediate effect of the devaluation will be to increase the c.i.f. price of imported items, expressed in domestic currency terms. Since a significant proportion of imports consist of intermediate and capital goods, the higher import costs will increase the costs of production of locally produced final manufactures. The increase in the relative price of traded goods may also lead to corresponding increases in the prices of non-traded goods and services. Resistance on the part of organized labour to a reduction in real income may lead to increased money wages (Schydlowsky, 1982).

Devaluation may also have an inflationary impact via an interest rate effect. The initial increase in prices following devaluation will reduce the real volume of bank credit. Firms are therefore forced to resort to other, informal sources of funds where the interest rate will be higher. The cost of working capital is increased, costs of production rise, and the aggregate supply curve is shifted upwards. The result is a decline in real output and increase in the price level (Buffie, 1984; van Wijnbergen, 1983).

There is empirical evidence to support the belief that devaluation will have inflationary repercussions. Donovan's (1981) cross-section study of a sample of countries following IMF stabilization programmes during the 1970s found that devaluation directly increased the price level and raised the underlying rate of inflation. Over the 3-year period following devaluation, annual inflation rates rose markedly, by about 5 to 7 percentage points on average. Lowinger's (1978) time-series study for Brazil, Colombia, Philippines and South Korea during 1959–72 shows a positive, statistically significant relation between exchange rate changes and the rate of inflation. Similar results are reported by Bautista (1982). An exception is Krueger (1978), who concludes that, for the 10 countries she studied, the contribution of exchange rates was small compared to other types of inflationary pressures. An explanation may be that Krueger was concerned with the impact of a general liberalization of the trade regime in the countries concerned. If devaluation is accompanied by a relaxation of import and exchange controls, the rents that accrued previously to those who held import and exchange licences will be reduced and the domestic market price will fall (Roemer, 1986). The effect on inflation will therefore depend on the degree of devaluation as compared to the extent of market liberalization.

A longer-term response to persistent BOP difficulties may be to follow a strategy of import substitution. Typically, this increases the dependence on 'essential' imports of intermediate and capital goods, thereby increasing the economy's vulnerability to 'imported inflation' which is passed on via higher costs of production to final prices.[18]

BOP adjustment and output levels

A second important structuralist criticism of the MABOP is directed towards the assumption that the process of adjusting to a BOP disequilibrium has no effect on the level of real output and employment. It is clear, however, that during the adjustment process a decline in the growth of domestic credit may be associated with a reduction in capacity utilization and increase in unemployment, since prices are not completely flexible downwards.

Structuralists maintain that the adverse effects of monetary contraction on economic activity are likely to be severe (Bruno, 1979; Taylor, 1981; van Wijnbergen, 1981). Khan and Knight (1985) assemble the empirical evidence on the effect of a contractionary monetary policy on the growth of output in LDCs. The results confirm that monetary contraction does tend to have a deflationary effect on real output, particularly in the short run, a 10 per cent reduction in the growth of money or domestic credit reducing the rate of growth of output by just under 1 per cent, over 1 year. Monetary contraction may also affect adversely longer-term growth, through its impact on investment. A reduction in the availability of bank financing, combined with an increase in interest rate costs, are likely to discourage private investment, thereby lowering economic growth. The results obtained by recent empirical studies confirm the hypothesis that variations in domestic credit can have a sizeable impact on real private capital formation in LDCs. The studies of Blejer and Khan (1984) and Tun Wai and Wong (1982), for example, both report finding a positive relationship between changes in domestic credit and private investment for a variety of LDCs. Since considerable evidence also exists on the positive relation between growth and investment in LDCs, these results imply a connection between domestic credit changes and growth through the effect on private investment. In addition, it has been well documented that significant declines in real output and employment have been features of recent stabilization programmes in various Latin American economies (Corbo and de Melo, 1985; Diaz Alejandro, 1981; Foxley, 1981, 1983).

5.5 The consequences of inflation

5.5.1 Inflation and growth

Much of the discussion of the consequences of inflation in LDCs has focused on the relationship between inflation and economic growth. The early structuralist literature argued that there was a positive relation between inflation and growth, and that inflation was unavoidable if economic growth was to occur. Various rigidities and inelasticities led to the emergence of sectoral disequilibria during the growth process, and because of downward rigidity of factor prices and factor immobility, excess demand and rising relative prices in some sectors were not offset by a decline in prices in the excess supply sectors (Canavese, 1982; Cardoso, 1981). These bottlenecks led to a build-up of inflationary pressures which had to be accommodated by monetary expansion if potential economic growth was to be realized. Inflation was therefore an inevitable and unavoidable feature of rapid growth.

Moreover, a theoretical literature argued in favour of using inflation as an instrument to increase economic growth in LDCs. One argument for inflationary financing built on the assumption that inflation would increase the overall level of saving and investment by transferring income from wage-earners as a group to profit-earners as a group. If prices rose faster than wages, and if the propensity to save out of profits was higher than the propensity to save out of wages, the level of real savings and investment would increase and economic growth would be accelerated (Thirlwall, 1974, chapter 4). It must be emphasized that this process of inflationary-financed saving rested on the assumption that inflation was unanticipated, or if anticipated, on the inability of wage-earners to obtain full compensation for the reduction in their real income.

A further way in which inflation could cause an increase in the growth rate was by redistributing resources from the private to the public sector. Even if inflation was fully anticipated and adjusted for, the operation of the 'inflation tax' would transfer resources to the government.[19] Inflation thus acted as a tax on money, redistributing resources from the private sector to the government sector where they could in principle be used to finance real investment. Provided that the public sector has a higher propensity to save than the private sector, the redistributive effect of inflation would increase aggregate investment and economic growth (Aghevli, 1977; Mundell, 1965).

The argument that inflation will provide a positive stimulus to economic growth has not gone unchallenged. McKinnon (1973) argues that inflation is likely to result in a lowering of the real rate of interest, creating a disequilibrium in the capital market. This will cause the supply of investment funds to fall, and as a result, private sector investment is 'repressed' below its equilibrium level by the limited supply of loanable funds. Therefore, in so far as inflation leads to low real rates of interest and capital market disequilibrium, it retards investment and growth.

Private investment may also be depressed by inflation if the resources transferred to the government would have been used for private sector investment in the absence of inflation. Furthermore, the increase in public sector investment may 'crowd out' private investment if it utilizes scarce resources that would otherwise be available to the private sector, or if it produces marketable output that competes with private output.[20]

If inflation is manifested by considerable variability, the composition of private sector investment may shift towards quick-yielding financial assets, with a reduction in longer-term investment. The quality of investment in the private sector may therefore deteriorate as the rate and variability of inflation increase.

Finally, the argument for inflationary growth must be modified to allow for open economy considerations (Johnson, 1974, 1984). The two-gap model shows how a developing economy's growth can be constrained by either a domestic savings or foreign exchange gap. If the latter is the effective constraint then additional domestic savings are redundant in the sense that they cannot be used for investment, since the necessary foreign inputs of capital goods are not available (Findlay, 1984; McKinnon, 1964). If the domestic inflation rate exceeds the general rate of world inflation, and if the exchange rate is not perfectly flexible, then inflation will lead to increased demand for imports and a reduction in export supply. The balance of trade will worsen, therefore, and the foreign exchange constraint becomes more severe.

The attempt to test empirically the relationship between inflation and growth has led to inconclusive results. The most straightforward approach has been to examine cross-country data to see if differences in GDP growth rates have had any association with differences in inflation rates. Few of these studies have produced strong statistical results in support of a positive relationship. Dorrance (1966) found some evidence of positive association at low inflation rates, but once inflation exceeded a certain level, rising prices and growth tended to be negatively linked. Similar findings are reported by Thirlwall and Barton (1971). In a later study, Thirlwall (1974) identified an inverted U-shaped relationship in his cross-section data, and suggested that the 'optimum' rate of inflation was below 10 per cent. A more recent study by the International Monetary Fund (1982) examined 112 non-oil developing countries over the period 1969–81, and concluded that, for the most part, 'relatively low inflation rates have been associated with relatively high growth rates and that reductions, or at least relative reductions, in inflation have been associated with an improvement, or relative improvement in growth rates' (p. 134).

Hanson's (1980) study used data from five Latin American countries over the period 1950–74 to study the short-run relation between growth and inflation. A distinction is drawn between expected and unexpected inflation, with increases in growth being achieved during the short-term disequilibrium caused by unexpected price rises. The empirical results show a positive correlation between unanticipated inflation and growth. Contrary findings are reported by Glezakos (1978). Using cross-section data for 41 LDCs in 1953–68, he included a measure of unanticipated changes in the rate of inflation as an independent variable to explain variations in the rate of growth. The results show a statistically significant negative relationship. The rate of inflation has a negative, but insignificant, effect on growth.

The evidence on the relationship between investment and inflation is also inconclusive. Thirlwall's (1974) results showed a negative coefficient between inflation and the aggregate investment ratio in the developing countries. Galbis's (1979) study of cross-section data for 16 Latin American countries during 1961–73 failed to find a significant relationship between the private sector investment ratio and inflation. When the individual countries were examined using time-series data, the results were mixed. The coefficient of the inflation variable was positive in nine countries (and statistically significant in three of them), and negative in the remaining seven countries. Finally, we can note the indirect evidence provided by Blejer and Khan's (1984) study of the behaviour of public and private sector investment. Using pooled cross-section data for 24 LDCs over the period 1971–9, they find that an increase in public sector investment leads to a fall in real private sector investment in the short run, although the degree of substitution is less than unity. In so far as inflation succeeds in transferring real resources to the public sector, therefore, the net increase in investment will be lower than the inter-sectoral resource shift.

5.5.2 Inflation, distribution and poverty

What is the likely effect of inflation on other aspects of the development process? The impact of inflation upon particular sectors or groups in the economy will depend upon the relative movements in prices during inflation. Inflation is seldom fully anticipated, and even when economic agents do anticipate future inflation, there are often institutional and other constraints preventing them from making the adjustments necessary to preserve their real incomes. A rise in the general rate of inflation is therefore associated with different relative price movements, depending upon the adjustment process in different factor and product markets.

The effect of price inflation on real income standards depends on the source of income receipts and the ability of the income group concerned to offset the effect of price increases. In the case of wages, many observers have argued that the resistance of organized labour to a reduction in real income standards creates a distributional conflict (Hirschman, 1981) which intensifies the relative price oscillations (di Tella, 1979), and perpetuates the inflationary process. Kaldor (1983) makes the same point, arguing that the price–wage relationship depends critically on the political strength of labour. The impact of inflation on the unorganized labour force is more difficult to analyse. If the prices of goods and services sold by self-employed informal urban households increase in line with the cost of their consumption purchases, their real incomes may be largely unaffected. In the rural sector, landless labourers are likely to suffer a reduction in real income as the prices of foodstuffs and other consumption goods increase. Rural households producing a marketed surplus of foodstuffs may gain, if food prices rise more rapidly than the general price level. Inflation may also affect the structure of the labour market, with labour shifting into the unionized and government sectors which offer the best prospects of maintaining real income levels; alternatively, if real incomes fall in the formal sector, workers may attempt to maintain their incomes by undertaking supplementary informal sector activities (Lagos and Tokman, 1984; Tokman, 1983).

Inflation may also favour one group of property-owners or capitalists at the expense of another. If inflation is combined with a fixed exchange rate and import controls, exporters experience a decline in real incomes, whereas those who are entitled to import at the overvalued exchange rate enjoy an equivalent gain. If inflation is combined with fixed nominal interest rates, capitalists with access to credit at low real interest rates will gain. Hirschman (1981, p. 191) cites the case of Brazil to illustrate the effects of inflation on different sections of the industrial sector. Beginning in 1964, an inflationary expansion of consumer credit facilities for the purchase of durables made possible a sustained boom in the automobile and appliance industries in the second half of the sixties and early seventies, at the expense of both the traditional consumer goods industries and the industries producing basic inputs and capital goods.

Differences in relative price movements and in the sources of income make it difficult to assess the impact of inflation on income distribution and poverty. Household income distribution data typically record household money income by percentile group. But households with the same money income have different consumption patterns, obtain their income from different sources, and may well face different prices for the same goods. Therefore, to assess the effect of inflation on household income distribution would require detailed information on individual price movements, household income receipts, and household consumption patterns. Similar considerations arise in attempting to assess the impact on poverty levels, since there is often considerable variation in household composition within the poverty percentiles.

Consider by way of illustration the case of increasing food prices. For the urban poor who purchase food, real income is likely to fall. For the rural poor the outcome will depend upon the extent to which households rely on purchased foodstuffs. A further complication may arise if the price of foodstuffs differs between the rural and urban areas. If food prices rise more rapidly than other prices, then since food forms a higher proportion of total expenditure for the poor, relative poverty will increase. Using Indian data for the mid-1960s, Mellor

(1978) shows that if foodgrain prices rose by 10 per cent, the real expenditure level of the lowest two deciles of households would decline by 5.5 per cent. In contrast, in the top 5 per cent in the expenditure distribution, the decline in expenditure is less than one-quarter as large as that experienced by the low-income groups. When the impact of the price rise on producers is considered, it is found that the income of the smallest farmers is reduced since they are net purchasers of foodgrain. It is only in the fourth and fifth deciles and above that a substantial rise in income occurs.

Given the methodological and data problems in assessing the impact of inflation on distribution and poverty, it is hardly surprising to find that the empirical evidence is scarce. Because of the complexity of the interrelationships between prices, patterns of production and consumption, and sources of income, only a general equilibrium analysis can unequivocally determine the effect of inflation on income distribution. It is difficult to generalize, but the conclusion reached by Johnson and Salop (1980, p. 3) in their discussion of the likely distributional repercussions of stabilization programmes in LDCs is probably applicable to most developing economies:

In general, lower-income groups tend to have the least access to assets whose values rise *pari passu* with inflation and are most likely to hold their savings in a monetary form. That these same groups are often the weakest in their ability to secure effective indexation of their wages strongly suggests that reducing inflation has egalitarian implications.

5.6 IMF stabilization programmes and the 'new structuralist' critique

The increasing involvement of LDCs with the IMF during the 1970s led to the emergence of a 'new' structuralist critique of the Fund's stabilization programmes.[21] While the focus of this critique is centred on the balance of payments policy rather than inflation control, it retains the original structuralist thesis that the characteristics of LDCs will often mean that the application of orthodox stabilization measures have undesirable and 'perverse' effects. Rather than reinforcing the stabilization efforts of the authorities, financial reform is likely to be associated with falling output and rising prices (Bruno, 1979; Taylor, 1983).

The immediate effect of an orthodox stabilization programme will be to alter certain key relative prices, including the exchange rate, nominal interest rates, and the price of public sector services. The 'liberalization' of the prices acts as a supply-side shock to the manufacturing sector in particular, raising firms' variable costs (imported inputs, working capital). The combined effect of limited substitution possibilities in production and the oligopolistic structures of the modern industrial structure in many LDCs (see Kirkpatrick *et al.*, 1984, chapter 3) will be that prices are more likely to be determined on a cost-of-production basis, rather than by competitive forces. Increases in input costs are passed on, therefore, on a mark-up basis.

Inflationary pressures may also be increased via the effect of monetary reforms on the balance of payments. The potential of devaluation to exercise an upward pressure on prices has already been considered.[22] In addition, changes in the exchange rate and domestic interest rates may result in a sudden inflow of short-term capital from abroad, which in the absence of an effective sterilization mechanism, will increase the domestic money supply (Diaz-Alejandro, 1981; Mathieson, 1979).

The empirical evidence on the economic consequences of Fund-supported adjustment programmes in LDCs appears to validate the structuralist argument.[23] Having reviewed various studies of pre- and post-stabilization programme performance in the main macroeconomic variables (balance of payments, inflation, growth rate), Killick (1984, p. 250) concluded that:

> The general outcome of the evidence surveyed so far is to throw doubt on the ability of Fund programmes to bring countries to BOP viability, to promote liberalization and to reduce inflation. . . . If (as we probably should) we confine ourselves to the statistically significant effects of Fund programmes, then they appear to make little difference to anything.

Cross-country studies of inflation performance point to a general inability of Fund programmes to bring down inflation rates. Reichmann and Stillson (1978) used quarterly data for 29 LDCs covering the period 1963–72 to compare inflation performance before and after the introduction of a programme, and found that only seven countries showed a statistically significant reduction in the eight quarters following the programme. Donovan (1982) found that over the period 1971–80 the annual rate of consumer inflation rose following the adoption of stabilization programmes in LDCs. Krueger (1978, p. 229) similarly reports little success in lowering inflation in the countries studied in her project. Kirkpatrick and Onis (1985) attempt to identify a systematic pattern in the behaviour of the inflation rate in a sample of Fund programmes, by relating inflation performance to selected indicators of the economic structure of the sample economies. The success of a stabilization programme in lowering the inflation rate is found to be (negatively) correlated with the level of urbanization and the degree of dependence on intermediate and capital goods imports. These results are interpreted as confirming the structuralist hypothesis that, given the structural characteristics of a 'typical' semi-industrialized LDC, the combined effect of monetary restraint and devaluation policies is likely to be an intensification of inflationary pressures.

5.7 Conclusions: towards a general theory of inflation for LDCs

Inflation is a problem endemic in most LDCs. The attempt to identify the causes of inflation still generates much controversy and the alleged 'cures' continue to impose high economic costs through reductions in output and employment.

The initial debate over the causes and consequences of inflation centred on the Latin American experience, and was in part responsible for the evolution and development of the structuralist school of thought. Structuralism has exerted great influence throughout the LDCs (although almost totally ignored, until recently, in developed, industrialized economies) but the relevance of the structuralist model of inflation to individual LDCs is not always obvious, and the attempt to generalize this model is not always successful.

It could be argued, for example, that the emphasis placed by structuralist writers on two or three specific bottlenecks and their presentation of a somewhat rigid and mechanical analysis of the operation of those bottlenecks is easy to refute with specific examples, and presents a misleading interpretation of policy choice in LDCs. In principle, all structural constraints are in a fundamental (though restricted) sense 'policy-induced', in that they are not immutable and can be removed or eased if the 'correct' policies are chosen. For example, the agricultural sector bottleneck can be broken or alleviated by land and agrarian reform; the foreign exchange constraint can be alleviated by the elimination of non-essential imports, the promotion of exports, and so on.

But within any given socio-political environment, governments are constrained with respect to the policy options that are *actually* open to them. A government consisting of, or dominated by, landed interests is, other things being equal, unlikely to pursue a policy of radical land redistribution. Politically influential middle- and upper-income groups are hardly likely to agree voluntarily to programmes that restrict the import or domestic production of durable consumer goods. The inability or unwillingness of governments to act in a manner consistent with the elimination of these constraints or bottlenecks implies that they are 'policy-induced' in the sense indicated above, but that nevertheless they are the result of particular economic, political, social and institutional structures. The concept of a structural constraint cannot be divorced from the specific social–political and historical framework within which it is operative.

From this perspective, some would agree that what is needed is a broadly based structural analysis of inflation, specific to each country, and encompassing a wide range of potential bottlenecks. Myrdal (1968, pp. 1928–9), for example, argues that bottlenecks in such sectors as electricity generation, fuel, imported raw materials, transport, repair facilities and credit facilities are all important in generating inflationary pressures. The problem with such an approach is that the inclusion of so many variables reduces the explanatory power of the model and provides only limited guidance to policy-makers.

The debate between the different schools of thought has largely focused on the *causes* of inflation. Most structuralists would accept that an increase in the supply of money was necessary for the manifestation of an inflationary spiral, but not a sufficient condition. At the same time, structuralists would argue that the control of the money supply was not a sufficient condition for the elimination of inflation. It has been argued that this is not a logically consistent perspective (Addison *et al.*, 1980) and that rather we should speak of the proximate and fundamental causes of inflation. 'The proximate determinants of inflation are the direct causes of an inflationary situation; by the fundamental determinants of inflation are meant those factors which themselves bring about the occurrence of the proximate determinants (Addison *et al.*, 1980, p. 147).

From this perspective, monetarists are mainly concerned with the issue of the proximate causes of inflation, the most important of which is argued to be monetary expansion in excess of real income growth. Structuralists, on the other hand, are concerned with the fundamental determinants – that is, those factors responsible for monetary growth itself. Put another way, monetarists view monetary growth as an exogenous variable whereas structuralists see it as endogenous (itself in need of explanation).

Most structuralist authors (for example, Seers, 1981a), now attach considerable importance to monetary and fiscal policy and countries undergoing profound structural change in particular require 'prudent short-term economic and financial management' (Griffith-Jones and Harvey, 1985, p. 346). Issues relating to the short- and medium-term macroeconomic management of LDCs have until recently been neglected in particular by structuralist writers, and the latter's recognition of the importance of these matters may well lead to a better appreciation of the monetarist perspective (although not necessarily to an acceptance of monetarist policy prescriptions!). As Seers (1981a, p. 9) argued:

neither structuralist nor monetarist explanations are adequate by themselves, and we need to draw on both to explain inflation. A government strong enough to suppress some of the propagating factors is a necessary but not a sufficient condition for slowing down inflation. In particular, monetary policy in itself will not eliminate inflationary pressures: it merely determines what its effects will be – price rises or social conflict, or some combination of the two.

It is perhaps too soon to look for real convergence between structuralist and monetarist perspectives, but the acceptance by the former of the importance of monetary policy, and the recognition by some economists sympathetic to the latter that 'there is an element of superficiality in monetarist explanations, which fail to examine the political circumstances which result in excess money creation' (Killick, 1981a, p. 16) holds out real hope for constructive dialogue between the two schools of thought and greater understanding of the causes of, and remedies for, inflation in LDCs in the future.

NOTES

1. More detailed data on both weighted average and median rates of inflation for different groupings of LDCs are given in IMF (1985, tables 10 and 11).
2. A positive covariance between the rate of inflation and its variability is reported by Blejer (1979) for Latin American countries, and by Khan and Abbas (1983) for Asian economies. Logue and Willett's (1976) study of 41 LDCs and DCs covering the period 1949–70 found that the positive relationship held only at high inflation rates.
3. The data on price increases in LDCs should be treated with caution. Data are limited, and those that are available often have severe limitations. The majority of LDCs do not compile GNP deflators so that cost of living indices and/or indices of wholesale prices are frequently the only price series available. Both of these measures have serious defects. The wholesale price index is frequently heavily weighted with the price of imports and exports, which tend to be domestic equivalents of international prices rather than measures of domestic prices, while the cost of living index is usually based upon a limited sample of goods and services purchased in the major urban areas and is thus unrepresentative of the consumption patterns of the majority of the population located in smaller urban centres and rural areas. In practice, cost of living indices are usually employed as they are often the only measure available, or are the least unsatisfactory of the measures of domestic price increases available.

4. Discussions of inflation theory in the context of the advanced industrialized economies can be found in Artis (1984), Frisch (1983), Hirsch and Goldthorpe (1978), Jackman *et al.* (1982).
5. The origins of the structuralist approach are discussed in Arndt (1985) and Jameson (1986).
6. However, as Hirschman (1965) noted, structuralism is a label that can be appropriated by all. Thus the current interest of the IMF in supply-side market liberalization policies has been labelled as 'a form of structuralism using orthodox instruments' (Foxley, 1981, p. 197).
7. The price increase stemming from the bottleneck is not a once-and-for-all change in relative prices, leading to a reallocation of resources and no change in the overall price level. Rather it may trigger off an inflationary spiral: 'Price increases that, in a different institutional setting, would be confined to a few items and carry their cure with them, will in an under-developed country tend to spread to other items and be self-defeating' (Myrdal, 1968, p. 1929).
8. Balogh (1961, p. 57) argued that it was not accurate to state that the owners of the latifundia and minifundia acted irrationally. Large-scale landowners were interested in the maximization of their incomes over time, constrained by the minimization of effort and risk (both economic and political); the small farmers and share-croppers had little interest in improvement: 'Their lack of capital and access to credit at reasonable terms makes risks connected with improvement unbearably high. Should anything go wrong, even their wretched existence would be jeopardized.'
9. It is recognized that monetarism is not monolithic and that there is 'a variety of monetarist analyses and models, with differing implications for the conduct of government policy' (Burton, 1982, p. 31). Nevertheless, there are 'certain basic ingredients that are common to all brands of monetarism' (p. 15).
10. Myrdal (1968, pp. 1257–8) commented: 'Prices of agricultural products and government price policies play, of course, a vital role in determining the course of agricultural output in the West, and naturally Western economists who happen to touch on the problems of underdeveloped countries often naively assume that these countries could stimulate agricultural production by raising farm prices. Western experts who have studied the South Asian agricultural situation are more careful. Like their South Asian colleagues, they do not count much on price support as a means of raising agricultural production.'
11. This argument perhaps understates the case. Output is likely to remain depressed and unemployment high for an even longer period, thus increasing the economic and social costs of orthodox stabilization policies. It is not certain that Vogel's regression results justify the conclusion he reaches. One critic argues that monetarists would not defend the use of the same monetarist model to every Latin American country, that there are significant differences in the inflationary process in Latin America, and that what is needed is a detailed comparative analysis of different groups of countries over some given time period. See Betancourt *et al.* (1976).
12. For an application of a similar 'hybrid' model to Argentina, see Sheehey (1976).
13. Aghevli and Khan obtain econometric estimates for Brazil, Colombia, Dominican Republic and Thailand, that appear to support their hypothesis.
14. Heller (1980) examines the various factors that affect the relative speed of adjustment of different types of revenue and expenditure to inflation. Econometric testing for 24 LDCs demonstrates a significant degree of variability in the relative adjustment rates of total expenditure and total revenue.
15. Misgivings about the 'conditionality' attached to the adjustment loans made by the IMF during the 1950s were an important factor in the emergence of the general struc-

turalist approach, of which the analysis of inflation reviewed in section 5.3.1 was an important part.
16. The definitive work was the collection of papers edited by Frenkel and Johnson (1976).
17. If domestic inflation rises faster than the world inflation rate, and the nominal exchange rate remains unaltered, the effective exchange rate will rise, with a loss in international competitiveness and deterioration in the current account. However, as Khan and Knight note (p. 830), the appreciation in the EER may be due to an increase in import prices, and cannot therefore be regarded as an indicator of domestic influences alone.
18. The relationship between import-substituting industrialization and inflation is discussed in detail in Kirkpatrick and Nixson (1976, pp. 158–62), Kirkpatrick and Onis (1985) and Onis (forthcoming).
19. The inflation tax is equivalent to the real income forgone by the private sector in maintaining its level of real cash balances constant. Since money balances must be accumulated at the same rate as the rate of inflation, the rate of tax is equal to the rate of inflation.
20. An equally plausible hypothesis is that public and private investment are complementary, and that public sector investment in infrastructure and the provision of public goods enhances the possibilities of private investment.
21. The IMF's involvement with LDCs during the 1970s is examined in Killick (1984). Foxley (1983) offers a critical appraisal from a structuralist perspective of the Fund's involvement with the Latin American economies.
22. Also see Bond (1980) for a discussion of this point.
23. There are serious difficulties in measuring performance in terms of a limited number of quantitative indicators. Ideally, one would wish to compare post-programme performance to the hypothetical no-programme results. The problems of devising appropriate performance criteria are considered in Donovan (1983).

REFERENCES

Addison, J. T., Burton, J. and Torrance, T. S. 1980. On the causes of inflation. *The Manchester School*, 48, 140–56.
Aghevli, B. B. 1977. Inflationary finance and growth. *Journal of Political Economy*, 85, 1295–1307.
Aghevli, B. J. and Khan, M. S. 1978. Government budget deficits and inflationary process in developing countries. *IMF Staff Papers*, 25, 383–416.
Aghevli, B. J. and Khan, M. S. 1980. Credit policy and the balance of payments in developing countries. In W. L. Coats Jr and D. R. Khatkhate (eds), *Money and Monetary Policy in Less Developed Countries*. New York: Pergamon Press, pp. 685–712.
Argy, V. 1970. Structural inflation in developing countries. *Oxford Economic Papers*, 22, 73–85.
Arndt, H. W. 1985. The origins of structuralism. *World Development*, 13, 151–9.
Artis, M. J. 1984. *Macroeconomics*. Oxford: Clarendon Press.
Ayre, P. C. I. 1982. Money, inflation and growth. In S. Ghatak, *Monetary Economics in Developing Countries*. London: Macmillan, pp. 66–90.
Baer, W. 1967. The inflation controversy in Latin America: a survey. *Latin American Research Review*, 2, 3–25.
Balogh, T. 1961. Economic policy and the price system. *UN Economic Bulletin for Latin America* (March). Reprinted in T. Balogh, 1974, *The Economics of Poverty*, 2nd edn. London: Weidenfeld and Nicolson, pp. 45–71.

Barro, R. J. 1979. Money and output in Mexico, Colombia, and Brazil. In J. Behrman and J. A. Hanson (eds), *Short-term macroeconomic policy in Latin America*. Cambridge, Mass.: National Bureau of Economic Research, pp. 177–200.

Bautista, R. M. 1982. Exchange rate variations and export competitiveness in less developed countries under generalized floating. *Journal of Development Studies*, 18, 354–78.

Betancourt, R. R., Sheehey, E. J. and Vogel, R. C. 1976. The dynamics of inflation in Latin America. *American Economic Review*, 66, 688–98.

Bhalla, S. S. 1981. The transmission of inflation into developing countries. In Cline and Associates, 1981, pp. 52–101.

Blejer, M. I. 1979. Inflation variability in Latin America: a note on the time series evidence. *Economics Letters*, 2, 337–41.

Blejer, M. I. and Khan, M. S. 1984. Government policy and private investment in developing countries. *IMF Staff Papers*, 31, 379–403.

Bond, M. E. 1980. Exchange rates, inflation and vicious circles. *IMF Staff Papers*, 27, 679–711.

Bruno, M. 1979. Stabilization and stagflation in a semi-industrialized economy. In R. Dornbusch and J. A. Frenkel (eds), *International Economic Policy: Theory and Evidence*. Baltimore: Johns Hopkins University Press, pp. 270–91.

Buffie, E. 1984. Financial repression, the new structuralists, and stabilization policy in semi-industrialized economies. *Journal of Development Economics*, 14, 305–22.

Burton, J. 1982. The varieties of monetarism and their policy implications. *Three Banks Review*, 134, 14–31.

Campos, R. de O. 1967. *Reflections on Latin American Development*. Austin, Texas: University of Texas Press.

Canavese, A. J. 1982. The structuralist explanation in the theory of inflation. *World Development*, 10, 523–30.

Cardoso, E. A. 1981. Food supply and inflation. *Journal of Development Economics*, 8, 269–84.

Cline, W. R. and Associates. 1981. *World Inflation and the Developing Countries*. Washington, DC: The Brookings Institution.

Cline, W. R. and Weintraub, S. (eds). 1981. *Economic Stabilization in Developing Countries*. Washington, DC: The Brookings Institution.

Corbo, V. and de Melo, J. (eds). 1985. Liberalization with stabilization in the Southern cone of Latin America *World Development*. (*Special Issue*), 13, 863–1015.

Dell, S. and Lawrence, R. 1980. *The Balance of Payments Adjustment Process in Developing Countries*. New York: Pergamon Press.

de Pablo, J. C. 1974. Relative prices, income distribution and stabilization plans: the Argentine experience 1967–70. *Journal of Development Studies*, 1, 187–9.

Diaz-Alejandro, C. 1981. Southern cone stabilization plans. In Cline and Weintraub, 1981, pp. 119–41.

di Tella, G. 1979. Price oscillations, oligopolistic behaviour and inflation: the Argentine case. *World Development*, 7, 1043–52.

Donovan, D. J. 1981. Real responses associated with exchange rate action in the upper credit tranche stabilization programs. *IMF Staff Papers*, 28, 698–727.

Donovan, D. 1982. Macroeconomic performance and adjustment under fund-supported programs: the experience of the seventies. *IMF Staff Papers*, 29, 171–203.

Donovan, D. 1983. Measuring macroeconomic performance. *Finance and Development*, 20(2), 2–5.

Dorrance, G. S. 1966. Inflation and growth: the statistical evidence. *IMF Staff Papers*, 13, 82–101.

Edel, M. 1969. *Food Supply and Inflation in Latin America*. New York: Praeger.

Edwards, S. 1983. The short-run relation between growth and inflation in Latin America: comment. *American Economic Review*, 73, 477–82.

Felix, D. 1961. An alternative view of the 'monetarist–structuralist' controversy. In A. O. Hirschman (ed.), *Latin American Issues: Essays and Comments*. New York: Twentieth Century Fund.

Findlay, R. 1984. Growth and development in trade models. In R. W. Jones and P. B. Kenen (eds), *Handbook of International Economics*, vol. 1. Amsterdam: North-Holland, pp. 185–236.

Foxley, A. 1981. Stabilization policies and their effects on employment and income distribution: A Latin American perspective. In Cline and Weintraub, 1981, 191–225.

Foxley, A. 1983. *Latin American Experiments in Neo-Conservative Economics*. Berkeley: University of California Press.

Frenkel, J. A. and Johnson, H. G. (eds). 1976. *The Monetary Approach to the Balance of Payments*. London: Allen and Unwin.

Frisch, H. 1983. *Theories of Inflation*. Cambridge Surveys of Economic Literature. Cambridge: Cambridge University Press.

Galbis, V. 1979. Money, investment and growth in Latin America, 1961–1973. *Economic Development and Cultural Change*, 27, 423–43.

Ghatak, S. 1981. *Monetary Economics in Developing Countries*. London: Macmillan.

Glezakos, C. 1978. Inflation and growth: a reconsideration of the evidence from the LDCs. *Journal of Developing Areas*, 12, 171–82.

Griffith-Jones, S. and Harvey, C. (eds). 1985. *World Prices and Development*. Aldershot: Gower.

Hanson, J. A. 1980. The short-run relation between growth and inflation in Latin America: a quasi-rational or consistent expectations approach. *American Economic Review*, 70, 972–89.

Hanson, J. A. 1983. The short-run relation between growth and inflation in Latin America: Reply. *American Economic Review*, 73, 483–5.

Harberger, A. C. 1963. The dynamics of inflation in Chile. In C. F. Christ *et al.* (eds), *Measurement in Economics: Studies in Mathematical Economics and Econometrics in Memory of Yehudi Grunfeld*. Stanford: Stanford University Press.

Harberger, A. C. 1978. A primer on inflation. *Journal of Money, Credit and Banking*, 10, 505–21. Reprinted in W. L. Coats Jr and D. R. Khatkhate (eds). 1980. *Money and Monetary Policy in Less Developed Countries: A Survey of Issues and Evidence*. New York: Pergamon Press, pp. 149–63.

Heller, P. S. 1980. Impact of inflation on fiscal policy in developing countries. *IMF Staff Papers*, 27, 712–48.

Hirsch, F. and Goldthorpe, J. H. 1978. *The Political Economy of Inflation*. Oxford: Martin Robertson.

Hirschman, A. O. 1965. *Journeys Toward Progress*. New York: Anchor Books.

Hirschman, A. O. 1981. The social and political matrix of inflation: elaborations on the Latin American experience. In *Essays in Trespassing: Economics to Politics and Beyond*. Cambridge: Cambridge University Press.

International Monetary Fund. 1982. *World Economic Outlook: A Survey by the Staff of the IMF*. Occasional Paper No. 9. Washington, DC: IMF.

International Monetary Fund. 1984. *Annual Report*, 1984. Washington, DC: IMF.

International Monetary Fund. 1985. *World Economic Outlook, 1985*. Washington, DC: IMF.

Jackman, R. Mulvey, C. and Trevithick, J. 1982. *The Economics of Inflation*, 2nd edn. Oxford: Martin Robertson.

Jameson, K. P. 1986. Latin American structuralism: a methodological perspective. *World Development*, 14, 223-32.

Jansen, K. (ed.). 1983. *Monetarism, Economic Crisis and the Third World*. London: Frank Cass.

Johnson, O. E. G. 1974. Credit controls as instruments of development policy in the light of economic theory. *Journal of Money, Credit and Banking*, 6, 85-99.

Johnson, O. E. G. 1984. On growth and inflation in developing countries. *IMF Staff Papers*, 31, 636-60.

Johnson, S. and Salop, J. 1980. Distributional aspects of stabilization programs in developing countries. *IMF Staff Papers*, 27, 1-23.

Kahil, R. 1973. *Inflation and Economic Development in Brazil, 1946-63*. Oxford: Clarendon Press.

Kaldor, N. 1983. Devaluation and adjustment in developing countries. *Finance and Development*, 20(2), 35-7.

Khan, A. H. and Abbas, K. 1983. Additional evidence on inflation variability: the experience of Asian countries. *Economics Letters*, 12, 157-61.

Khan, M. S. and Knight, M. D. 1983. Determinants of current account balances of non-oil developing countries in the 1970s: an empirical analysis. *IMF Staff Papers*, 30, 819-42.

Khan, M. S. and Knight, M. D. 1985. *Fund Supported Adjustment Programs and Economic Growth*. Occasional Paper 41. Washington, DC: IMF.

Killick, T. 1981a. Inflation in developing countries: an interpretive survey. *ODI Review*, 1, 1-17.

Killick, T. 1981b. *Policy Economics: a Textbook of Applied Economics on Developing Countries*. London: Heinemann.

Killick, T. (ed.). 1984. *The Quest for Economic Stabilization*. London: Heinemann.

Kirkpatrick, C. and Nixson, F. 1976. The origins of inflation in less developed countries: a selective review. In M. Parkin and G. Zis (eds), *Inflation in Open Economies*. Manchester: Manchester University Press, pp. 126-74.

Kirkpatrick, C. and Onis, Z. 1985. Industrialization as a structural determinant of inflation performance in IMF stabilization programmes in less developed countries. *Journal of Development Studies*, 21, 347-61.

Kirkpatrick, C., Lee, N. and Nixson, F. 1984. *Industrial Structure and Policy in Less Developed Countries*. London: Allen and Unwin.

Krueger, A. O. 1978. *Liberalization Attempts and Consequences*. Cambridge, Mass.: Ballinger.

Lagos, R. and Tokman, V. 1984. Monetarism, employment and social stratification. *World Development*, 12, 43-66.

Laidler, D. and Parkin, M. 1975. Inflation - a survey. *Economic Journal*, 85, 741-809.

Logue, D. and Willett, T. 1976. A note on the relation between the rate and variability of inflation. *Economica*, 43, 151-8.

Lowinger, T. C. 1978. Domestic inflation and exchange rate changes: the less developed countries' case. *Weltwirtschaftliches Archiv*, 114, 85-100.

Mathieson, D. J. 1979. Financial reform and capital flows in a developing economy. *IMF Staff Papers*, 26, 450-89.

McKinnon, R. I. 1964. Foreign exchange constraints in economic development and efficient aid allocation. *Economic Journal*, 74, 388-409.

McKinnon, R. 1973. *Money and Capital in Economic Development*. Washington, DC: The Brookings Institution.

Mellor, J. W. 1978. Food price policy and income distribution in low-income countries. *Economic Development and Cultural Change*, 27, 1-26.

Mundell, R. 1965. Growth, stability and inflationary finance. *Journal of Political Economy*, 73, 97–109.

Myrdal, G. 1968. *Asian Drama: An Inquiry into the Poverty of Nations*. Harmondsworth: Penguin Books.

Onis, Z. Forthcoming. Persistent inflation in semi-industrial economies: a conceptual framework for analysis. Manchester Papers on Development.

Polak, J. J. 1957. Monetary analysis of income formation and payments problems. *IMF Staff Papers*, 6, 1–50.

Ram, R. 1985. Level and variability of inflation: time-series and cross-section evidence from 117 countries. *Economica*, 52, 209–23.

Reichmann, T. M. and Stillson, R. 1978. Experience with programs of balance of payments adjustment: Stand-by arrangements in the higher tranches 1963–72. *IMF Staff Papers*, 25, 293–309.

Roemer, M. 1986. Simple analytics of segmented markets: what case for liberalization? *World Development*, 14, 429–40.

Schydlowsky, D. M. 1982. Alternative approaches to short-term economic management in developing countries. In T. Killick (ed.), *Adjustment and Financing in the Developing World: The Role of the IMF*. Washington, DC: IMF and Overseas Development Institute.

Seers, D. 1964. Inflation and growth: the heart of the controversy. In W. Baer and I. Kerstenetzky (eds), *Inflation and Growth in Latin America*. Homewood, Ill.: Irwin, pp. 89–163.

Seers, D. 1981a. *Inflation: The Latin American experience*. IDS Discussion Paper, DP 168, November.

Seers, D. 1981b. *Inflation: A Sketch for a Theory of World Inflation*. IDS Discussion Paper, DP 169, November.

Sheehey, E. J. 1976. The dynamics of inflation in Latin America: comment. *American Economic Review*, 66, 692–4.

Sunkel, O. 1960. Inflation in Chile: an unorthodox approach. *International Economic Papers*, 10, 107–31.

Taylor, L. 1981. IS-LM in the tropics: diagrammatics of the new structuralist macrocritique. In Cline and Weintraub, 1981, pp. 465–503.

Taylor, L. 1983. *Structuralist Macroeconomics*. London: Harper and Row.

Thirlwall, A. P. 1974. *Inflation, Saving and Growth in Developing Economies*. London: Macmillan.

Thirlwall, A. P. and Barton, C. A. 1971. Inflation and growth: the international evidence. *Banca Nazionale del Lavoro Quarterly Review*, 98, 263–75.

Thorp, R. 1971. Inflation and the financing of economic development. In K. Griffin (ed.), *Financing Development in Latin America*. London: Macmillan, pp. 182–224.

Tokman, V. E. 1983. The influence of the urban informal sector on economic inequality. In F. Stewart (ed.), *Work, Income and Inequality*. London: Macmillan, pp. 108–37.

Tun Wai, U. and Wong, C. 1982. Determinants of private investment in developing countries. *Journal of Development Studies*, 19, 19–36.

van Wijnbergen, S. 1982. Stagflationary effects of monetary stabilization policies: a quantitative analysis of South Korea. *Journal of Development Economics*, 10, 133–69.

van Wijnbergen, S. 1983. Credit policy, inflation and growth in financially repressed economies. *Journal of Development Economics*, 13, 45–65.

Vogel, R. C. 1974. The dynamics of inflation in Latin America 1950–1969. *American Economic Review*, 64, 102–14.

Wachter, S. 1976. *Latin American Inflation*. Lexington, Mass.: D.C. Heath.

Whitman, M. 1975. Global monetarism and the monetary approach to the balance of payments. *Brookings Papers on Economic Activity*, 3, 491–536.

PART III

Factor markets in LDCs

6

The labour market and human capital in LDCs

Albert Berry

6.1 Introduction

The labour market has been close to the heart of much discussion of developing economies and what is special about them, and has accordingly figured prominently in distinguishing different views or models of 'how developing countries work'. The labour-abundant character of most poor countries is obviously a key distinguishing feature between them and the developed countries; the Lewis 'labour-surplus' model highlights this feature. Most workers are poor in developing countries, and since their earnings (or potential earnings for the many who are self-employed rather than paid workers) are determined in the labour market, a sort of spotlight naturally falls on this market. The massive rural to urban migration occurring in many countries, and the sometimes dramatically fast growth of urban labour forces which it fuels, are a labour market adjustment process which can hardly escape notice. Rapid expansion of the coverage of education in most less developed countries (LDCs) has, inevitably, had significant effects in the labour market. High levels of urban unemployment, especially for certain groups, are a natural cause for concern; further, many observers have worried that unemployment has been rising over time. Since in any reasonable social welfare function the earnings levels of workers and the ease of their access to jobs must figure prominently, it is in terms of such labour market outcomes that the evidence of an economy's success or failure is manifested and frequently measured.

The major focus of this survey is on the sort of understanding of the labour market which may contribute to policy-making. We review the evidence bearing on the explanatory power of some of the major broad models or paradigms of labour market functioning since which of those broad paradigms correspond most clearly to the facts is of relevance in many ways. Thus, how much 'surplus labour' exists clearly contributes to any guess as to how much output could rise were it possible to put that surplus to use, for example, in public works programmes. Other aspects of labour market functioning which do not define the differences between broad paradigms, but are important in the context of specific policy issues, will be given equal attention.

In the evolution of thought about LDC labour markets, the search for paradigms which would explain the set of phenomena believed to characterize the market has reflected special attention to those features which are perceived as negative or as problems (high urban unemployment, rapid growth of urban slums, low levels of earnings, and the like). It has also focused especially on phenomena or issues which seem particularly related to policy. The search for paradigms is in part the search for basic understanding; but we are more anxious to understand some things than others, so emphasis is naturally and appropriately placed on those things which are problems and on the implications of the manipulation of actual or potential policy tools (minimum wage legislation, etc.).

Broadly speaking, what one wants to know about labour market functioning in LDC settings is:

1 how well labour is allocated among competing uses or – the other side of the coin – how serious are the phenomena which inhibit an efficient allocation at any given time;
2 how well the labour market contributes to assuring adequate and stable incomes for the poorer groups;
3 how effectively the information generated in the labour market contributes to public and private decisions about human capital formation (education, training, etc.).

Before turning in sections 6.3–6.5 to discussions of underutilization and misallocation of labour, of the determinants of labour earnings (including education and other selected policies) and of participation and discrimination, we review briefly in section 6.2 the evolution of thought on how labour markets function in LDCs. A look at this evolution helps to put the major paradigms in historical context.

As is true of most areas of research, certain ideas and paradigms have held sway for a period, and have later lost ground and/or been significantly qualified. Major attention has been directed to the idea that labour is in surplus supply leading to various types of underutilization and to the idea that the labour market is seriously segmented. Empirical analysis and theoretical refinement, while by no means rendering these ideas irrelevant, have in our judgment shown them to be less central to decision-making in many policy areas than was at one time commonly believed. But a good understanding of labour markets is essential to good policy-making on education, wage policy, and several other areas.

Unfortunately, our understanding is still rather far from being adequate, partly because of the modest amount of research which has been carried out on LDC labour markets, and partly because of the limited extent to which the results of research on industrialized countries' (IC) labour markets can be transferred to the LDC setting. The outsider to this area would probably be surprised by the limited interaction between the labour market literatures for industrialized countries and for LDCs. Many major participants in the latter literature have clearly viewed the issues as being distinctly different. This is partly a normal reaction to the very different contexts; in the early post-war period especially, in nearly all Third World countries agriculture employed the great majority of the labour force in rural areas and the 'modern' sector was small indeed. The relatively impersonal labour market characteristic of urban industrial societies was small, if present at all, and the role of family and community decision-making and collective action seemed to constitute a significant difference from the developed country cases with which the IC economists were familiar.

In spite of the fact that the labour surplus and Harris–Todaro models are usually viewed as specific to Third World contexts,[1] and most writing on Third World labour markets does have a quite different set of orientations from the corresponding developed country literature, it has at the same time been said with some reason that labour market concepts from the industrialized countries have been misapplied in the LDCs; the rate of open unemployment as a gauge of employment access and opportunities is often cited in this context. The ILO is often criticized for a rigid adherence to the idea that policies which are widely believed to be in the interests of workers in ICs are also in their interest in the LDC context.

While some transfer of ideas has no doubt been inappropriate, it is also true that many benefits can be reaped from a careful consideration by students of LDC labour markets of what has been learned in the IC counterparts of late. And an important task remains largely to be performed: the development of a more wide-ranging theory or picture of how labour markets function, with ICs as a special case – 'at one end of a spectrum' perhaps – and with recognition of how the major labour market phenomena of interest and importance change as a country undergoes development and structural change. In very poor countries, as has often been pointed out, many of the urban unemployed cannot be thought of as falling near the bottom of the economic totem pole; sometimes the term 'luxury unemployment' is used to describe them (Udall and Sinclair, 1982). In industrialized countries, unemployment seems to be more systematically correlated with poverty. Where, in the process of development, does the phenomenon of open unemployment switch from being mainly of the 'luxury type' (if that description is indeed accurate) to being mainly of the poverty type, or is the change a gradual, continuous one? We need more work of an integrative nature to both explain and learn from how such labour market phenomena differ across the spectrum of countries. The same goes for the 'Phillips curve' concept, relating wage and price increases on the one hand to the level of unemployment on the other. This relationship, much discussed in the ICs, has been given little attention in the LDCs, and few studies have reported its presence. Many facts make this difference plausible, but again one would like to have some feel for the stage of development at which the inflation/unemployment link might be expected to tighten. More generally, labour market research on LDCs has been very micro-oriented, as indeed has come increasingly to be the case in ICs. In LDCs the balance probably should be adjusted. Too few serious attempts have been made to link macroeconomic events and labour market outcomes.

There are of course many important labour market phenomena which exist both in LDCs and in ICs. The nature and extent of labour market dualism has been the subject of much discussion in both contexts over recent years, and though the contexts differ in important ways, perceptions as to the mechanisms at work in the two cases have considerable overlap.[2]

6.2 The evolution of ideas on LDC labour market functioning and the major paradigms

The benchmark paradigm in labour market analysis, both because of its usefulness and its simplicity, is the neoclassical model in which all markets function smoothly and efficiently, or are close enough to this state that the implications of their divergences from it can still be best analysed by starting with the predictions of the model itself. But at least early on, this paradigm did not by any means dominate the literature, nor it would seem the thinking, on LDC labour markets.[3] Lewis's (1954) labour surplus model, further elaborated by Fei and Ranis (1964), introduced labour market dualism into our intellectual process. Like all models, its message was exaggerated and/or misapplied by some exponents and, partly for this reason, it came under counterattack (see Berry and Sabot, 1978, pp. 1222–5; Kao *et al.*, 1964). The subtlety required to test properly the proposition that a given country may harbour a sizeable amount of labour with marginal productivity well below the going wage rate has greatly constrained what can be learned from the empirical work done in this area so far. A reasonable guess would be that labour surplus so defined does not reach drastic proportions in many countries. Perhaps more to the point, the record, at least from market economies in the Third World, seems rather clear on the difficulty involved in harnessing this surplus for productive uses. The facts that much surplus may be only seasonal, that the organization necessary to put it to effective use in public works seems to exceed the administrative capacity of many countries (for an interesting discussion see J. P. Lewis, 1977), and that some 'surplus' labour is relatively immobile, have conspired to lower hopes that utilization of surplus labour could lead to easy increases in output and investment. Encouragement of increased utilization of labour by such policies as subsidies to the hiring firms, the use of a low shadow price for labour in the selection of technologies for public sector projects, and the like may have had modest impacts in some LDCs, but these policy instruments have yet to demonstrate that combination of power and administrative simplicity which would give them first rank importance.

Though early post-war conceptualizations of the labour surplus character of an economy tended to suggest that the modern sector was mainly urban and the traditional sector mainly rural, it was not long before this 'surplus' designation came to be applied to many urban workers as well, both by people whose thought fell squarely in the Lewis/Fei/Ranis tradition (e.g. Reynolds, 1969), and by many others who perceived much of the burgeoning urban population as simply unproductive, not to mention poor, and who decried the exploding urban slums as a more or less obviously undesirable development. A major literature evolved which suggested that rural–urban migration was excessive, adducing as evidence high and rising rates of open unemployment in the urban areas and urban poverty, and which groped in various ways for explanations of the phenomenon. An irrational attraction to the cities, education which made youth less well fitted for agricultural than for other work, and displacement of rural workers by labour-saving technological change in agriculture and by increasing land concentration, all came in for their share of the blame for the existence of a rapidly expanding and allegedly marginalized mass of urban poor people. But the accuracy of the observation that the urban masses in most LDCs were quite poor was not matched by accuracy of most of these early interpretations. In short, the empirical evidence has provided almost no support for the idea that migration has been based on misinformation as to urban employment opportunities or to 'irrational' behaviour by the migrants. Instead, it has made it clear that economic motivation is the dominant factor, and that a large majority of migrants judge *ex-post* that the move did improve their economic prospects and situation (Yap, 1977).

Whether the migration process implies a socially efficient allocation of labour between rural and urban settings is, however, much less clear than whether it results from conscious and apparently rather efficient private maximization by the participants. Several ideas/arguments are particularly relevant here. Urbanization could be excessive as a result of some combination of the following factors (though other factors could tend to offset these): (1) if, as per the Harris–Todaro models, migrants maximize their expected welfare by taking a chance on getting a 'good' urban job even when there are definitely not enough such jobs for all of them (the source of the risk of not finding one); (2) if public expenditure subsidizes urban living and urban activities relative to rural ones; or (3) if such structural features as widespread monopolistic competition in urban areas push the marginal social productivity of labour below the marginal private productivity. Of these arguments, the most developed in the literature, certainly, is the Harris–Todaro model.[4] The essence of the model is that earnings in a protected high-productivity urban sector composed of the public sector, large-scale private firms and some other activities, are well above those of other sectors and, in particular, of the rural sector. Institutional factors keep these earnings above the supply price of labour. It is reasonable for a person to move to the city in search of one of these jobs, as long as the probability of getting one is high enough, in relation to the income gains which would result. This Harris–Todaro model provides an interpretation of labour market functioning substantially different from both the neoclassical and the labour surplus models, and under some circumstances implies that urban job creation may increase the level of unemployment and be economically inefficient (see, for example, Arellano, 1981). Although it remains a prominent model, it appears to have been losing some ground to more neoclassical interpretations in the recent literature which reports attempts to test the explanatory power of competing versions. We return later to the empirical evidence (see section 6.3.4).

More recent formulations have tended to include the urban informal sector as an explicit part of the Harris–Todaro model. More generally, the definition and interpretation of the extensive low-income, small-scale and generally not very modern activities in the urban sector have been the object of great attention and a fair amount of serious study over the past two decades. This sector is important to our discussion both because of its size and because it is not self-evident how it is connected with the modern sector, nor how its labour market (if indeed it needs to be distinguished from that of the modern sector) functions.

The growth of the informal urban sector, and the much more rapid growth of our awareness of it, underlies the interest in how its labour market functions. Another striking development of recent decades in many developing countries is the increase in female labour force participation. Explaining it and deducing its economic implications has been the objective of another group of researchers.

Finally, the great and increasing importance of both public and private expenditures on education in LDCs has put a spotlight on the economic payoffs to education. The traditional 'human capital model' approach to an economic measurement of those payoffs relies on a specific interpretation of how labour markets function. The attempt to provide more robust and hence persuasive assessments of education's payoff has led to discussion and controversy over how wage structures are set and jobs allocated among candidates.

In the rest of this survey an attempt is made to review the evidence on what seem to me the more important research issues on LDC labour markets. Importance is not based solely on whether evidence on an issue might throw light on how labour market policy *per se* should be managed (for example, how the public sector pay structure should be set), but on whether study of the labour market and its outcomes throws light on how any policy (macro, trade or whatever) should be managed. In fact, a useful null hypothesis in dealing with the economics of the labour market is that very few direct policy interventions in that market are likely to have significantly beneficial effects, after allowance is made for the fact that when undertaken they are unlikely to be carried out in an optimal fashion because of lack of information, lack of efficient policy instruments, political biases, or administrative incompetence and corruption. That the labour market functions in a seriously inefficient way is nowhere nearly as evident as that the capital market does. But labour market functioning and outcomes can certainly provide a good window into the broader socio-economic reality of a country and useful ideas on appropriate policy in many areas, including education, population, urbanization and so on.

The labour market issues where I believe research most likely to provide policy relevant insights include:

1 Those aspects of wage structure and the determination of who gets what job which help to assess the *economic payoffs to education*. These aspects include many which are also relevant to an understanding of other labour market issues such as appropriate public sector pay structures and such possible interventions in the labour market as minimum wage legislation, support or opposition to unions, establishment of social security systems, severance pay procedures, etc.

2 The extent of various types of *dualism or segmentation of labour markets* and its implications for output, employment, and income distribution in the economy. Under this umbrella one may distinguish the following.

  (a) The extent of labour surplus of the Lewis–Fei–Ranis variety, and its implications for the feasibility of low-cost inputs of labour on infrastructure and other public sector uses, and on the desirability of inducing the modern private sector to absorb more workers.

  (b) The prevalence of the combination, formalized in the Harris–Todaro model, of (i) a high-wage modern sector, where the wage level is set by institutional (the usual assumption) or even market forces, and (ii) willingness of workers to risk unemployment in order to move to a place from which such jobs can be effectively pursued. The prevalence of this combination is important to understanding both the social cost of urban unemployment or underemployment and the appropriate means to cutting the loss associated with excessive pursuit of these jobs.

  (c) The extent of labour market discrimination by sex, age, ethnic group and the like, and the implications for output and income distribution.

    Both (a) and (b) are likely to bear significantly on the much-debated question of the appropriate rate of urbanization in LDCs. Lewis (1977) has recently argued that urbanization is a very expensive business in developing countries, and there is enough evidence to support that proposition to give special interest to how, and in response to what incentives, rural–urban migration occurs.

3 The character and hence the *social cost of open unemployment*. Is it productive job search, a reflection of unrealistic aspirations, or a reflection of very scarce jobs of any sort?

4 *The determinants and effects of female labour force participation*. There may be no reason to believe that levels of, or changes in, participation rates signal market imperfections, and it might therefore be argued that those rates are not a matter of much purely economic interest. But they may be related in important ways both to income distribution between men and women and the question of discrimination by sex, and to the population growth rate.

The next section reviews evidence and thinking on these issues, beginning with the simpler ones.

6.3 The extent of labour surplus or underutilization

The most prevalent theme in the literature on LDC labour markets is probably still the extent of underutilization of labour, underutilization hypothesized to occur either because there simply is not enough work to go around, given the high ratio of population to other resources in most of these countries, or because the use of inappropriate technologies or bad distribution of land and capital among workers greatly curtails the number of jobs available. These ideas have a common-sense basis and much casual observation is consistent with them. But it is important to distinguish the more relevant models or interpretations from the less persuasive.

6.3.1. Lewis-type labour surplus

Within economics it was the writing of Arthur Lewis which provided the model to reconcile the perception that there was a great deal more labour available than could productively be used with the fact that there was little open unemployment of the type which characterized Western industrial countries. (Later open unemployment did become more prevalent as LDCs became more urbanized.) Beginning with some writings of the inter-war period, it has not been uncommon to see the claim that open and disguised unemployment amounted to 25–50 per cent or even more, of a country's labour force. Careful measurement and interpretation casts much doubt on these extreme contentions but leaves a good deal of uncertainty as to just how important is the reservoir of underutilized labour. That reservoir would include: (1) disguisedly unemployed workers in the Lewis sense – those who are not necessary to the operation of the firm (usually farm) but are kept on, sharing the work with others, because of family or other obligations; (2) the openly unemployed; and (3) discouraged workers who would enter the labour force under more favourable conditions (better remuneration, less logistical problems, etc.). Also prominent in the literature for a time was the suggestion that people be treated as underemployed if their income was below a certain level.[5] This unfortunate confusion of the issues of income distribution and of labour utilization seems to have largely faded from view in the past few years.[6]

Most of the dispute has centred around the extent of Lewis-type disguised unemployment, and the overall upshot would seem to be (1) that its extent is not so great as is often believed, and (2) that its extent cannot be satisfactorily described in a single number, but requires distinguishing, for example, between activities where the surplus could be utilized and where it could not. Contributing, it seems, to the large numbers often cited as being underemployed were (1) a tendency to extrapolate incorrectly from the casual observation that there were many people in urban areas 'standing around doing nothing', (2) a tendency to assume a given task required a similar complement of labour in an LDC as it would in an IC, and (3) a tendency to be dramatic. As the stage of impressions gradually gave way to the stage of more careful study, much of the apparent surplus in agriculture was seen to be so only on a seasonal basis; the quite labour-intensive techniques in use were better recognized; and the considerable use of labour in secondary activities was perceived. Guesses as to the extent of surplus were accordingly scaled down. Unfortunately little attention seems to have been paid till quite recently to the question of how family decision-making occurs, and whether it would typically be consistent with the support of workers whose marginal product was less than their consumption.[7]

In some of the practical attempts to take advantage of the existence of surplus labour (whether seasonal or permanent) to generate infrastructure or other public works, the fact that labour has been less forthcoming than anticipated has led to a recognition that there may be an element of the voluntary in the failure to be productively occupied, and that the extent to which underutilized labour can be marshalled depends on the conditions: the wages paid, how far the job is from the person's home, the job conditions, etc. In short the supply curve of such labour is in practice unlikely to be horizontal, as in the simpler conceptualizations of the model.

More generally, some confusion has surrounded the matter of how a labour surplus condition may be identified. Some authors have attempted to identify directly a low or zero marginal product of labour, for example, by cross-section regression analysis designed to reflect the production function (see for example, Desai and Mazumdar, 1970). Many have attempted to demonstrate that more labour was available in a given sector than was needed (see, for example, Mehra, 1966). Some authors have used less direct approaches, in particular a focus on the character of the labour supply curve. Hansen (1969) argued that seasonal fluctuations in wage rates demonstrate that labour supply is not unlimited at an institutionally fixed level; other authors have suggested or assumed that when labour supply elasticity is not infinite the labour surplus condition does not hold (for example, Jorgenson, 1966). In fact, however, there is nothing inconsistent between labour surplus and a positively sloped supply curve or a supply curve which shifts with economic conditions; many of the more careful students have recognized this point (for example, Minami, 1970, p. 27). It is not true, as these discussions sometimes seem to suggest, that when labour surplus exists, the market forces determining levels of wages and employment in a neoclassical world are simply replaced (on the supply side) by an 'institutional mechanism'. Better conceived, the institutional setting becomes more complicated by the fact that an individual's consumption may be subsidized as long as he/she stays in the traditional sector. But if the level of that subsidy depends on average labour productivity in the traditional sector farm or firm (in which case it would rise, and with it the supply price of labour as labour shifts to the modern sector), or if it varies across traditional sector units, or if supply price depends also on region of origin and hence logistical costs, then the labour supply curve will still slope upward even in the presence of surplus labour. Labour surplus would no doubt lead one to expect a *flatter* labour supply to the modern sector *than otherwise*, and indeed the lengthy period of wage stability in a number of developing countries (even as per capita income rose) has been one of the arguments wielded by the proponents of labour surplus.[8] But their argument, too, requires additional testing and buttressing since such stability may have origins other than labour surplus.

The existence of *some* surplus labour in LDCs, or in almost any economy for that matter, seems unexceptionable. Overstaffing in the public sector, including public companies, is one obvious context in which workers are paid more than their marginal product. The *extent* of underutilization which can be traced to the *income-sharing phenomenon* is the main issue of contention. Most evidence suggests it is more likely in LDCs to involve 5–15 per cent of the labour force than the 20–40 per cent sometimes talked of earlier.[9] And, as noted earlier, its perceived significance for economic efficiency has also fallen because of the recognized difficulties in making effective use of the surplus, at least in market economies. It is an interesting question whether the presence of surplus labour constitutes a source of advantage for a system with centrally controlled allocation of labour, as more or less characterized China till recently, since the surplus is much more readily mobilized in that setting than in a comparable market economy such as India's.

6.3.2 Open unemployment

Discussion of open, primarily urban, unemployment as a form of under-utilization of labour has gone through phases not unlike the discussion of disguised unemployment. The phenomenon did not receive much attention prior to the 1960s, probably in part because it was not too prevalent, and also because few reliable statistics were available. But when evidence was produced in the 1960s showing rates of unemployment 10 per cent or higher in a number of LDC cities, at a time when in most ICs the rates were in the range of 2–6 per cent, notice was taken. And with rural–urban migration seeming to swamp the decent job possibilities in the urban areas, many feared a rising pattern of unemployment leading to who knew what sort of disaster (Grant, 1971). The difficulty LDC economies faced in generating enough new jobs was dramatized in the work of the ILO (1970, 1971, 1972) and others. The proposition that unemployment was a problem of *increasing* severity became, if not the conventional wisdom, certainly a very widespread belief.

By 1980 the pendulum had swung once more. There was no evidence of a general pattern of rising open unemployment in the urban areas of LDCs, in spite of their rapid population growth (see especially Gregory, 1980). In many countries the rates of unemployment remained high, at least in comparison with the experience of ICs up till that time. But by the 1970s many ICs were living with unemployment rates in the 6–12 per cent range as well. Awareness increased that open unemployment was at least in part a result of a preference not to accept available low-income/low-status jobs (see Udall and Sinclair, 1982), a tendency more marked among, and helping to explain, the sometimes high rates of unemployment of people with middle levels of education (see, for example, Fields, 1980). While unemployment was certainly not just a matter of unrealistic middle-class youth holding out for good jobs,[10] and in fact it appears that the incidence of open unemployment is greater among poorer urban families than better-off ones (see Tenjo, 1985; Visaria, 1980), it was clear that supply-side considerations such as reservation wages and expectations as to type of job were important. The Harris–Todaro model, in fact, suggested that an increase in the modern sector demand for labour could increase the absolute amount of unemployment and would not necessarily decrease the unemployment rate at all (see Todaro, 1976).

Such an extreme prediction would seem to go too far. Certainly the economic slowdowns of the 1980s have been reflected in marked increases in the rate of unemployment in most Latin American countries (see Garcia and Tokman, 1985, p. 83). How true this is in African countries is less clear, but an important matter, since evidence on the character of rural–urban migration there suggests much more potential for reverse flow back to rural areas when the economy ceases to move ahead (Nelson, 1976). Considerable ties with the rural area are maintained by African migrants, whereas this has not been the norm in Latin America.

More generally, empirical support for the Harris-Todaro model is at this time limited and ambiguous. Though few countries have very adequate open unemployment figures, there seems little evidence that urban rates have often exceeded the 10–15 per cent range for any length of time, and even less evidence that this has been true of migrants or of labour markets with unusually rapid influx of migrants. Similarly infrequent have been the occasions where a real case could be made that migrants could have earned more in rural areas than they in fact did in the urban setting. It seems that urban informal sector incomes are typically higher than rural incomes. These reservations do not imply that the model has no relevance; in fact it would be hard to imagine that the mechanisms it outlines play no role at all in migration. The issue is one of degree. And it is true that in many of the (especially African) countries where it would seem most plausible, there is less empirical information available than elsewhere. Statistical analysis sufficiently refined to provide a definitive test of the model has not yet been possible.[11]

6.3.3 The informal sector: marginalization

With urban populations expanding usually at 3–5 per cent per year over the past few decades, it soon became evident to observers that in most cases the bulk of the new jobs were not being generated in the modern sector (usually thought of as consisting mainly of larger establishments with fairly modern technology, plus the public sector), but in what became variously known as the urban traditional sector, the informal sector, the murky sector, and so on. The fact that this sector was 'murky' to us, the outsiders, reflected our failure to generate organized data on the small-scale, unmodern part of the urban economy. Some authors quickly jumped to the conclusion that the sector (whatever exactly it was) consisted of quite low-income people doing jobs of little social productivity, and who should be discouraged from moving to the city (Mangin, 1967). Fascination with things modern (the 'fatal' fascination?) contributed to this tendency to presume that what escaped the normal data-gathering processes was not of much significance. Ideological predilection was a factor; some authors anticipated a large-scale 'marginalization' of the poor, and wasted no time in presuming that the growth of this informal sector was it.

That most informal sector earnings are low relative to those of the modern sector has proven to be a valid (though hardly surprising) perception. The not insignificant share of incomes which are fairly high has surprised some observers; many informal sector workers earn more than people towards the bottom of the formal sector earnings hierarchy. The idea that persons in this sector were isolated or marginalized from the formal sector (Vekemans and Silva, 1969) proved to have little validity, and has more or less fallen by the wayside (one of the dramatic critiques is Perlman, 1976), as befits an idea which picked up a considerable following prior to any serious empirical evidence appearing on the table.

A more interesting issue is the economic efficiency and contribution of the urban informal sector. Its role in creating at least subsistence income levels for quite a few people is generally recognized. But is it just a sort of 'welfare' sector in which people are saved from destitution? Or is its role more positive than that? The fascination with modernity of technology, size, and capital intensity, which seems to have characterized so many students of development and policy-makers in the earlier years of the post-World War II period, has certainly waned since then. Small farms were shown routinely to achieve higher land productivity than large ones (Berry and Cline, 1979) and higher capital productivity in small and/or medium-sized manufacturing establishments than in large ones was reported in some countries or industries (Sutcliffe, 1971, chapter 6). Everyone agreed that large-scale capital-intensive establishments, even if they were economically efficient, contributed to employment and income distribution problems by using so much capital to create only a few jobs, thereby benefiting only a few workers and a few capitalists when less capital-intensive technologies could have created benefits for many more people. 'Small is beautiful' became a familiar refrain (from the important book by E. F. Schumacher, 1974).

It will, in fact, be a long time before the informal or small-scale sector is understood well enough to clarify its potential role in development, and the overlapping question of whether it is a sector of major underutilization (or misutilization) of labour. Part of the problem is its heterogeneity: there is no doubt that some of the activities it encompasses are carried out as efficiently as in the modern sector, or more so, but it also includes monopolistically competitive sectors such as retail commerce, and socially unproductive activities such as petty theft.[12] As commonly defined, the sector includes substantial manufacturing, commerce, and service employment. Thus far, little evidence has been adduced to suggest that the sector as a whole suffers from low social productivity (relative to private earnings) under normal conditions of reasonable economic growth. Whether this might still be true when a serious economic downturn occurs remains to be seen, perhaps in the experience of the Latin American nations now undergoing that ordeal. Certainly informal activities permit the creation of many jobs with little capital, a fact now recognized in the government and international agency projects to support micro-enterprise in many developing countries.

At this time there seems no reason to believe that the urban informal sector has, in most countries, been chronically and seriously overexpanded relative to its optimal size. Certainly the society would be better without some parts (for example, the criminal activities) and some activities are no doubt larger than would be optimal. But given the evident difficulty of controlling the size and character of the sector, it seems implausible to conceive of policy tools which could be wielded to curtail its size with enough efficiency in an essentially market economy to make their benefits greater than their costs. Direct attempts to curb rural–urban migration, for example, are unlikely to get too far except in societies with very strong central control.

While the urban informal sector is clearly not just a mass of socially unproductive workers in economically suspended animation until they are really needed for some useful purpose, it is not true on the other side that the sector is just one more place where the simple neoclassical model is all one needs to understand what is going on, and where incomes neatly reflect marginal social productivity, as they are sometimes assumed to do in the modern sector. For the urban economy as a whole, for which our information is considerably more complete than for the rural sector, it seems likely that considerable imperfection exists in the labour market, including some introduced by the government via minimum wage legislation or inappropriate public sector pay scales. These imperfections and segmentations it is convenient to discuss below (see section 6.4) in the context of what seem to be the major labour market-related policy issues: educational policy and wage/employment policy.

6.3.4 Urbanization: rural–urban migration

The theories involving major labour underutilization (labour surplus, open unemployment related to the Harris–Todaro or other mechanisms, unproductive informal sector) have had various implications for the appropriate rate of rural–urban migration. When the labour surplus theory was the dominant version of underutilization, it could have been used as a rationale for higher rural–urban migration since the labour surplus was usually viewed as being mainly rural, and awareness of the importance of the urban informal sector was limited. Instead, the more commonly drawn policy implication was in favour of labour-intensive public works (Nurkse, 1953). And soon there was recognition of urban labour surplus too (Reynolds, 1969). The magnitude both of open urban unemployment and of the urban informal sector have generally been construed as reason to believe that rural–urban migration has been excessive (Friedmann and Sullivan, 1974).

If one concludes that none of these three phenomena implies the degree of underutilization sometimes attributed to them, the associated arguments to the effect that rural–urban migration is often excessive in LDCs are correspondingly weakened. Plausible assumptions about their magnitude suggest rather modest misallocation of labour resources between rural and urban areas, making the whole issue of distinctly secondary importance (for some tentative quantifications see Berry, 1985). If migration is excessive, it would seem that the fault lies not with any inefficiency in the process itself, or with any broad features of labour market functioning (like the sources of underutilization mentioned), but with public policies which favour urban dwellers and urban economic activities. Public spending on urban areas is substantial; apart from better employment opportunities, urban residence usually improves one's (or one's children's) chances for education, health services and other benefits. And public policy normally involves a bias towards the creation of urban jobs; neither labour-intensive agriculture nor small non-agricultural enterprises which may locate in rural areas tend to receive a great deal of public support (see Lipton, 1977). The magnitude of these biases is very hard to gauge. Urbanization is in many countries a very expensive process; Arthur Lewis (1977) has even linked it to the debt problem of many LDCs. Certainly it is true that the Western middle-class style of life, intensive directly and indirectly in imports, is primarily an urban style in most LDCs (Keyfitz, 1982). Unfortunately it is extremely hard to get the sort of quantitative information which would enable one to disentangle the inevitable and natural costs associated with an economy's structural shift away from agriculture and towards more capital-intensive sectors and techniques, from unnecessary costs associated with a favouring of urban dwellers and activities (one attempt to get at some of the relevant magnitudes is Linn, 1982). Research is urgently needed in this area. About all one can say with some confidence is that, if urbanization has generally proceeded too fast and been too expensive, this is not mainly attributable to what one would normally call labour market failures (for example migration to urban areas even though employment opportunities are inferior to rural ones), but to errors of public policy (for example excess subsidization to urban dwellers and urban-based activities).

6.4 The determinants of labour earnings

6.4.1 The returns to education

The evidence reviewed above casts doubt on the various propositions which have become popular at one time or another during the past three or four decades to the effect that major portions of the labour force are unproductive. Perhaps, indeed, quite a portion is; but this has not yet been well demonstrated, and the policy implications of such contentions for governments of market economies seem quite limited, especially since the desirability of policies to raise the demand for labour is already an obvious implication of the high levels of economic inequality and the low labour earnings in most LDCs. Characteristics of the labour market other than the level of underutilization may be more important for policy purposes. Probably the most important policy area where the evidence available to decision-makers calls for a good understanding of that market is education. Whereas we do not need to understand the workings of the labour market with great precision to conclude that little loss associated with underutilization of labour could be avoided by any feasible policy steps, in the case of education major expenditures occur each year whose economic payoff is rather sensitive to exactly how one believes the labour market works. Worse, for one to have a high degree of confidence in one's estimates of the economic payoff to investment in education, one must believe that the labour market functions in a fairly close to neoclassical way.

A review of the issues surrounding the estimation of the economic returns to education provides a window onto a whole set of interesting aspects of labour market functioning. And the importance of the issue is immediately apparent in the sums of money involved. As of about 1980 the share of GNP which governments spent on education was probably around 4–5 per cent in LDCs and the share of the national budget averaged 15–20 per cent (extrapolating from figures in World Bank, 1980, p. 67). Were private outlays and opportunity costs included, the former figure might be in the range of 7–8 per cent of GNP, and of course higher in some countries. With gross domestic investment as conventionally measured falling in the range of 15–25 per cent in many LDCs, and net domestic investment rather lower, it becomes clear that expenditures on education are not a trivial share of total investment in human and physical capital. Whether those expenditures 'pay off' is an increasingly important issue from an overall economic point of view.

The human capital model and its problems

Since the estimated returns to education reflect the magnitude of earnings differentials by level of education, and since those differentials are a major factor in the serious income inequalities afflicting many LDCs, the study of those differentials is of interest for more than one reason. In Latin American countries, with their extreme levels of inequality, the average gap in earnings between university-trained people and illiterates, for example, reaches levels like ten to one and higher (see Psacharopoulos, 1973).

Estimates of the economic rate of return to education have been based almost exclusively on the 'human capital model' with or (usually) without any complications beyond its simplest neoclassical format. They are therefore usually vulnerable to any misspecification which that model may entail. Typically the methodology involves estimating, for a cross-section data set, the human capital equation

$$R = f(S, E)$$

where R is the level of remuneration, S is level of schooling, and E is years of experience. The precise functional form varies from study to study, as do the inclusion of other variables whose omission might bias the coefficients of S and E (for example, quality of education, location of residence and so on).[13]

This human capital methodology has usually produced rather high estimates of the social (as well as the private) returns to education, with a tendency for these to be higher at the primary level and substantially lower for higher education. Estimated private rates of return have tended to be high for all levels of education (Psacharopoulos, 1973, 1980). Less evidence is available for technical education, though here too satisfactory returns have been reported with frequency. As noted above, the generally high 'returns' to education reflect wide earnings gaps by level of education in most LDCs. At the primary level, especially, the relatively low costs of education also contribute to the high estimated returns (Zymelman, 1976).

Though the accuracy of human capital model estimates of the private returns to education is subject to problems of omitted variables, functional form, and the use of cross-section data to predict over-time profiles, there is reasonable hope that the resulting uncertainties can be diminished, and that the estimates have some meaning. Certainly the existence of high private rates of return is consistent with the obviously great demand for education in LDCs. When it comes to the *social* returns to education – the estimates of relevance for public policy – one cannot be so sanguine. Here, for the estimates to hold water, one must accept that earnings differentials within a cross-section of workers accurately reflect productivity differentials. The debate around the validity of this assumption leads one into a number of aspects of labour market functioning, and in particular into the matter of the determinants of wage or earnings structure.

Probably no one doubts that productivity is an important determinant of earnings; the question here is, 'how close is it to being the sole determinant of earnings'? And on this point our knowledge becomes inadequate to the task at hand. Assessing the payoff to various levels and types of education with the set of information typically available – the average and variance of the earnings of people with different levels of education, experience and other measurable variables – involves dealing with questions of how earnings structures are set and how people are selected for specific jobs. At one extreme is the proposition that, for each and every worker, earnings are equal to the value of the marginal product or, equally facilitating, that for a given category of workers (for example those with a given level of education and a given length of work experience) the average earnings equal the average value of the marginal product. The typical regression analysis is successful as long as the introduction of other determinants of productivity and of earnings leave the equation capable of detecting the marginal impact of education and experience on productivity/earnings.

But there are serious reasons for doubting whether either the education to productivity or the productivity to earnings links, which are essential to the human capital approach to measurement of the payoff to education, are accurately reflected in the typical human capital regression. Probably the major sources of concern are the following:

1 The hard-to-measure role of ability as a determinant of productivity and earnings, and the possibility that a positive correlation between level of education and ability will lead to overestimates of the positive effects of education when ability is omitted from the regression.

2 The possibility that many wage or earnings structures do not reflect relative marginal productivities but rather institutional factors (such as beliefs as to appropriate relative pay for different types of activities or different levels of education, or inertia) (for a detailed discussion, see Phelps-Brown, 1977) and the associated possibility that, because it is not really productivity which determines earnings, both students and educational institutions focus unduly on the 'credentials' provided by those institutions (Dore, 1976).

3 The possibility that employers take account of job candidates' levels of education and performance in school, not so much because what was learned there is important to their potential performance in the job, but because it signals the candidates' general levels of ability; that is, it is a good screening device (Arrow, 1973; Bowman, 1976).

4 The probability that earnings differentials at a point of time (the raw material for nearly all rate-of-return calculations) do not accurately predict the differentials which will exist in the future.

Few rate-of-return studies have worried a great deal about these or other sources of bias in their estimates, so there is not much empirical evidence on which to judge the sensitivity of estimates to the sources of possible bias. There seems little reason to doubt that the biases related to the factors cited above are positive; that is, their impact is to lead to overestimates of the true return. But there are probably biases in the other direction as well, including the failure of the standard methodology to take account of some social benefits which are not captured in private earnings – for example, the benefits resulting from technological improvements fostered by education, the benefits of smaller family size related to education, and so on (Berry, 1980; Bowman, 1980). So, in spite of the putative precision of the figures, much uncertainty remains. But since alternative methodologies for judging the benefits of education and training are not promising at this time, it is important to get as much as is possible out of the human capital approach, with its focus on how the labour market works. In this connection the studies which should be taken most seriously are those which attempt to deal with the above-cited problems of the simple human capital approach, as well as with other sources of possible bias. They should provide both the most reliable assessments of the payoffs to various levels of education available, and useful insights into how labour markets work.

Advances in human capital model analysis

The first generation of rate of return studies, as noted above, produced generally high figures for both private and social returns. Too seldom have there been studies for a given country at two separate points of time but with similar methodologies to permit an assessment of whether and how rates of return have changed over time. (Among the few examples are Knight and Sabot, 1981; Mohan, 1981.) One would expect these rates to have fallen in many countries in the wake of the very rapid increase in levels of education.[14] In a number of countries it does appear that the relative earnings of lower-level white-collar workers (for example, clerical personnel) have fallen relative to those of blue-collar workers (this result is documented for Colombia by Urrutia, 1985), which might suggest a declining rate of return to secondary-level education.

What we might refer to as a second generation of rate-of-return or earnings function studies attempt to take account of the effects of obviously relevant variables omitted in the simplest formulations, including ability, quality of schooling, social connections, place of residence and a few others (for example, Behrman and Birdsall, 1983; Behrman and Wolfe, 1984). The results provide some hints on labour market functioning. Of particular interest is the fact that attempts to allow for socioeconomic background and connections, invariably recognized as helping people to get good jobs in developing countries, have not uncovered evidence that these connections have really dramatic effects on the earnings experience of a person (Psacharopolous, 1977). While failure to take account of such connections does tend to bias the returns to education upward, it does not appear to do so excessively.

Allowance for ability involves much subtler questions, since little evidence is available in most data sets, and since the type of ability which pays off in higher earnings may not be the type measured by IQ or other available standard measures. It has been generally presumed that failure to include ability as a determinant of earnings would lead to an overestimate of the benefits of education. Some analysts have, for want of a better way, simply assumed (following Denison, 1974), that a third of the effects of education on earnings, as estimated in a regression without a measure of ability, are due to ability and only the remaining two-thirds to education (Blaug, 1976, p. 842).

A rate-of-return analysis must be considered methodologically incomplete if it does not incorporate in some testable way both the neoclassical assumption that the labour market works smoothly and that earnings reflect marginal social productivity, and the competing idea that credentials are important as a determinant of earnings and employment access either because they are believed to reflect ability or for other more institutional reasons. Too few studies have met these requirements to provide much feel for the relative explanatory power of the various competing mechanisms, and hence to permit a more solidly based judgment on the social returns to education. In a recent effort based on data from Kenya, Boissière *et al.* (1985) have made an interesting initiative in this direction. Using Raven's Progressive Matrices as a measure of reasoning ability, and the sum of scores on literacy and numeracy tests as a measure of cognitive skills, they estimated that whereas the standard earnings equation (with level of education and years of experience as independent variables) implied a rate of return to secondary education (over completed primary) of 13 per cent,[15] the gain in cognitive skills by itself would imply a rate of return in the range of 4–11 per cent, closer to the higher figure the more the independent variable 'level of schooling' was picking up cognitive gains not picked up by the proxy used to that end. It is clear that many more tests of this sort are required before strong views will be warranted on the relative earnings effects of cognitive skills gained in the educational process vis-à-vis those of credentials.

6.4.2　Labour market interventions versus other economic policies

Apart from education, where government policy can clearly have a major impact on the labour market, and probably on overall development, the next most important labour market-related issues involve possible interventions or attitudes of the government on how that market should function, in particular, policy on minimum or other wage legislation, public sector pay scales, unionization, non-wage labour costs (such as social security, severance pay, etc.), discrimination by sex, ethnic group, etc. Thus far empirical analysis has made only a modest contribution to understanding on these matters, because of their inherent complexity.

Policies affecting labour costs

In most countries the more progressive political forces, typically representing middle-strata groups such as modern sector employees, take a stand in favour of labour market interventions, with the conservative groups opposing them. Usually the poor, including most of the rural sector and the informal urban sector, have no real champions in the political process, so their welfare is essentially left out of these discussions (Ascher, 1984; Webb, 1977, p. 87). In some countries the government intervenes very little, neither supporting nor actively blocking the development of union power, for example, and keeping legislated minimum wages close to market-determined levels; in others it appears that these phenomena do affect the real cost of labour significantly. Labour policy is a heated issue in many countries, since the advantages of higher wages and of protection against the exploitative practices which are endemic in the labour markets of many Third World countries are so obvious, while the conservative views are often held with the fervour of divine right. But the issues are complicated even for the dispassionate outsider. The question of how much employment will be reduced (and unemployment perhaps increased) when the cost of labour is raised above its market level is central here, and has not been easy to come to grips with empirically.

It is necessary to consider both (1) the question of how large are the gaps created by union power and public sector interventions between the actual cost of labour and its opportunity cost, and (2) the impact of those gaps on GNP and on the incomes of various groups. The literature on labour market segmentation has often suggested that the cost of labour in the modern, protected sector was far above its opportunity cost. This proposition is of course fortified if one accepts, as per the labour surplus model, that the marginal product of labour is below its wage in much of the traditional sector. Clearly, countries are likely to differ, perhaps quite importantly, on both counts. Research efforts aimed at assessing the extent of labour surplus and/or the degree of labour market segmentation have tended to scale down some early guesses as to the magnitude of these phenomena, and to provide alternative interpretations of substantial wage gaps.[16] Still, it seems likely that labour market interventions and imperfections do push actual labour cost well above opportunity cost in some settings, and thereby lead to lower employment than would otherwise occur, especially in the longer run when the effects of high labour costs on technology choice have been felt.

It is useful for our purposes to distinguish these types of situations where respectively:

1 A combination of limited pressure on wages from the supply side (for example because minimum wages are set not far above the equilibrium level) and obvious inelasticity on the demand side creates a situation where the interventions/imperfections simply have little impact on employment, output, or income distribution.
2 The economy can, for purposes of analysing this issue, be considered to be one sector, and the effects on employment and output can fairly easily be shown to be large (discussions falling into this category include Meade, 1961 and Brecher, 1974). Predicting the impact on income distribution requires more information than predicting those on employment and output.
3 Because of the existence of other imperfections, and/or the need to distinguish a sector where an above-equilibrium wage exists and one where this is not the case, analysis of the impact of labour market interventions/imperfections is in

fact very complicated, and there is no presumption that the effects are either large or small.

The ambiguous case (3) seems the most likely in LDC settings. Even where there is strong evidence that above-equilibrium wages, restraints on firing, and employer insecurity as to degree of control over future labour costs do make the affected sector of the economy more capital-intensive,[17] and do lower its competitiveness and slow its expansion, it may be necessary to know how other sectors are affected, and how well they perform, before one can reach useful overall conclusions. Neither the agricultural nor the informal sector are normally affected directly by unions, wage legislation and the like. One of the essential questions is how well the high-wage sector performs relative to these parts of the economy in terms of whatever combination of output, employment and income distribution make up one's objective function. If the answer is 'well',[18] then impediments to its growth and labour intensity are likely to worsen overall economic performance. If the answer is 'not well', or is ambiguous, the picture becomes clouded. We do know, of course, that comparisons across firms of different sizes and levels of technological modernity show up tremendous gaps in factor proportions, and hence in single factor productivities. We no longer accept the idea that efficiency is always related positively to either size or technological modernity. Hence a market imperfection which slows the expansion of the large-scale modern sector *may* increase overall efficiency of the economy by shrinking the relative size of that inefficient sector. In a case where that *is* true, however, the imperfection may simultaneously lower the efficiency of the modern sector (causing a loss), so its overall effect could still be negative.

A two-sector breakdown may still fail to capture the relevant distinctions needed to analyse adequately the impact of labour market imperfections. In many countries, while the economic and social efficiency of the modern large-scale sector is not high, the very small informal sector may have so high a labour-capital ratio, and/or such unproductive technology, that its efficiency is also not high. There may be, in fact or in prospect, a middle sector which has more capacity to contribute to the country's development than either the larger, more capital-intensive or the smaller, more traditional, sector. This middle sector may be subject to the higher than equilibrium wages which hold in the modern sector, or it may not. Usually it gets rather little subsidized capital. In an economy where it is meaningful to distinguish among these three sectors, labour market imperfections which raise the cost of labour might be beneficial as long as they are limited to the large-scale capital-intensive sector, whose competitiveness they diminish, but damaging if they impinge also on this middle sector. The dynamism of small and medium-sized manufacturing firms in Colombia during the 1970s illustrates the potential of this sector; aggregate employment of plants with 5–50 workers probably grew at 8–10 per cent per year, profits were good, labour productivity was rising and so on (see Cortes *et al.*, 1987). It is doubtful that such dynamism could have occurred had both (a) wages been as high as in the country's largest manufacturing establishments and (b) impediments to firing workers been great. Many of the firms were experiencing dramatic fluctuations in employment and output during the decade of rapid aggregate growth, and any restriction on their freedom to expand and contract quickly would have no doubt discouraged their expansion or continuance in the market. Such a case suggests that the overall effects of labour market interventions/imperfections may depend very much on what part of the economy is directly affected by them.

Wage policy and trade policy

The simpler analysis in which the modern sector, which is or would be adversely affected by labour market interventions/imperfections, is efficient may be most relevant for trading economies such as Korea, Taiwan, Hong Kong or Singapore. They have been able to take advantage of their abundant cheap labour in order to export, grow rapidly, accumulate capital and quickly graduate from the labour-abundant category as wages rise quickly. One certainly cannot discount the possibility that in such countries strongly organized labour is a major threat to the future welfare of the labouring class itself. (In cases such as Colombia, this might be true only if labour costs were also pushed well above equilibrium in the small and medium enterprises.) To take a suggestive comparison, while it comes as no surprise that Argentina has grown less rapidly in the post-war period than Korea, it may be less widely known that wages kept pace with growth in Korea, rising by 6.2 per cent per year (in the manufacturing sector) over 1957–82 while the comparable series for Argentina fell by 1.3 per cent per year over 1950–82 and rose by only a modest 1 per cent per year over 1950–74, prior to the recent crisis (see table 6.1).

The Taiwanese case, where employment generation has also been rapid and where an impressively egalitarian distribution of income has been achieved, is also consistent with the argument that an equilibrium wage policy (that is, non-intervention and, if necessary, repression of labour organizations) can contribute to rising labour incomes by permitting rapid growth of employment via specialization on labour-intensive exports, and a rapid associated growth of output. While little detailed evidence has yet been adduced on the precise role of equilibrium wages in successful labour-intensive export growth (due to the problem of disentangling the effects of trade policy and of wage policy) it is plausible to expect that role to be positive. There seems no reason to doubt that outward orientation often contributes to rapid employment growth in the tradeables sector, due to the generally higher intensity of less skilled labour in the export industries of LDCs than in the import competing industries, though the case of natural resource exports is of course an exception to this proposition. Its impact on income distribution is harder to assess. In fact there have been only a few serious attempts to test for the effects of trade strategy in individual countries on employment, unemployment, or income distribution using macro-data over time. Fei *et al.*'s (1979) effort in the case of Taiwan is, I believe, the most detailed attempt to link trade strategy to income distribution. Some of the studies included in a recent volume by Krueger *et al.* (1981) provide reasonably strong evidence of favourable employment effects.[19] These various results are reassuring for the outward orientation view, though it remains to be seen how

Table 6.1 Wages and GNP Growth in Argentina and Korea

	Argentina	Korea
GNP per capita: 1982[a] (US dollars)	2520	1910
Average annual growth of GDP, 1950–82[c]	2.84%	7.70[b]%
Average annual increase in manufacturing real wages:		
1950–82[d]	− 1.3%	6.2[e]%
1950–74	0.95%	−

[a] World Bank (1984, p. 219).
[b] 1955–82, since the 1955 figure was far above 1950's figure as a result of the impact of the Korean war on the latter.
[c] World Bank, *World Tables*, 1976 and *World Tables: The Third Edition*.
[d] For Korea, for the period 1957–75, Kim and Roemer (1979, p. 73); and ILO *Yearbook of Labour Statistics* for earlier and later years. For Argentina, 1950–2 to 1959–61, Diaz-Alejandro (1970, p. 129); for later years, ILO *Yearbook of Labour Statistics*.
[e] 1957–82.

general they may be, or how quantitatively important are the effects of trade policy on these variables. And, from our perspective here, it remains to be seen just how central a market wage policy is to a successful outward orientation. In a recent study, Fields (1984) has argued that wage policy (allowing the market to determine wages) and trade policy are related sources of the high growth of exports and of output in the four East Asian countries; he contrasts their experiences with those of Barbados, Jamaica and Trinidad–Tobago, where he believes the 'interventions' in the form of minimum wage legislation and high public sector wages have raised inequality among wage-earners. The comparison is suggestive but not conclusive; Trinidad–Tobago has recorded Gini coefficients comparable to those for Hong Kong and Singapore, while those for Jamaica are so high that it is evident that the major factor at work is not wage differentials between protected and unprotected workers. There is no doubt that inequality is lower in Korea and Taiwan than in most LDCs, and the outward orientation period has coincided with a decline in inequality in Taiwan; whether this is the case for Korea is a matter of dispute. Inequality is not atypically low in either Hong Kong or Singapore, nor does it appear to have shown a systematic downward trend. The low level of inequality in Taiwan and Korea is probably related much more to the postwar land reforms, from which these countries benefited, than to trade policy.

Direct and strong evidence on the effects of an outward-oriented strategy or a market wage policy on income distribution may not be soon forthcoming; in most countries data on distribution are neither very accurate nor very comparable over time, and sorting out the effects of other relevant factors is hard. Nonetheless, a reasonable best guess is that the supporters of outward orientation have a generally valid point here, though results will vary from country to country.[20] If wage policy is central to successful labour-intensive export expansion, it is likely to be particularly important in countries where such expansion is a serious possibility, but of less importance in other countries.

Attempts to isolate the direct impact of above-equilibrium wages in a subsector of an LDC economy on income distribution have, like counterpart efforts in ICs, had a difficult time. The presumption that distribution among workers is worsened is based on the reasonable guess that raising wages for a protected group will lower them for the unprotected. But how this influences the household income distribution is not so clear. Nor, more generally, is the overall distributional impact when capitalists are also taken into account. Although any conclusion would be premature at this time, it seems likely that wage policy is a far less important direct determinant of income distribution than is educational policy. Its indirect effects could be crucial, though, if it has major impacts on a country's strategic options, and especially on the option of labour-intensive exports.

6.5 Labour market participation and discrimination

Economists have dedicated considerable attention to the study of determinants of labour market participation in LDCs (see Standing, 1978). In the absence of a belief that malfunction of that market implies that non-participants 'should' be participating, or vice-versa, the policy significance of this work would be unclear, and it might be argued that the rate of labour force participation was more a matter of curiosity than of policy significance. If one believes that there are many 'discouraged workers' who would participate were the payoffs more attractive, there might be logic to such study. More relevant at this time, trends in the rate of female participation in urban labour forces are worthy of analysis. In most cases such participation is both reflection of, and contributor to, a process of broad social change. From a narrowly economic point of view, one of its significant impacts may be on the rate of population growth, which is of obvious importance to the future of LDCs. It may also have significant impacts on personal and family income distribution (though the direction of those effects is not clear), and on female education.

It is well known that official census and survey figures on female labour force participation are misleading; they show little participation in rural, agricultural areas but greater involvement in urban areas, but it is well known that the difference being picked up is in the *type* of work, not in the *amount*. In terms of the impact on fertility, however, it does seem to be the type of work which matters. Research tends to show that urban women who work full-time, particularly in 'modern' jobs, have fewer children. For one thing they tend to delay marriage – by 1½–2 years according to a study of five Asian countries. In addition, they are most frequent users of contraceptives (World Bank, 1984, p. 110). The opportunity of employment may affect fertility indirectly by raising the incentive for parents to educate girls given the now higher status of women in the family. But fertility doubtless affects participation, so it is very hard to assess the magnitude of the causal effects from participation to fertility.[21]

228   *Factor markets in LDCs*

For students of labour markets, the potentially beneficial effects of higher female labour force participation are of major interest to the extent that they are affected by how labour markets work. With smoothly functioning labour markets it might turn out that the rising presence of women in modern sector activities was mainly a matter of the education they received, and the absence of the social pressures exercised in the family against such participation. Alternatively, though, labour market discrimination against women could be a significant determinant of participation as well, of course, as being important in its own right. It requires no refined techniques to detect sex discrimination of various types in many LDCs, reflecting the strongly type-cast roles of the sexes, and the usually strongly dominant position of men. Earnings gaps for urban men and women of similar education and experience are frequently in the range of 20–40 per cent, and perhaps somewhat greater than the corresponding figures for industrial countries, though too little evidence is available yet to be sure.[22] And other forms of exploitation of women are of course present and probably frequent, as well.

What labour market interventions would have a reasonable chance to diminish the negative welfare and distributional impacts of discrimination is not clear; the discrimination may occur in the labour market context, but it reflects attitudes widely held in the society and, as is the case of the overall impact of many interventions, there are likely to be offsetting mechanisms. Minimum wage legislation, for example, could help to erase male–female earnings differentials, but might at the same time cut female employment, as employers who previously hired women only because they were cheaper would now exercise their basic discriminatory preference to hire men. How discrimination or other imperfections impinge on fertility behaviour, through the rate of female labour force participation and the sort of jobs women get, also remains at this time unclear. To the extent that imperfections impede female involvement in the 'modern' sector this effect must be negative. To the extent that rigid sex roles preserve lower-paid but still modern sector activities like domestic service and secretarial work for women, there may be some offset. In short, both the direct effects of discrimination on welfare, and the indirect effects via fertility behaviour, deserve more attention and research.

6.6 Summary

The obvious labour abundance in most LDCs has contributed to both useful and not so useful conceptualization of the processes determining the allocation and utilization of the labour force. The Lewis labour surplus model, the Harris–Todaro model, technological rigidity, concepts of marginalization and segmentation, the informal sector and various other ideas have had their day in court. Each has provided relevant questions and insights, with the result that we now understand a great deal more about labour markets than was the case 30–40 years ago. Our assumptions are more refined, and in general more defensible. In terms of how adequate our current understanding is in relation to the needs of wise policy-making, both labour market-related policy and other policy, the situation is a much less happy one. In the words of Kannappan (1985) 'Economic analysis of the growth and functioning of urban labour markets in developing nations is in an undeveloped state' (p. 719) (see also Kannappan, 1983). The advance in understanding would, to be sure, discourage informed policy-makers from anticipating a major output or investment increase by putting surplus labour to work, or from trying to block rural–urban migration on the grounds that it would lead either to explosive levels of open unemployment or to an excessively large and socially unproductive urban informal sector. But in neither of these cases do available policy instruments appear capable of doing much for good or ill anyway. When it comes to areas where policy can and does have impacts – such as educational expenditures and labour market interventions which create or attempt to remove 'imperfections' in that market – we are as yet in a quite unsatisfactory position.

Hopefully ongoing research will gradually shrink the extent of our ignorance, but the task will probably not be easy.

NOTES

1. Though the phenomena they describe are clearly not exclusive to those contexts and have certainly been discussed in industrial countries too.
2. Prominent authors in the IC literature include Doeringer and Piore (1971) and Gordon (1972). A review article is that of Cain (1976). The literature on segmented or dualistic labour markets in LDCs is large; in fact much of the literature tends to take dualism for granted. Important studies are Mazumdar (1976, 1983).
3. I distinguish literature and thinking since, inevitably, a new model or paradigm will tend to get much exposure in the literature as it is being worked out and elaborated, even if only a minority of specialists become its adherents. Perhaps accidentally, at about the time that a literature on LDC labour markets was being born, standard labour market theory was being challenged by Reynolds and others for the over-simplification resulting from its severe abstraction. See, especially, Reynolds (1951).
4. The original published statement of the model is Todaro (1969).
5. The ILO Kenya study (ILO, 1972) gave impetus to this view. A number of studies in India have also used unemployment as a criterion. For a helpful review of alternative approaches to the estimation of unemployment in India see Krishna (1973).
6. An articulate criticism of this idea is found in Sen (1975). Note that careful study of the employment context of low-income workers may be very useful in guessing the extent and manifestations of labour surplus (see, for example, Turnham, 1970, p. 69). But this does not mean that the *number* of low-income workers has much to do with the degree of surplus labour.
7. Studies of decision-making on separation of family members, including recent work on the determinants of conjugal separation (for example, Banerjee, 1984) may help in understanding this more general question. The same goes for the recent body of work on family and farm modelling, reviewed by Singh *et al.* (1986).
8. Particular attention has been given to the Japanese case, where Minami's (1970) work has been central. Agricultural wages appear to have shown no positive trend over periods of substantial growth in a number of countries, including Brazil, 1940s to late 1960s (Pfefferman and Webb, 1983), and Colombia (Berry and Urrutia, 1976, pp. 66–7).

9. A somewhat fuller discussion of this issue is presented in Berry and Sabot (1978).

10. Though the Malaysia case illustrated just how far this pattern could go; there, as of 1967, half of persons aged 15-24 who were first-time unemployed had been unemployed for a year or more (Mazumdar, 1980, p. 262).

11. Among the interesting contributions in this area are studies by Schultz (1982) for Venezuela and Fields (1982) for Colombia. These authors found limited (Schultz) or no (Fields) explanatory power for an employment variable (defined as one minus the rate of unemployment), as opposed to wage differentials, in explaining the rate of migration. These studies, and many others like them, suffer from the fact that the use of open unemployment, however defined, as a measure of the prevalence of failure does not give a fair hearing to the Harris–Todaro idea, that migration is undertaken in the face of uncertainty with respect to the income which will be received, and is stimulated by the possibility of much higher incomes than are obtainable in the region of origin. Schultz's wage data, for example, refer to the average earnings of a given group; where a low-income job rather than unemployment is the manifestation of failure to get the 'hoped-for' high-income job, those average wages may already incorporate the 'failures' which Schultz (and much of the literature) identifies with open unemployment. The appropriate specification would have to include the variance of earnings for a given group as well as average earnings. The Harris–Todaro hypothesis might require even more novel testing, by using direct evidence on pre-migration expectations. Yet even the test performed by Schultz could not be undertaken in most African countries for want of data.

12. Though whether theft is any more prevalent in the informal than in the formal sector is not entirely clear.

13. Other ways of calculating the payoff to education, training, and experience are theoretically possible, but none has proven helpful thus far. Cross-country or over-time production function analysis can in principle quantify the effects of an input such as education-based skills, but the adequate specification of such a production function is at this time so far beyond our capacity as to render this a rather forlorn hope, especially when one wishes to distinguish among different levels and types of education. Work in this area is desirable, but is unlikely to provide a substitute methodology in the near future.

14. The impressive increases recorded in most LDCs are apparent in the figures presented each year in the World Bank's *World Development Report*.

15. For the sub-sample on which they had the full information needed to perform the tests to which we refer here. For the full sample, the rate of return was estimated at 16 per cent.

16. Mazumdar's (1979) argument to the effect that the wage gap between casual labour and permanent labour mainly reflects a difference in the supply price of permanent and temporary migrants is one such alternative.

17. When these phenomena are coupled with subsidies to capital, the resulting degree of capital intensity may be great.

18. As might clearly be the case if the sector has a good output–capital ratio and creates a lot of jobs for persons currently in the lower part of the income distribution.

19. This volume includes the results of 10 country studies, which focus on how the trade regime affects manufacturing employment via its effect on the composition of output (between export-oriented and import-substitution industries) and on choice of technique and capital–labour ratios. The study reports that the Heckscher–Ohlin-type prediction, that export industries not based on availability of some natural resource (here called HOS goods in distinction from NRB goods) will be more labour-intensive than import-substituting ones, generally holds, as does the proposition that certain

features of trade policy (e.g. relatively low tariffs on imported capital goods) and other market distortions (e.g. interest rate subsidies) frequently bias factor proportions toward an excessive use of capital.

20. Factor proportions are correlated not only with industry (the correlation which makes the Hecksher–Ohlin model of interest) but also with firm and plant size. Large firms tend, even within a given industry, to have higher capital–labour ratios than do smaller ones. Large firms also can more successfully move into the large arena of international trade. This combination of circumstances could offset any income-distribution benefits coming from the Hecksher–Ohlin effect; the issue is an empirical one and very little evidence has to date been adduced. (For a discussion see Berry and Diaz-Alejandro, 1980.)

21. A point emphasized, for example, by Schultz (1981, p. 105). For an extensive treatment of the relationships between the two variables, see Standing (1978, chapter 7).

22. Differentials in wage rates, without allowance for education or experience, are not clearly either greater or smaller in LDCs than in ICs, though again the data are very sparse in the LDCs (Schultz, 1981, pp. 210–11).

REFERENCES

Arellano, K. 1981. Do more jobs in the modern sector increase urban unemployment? *Journal of Development Economics*, 8, 241–7.

Arrow, K. J. 1973. Higher education as a filter. *Journal of Public Economics*, 2, 193–216.

Ascher, W. 1984. *Scheming for the Poor: The Politics of Redistribution in Latin America*. Cambridge, Mass.: Harvard University Press.

Banerjee, B. 1984. Rural to urban migration and conjugal separation: an Indian case study. *Economic Development and Cultural Change*, 32, 767–80.

Behrman, J. and Birdsall, N. 1983. The quality of schooling: quantity alone is misleading. *American Economic Review*, 73, 928–46.

Behrman, J. and Wolfe, B. 1984. The socio-economic impact of schooling in a developing country. *Review of Economics and Statistics*, 66, 296–303.

Berry, A. 1980. Education, income, productivity and urban poverty. In T. King (ed.), *Education and Income*. World Bank Staff Working Paper No. 402, Washington DC: World Bank.

Berry, A. 1985. 'The social efficiency of rural–urban migration in developing countries'. Mimeo.

Berry, A. and Cline, W. 1979. *Agrarian Structure and Productivity in Developing Countries*. Baltimore: Johns Hopkins University Press.

Berry, A. and Diaz-Alejandro, C. 1980. The new Colombian exports: possible effects on the distribution of income. In A. Berry and R. Soligo (eds), *Economic Policy and Income Distribution in Colombia*. Boulder, Col.: Westview.

Berry, A. and Sabot, R. H. 1978. Labour market performance in developing countries: a survey. *World Development*, 6, 1199–1242.

Berry, A. and Soligo, R. (eds). 1980. *Economic Policy and Income Distribution in Colombia*. Boulder, Col.: Westview.

Berry, A. and Urrutia, M. 1976. *Income Distribution in Colombia*. New Haven: Yale University Press.

Blaug, M. 1976. The empirical status of human capital theory: a slightly jaundiced survey. *Journal of Economic Literature*, 14, 827–55.

Boissière, M., Knight, J. B. and Sabot, R. H. 1985. Earnings, schooling, ability and cognitive skills. *American Economic Review*, 75, 1016–30.

Bowman, M. J. 1976. Through education to earnings. *Proceedings of the National Academy of Education*, 3, 221-92.

Bowman, M. J. 1980. Education and economic growth: an overview. In T. King (ed.), *Education and Income*. World Bank Staff Working Paper No. 402. Washington, DC: World Bank.

Brecher, R. 1974. Minimum wage rates and the pure theory of international trade. *Quarterly Journal of Economics*, 88, 98-116.

Cain, G. 1976. The challenge of segmented labour market theories to orthodox theory: a survey. *Journal of Economic Literature*, 14, 1215-57.

Cortes, M., Berry, A. and Ishag, A. 1987. *What Makes for Success in Small and Medium Scale Enterprises: The Evidence from Colombia*. Baltimore: Johns Hopkins University Press.

Denison, E. F. 1974. *Accounting for U.S. Growth, 1929-1969*. Washington, DC: The Brookings Institution.

Desai, M. and Mazumdar, D. 1970. A test of the hypothesis of disguised unemployment. *Economica*, 37, 39-53.

Diaz-Alejandro, C. 1970. *Essays on the Economic History of the Argentine Republic*. New Haven: Yale University Press.

Doeringer, P. B. and Piore, M. J. 1971. *Internal Labour Markets and Manpower Analysis*. Lexington, Mass.: D.C. Heath.

Dore, R. 1976. *The Diploma Disease: Education, Qualification and Development*. Berkeley: University of California Press.

Fei, J. C. H. and Ranis, G. 1964. *Development of the Labour Surplus Economy*. Homewood, Ill.: Irwin.

Fei, J. C. H., Ranis, G. and Kuo, S. W. Y. 1979. *Growth with Equity: the Taiwan Case*. New York: Oxford University Press.

Fields, G. S. 1980. Education and income distribution in developing countries: a review of literature. In T. King (ed.), *Education and Income*. World Bank Staff Working Paper No. 402. Washington, D.C.: World Bank.

Fields, G. S. 1982. Place to place migration in Colombia. *Economic Development and Cultural Change*, 30, 539-58.

Fields, G. S. 1984. Employment, income distribution and economic growth in seven small open economies. *Economic Journal*, 94, 74-83.

Friedmann, J. and Sullivan, F. 1974. The absorption of labour in the urban economy: the case of developing economies. *Economic Development and Cultural Change*, 22, 385-413.

Garcia, N. and Tokman, V. 1985. *Acumulacion, Empleo y Crisis*. Santiago, Chile: Oficina Internacional del Trabajo, PREALC, Investigaciones Sobre Empleo 25.

Gordon, D. 1972. *Theories of Poverty and Unemployment*. Lexington, Mass.: D.C. Heath.

Grant, J. P. 1971. 'Marginal man': the global unemployment crisis. *Foreign Affairs*, 50, 112-24.

Gregory, P. 1980. An assessment of changes in employment conditions in LDCs. *Economic Development and Cultural Change*, 28, 673-700.

Hansen, B. 1969. Employment and wages in rural Egypt. *American Economic Review*, 59, 298-313.

Harris, J. R. and Todaro, M. P. 1970. Migration, unemployment and development: a two-sector analysis. *American Economic Review*, 60, 126-42.

ILO. 1970. *Towards Full Employment: A Programme for Colombia*. Geneva: ILO.

ILO. 1971. *Matching Employment Opportunities and Expectations. A Programme of Action for Ceylon*. Geneva: ILO.

ILO. 1972. *Employment, Incomes and Equality: A Strategy for Increasing Productive Employment in Kenya*. Geneva: ILO.

Jorgenson, D. W. 1966. Testing alternative theories of the development of a dual economy. In I. Adelman and E. Thorbecke (eds), *The Theory and Design of Economic Development*. Baltimore: Johns Hopkins University Press.

Kannappan, S. 1983. *Employment Problems and the Urban Labour Market in Developing Nations*. Ann Arbor, Michigan: University of Michigan, Graduate School of Business Administration, Division of Research.

Kannappan, S. 1985. Urban employment and the labour market in developing countries. *Economic Development and Cultural Change*, 33, 699–730.

Kao, C., Anschel, K. and Eicher, C. 1964. Disguised unemployment in agriculture: a survey. In C. Eicher and L. Witt (eds), *Agriculture in Economic Development*. New York: McGraw-Hill.

Keyfitz, N. 1982. Development and the elimination of poverty. *Economic Development and Cultural Change*, 30, 649–70.

Kim, K. S. and Roemer, M. 1971. *Growth and Structural Transformation*. Cambridge, Mass.: Harvard University Press.

Knight, J. B. and Sabot, R. H. 1981. The returns to education: increasing with experience or decreasing with expansion? *Oxford Bulletin of Economics and Statistics*, 43, 51–72.

Krishna, R. 1973. Unemployment in India. *Economic and Political Weekly*, 8, 475–84.

Krueger, A. O. 1981. *Trade and Employment in Developing Countries*. Chicago: University of Chicago Press.

Krueger, A. O., Lary, H. B., Monson, T. and Akransanee, N. 1981. *Trade and Employment in Developing Countries: I. Individual Studies*. Chicago: University of Chicago Press.

Lewis, J. P. 1977. Designing the public works mode of anti-poverty policy. In C. R. Frank Jr and R. C. Webb (eds), *Income Distribution in Less-Developed Countries*. Washington, DC: The Brookings Institution.

Lewis, W. A. 1954. Economic development with unlimited supplies of labour. *Manchester School*, 22, 131–91.

Lewis, W.A. 1977. *The Evolution of the International Economic Order*. Princeton, NJ: Princeton University Press.

Linn, J. 1982. The costs of urbanization in developing countries. *Economic Development and Cultural Change*, 30, 625–48.

Lipton, M. 1977. *Why Poor People Stay Poor: Urban Bias in World Development*. Cambridge, Mass.: Harvard University Press.

Mangin, W. 1967. Latin American squatter settlements: a problem and a solution. *Latin American Research Review*, 2, 65–98.

Mazumdar, D. 1976. The urban informal sector. *World Development*, 4, 655–79.

Mazumdar, D. 1979. *Paradigms in the Study of Urban Labour Markets in LDCs: A Reassessment in the Light of an Empirical Study in Bombay City*. World Bank Staff Working Paper No. 366. Washington, DC: World Bank.

Mazumdar, D. 1980. *Urban Labour Markets and Income Distribution in Malaysia*. New York: Oxford University Press.

Mazumdar, D. 1983. Segmented labour markets in LDCs. *American Economic Review*, 73, 254–9.

Meade, J. E. 1961. Mauritius: a case study in Malthusian economics. *Economic Journal* 71, 521–34.

Mehra, S. 1966. Surplus labour in Indian agriculture. *Indian Economic Review*, 1, 111–29. Reprinted in P. Chaudhury (ed.). 1972. *Readings in Indian Agricultural Development*. London: George Allen and Unwin.

Minami, R. 1970. Further considerations on the turning point in the Japanese economy, parts 1 and 2. *Hitotsubashi Journal of Economics*, 10, 18–60.

Mohan, R. 1981. *The Determinants of Labour Earnings in Developing Metropoli: Estimates from Bogota and Cali, Colombia.* World Bank Staff Working Paper No. 498. Washington, DC: World Bank.

Nelson, J. 1976. Sojourners versus new urbanites: causes and consequences of temporary versus permanent cityward migration in developing countries. *Economic Development and Cultural Change*, 24, 721-57.

Nurkse, R. 1953. *Problems of Capital Formation in Underdeveloped Countries.* New York: Oxford University Press.

Perlman, J. 1976. *The Myth of Marginality: Urban Poverty and Policies in Rio de Janeiro.* Berkeley: University of California Press.

Phelps-Brown, H. 1977. *The Inequality of Pay.* Berkeley: University of California Press, and Oxford: Oxford University Press.

Pfefferman, G. and Webb, R. 1983. Poverty and income distribution in Brazil. *Review of Income and Wealth*, 29, 101-24.

Psacharopoulos, G. 1973. *Returns to Education.* San Francisco: Jossey-Bass.

Psacharopoulos, G. 1977. Family background, education, and achievement: a path model of earnings determinants in the UK and some alternatives. *British Journal of Sociology*, 28, 321-35.

Psacharopoulos, G. 1980. Returns to education: An updated international comparison. In T. King (ed.), *Education and Income.* World Bank Staff Working Paper No. 402. Washington, DC: World Bank.

Reynolds, L. G. 1951. *The Structure of Labour Markets.* New York: Harper and Row.

Reynolds, L. G. 1969. Economic development with surplus labour: some complications. *Oxford Economic Papers*, 21, 89-103.

Schultz, T.P. 1981. *Economics of Population.* Reading, Mass.: Addison-Wesley.

Schultz, T. P. 1982. Lifetime migration within educational strata in Venezuela: estimates on a logistic model. *Economic Development and Cultural Change*, 30, 559-93.

Schumacher, E. F. 1974. *Small is Beautiful: A Study of Economics as if People Mattered.* London: ABACUS.

Sen, A. K. 1975. *Employment, Technology and Development.* Oxford: Clarendon Press.

Singh, I. J., Squire, L., and Strauss, J. (eds). 1986. *Agricultural Household Models: Extensions, Applications and Policy.* Washington, DC: World Bank (forthcoming).

Standing, G. 1978. *Labour Force Participation and Development.* Geneva: ILO.

Sutcliffe, R. B. 1971. *Industry and Underdevelopment.* Reading, Mass.: Addison-Wesley.

Tenjo, J. 1985. 'Aspirations, opportunities and unemployment in urban Colombia'. Unpublished Ph.D. dissertation, University of Toronto.

Todaro, M. P. 1969. A model of labour migration in less developed countries. *American Economic Review*, 59, 138-48.

Todaro, M. P. 1976. Urban job expansion, induced migration and rising unemployment. *Journal of Development Economics*, 3, 211-25.

Turnham, D. 1970. *The Employment Problem in Less Developed Countries: a Review of Evidence.* Paris: OECD.

Udall, A. and Sinclair, S. 1982. The 'luxury unemployment' hypothesis: a review of recent evidence. *World Development*, 10, 49-62.

Urrutia, M. 1985. *Winners and Losers in Colombia's Economic Growth of the 1970s.* Oxford: Oxford University Press.

Vekemans, R. and Silva, I. 1969. *Marginalidad en America Latina: Un Ensayo Diagnostico.* Barcelona: Herdes.

Visaria, P. 1980. *Poverty and Unemployment in India: An Analysis of Recent Evidence.* World Bank Staff Working Paper No. 417. Washington, DC: World Bank.

Webb, R. C. 1977. *Government Policy and the Distribution of Income in Peru.* Cambridge, Mass.: Harvard University Press.

World Bank, 1980. *Education Sector Policy Paper*, 3rd edn. Washington, DC: World Bank.

World Bank. 1984. *World Development Report.* Washington, DC: World Bank.

Yap, L. Y. L. 1977. The attraction of cities: a review of the migration literature. *Journal of Development Economics*, 4, 239–64.

Zymelman, M. 1976. *Patterns of Educational Expenditures.* World Bank Staff Working Paper No. 246. Washington, DC: World Bank.

7
Technology choice and factor proportions problems in LDCs

Henry Bruton

7.1 Introduction

An economy at a given time has an array of productive resources available to it. These resources include physical capital in the form of vehicles, chemical plants, textile mills, shoe factories, and thousands of other items. Included also is labour. The existing labour force will have a great variety of inherent talents and acquired skills, experience and commitment, initiative and ambition. Other categories of resources may also be identified, of which land is the most important. The economy has available to it at this particular time a body of knowledge; knowledge about the technology of production, its administration, and its organization. The factor proportion issue, in its broadest terms, is concerned with finding the ways to use this array of resources in order to achieve the maximum social welfare that is technologically possible. More narrowly, the factor proportion issue refers to the various considerations that are relevant in understanding how productive resources are combined to produce output and to provide employment opportunities. For many less developed countries, the creating of employment opportunities is as important a source of welfare as is the output of goods and services.

Technology is an essential part of any discussion of factor proportions. It is the existing technology that determines how, and the extent to which, it is possible to combine the productive factors and the productivity of these factors in their several combinations. The factor proportion question and the choice of technique problems are therefore essentially the same. Factor prices provide a major inducement for an enterprise to combine resources in one way rather than another. Factor prices, along with technology, must occupy considerable attention in any discussion of this range of issues.

The treatment of this material in most elementary textbooks is such that all problems virtually disappear. Suppose that all factors may be classified as either capital or labour. Suppose further that the existing technology permits a very great deal of substitution of one factor by another, of labour by capital and of capital by labour. The substitutability is great enough, and can be done quickly and cheaply enough, that it is technologically possible for firms to respond immediately to factor price signals. Now suppose that all factors are thrown on the market and accept the price that clears the market. These factor prices will measure relative factor supplies in the economy, and firm decision-makers will be induced to combine the factors in a way that results in the full utilization of all the factors that are thrown on the market. The prevailing technology allows them to do this, and they are induced to do this because they seek the least-cost combination of inputs. So: if factor substitution is great enough and known to be great enough, if relative factor prices measure relative factor scarcities, if all enterprises seek and find the least-cost method of production, and if any possible aggregate demand problem is solved by government fiscal and monetary policy, there is no specific problem identified as the factor proportion problem. It is resolved immediately by a smooth working market mechanism and an exceptionally flexible technology.

Specific questions about factor proportions arose because the story told in the preceding paragraph did not appear to be very helpful in the modern less developed country. There are several areas of failure, five of which are of direct relevance in the present context.

1 Is there in fact as much substitutability among factors as the preceding argument requires to make it applicable? In particular, is there sufficient substitutability between labour and non-labour inputs, usually called capital, to justify assuming the smooth downward-sloping isoquant?

2 Factor markets inevitably are distorted, some more some less, but all are. Therefore relative prices cannot be assumed to measure relative factor supplies in a very accurate way. Private costs will differ from social costs, and the firm that seeks the least-cost combination of inputs on the basis of market prices will not be minimizing social costs.

3 Technology is a much more complex issue than the conventional argument allows, even if extensive substitution between labour and other inputs is possible. In particular, the assumption that all combinations of capital and labour are known, and blueprints are available, is a very strong assumption. So too does the possibility of the importation of technology created elsewhere add to the difficulty of defining a 'given' technology and assuming it to be widely known.

4 There are many reasons why an enterprise might not employ the least-cost combination of factors, even if it is known to the firm. Firm managers may simply like nice new machines, and may have enough monopoly power to enable this preference to be accommodated. They may fear labour unions, they may be convinced quality varies with the use or non-use of machines, and many other considerations. If each enterprise has more or less its own criterion the results noted above do not follow.

5 The choice of technique may have effects in addition to those on output and factor utilization. It may, for example, affect saving and investment rates, it may affect the regularity of the flow of output, and it may have learning

consequences of one kind or another. In the development context these considerations may well be of great importance.

The introduction of consequences flowing from these five considerations turns the factor proportions question, the choice of technique problem, into a significant conceptual and policy matter. The purpose of this survey is to examine this set of issues in the context of a developing country. In particular our concern will be with the difficulties and process by which a country seeks to employ all its productive resources in an optimal manner. While any nation is interested in the employment of all of its resources, many developing countries, as noted earlier, give special attention to labour. So too will this survey.

There are six major sections. In the first (section 7.2) attention is given to the meaning of labour and capital intensity, to the meaning and role of substitutability between these two factors, and how factor proportions are relevant to a theory of growth. After this some further complications are considered in section 7.3. Chief among these are the role of intermediate inputs and the substitutability among factors that can be introduced through the choice of the products to produce. Foreign trade and income distribution are, of course, directly relevant in the choice of product. In section 7.4 the role of technology is studied. Some attention is given to importing technical knowledge, but the main attention is given (in the fifth section) to the emergence of an indigenous technological capacity that itself evolves in response to relative factor supplies. Section 7.6 is a brief summary of the analytical issues, and in the last section there is a short reference to empirical work in this field.

It is perhaps useful to summarize briefly the main theme of the survey. Firms combine productive factors in the way they do for a number of reasons. Chief among these reasons are the relative costs of the factors, the objectives and constraints which govern and limit the firm's actions, and the available technical knowledge. To produce any given output at the least cost is an important objective of a firm, but by no means the only one. The other objectives and constraints that a firm responds to emerge from the social and economic environment of which it is a part. A technology that allows full utilization of resources is one that is an essential component of this economic and social environment. We need, then, to study how a technology can evolve along with the economy in such a way that it fits the economy.

7.2 The factor proportions problem

The earliest concern with the factor proportions problem arose from the application of the Harrod (1939) growth model to developing economies. That growth model recognized that, while investment in the Keynesian explanation of income determination was a part of aggregate demand today, it contributed to an increase in the capacity of the economy to produce goods and services tomorrow. This it did by adding to capital stock. Investment today equalled the increment in capital tomorrow. To maintain full utilization of capacity, aggregate demand had to grow along with capacity. How much productive capacity increased depended on the productivity of the new capital. This productivity was measured by the capital-output ratio, the reciprocal of the average product of capital, and this ratio became in numerous theoretical models, planning exercises, and applications for foreign loans and aid a fixed technological parameter, a supply parameter. If the capital-output ratio were fixed and technology remained unchanged the ratio of capital to labour remained fixed, and factor proportions were determined by technology alone. Factor prices did not enter into the analysis.

The argument fits well with Arthur Lewis's (1954) 'unlimited supplies of labour' model of development. In that model the developing economy has two sectors: a large and stagnant traditional sector and a small, growing modern sector. All investment, and so all growth, takes place in the latter sector, and the traditional sector supplies the labour as it is demanded by the expansion of the modern sector. Suppose a single good is produced in the modern sector, then the Harrod argument goes as follows:

$$Q = K \bigg/ \frac{K}{Q} = \frac{K}{k}$$

$$\Delta Q = \Delta K / k = I / k$$

$$\frac{\Delta Q}{Q} = \frac{I}{Qk}$$

$$= \frac{S}{Qk}$$

$$= s/k$$

where:

Q = productive capacity;
K = capital stock;
I = investment;
S = saving (= investment);
k = capital–output ratio;
s = saving–income ratio.

The rate of growth of the capacity to produce the modern sector output is given by the ratio of two ratios: that of saving to output and that of capital to output. The fixed savings ratio was inherited from Keynes and the fixed capital–output ratio, as just noted, was the measure of the productivity of the new investment, once it became part of capital stock.

Figure 7.1 helps to clarify the argument. At the beginning of the story, there is OK_1 of capital in the modern sector, and this amount of capital creates job places for OL_1 of labour. Job places in the modern sector are determined entirely by the amount of non-labour inputs (called capital) available in that sector. Output is

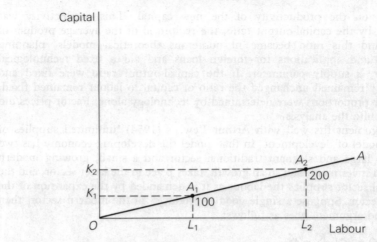

FIGURE 7.1 The Harrod model of growth

100 units as shown by the interval OA_1. The capital–output ratio is OK_1/OA_1 and the capital labour ratio is OK_1/OL_1. The latter is a measure of the slope of the production ray OA. The argument applies to a particular period of time. In one shift of work output of OA_1 is produced. One method, therefore, of increasing the effective capital stock is to use the capital more shifts per day or week. Therefore 'K' here refers to capital services supplied.

In this first year of development net investment equal to K_1K_2 takes place in the modern sector, so that at the beginning of the second year there is OK_2 of capital. This new amount of capital will employ an additional L_1L_2 of labour attracted to the modern sector from the traditional sector, and the increase in output is A_1A_2. Evidently the productivity of capital (and labour) is the same at A_2 as at A_1 and factor proportions – the amount of labour used per one dollar of capital – is also the same at both output levels. So the figure and the equations tell the same story.

Figure 7.1 helps identify several additional points of considerable relevance to the factor proportions question. The diagram, as drawn, states that there is only one technique of production, only one possible combination of capital and labour. There is no choice of technique problem, and, since there is only the one good, no choice of product. To expand the modern sector, saving and investment take place and the new capital is combined with labour in the ratio shown by the slope of OA. To grow faster – to move out along OA more rapidly – either the society must save more or it must convince another society to save and lend or grant this economy the use of the investible resources made available by the foreign saving.

A different interpretation is possible. There is, as development begins, a traditional sector with an abundance of labour available for employment in the modern sector. The wage rate then is assumed to remain constant, as long as the supply curve of labour to the modern sector is horizontal. The cost of capital also remains constant, so the optimal technique remains unchanged as growth occurs. Suppose that technique OA is the most labour-using technique known and the wage rate reflects the abundance of labour. In this case OA is the optimal technique, and optimal means that it is the technique – the factor proportions – that best meets an explicit criterion; in this case, the lowest cost of the production of a rate of output of 100. Figure 7.2 shows that there are three possible factor combinations that could be used to produce the modern sector output. Lines r_1w_1 and r_2w_2 are isocost lines and their slope is that ratio of the cost of capital to the cost of labour. Then, by conventional argument, technique A can be identified as the least-cost way of producing any predetermined rate of output. Whether the price of the product equals this cost figure, of course, requires additional argument.

In both instances technique A is used. Does it then matter which diagram is considered applicable? The answer is unequivocal: it matters greatly. Figure 7.2 allows choice, indeed requires choice, and mistakes can be made in exercising that choice. In particular in figure 7.2 factor prices matter, while in figure 7.1 they do not. This means that distortions can occur because the factor markets do not reflect relative supplies of the factors accurately or because the decision-maker is less than completely informed as to the choices available. Evidently, a choice of technique B in figure 7.2 would mean less labour absorbed from the traditional sector and a smaller increment of output obtained from a given increment in the capital stock. Nothing like this is possible if figure 7.1 is the appropriate metaphor. It matters in another way. Suppose, for example, a

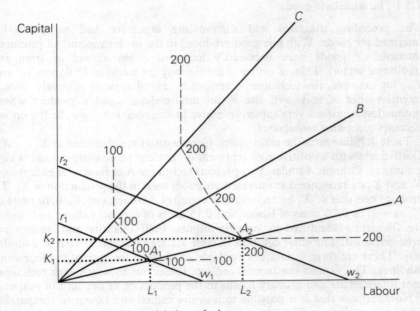

FIGURE 7.2 Growth with multiple techniques

government wished to increase the income of workers relative to that of capitalists. It therefore mandates an increase in wage rates above that reflected in the line r_1w_1. In figure 7.1 employment growth associated with capital growth would not be penalized by this policy, while in figure 7.2 employment would grow more slowly if wage rates were artificially raised in order to meet an income distribution objective.

The production rays – A, B, C – reflect the prevailing technologies. At the beginning of the development story they are 'given'. Given, in this context, means that no questions are asked about origins. Similarly, the techniques are assumed to be known by everyone in the modern sector. The modern sector decision-maker, in effect, has blueprints for all three technologies readily available. This is a strong assumption, and its justification for a developing country is no small matter. In a later section it will be argued that alternative assumptions are more helpful to understanding.

7.3 Some modifications and extensions

The preceding analysis provides the simplest picture of the factor proportions issue. A number of extensions and modifications are necessary to make the analysis more complete, and in order to understand the issues in the context of a particular country. In this section several such considerations are introduced.

7.3.1 Intermediate goods

The preceding diagrams and surrounding argument had no place for intermediate goods. With one good produced in the modern sector, all produced intermediate goods were necessarily imported (from abroad or from the traditional sector). This, of course is not the way the world is. In figures 7.1 and 7.2, for example, the technique described by ray A appears relatively labour-intensive, but it may well use as an intermediate input a product whose production requires a very capital-intensive production technique. So the notion becomes somewhat ambiguous.

Table 7.1 illustrates the main issues. Commodities are identified as $X_1 \ldots X_4$. Coefficients with a positive sign represent output and those with a negative sign are inputs. Column A under X_1 represents technique A of figure 7.2 except now X_2 and X_3 are recognized as intermediate goods used in the production of X_1. To produce one unit of X_1 by technique A requires 0.60 units of X_2, 0.40 units of X_3 as well as 0.70 units of labour and 0.15 units of capital. Labour and capital are frequently identified as primary inputs, their quantity and quality are predetermined. The other columns in table 7.1 are to be interpreted in a similar way. There are three techniques available and known for each of the four commodities. The various coefficients indicate the extent to which each technique uses intermediate and primary inputs in the production of one unit of output.

Now suppose that it is possible to measure capital and labour in comparable units so that their coefficients indicate the relative intensity with which each is

Table 7.1 The role of intermediate goods

	X₁			X₂			X₃			X₄		
	A	B	C	A	B	C	A	B	C	A	B	C
X_1	1.00	1.00	1.00	-0.90	-0.95	-0.95	-0.40	-0.70	-0.80	-0.75	-0.70	-0.70
X_2	-0.60	-0.60	-0.60	1.00	1.00	1.00						
X_3	-0.40	-0.30	-0.35	-0.25	-0.25	-0.20	1.00	1.00	1.00			
X_4										1.00	1.00	1.00
L	-0.70	-0.60	-0.50	-0.20	-0.15	-0.12	-0.12	-0.08	-0.05	-0.85	-0.70	-0.62
K	-0.15	-0.20	-0.30	-0.80	-0.85	-0.95	-0.90	-0.90	-0.92	-0.20	-0.28	-0.35

used. Technique A is more labour-intensive than technique B for the production of X_1 and all three known techniques for the production of X_2 are relatively capital-intensive compared to those available for X_1 and X_4.

The production of X_2 appears relatively capital-intensive if one looks only at the primary input rows. Table 7.1 tells us, however, that X_1 and X_4 are necessary as intermediate inputs into the production of X_2, and their production is relatively labour-intensive. Recognition of produced intermediate products means that factor proportions must refer to the direct plus the indirect use of each factor. Indirect use refers, of course, to the use of primary factors in the production of the intermediate good. The cost of production of a predetermined output now includes the cost of primary inputs used directly and indirectly in the production of the commodities. Given the cost of labour and capital, these production costs can be determined in a straightforward, though complex, manner. If the prices of all primary inputs equal their 'true' shadow prices, the resulting costs of production represent the social cost of producing the given output by each technique, from which the least-cost method of producing the predetermined target output can be identified. Hollis Chenery (1961) has a particularly useful discussion and numerical illustration of these issues.

7.3.2 Human capital

In table 7.1 there is a single labour category. It is useful to recognize that any productive activity requires a variety of labour skills and experience, so the labour coefficient may be thought of as representing a set of labour skills. More important, however, is the fact that the acquisition of skills and experience is a form of capital formation. It requires saving. There is therefore some capital embodied in the labour input. A technique that has a large labour coefficient may also represent a substantial amount of capital in the form of training and accumulated experience. Another technique may have the same labour and capital coefficients, but the labour required is essentially untrained and unskilled. Evidently the amount of capital used is very different in the two instances, and an additional complexity is added to the factor proportions question. It may also be noted that substitution between well-trained, skilled labour and poorly trained labour is limited. Three poorly prepared economists can rarely substitute for one who is well prepared! However an economist (or engineer, or mechanic, or . . .) may embody more capital than is required for the activity. If this is in fact the case, then it is evident that some capital is underutilized, and hence its productivity reduced.

The human capital issue can be merged with the intermediate good question. Dahlman and Westphal (1982) note that in weaving the firm often chooses between automatic and semi-automatic looms. The latter are of course much more labour-intensive. The probability of yarn breakage, however, is much higher with the semi-automatic loom. How much higher depends in turn on the quality of yarn used. Whether yarn breakage can be repaired with little damage to the cloth depends on the skill and experience of the worker. So the least-cost combination of inputs involves a wide range of trade-offs, not just two.

There are two issues of relevance to our story: the first is that labour embodies capital in the form of skill and experience. The accumulation of this capital requires saving, just as does the construction of a dam or the building of a steel mill. The second issue refers to the determination of the optimal amount of capital to be embodied in the labour. 'Too much' training means that the incremental cost of the training exceeds the increment in productivity it produces. Too little means the opposite. The main point, however, is that factor proportions are affected in a direct way.

The recognition of intermediate goods and capital embodied in labour adds to the difficulties of identifying labour or capital-intensive activities. A great deal of information and data are required. There is abundant evidence that many less developed countries have run into difficulties because of the inability to take into account all the intermediate inputs that a particular activity requires. An apparently labour-intensive activity turns out to require extremely capital-intensive inputs. Similarly, an apparently large labour input may hide the fact that a lot of capital is required because of the failure to recognize the cost of equipping the labour to perform its assigned tasks.

7.3.3 Choice of product

The preceding discussion did not allow for international trade. Suppose there is trade between two countries, and further that the exchange rate is such that the balance of payments is protected without tariffs or other impediments to importing or exporting. Finally, suppose that relative factor prices reflect relative factor availability and that technical knowledge is the same in both countries. Then a country will find that the relative cost of producing a particular commodity is determined by the relative factor combination employed. A technique that makes intensive use of the more abundant factor (the factor whose relative price is lower) will have a lower cost than one that uses large quantities of the factor whose relative price is higher. A country will then export the commodities whose production makes more use of the relatively plentiful resource, and import those whose production makes less use of that resource. This argument is usually identified as the Heckscher–Ohlin theory of international trade.

This obvious argument is relevant for the factor proportions questions because it shows that foreign trade is a means for factor substitution. Suppose that all products could each be produced by only one technique, but that the one technique for the products varied from very labour-intensive to very capital-intensive. Then the labour plentiful country may concentrate its production on those products that are at the labour-intensive end of the spectrum. This factor substitution takes place through the substitution of imports for the domestic production of those products whose production requires the least plentiful resource. Evidently, then, the country that limits its foreign trade is also, to some extent, dampening its capacity to find ways to use all its resources. For a small country this source of adjustment may be of considerable importance.

7.3.4 Demand

Demand enters the story in a more ambiguous way. Suppose again that there is no foreign trade, and that there are two products whose production technologies are as shown in figures 7.3a and 7.3b. Production of commodity a is more capital-intensive than b even if technique A, the least capital-intensive technique, is used. Similarly all the techniques available to produce commodity b would be identified as labour-intensive. Now suppose that in a labour-plentiful economy, the demand curve for b is very near the origin; that is there is virtually no demand for this product. Demand for a, on the other hand, is strong, so a is produced, but b is not. The labour-plentiful economy must use a capital-intensive technique, even though a labour-intensive technique is available. This result is due to the composition of demand.

Foreign trade may provide demand for b, and all is well. In the absence of foreign trade, internal income distribution is the most important single factor affecting the composition of demand. There is a bit of evidence that suggests that households in lower-income brackets may be expected to buy food, textiles, and unsophisticated home-produced products that lend themselves to production by labour-intensive means. If the income of the poorer groups is growing slowly, or not at all, then demand for b-type goods will also grow slowly, and the use of labour-intensive production techniques will face a demand constraint. The empirical evidence is open to doubt, and the main point here is to call attention to the role of the composition of demand in the choice of technique question, and so also the role of foreign trade and income distribution.

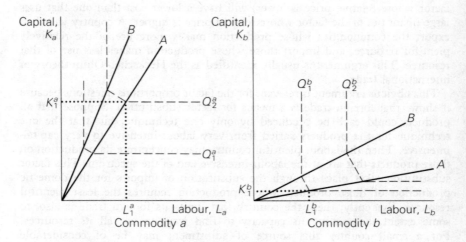

FIGURE 7.3   Effect of demand on factor proportions

7.4   Sources of the given technology

In all the preceding discussion technology was assumed 'given'. In the diagrams the several rays reflect this given technology. In table 7.1 the columns reflect the 'given' technology. This technology is assumed known and understood by all enterprises in the economy. The labour available is assumed to be trained and to have the skills to operate with each of these known techniques. In figure 7.2, for example, the labour that is measured along the horizontal axis can be employed in any of the three techniques shown there. Labour can work equally well with very little complementary capital, or with a great deal of capital. The purpose of this section is to study some aspects of the role of technology in the determination of factor proportions. The main theme of the discussion is that technology is not 'given', it is found and learned, and that there is at any one time widespread ignorance about the technology that is, in some sense, available. This means that a *search and learning process* is central to the understanding of the choice of technology that a firm makes.

7.4.1   Appropriate technology

In an economy that has experienced very little change over past decades, the technical knowledge available and in use is well known and widely applied. This technology has evolved over the years by a variety of routes, mainly learning, experimenting, watching one's neighbours, and gaining wisdom by performing tasks day after day. One may then speak of an indigenous technology, a technology that has emerged from within the society itself and has, indeed, evolved with that society as an essential part of it. It is therefore a technology that is compatible with the other characteristics and institutions of the society. It is appropriate. Factor proportions are right. There is full employment of labour in the sense that everyone has a role that is recognized by the members of society. This role in turn creates a recognized claim on resources. There may be unemployment or underemployment in the more conventional meaning of some people not 'working full-time'. Working full-time, however, is a term that has content only in a particular society, and the main point is that everyone in this society has a claim on a share of the output.

This technology, however, is relatively unproductive, and labour productivity is low, with the availability of goods and services per capita just above subsistence. The objective is to find a new technology that is more productive and that is equally appropriate. The new technology should raise per capita output, but do so in a manner that does not create employment or distribution difficulties that the society is unable to resolve. The community has two evident approaches to this objective: it may seek to create a more productive technology within its own borders, or it may seek to borrow or otherwise obtain technology from abroad. Evidently these approaches are not mutually exclusive, but it is helpful at the beginning to treat them separately.

7.4.2   The importation of technology

The international transfer of technology from one country to another is one of
the oldest ideas in the development literature, and of course has taken place in
various forms throughout recorded history. If in one society a body of technical
knowledge exists that is much more productive than that available in another
society, then it would seem virtually self-evident that the latter country could
profit from importing the knowledge already created in the former country. To
re-create knowledge in one country that already exists in another is, it would
seem, an obvious misuse of resources. A substantial range of problems, however,
appeared almost immediately as efforts to transfer technology accelerated. There
are three of direct relevance to the factor proportions issue.

Relative factor use

The first follows from the story told at the beginning of this section. The
knowledge that is created in a particular society reflects the characteristics of that
society. The most obvious of these characteristics is the relative use of factors. If
a country that, throughout most of its history, has been land- and physical
capital-rich and labour-poor, achieves regular, sustained technological
improvements, those improvements will reflect these characteristics. Such a
statement means simply that the technology creation is indigenous to that
society, and thereby reflects its characteristics.

In a capital- and land-rich, labour-poor society primary interest is in finding
new techniques that replace current labour with land or physical capital. In
terms of the capital–labour diagrams used previously, the search for new
technologies will be concentrated in the capital-intensive areas. In figure 7.4a the
relative factor prices in a capital-rich, labour-poor country is shown, and in
figure 7.4b those of a labour-rich, capital-poor country. In year 1 exactly the
same technology is available and used in both countries. This means that a
specific distance along the same ray represents the same rate of output in both
countries. We may expect that the labour-rich country will employ technique A
and the capital-rich country of figure 7.4a, technique C.

Now suppose that, in the capital-rich country, technical change is occurring at
a fairly rapid rate, but there is little accumulation of new knowledge in the
labour-poor country. In country a the search activity will be concentrated in
the area of technique C as technique A is of little interest to anyone in that
country, and no-one searches for new knowledge in that factor combination area.
As new technical knowledge is accumulated in a one or both of two changes
occur to the diagram. Productivity of capital and labour increase only along ray
C, not on all rays uniformly. Now a given distance along ray C represents a
larger rate of output than it did in year 1. Also a new ray may appear between the
vertical axis and ray C, so that an even more capital-intensive technique than C
becomes available. The new knowledge and new techniques will doubtless
impose changes in the quality of labour that is usable; possibly also changes in
the composition of intermediate inputs or in the coefficients defining the extent

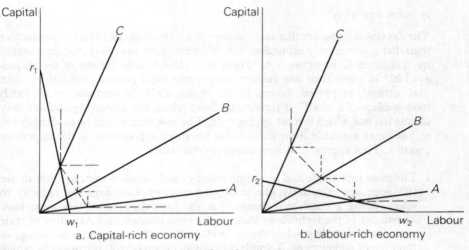

FIGURE 7.4 Factor supplies and transfer of technology
(a) Capital-rich economy
(b) Labour-rich economy

of their use are necessary. Availability of intermediate inputs may indeed affect the direction that search takes. Technology is changing and productivity is rising in the capital-rich country, but such change is limited to the capital-intensive area of activity.

Nothing has happened in the labour-rich country, and the diagram is the same in year 10 as it was in year 1. The country now, however, commits itself to increased productivity, and recognizes that the technology employed within its boundaries is much less productive than that available in the country represented by a. It is immediately evident, however, that transferring a's technology to b will create difficulties. The most obvious of these difficulties is that the availability of capital in the latter country will not allow all labour to be employed with the more productive technique. Suppose that the new technology is limited to the modern sector, and the expansion of the sector is governed by the rate of capital formation. If country a continues to achieve technical change that applies only to the very capital-intensive activities of the economy and country b imports this new technology, its modern sector will face ever-greater difficulties in expanding because of the rising capital intensity of production. The technology-importing country may also have difficulties providing the appropriate labour to use the imported technology. For all these reasons the productivity of the resources using the newly imported technology is below that in the community in which the technology was originally developed.

A technology 'shelf'

The developing country that seeks to import a technology that is more productive than that it is currently using does not, of course, have to import that represented by technique C in figure 7.4a There is a considerable variety of techniques available in more than one country that would yield greater productivity than that currently employed. Several people (Ranis, 1979; Stewart and James, 1982) have spoken of a 'shelf' of technology from which the importing country may choose the one which is most appropriate. The task then would be to identify the technologies available from abroad that are most appropriate in the importing country. This approach in turn raises several issues:

1 The most immediate and most important consideration is that, in order to use this approach effectively, the importing country must have the capacity to select. More accurately it means that the firm decision-makers must have knowledge of the technology shelf, and a clear enough understanding of their own needs that they select the technology that takes maximum advantage of their factor endowment. There is, in such an arrangement, no means by which managers can learn to choose the right technique, even if they can see the entire shelf. Decisions are further complicated by the presence of sales people, advertisements, tied aid projects, and the like.

2 In this approach factor prices in the importing country become an important consideration in the choice of the technology to be imported, and so in the factor combinations that are employed. If market prices of the factors are distorted, if they do not measure relative scarcities in the economy, then the firm that seeks that combination of inputs that results in the least cost to it will not thereby combine resources in the way that results in the achievement of the least *social* costs. Where distorted market signals prevail because of institutional reasons – segmented labour markets, incomplete capital markets, inadequate information flows, monopoly or monopsony power, etc. – a government may seek to establish a system of subsidies or taxes that correct these distortions. This is a simple idea, of course, but its implementation is far from simple, and few governments have been able to put effective tax/subsidy systems into operation. It is therefore to be expected that factor market distortions will add to the burdens of choosing the appropriate technology from the international shelf.

3 Imported technology is not free technology. In choosing the technology from the shelf, the firm must not only have a great deal of technical information, it must also be able to make decisions on costs and, almost invariably, to bargain. Bargaining is usually necessary because the market for technology rarely meets the conditions for a competitive one, although there is, of course, much competition among suppliers. The product is always differentiated; the full details of the product can hardly be known to the buyer; and, in general, the marginal cost to the owner of the technology is essentially zero. This last consideration means that the seller has room to bargain, but it does not mean, for obvious reasons, that the seller is prepared to provide the technology at zero cost. The fact that the enterprise cannot be completely sure of what is being purchased,

and so cannot be sure of its value to the firm, puts the buyer at a disadvantage in any negotiation.

These arguments add up to a simple conclusion: for a nation with little indigenous technological capacity to select knowledge that makes best use of its available resources requires it to have a great deal of technical knowledge and understanding, to know a great deal about pricing and bargaining, and to be able to offset domestic price distortions in some way or other. It is a demanding requirement, and if nothing else happens the country can rarely expect to establish in this way a domestic technology that helps to resolve the factor proportions problem.

Direct foreign investment

A final means through which a country may import technology is by encouraging direct foreign investment. Policies with respect to private foreign investment vary greatly among developing countries, and generalizations are risky. Since the multinational enterprise (MNE) plays such an important role in transferring technology, and the technology that it transfers is so crucial, in many countries, to the choice of technique in the host country, it cannot be ignored in any discussion of the issues surrounding this topic. It is discussed more fully in survey 3.

That the MNE can build a plant in a less developed country with a technology that yields a larger rate of output per unit of conventionally measured inputs than a domestic firm is, of course, clear. The question here is will they do it in such a way that fits the economy – that uses domestic resources in accordance with their relative supplies? This question involves a number of sub-questions: (1) to what extent does an MNE have an incentive to do so? (2) to what extent can the host country establish policies that will induce the MNE to find and to use appropriate techniques? and (3) to what extent does the MNE contribute, or can be induced to contribute, to the creation of indigenous technological development?

Two main factors seem to affect the technology that the MNE uses in a less developed country. On the one hand there is a great advantage in reproducing exactly a tried and true technology from home, and operating it as nearly as possible as the home firm is operated. To proceed in this way almost surely reduces costs, but it also means that the MNE fails to take full advantage of the environment of the host country. On the other hand the MNE will have a great deal of knowledge and experience about productive techniques in several, possibly many, countries in many parts of the world. It may be possible to bring to bear this knowledge quickly and inexpensively in a given host country to make the choice of technique more compatible with the host country's factor endowment. It is surely acceptable to say that the MNE has the capacity to make some, in many instances considerable, adaptations in the home technology so that techniques more appropriate to the host country environment are used. To accept this latter statement implies that a government policy that provides the MNE with incentives to make some adaptations in its home technology would be effective. A sequence along the following lines is at least possible, if host government policies push in the right direction: the MNE establishes an activity abroad that is virtually identical to the one at home that has been most thoroughly tested. Once it is in place, managers and foremen begin to search and to learn what resources a particular community offers, and how these might be exploited to reduce costs. The obvious point here is that this more appropriate technology is not given; it must be created. The MNE is not pulling off the shelf the right technology, it is rather using its knowledge about technologies around the world to help it find ways to take advantage of a new environment.

The other question to be asked of the MNE is, does its operation in the developing country contribute to the creation of an indigenous knowledge accumulating process? The record is not clear by any means, nor is it clear what the principal factors are that determine whether an MNE does or does not so contribute. The following observations must be looked upon as tentative, and in no sense firmly established.

The MNEs seem more adept at creating and introducing new products than at devising and establishing new processes for the production of existing products. Similarly, the MNEs do not have a very favourable record on the introduction of routine innovations in their host countries. Also the MNE tends to develop new products with only its home country in mind. There are, of course, exceptions and qualifications, but in general these characteristics seem quite common among multinationals (Caves, 1982; Dunning, 1974; Vernon, 1977).

Such characteristics are relevant to the factor proportions issue in a number of ways. The line between a new product innovation and a process innovation is ambiguous, but it does appear that general information about design, testing procedure, and properties of materials is of greater use to developing countries than knowledge about a new product. The MNEs seem to have difficulty transferring the former forms of technical knowledge compared with their capacity to transfer knowledge about new products. Production of new products often means that linkages with other sectors of the economy are rare, and induce-ment for the creation of new firms to supply intermediate goods for the production of new products is also small. There does not, for example, appear to be many examples of skilled workmen leaving an MNE and starting up a small, independent firm. The evidence is much clearer that the multinational does virtually all of its R and D in the country it considers home, and this R and D is done in response to the market conditions – factor prices, composition of demand – that obtain in that country. Links between the R and D in the host country and that of the MNE are therefore extremely limited, (Stobaugh and Wells, 1984; Vernon, 1977).

These observations suggest that the MNE is not very well equipped to con-tribute to the creation or the evolution of an indigenous technological capacity in a developing country. Evidently the story varies across MNEs and industries. It is most extreme where the MNE builds a plant to its own specification, and operates it with minimal use of domestically available resources. Even in those instances where the plant, once built and ready to function, is turned over to host country nationals, there is likely to be little learning. The recipient is usually provided with instruction for operating the plant in the exact manner called for in the design. At this stage it is difficult to help the host country operators understand why the plant operates the way it does. Any effort to improve the plant's productivity, or to make it more compatible with factor supplies, is therefore extremely difficult. At the other end of the spectrum, one could imagine an MNE that encouraged local participation at every stage of the construction of a plant, and thereby host country nationals gained considerable knowledge and insight into how the plant functions. This procedure, at least, helps domestic engineers, skilled workers, etc. Where the MNE maintains full control, collaboration at all stages will facilitate the MNE's search and adaptation efforts. To include host country nationals in the planning and construction stages does not, however, appear to be a common practice among MNEs (Dahlman and Westphal, 1982).

Two important results seem to follow from the preceding discussion. The first is simple and straightforward: a developing country cannot rely on the importation of foreign technology as a means of resolving its technological difficulties. Imported technology is almost certain to be ill-suited to the importing country in a variety of ways. In particular, complete reliance on imported technology is virtually certain to exacerbate the factor proportions problem. The second result is a bit less simple: to profit fully from the importation of the technology – by selecting wisely from the world's technology shelf, by creating inducements for foreign-owned firms to search and modify in light of what they learn about their new environment, by inducing MNEs to find ways to make genuine contributions to the creation of an indigenous technological capacity – the country must already have considerable technological capacity, considerable technological knowledge. To use foreign technical knowledge in a manner that contributes both to the increased use of the country's available resources and to their increased productivity requires, therefore, that the country have considerable technological capacity already. Where then does this indigenous knowledge come from?

7.5 Factor proportions and indigenous technology

The resolution of technological choice and factor proportions problems is therefore closely linked to the emergence of an indigenous technological capacity. This indigenous technological capacity must also be continuously improving, if social welfare is to continue to rise. Finally, the indigenous technological capacity must be created and exist alongside the more 'advanced' technologies of the GNP-rich countries (see Ranis, 1984). The notion of indigenous technology is that elaborated upon in the opening paragraphs of section 7.4.1.

7.5.1 Creating indigenous technology

There are three principal notions that must underlie any approach to understanding how this process takes place, or can be induced to take place.

Searching and testing

Technology choices and factor proportions are not static and given, and knowledge is always and inevitably incomplete in a growing economy. Searching, testing, probing are always occurring. Technology and factor proportions are always in a state of flux, a state of change. In this way of thinking, the diagrams employed above are at best helpful in fixing ideas, but misleading if looked upon as realistic pictures of what is happening in a growing economy. Searching and learning are the central concepts, not least-cost equilibria or fixed coefficients. Relative factor prices are important as signals for the direction that search should take, rather than as parameters to which a final adjustment is attempted.

Continuous progress

In a growing economy the growth of productivity of the direct and indirect inputs must occur fairly consistently and over a wide range of the economy. The notion of a sharp, explicit change in technology that produces a shift in the insoquants to a new position where they remain until the next sharp, explicit technical change is a misleading one. Adjustments are always occurring, so productivity is always increasing, or the economy stagnates.

Underutilized knowledge

The third point is less clear, but no less central to the argument. There is at any given time a substantial amount of unutilized and underutilized knowledge in the community. This is the knowledge that the routine search and probing, the trial-and-error experiments uncover. The notion of underutilized knowledge may be illuminated by reference to the familiar production possibility curve. Textbook arguments show why an economy will be on this curve, rather than within it. To be within the feasible area defined by the curve, rather than on the curve, it is usually said, means that all resources are not fully utilized. There is idle labour or idle capital or both. If all activities are not employing all the knowledge that is available at the particular time, however, then evidently the economy is not on its production frontier. It is at least conceptually possible for all of physical capital and all individuals who so wish to be fully employed, and the economy to be within a curve drawn on the assumption that all underutilized knowledge is fully exploited. Such a situation is conceivable conceptually, but conceals the crucially relevant tasks of searching and testing. In an economy where knowledge is increasing, and the economy is growing, it is difficult even to define the full employment of all knowledge. There are countless practical difficulties: knowledge must be diffused through the system, and this takes time; some knowledge must be embodied in physical capital; some knowledge requires the creation of new human capital and this too takes time, etc. The basic reason, however, is that knowledge, by its nature, cannot be 'given'; it must be found and applied in each particular context. So the underutilization of knowledge may be said to exist in any economy where knowledge is being accumulated in a fairly regular way (Bruton, 1985; Lindblom and Cohen, 1979).

The jumble of lines shown in figure 7.5 is intended to suggest the argument just developed. Rather than a well-defined production possibility frontier, there is an increasingly grey, foggy barrier through which economic agents must find their way. Up to the first set of marks, knowledge is general and widespread, and producers know what there is to know about techniques of production in this area. In the non-growing economy of section 7.4.1, point *A* of figure 7.5 would represent the position of producers, but there would be nothing beyond *A*. Point *A* would then be the maximum output that could be achieved in this economy as in the conventional formulation of the production possibility curve. The existence of unutilized and underutilized knowledge – the knowledge that can be found by searching and learning – is reflected by the hash marks. Such marks are intended to suggest that moving past *A* is not free and easy; it requires search. The further the economic actor moves into this murky area, the harder, the more costly it is to move still further. Search becomes more costly, the probability of finding lower. A big breakthrough – a major invention – moves the whole jumble out and identifies routes that seem clearer and most easily travelled (Bruton, 1985).

As an illustration of all this, consider the development of high-yielding seeds, sometimes identified as the Green Revolution. In formal research laboratories there has been developed a set of general principles that underlie the production of seeds that are, compared to older seeds, exceptionally responsive to fertilizer and water. It is this development of these general principles about seed production that pushes back the outer barriers of figure 7.5. To exploit the potential of these general principles in a particular geographic area, however, requires a great amount of additional testing and learning. Seeds must be designed specifically for a particular area; the appropriate fertilizer and its use must be learned; effective water management, a complex task, is crucial to obtaining the higher yields. The actual realization of the high yields, therefore, in a particular

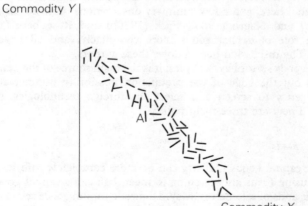

FIGURE 7.5 Knowledge and the production possibility frontier

region depends on a large number of farmers being able to find their specific way to exploit this new basic knowledge. The high-yielding seeds therefore did not provide a new 'given' knowledge, rather they created an opportunity of such a kind that search and learning by individual actors would yield substantial returns.

This argument seeks to capitalize on the understanding and insight that individual economic actors have or can be induced to acquire. It depends strongly on the assumption that there does exist what we have called underutilized knowledge. It further requires that government policies, chiefly price policies, be such that active and conscious search is induced, and the search goes in the direction that exploits with increasing effectiveness the factor proportions of the society. Technological development may then resolve any factor proportions difficulty.

7.5.2 The role of the capital goods sector

There is one more link in the argument. Suppose that the search and learning effort does proceed, and do take most economic units near the outer edge of figure 7.5. What happens then? It is then that links with the technologies from abroad become important as well as domestic R and D. The basic means by which these links are effected, and this domestic research occurs, is the capital goods sector.

In recent years a number of economists have argued that a domestic capital goods sector plays, or can play, an important role in the establishment of an indigenous technology. This position is quite different from the conventional wisdom of a decade and more ago. The argument then was that capital goods were to be imported because of cost considerations, and domestic production should concentrate on consumer goods. Of course many countries did just this, and most of these countries have experienced major and continuing problems. It is not possible to review the arguments supporting a domestic capital goods sector in detail here, and a few summary observations must do. Bruton (1985), Chudnovsky and Nagao (1983), Pack (1980b) and Rosenberg (1976, 1982) discuss the role of capital goods more completely, and all have additional references. The discussion here follows these authors.

A capital goods sector has two roles: it is the main source of the new knowledge that moves out the edge of the production possibility jumble, and it is the principal agency to screen and select the foreign technologies available for importing. There are three main points:

Local firms' needs

A domestic capital goods industry can be more completely informed about the needs that using firms are searching to meet than can a capital goods producer several thousands of kilometres away. Domestic capital goods sectors function in the same environment as the using firm, face the same constraints, the same input situation, and the same market structure. Several surveys have found that the single most important characteristic of successful new knowledge is that it emerges from an understanding of the needs of the user (Freeman, 1973). Nathan Rosenberg (1982) emphasizes that the full implications of a new capital item can be appreciated only over an extended period of use. He speaks of learning by using. This process is difficult, virtually impossible, unless the builder of the capital goods is readily available.

Specific learning

A capital goods activity can offer opportunities for special kinds of learning. The opportunity to develop a technology that recognizes specific environmental characteristics and meets specific objectives provides a sharp focus for research. It helps to identify specific questions to explore, possibly with foreign producers and foreign research organizations. This kind of activity helps to create a category of people who not only have certain skills, but also have a confidence that research can be profitable, can be problem-solving. This attitude in turn helps clients to have confidence in the capital goods sector. The difference between this approach and the importation of ready-made plant and equipment is marked. In the latter event, any puzzling through is effectively discouraged, and learning is severely circumscribed.

The real cost of capital

If there is a capital goods sector in a country, and productivity increases in that sector, then the real cost of capital to the society falls, no matter what happens to its price. If productivity in the capital goods sectors abroad falls, the price of imported capital must also fall before the importer is helped. Producing one's own capital goods eliminates the possibility that the society that uses the capital will not profit from its reduced costs of production, unless monopoly power is so great that prices do not follow productivity. That the capital goods sector is to serve existing economic activities implies, of course, that the capital goods sector will not simply duplicate that in other countries.

There is one final thing to say about importing knowledge from abroad. An effective way, perhaps the most effective way, to accomplish this is through exporting. Dahlman and Westphal (1982) put great emphasis on this, and cite the experience of the Republic of Korea as a prime example. Exporting, they write, provides 'virtually costless access to a tremendous range of information, diffused to them in various ways by the buyers of their exports. The resulting minor technological changes have significantly increased production efficiency, changed product designs, upgraded quality, and improved management practices' (p. 129). These changes have all occurred within the context of essentially Korean-owned and operated activities, activities that were compatible with Korean society in general and factor supplies in particular. It is exporting to learn, not exporting simply to earn foreign exchange that matters. The difference in these two objectives represents the basic message of this review.

7.6   Summary of analytical issues

In the introduction conditions were stated that would effectively eliminate technological choice and factor proportions as an analytical issue. These conditions were ruled out as unhelpful, and reasons were given as to why the selection of technology and of factor proportions constitute an important area of research inquiry and are of practical concern to the policy-maker. Chief among these reasons is the great complexity of the technology question, the difficulties of the spreading of knowledge, the learning process, and the inevitability of distorted markets.

In section 7.2 the simplest kind of factor proportion discussion was presented, initially in the context of the Harrod growth model. There are two primary factors and no produced intermediate inputs. There are a small number of techniques known by everyone, and relative factor prices represent relative factor supplies. Even here problems can arise if technological improvements do not affect all techniques more or less equally. In this case a conflict can arise between output and employment objectives.

In section 7.3 some modifications were added. These modifications include the recognition that produced intermediate goods complicate the definition, and especially the recognition of labour (and capital) intensity. Also of relevance is the fact that highly skilled labour includes a great deal of capital. Finally, products are recognized as a variable that may add flexibility to technology choice and resulting factor proportions. Product choice is especially important if foreign trade is widespread.

Section 7.4 began by emphasizing the importance of the assumption of a 'given' technology in sections 7.2 and 7.3, and the important role that technology plays in the arguments. Appropriate technology was defined in section 7.4.1, where an attempt was made to describe an economy in which prevailing technology was compatible with all aspects of the society. There followed a discussion of the advantage and difficulties of relying on the importation of technology from abroad. The main conclusion was that full reliance on imported technology created many problems, and rarely made much of a contribution to the creation of an indigenous technological capacity. It is the creation of the latter that is at the heart of the effective solution to the technology choice/factor proportions questions. The creation of an indigenous technological capacity was briefly examined in section 7.5, where primary emphasis was placed on searching and learning, on the creation of a relevant capital goods sector, and on exporting.

7.7   Some empirical reflections

In the preceding sections a broad view of factor proportions/technological choice has been presented. This material is intended to provide the student with a working acquaintance with principal concepts and theories of this body of material. Much detail and qualification and elaboration could be added, and for anyone probing deeply into these matters such detail is, of course, essential. Rather than proceed along those lines, however, it seems more profitable to examine, in similar broad strokes, the empirical and historical evidence on this topic. It is the purpose of this final section, therefore, to review the various bits and pieces of evidence that bear on the several issues raised in earlier sections. 'Bit and pieces' is a term used advisedly, because there does not appear to be a body of evidence to which one may refer as definitive or as presenting conventional wisdom. There are, of course, uncounted books and articles available, and one cannot claim to have read, not to say absorbed, all, or even most, of them.

There are several valuable surveys. David Morawetz (1974) and Lawrence White (1978) cover many of the considerations reviewed above, and have a great deal to say about the available evidence. Both have very rich bibliographies. There is now a considerable number of case studies, and these provide an abundance of evidence. There is now a considerable number of case studies, and these provide an abundance of evidence, insight, and hypotheses that help one gain a feel and an intuition for the considerations discussed above. Any list of such case studies is necessarily incomplete, but one might begin with Amsalem (1983), Bhalla (1981), Fransman and King (1984), Ginneken and Baron (1984), International Labour Office (1984), Pack (1980a), Pickett (1977), Sansom (1969), Stewart and James (1982), and Stobaugh and Wells (1984). All of these studies also have extensive bibliographies.

The most discussed empirical question has been whether or not it makes sense to speak of the substitutability between capital and labour. Prevailing views have changed in important ways over the past three or so decades. In the 1950s the assumption of fixed production coefficients was routinely made. As noted earlier, this assumption flowed conveniently from the Harrod growth model, and it also made the large-scale planning models more manageable. Soon, however, empirical evidence and theoretical argument began to cast considerable doubt on this assumption, and there emerged widespread agreement that multiple techniques of production were available, and hence relative factor prices are of significance in determining factor proportions and choice of technique. Further research qualified this position in important ways: yes, multiple techniques are available, but the process of substitutability is limited and complex. A brief comment on each of these follows.

Fixed or flexible production techniques

The argument, more accurately assumption, of fixed coefficients rested mainly on the technological efficiency of one technique compared to all others. The argument was not that there was only one technique that would produce a given product, but that one technique – the one employed in the GNP-rich countries – used less of all factors than did other techniques, and so would be chosen irrespective of factor prices. Accumulated econometric exercises and case studies offer convincing evidence that this argument is not generally valid.

A production function created by Arrow *et al.* (1961) made simple, at least conceptually, the estimation of the elasticity of substitution. There followed a great array of such estimates for developed as well as developing countries. There are problems all along the way in using this means of estimating this coefficient, and one can easily argue that the problems are such that the estimates are without value. Lawrence White (1978) and Morawetz (1976) have good, succinct reviews of the difficulties involved, and a summary of results.

These estimates of the elasticity of substitution are almost always significantly different from zero, and often exceed unity. They vary markedly among industries and over time. One of the important results from this material is, indeed, the fact that substitution possibilities seem to vary greatly from sector to sector. A sector in which substitution possibilities loom large is obviously more suitable (*ceteris paribus*) for a developing country than one where such possibilities are limited. The variation of substitutability among sectors is, however, not consistent among countries. Thus one sector may show high substitutable possibilities in one country and much lower in another (Morawetz, 1976). The most charitable interpretation of this result is that the more narrowly defined activities within a given sector are different from one country to another. There are of course less charitable interpretations. The estimates from these exercises are such, however, that it seems fair to say they have greatly influenced the view of many economists, despite the acknowledged shortcomings in the methods of estimation and in the quality and appropriateness of the data used.

Additional evidence, largely of a case study form rather than an econometric exercise, suggest that substitution is indeed present – there do exist multiple efficient techniques – but it is limited in various ways. In manufacturing activities the 'core' work rarely allows much substitution. Core refers to the explicit engineering process that often defines a product. The substitutability that is allowed takes place then in peripheral activities, transporting inputs from here to there, preparation of product for the core run, storage and packing, and similar activities. In some instances where core is a rather extensive function, then it is probably correct to say that to produce exactly the same product in two different localities requires exactly the same process. Different labour intensities of production often mean differences in the products, maybe small differences, but maybe not so small. Heavy-equipment producers seem to be able to respond less to factor prices than do manufacturers of lighter industrial products (Yeoman, in Stobaugh and Wells, 1984). Scale also seems to matter. There is less substitutability in very large productive units than in small and medium-sized units. Automobile assembly is an example of a continuous-flow technology that is very efficient for large runs and very inefficient for small runs. Automobile assembly has often been cited as an activity ill-suited for less developed countries, but also frequently found. Finally quality and other controls are often relevant. The example of automatic and semi-automatic looms for the weaving of wool and the breakage problem has already been mentioned. Fruit handling is another example. Machines can often handle fruit more carefully than can humans. Similarly, machines can frequently meet tolerance requirements that humans cannot. One often reads that it would take 25,000 people 1 week to perform calculations that a computer can perform in 5 to 10 minutes. No-one, however, thinks of this as an example of substitution, simply because the mobilization and organization of 25,000 people for this purpose is, for all practical considerations, impossible. Machines often provide a means of monitoring the honesty of employees that is of relevance to the firm. All of these issues are reasonable and can be important – and modify how one thinks about substitution of labour of capital.

Profits and other objectives

From this argument it is a relatively small step to another general notion. As individual firms are examined in a country or across countries, one uncovers many specific factors that affect a firm's decisions. Jorge Katz (in Fransman and King, 1984, p. 115) speaks of the 'idiosyncratic nature of manufacturing firms in LDCs'. The vast number of orgnaizational and economic characteristics that operate on a firm's decision-makers will affect some of them one way and others another way, and deciding factors are difficult to generalize about. This seems especially the case as the firm begins operations, but often even later as well. A few examples will illustrate.

1 A firm that puts heavy emphasis on product differentiation, and that competes on the basis of product quality, will concentrate more on market research than on finding the right technology. Those that compete with respect to price and operate in a competitive market will, more likely, seek to get their costs down (Lecraw, in Fransman and King, 1984, p. 99).
2 Several people have found that firms managed by experienced people, knowledgeable of the economic environment in which the firm operated, were more likely to use a low-cost technology than the less experienced.
3 Parastatals seem inevitably and everywhere to be less successful than private firms in finding and employing a technology that fits the country's factor endowment. In some countries (Egypt, for example) state-owned firms are often required to hire workers that are not needed, but this hardly meets the condition of appropriate technology.
4 In several activities the possibilities of a trade-off between capital and labour is swamped by considerations with respect to other inputs. Amsalem (1983) found, for example, that in the pulp and paper industry technology choice was dominated by the effort to minimize the use of chemicals, power and steam, and to maximize machine efficiency, and little heed was paid to labour and capital as such. C. G. Baron (in Bhalla, 1981) found similar evidence with respect to sugar cane manufacture, where the amount of cane used (or saved) seemed to be the over-riding consideration.
5 There is little doubt that many firms that select a technology that is more capital-intensive than is appropriate do so due to the predominance of 'engineering man' over 'economic man' in the firm's decision-making. Louis T. Wells, Jr (in Stobaugh and Wells, 1984) makes a strong case for this point with respect to a sample of Indonesian industries. A firm's managers gain

satisfaction from working with modern, advanced machinery, and are often, to the extent possible, willing to pay a price to do so. This argument seems to apply to both domestic and international firms, and even more clearly to state-owned firms.

6 Technological knowledge is costly to acquire and difficult to evaluate. Firms often content themselves with a quick search in familiar surroundings. There is, for example, little evidence to suggest that firms, domestic or multinational, examine a great number of technologies before deciding on the one to use. The same observation applies to other environmental characteristics, the strength of the labour movement, the attitude of the government, the stability of the community, etc. The effort to keep risk at the lowest possible level seems always to induce greater capital intensity than factor prices alone would dictate.

All of these considerations are understandable. They do not mean that the firms are 'irrational' or are not interested in making money. They mean rather that firms are subject to many constraints and face many sources of costs. In his imaginative study of the textile and pulp and paper industries Amsalem (1983) found that while adaptation to factor prices did take place among firms in these industries, that adaptation was rarely complete. This is surely the case in most new manufacturing activities in most developing countries.

Carrots and sticks

These considerations have one important implication for the way we think about factor proportions, and for policies to ensure that appropriate proportions are continuously sought. Firms must be subjected to a substantial number of carrots and sticks to induce them to move towards the use of increasingly more appropriate techniques of production. With protection from foreign and domestic competition, with heavy subsidies, with tax holidays, with price and wage controls, and a variety of other policies that permit the firm to enjoy its idiosyncrasies without penalty, firms often have no inducement to select appropriate techniques, and these other considerations dominate. Thus techniques employed are less appropriate than they might be.

Note that the argument here is not the conventional textbook argument that, if factor prices reflect relative factor supplies, firms will automatically and forthwith choose the optimal, the least-cost, technique. In an important sense there is no least-cost technique. There are rather a complex of circumstances of constraints, of objectives, of available resources, and within these the firm seeks to make as much money as it can.

Several analysts make the point that at any given time a progressive firm is producing two things: a flow of output of goods and services and a flow of new knowledge and information that leads to modification and adjustments. Policy, in this way of thinking, is aimed at making sure this second activity does in fact take place, and that the new knowledge and adjustments lead to products and production techniques that are increasingly appropriate for the society.

It is at this point that the notions of search and learning become important. Empirical or case study evidence on search and learning in developing countries is just beginning to be done. The most complete discussion of these processes is Nelson and Winter (1982). Their several simulations illuminate how search occurs and how it produces learning and where it leads to. Nelson and Winter have a good bibliography, and the articles of Bell and Lall in Fransman and King (1984) are also helpful. In a more general context Rosenberg (1976, 1982) has much historical argument and many examples to demonstrate the learning process. Perhaps the most revealing evidence of these phenomena is in the development of some of the new export activities of the developing countries and in the stories of specific inventions in developing countries.

The Republic of Korea has achieved a remarkable export record over the years since the early 1960s. Larry Westphal and his colleagues have documented in several articles (especially Westphal *et al.*, 1981) that this record is largely a matter of domestic Korean firms' mastery of the technical aspects of production processes. Koreans concentrated on activities where the technology was well established and the products were fairly standardized. This mastery was of course accomplished by learning by doing, and this in turn fostered domestic innovative activity. The strong inducements to export created many forms of contacts with foreign buyers who defined their product needs. In all this the principal point is that emphasized above in section 7.5: Korea did not acquire a 'given' technology that was 'appropriate' and that met its factor endowment situation. Rather it found a way to create an environment in which Korean economic agents were induced to keep searching and keep learning, so that new knowledge was continually appearing and being applied. Why did this process work so well in Korea? There are doubtless many factors, but it is worth noting that several observers (for example Stewart and Dore in their article in Fransman and King, 1984) emphasize historical backgrounds, culture and traditions, and ideology. The Korean approach might not work, might not be do-able in (say) an African or Latin American society.

R. M. Bell (in Fransman and King, 1984, p. 192) argues that one may 'learn little from using improved methods, but a great deal from defining and implementing them'. He cites evidence from a study of J. M. Katz and E. Ablin that shows that an Argentinian manufacturer of bakery equipment had 'in the course of production, . . . found solutions to various technical problems'. In the course of these typical 'trouble-shooting' activities it designed special equipment for the sector.

What the literature now offers in increasing number are examples and episodes of search and learning, and descriptions of the environments that have produced or induced these processes to be undertaken. Formal general theories or general principles that lead to specific policies are not yet available, and it may be that their development will be slow. The evidence now available does, however, make convincing the argument of section 7.5 that it is this indigenous process of technological search and learning that resolves the factor proportions/technology choice questions.

REFERENCES

Amsalem, M. A. 1983. *Technology Choice in Developing Countries.* Cambridge, Mass. and London: MIT Press.

Arrow, K. Chenery, H., Minhas, B. and Solow, R. 1961. Capital–substitution and economic efficiency. *Review of Economics and Statistics,* 43, 225–50.

Bhalla, A. S. (ed.). 1981. *Technology and Employment in Industry.* Geneva: International Labour Office.

Bruton, H. J. 1985. On the production of a national technology. In J. James and S. Watanabe (eds), *Technology, Institutions, and Government Policy.* London: Macmillan.

Caves, R. E. 1982. *Multinational Enterprise and Economic Analysis.* Cambridge: Cambridge University Press.

Chenery, H. B. 1961. Comparative advantage and development policy. *American Economic Review,* 51, 18–51.

Chudnovsky, D. and Nagao, N. 1983. *Capital Goods Production in the Third World.* New York: St Martin's Press.

Dahlman, C. and Westphal, L. 1982. Technological effort in industrial development – an interpretative survey of recent research. In F. Stewart and J. James (eds), *The Economics of New Technology in Developing Countries.* London: Frances Pinter.

Dunning, J. H. 1974. *Economic Analysis and the Multinational Enterprise.* London: Allen and Unwin.

Eckaus, R. S. 1955. Factor proportions in underdeveloped areas. *American Economic Review,* 45, 539–65.

Fransman, M. and King, K. (eds). 1984. *Technological Capacity in the Third World.* New York: St Martin's Press.

Freeman, C. 1973. A study of the success and failure in industrial innovation. In B. R. Williams (ed.), *Science and Technology in Economic Growth.* New York: John Wiley and Sons.

Ginneken van, W. and Baron, C. 1984. *Appropriate Products Employment and Technology.* New York: St Martin's Press.

Harrod, R. F. 1939. An essay in dynamic theory. *Economic Journal,* 49, 14–33.

International Labour Office. 1984. *Technology Choice and Employment Generation by Multinational Enterprises in Developing Countries.* Geneva: International Labour Office.

Lewis, W. A. 1954. Economic development with unlimited supplies of labour. *Manchester School,* 22, 131–91.

Lindblom, C. E. and Cohen, D. 1979. *Usable Knowledge.* New Haven and London: Yale University Press.

Morawetz, D. 1974. Employment implications of industrialization in developing countries: a survey. *Economic Journal,* 84, 491–542.

Morawetz, D. 1976. Elasticities of substitution in industry: what do we learn from such estimates? *World Development,* 4, 11–15.

Nelson, R. R. and Winter, S. G. 1982. *An Evolutionary Theory of Economic Change.* Cambridge, Mass. and London: Harvard University Press.

Pack, H. 1980a. *Fostering the Capital Goods Sector in LDCs.* Washington, DC: World Bank.

Pack, H. 1980b. *Macroeconomic Implications of Factor Substitution Industrial Processes.* Washington, DC: World Bank.

Pickett, J. (ed.). 1977. The work of the Livingstone Institute on 'appropriate' technology. *World Development,* 5, 773–882.

Ranis, G. 1979. Appropriate technology: obstacles and opportunities. In S. Rosenblatt (ed.), *Technology and Economic Development: a Realistic Perspective*. Boulder, Col.: Westview Press.

Ranis, G. 1984. Determinants and consequences of indigenous technological activity. In M. Fransman and K. King (eds), *Technological Capability in the Third World*. New York: St Martin's Press.

Rosenberg, N. 1976. *Perspective on Technology*. London and New York: Cambridge University Press.

Sansom, R. L. 1969. The motor pump: a case study of innovation and development. *Oxford Economic Papers*, 21, 109–91.

Stewart, F. 1974. Technology and employment in LDCs. In E. O. Edwards (ed.), *Employment in Developing Countries*. New York/London: Columbia University Press.

Stewart, F. 1984. Facilitating indigenous technical change in Third World countries. In M. Fransman and K. King (eds), *Technological Capability in the Third World*. New York: St Martin's Press.

Stewart, F. and James, J. (eds). 1982. *The Economics of the New Technology in Developing Countries*. London: Frances Pinter.

Stobaugh, R. and Wells, L. T. Jr (eds). 1984. *Technology Crossing Borders*. Boston: Harvard Business School Press.

Streeten, P. and Stewart, F. 1972. Conflicts between output and employment objectives in developing countries. In P. Streeten (ed.), *The Frontiers of Development Studies*. New York: John Wiley and Sons.

Vernon, R. 1977. *Storm over Multinationals*. Cambridge, Mass.: Harvard University Press.

Wells, L. T. Jr. 1983. *Third World Multinationals*. Cambridge and London: MIT Press.

Wells, L. T. Jr. 1984. Economic man and engineering man. In R. Stobaugh and L. T. Wells, Jr. (eds), *Technology Crossing Borders*. Boston: Harvard Business School Press.

Westphal, L. E., Rhee, Y. W. and Purcell, G. 1981. *Korean Industrial Competence: Where It Came From*. Washington, DC: World Bank.

White, L. J. 1978. The evidence on appropriate factor proportions for manufacturing in less developed countries: a survey. *Economic Development and Cultural Change*, 27, 27–60.

PART IV

The public sector and development

8

Taxation and development

Norman Gemmell

8.1 Introduction

This survey is concerned with the role played by taxation in the development process, and especially with the operation of tax systems in less developed countries (LDCs). The tax system in many LDCs is, according to Bird (1982, p. 212), 'perhaps . . . the most pervasive and far-reaching policy instrument available to the government'. Among various government objectives it is in the pursuit of economic growth that the tax instrument has perhaps most often been identified, particularly in the Keynesian tradition, as of critical importance. Thus Kaldor (1964, p. 55) suggests that 'the importance of public revenue to the underdeveloped country can hardly be exaggerated if they are to achieve their hopes of accelerated economic progress. . . . [Government] must steadily expand a whole host of non revenue-yielding services – education, health, communication systems and so on – as a prerequisite to a country's economic and cultural development'. Notwithstanding Kaldor's use of hyperbola, and some subsequent revision of opinions among many economists concerning the effects of government intervention, the economic role of government, and its funding, remain important areas of research for LDCs. Although the size of the public sector in LDCs, as measured by various statistical indicators (see section 8.2), is typically smaller than in most developed countries (DCs) – excluding centrally planned economies – its direct impact on production is often more widespread.

The purpose of this survey is to review useful economic analysis which can be applied to tax issues in LDCs, and to survey the empirical evidence which has sought both to advance knowledge of important tax parameters and to test hypotheses thrown up by economic analysis. This is not to suggest that economics alone provides the appropriate approach to the analysis of government policies. Many factors, often of a political and social nature, can influence government decision-making, and tax policies clearly can only be understood within that context. Nevertheless careful economic analysis is an important component of the study of taxation in LDCs, as elsewhere.

Both positive and normative aspects of taxation have been extensively studied, the former being concerned with such issues as how tax systems operate in various countries, what effects on income distribution or tax revenue might result from certain tax changes, and so on. This therefore includes both empirical study and positive theorizing and forms the basis of sections 8.2 to 8.5 below. Normative aspects of taxation which explore the *desirability* of alternative tax regimes and tax changes, and therefore must incorporate value judgments, are examined in section 8.6.

Section 8.2 considers alternative tax structures employed in different countries and reviews evidence on the sources of differences in tax systems. Sections 8.3 and 8.4 respectively survey the literature on the effects of taxation on economic growth and equity. The application of positive analysis to tax problems has provided valuable insights, and some of these are examined in section 8.5, while the normative issues of optimal taxation and tax reform in LDCs are the focus of section 8.6. Section 8.7 offers some concluding observations. Necessarily, some aspects of taxation in LDCs must be omitted. This survey does not examine the properties of particular tax *types* in any detail; three useful books which do so are Bird and Oldman (1975), Goode (1984) and Lewis (1984). A major area of the tax literature is concerned with the taxation of agriculture. Some of this material is reviewed in Ahmad and Stern (forthcoming) and Ghatak and Ingersent (1984), in addition to the three books above. Finally the interactions between the tax system and inflation/stabilization are not pursued here; some are discussed in survey 5. (See also Cline and Weintraub, 1981; Fitzgerald, 1978; Goode, 1984, chapters 5, 9 and 11; Lam, 1978; Tanzi, 1978, 1983).

8.2 Tax systems and development

This section concentrates on the main characteristics of tax systems in different countries which have been examined in recent literature. Section 8.2.1 looks at alternative tax structures and how these are related to development. Two tax parameters which have been extensively studied are tax 'buoyancy' and 'elasticity', and these are considered in section 8.2.2. Studies of tax 'effort' and tax 'capacity' – which have attempted to assess how successfully countries are tapping available tax resources – are reviewed in section 8.2.3, and section 8.2.4 examines the extent to which tax revenues have constrained public expenditure growth in LDCs.

8.2.1 Tax structures

Developed and developing country systems

Tax systems are used by governments to achieve a variety of objectives, including income redistribution, stabilization, financing publicly provided goods and services, and fostering economic growth. The weighting of these and other objectives is likely to vary across countries and over time, depending on such factors as the economic environment and political outlook, and it is therefore not surprising that tax systems vary enormously across countries. Differences in the ease with which different households, firms or sectors within an economy can be taxed also give rise to many alternative specifications of particular taxes which may have different associated economic effects. Taxes common to many structures include 'direct' taxes on income, profits and property (e.g. land, wealth) and indirect taxes on domestically produced goods and services (general sales taxes, value added taxes, excises), imports and exports. For purposes of many tax analyses social security contributions can also be treated as taxes. The contributions of these broad categories to government revenue in a sample of countries are shown in table 8.1. It is immediately obvious that the main differences between the 'developed' countries in group A (the main OECD countries) and the various groups of 'developing' countries (B, C and D) are (1) the greater share of revenue from income and profit taxes and social security contributions in the former group, and (2) the greater importance of various trade taxes in the latter groups. Interestingly, domestic indirect taxes provide a broadly similar share of revenue across the four groups. This may result partly from the omission of production subsidies which, though usually classified with public expenditure, are effectively negative indirect taxes, and tend to be more prevalent among the developing country groups.

Although income taxes are less important in revenue terms in LDCs they are often more complex than in developed countries, with greater use of 'schedular' income taxes which tax different sources of income using different schedules, with a variety of thresholds and rates[1]. In some countries (for example Egypt) this is combined with a 'general' income tax applying to all or most income sources. As a consequence a complex interaction of rates and thresholds can result, so adding to the more fundamental difficulties of operating income taxation in LDCs – problems of defining, measuring and assessing 'income' and the administration of tax collections. The greater the extent of subsistence consumption in LDCs the more difficult income tax administration becomes and, partly for this reason, the agricultural sector is often excluded from such taxes.

With indirect taxation a similar picture emerges; LDCs use a more complex set of consumption and commodity-specific taxes (excises) than DCs. Subsidies on basic wage-goods (for example, bread, rice, beans) are frequently used and implicit taxes and subsidies occur when 'marketing boards' – government agencies which act as intermediaries between producers and consumers in the market, and to whom producers are usually obliged to sell – fix prices above or below 'market' rates. Such schemes are particularly associated with African countries (see Abdel-Fadil, 1980; Prest, 1972). In recent years, however, following the adoption of value added taxes (VAT) in the EEC, a number of LDCs have introduced or experimented with VAT-type taxes and other general sales taxes. VAT now exists in such countries as Brazil, Argentina, Mexico, Israel, Korea, Ivory Coast and Senegal. Not surprisingly it is generally in the more developed LDCs – mainly in Latin America – where VAT is most important, since the tax requires well-developed administrative and accounting systems.

Table 8.1 Shares of different taxes in total government revenue (%) around 1980

Country group[a] (number)	Taxes				Social security contributions
	Income and profit	Domestic goods and services	International trade		
A: Industrial countries (20)	33.3	26.0	3.7		25.0
B: Semi-industrial countries (15)	25.3	30.6	14.5		13.0
C: Middle-income countries (55)	23.7	23.1	28.9		4.1
D: Least developed countries (14)	17.0	21.7	41.6		1.6

[a] For a list of countries included in each group see Goode (1984, pp. 6, 91). Countries have generally been assigned to groups following IMF practice.

Source: Goode (1984, p. 91).

Among the problems created by the extensive and complex set of taxes used in LDCs are (1) widespread evasion because the tax system cannot be adequately monitored; (2) unintended economic effects resulting from unforeseen inter-actions between different component taxes; and (3) partly as a result of (2), problems identifying whether tax policies are achieving government objectives. For details of the operation of particular taxes in LDCs, see Bird and Oldman (1975), Goode (1984), Lewis (1984) and Prest (1972). Finally evidence from a number of sources (see Chelliah *et al.*, 1975; Tait *et al.*, 1979) suggests strongly that the ratios of total tax revenue to GDP are higher on average in developed than in less developed countries, due primarily to higher ratios of *income* tax revenue to GDP. Chelliah *et al.* (1975) also found that splitting a sample of 47 LDCs into 'high' and 'low' per capita income subsamples, both groups had similar ratios of international trade taxes and internal production taxes to GNP but the 'high' income group had higher income tax : GNP ratios on average.[2]

Tax revenues and development

While there may be general agreement on major differences between DC and LDC tax systems there is much less agreement on how *changes* in tax structure are related to development, normally measured in this context by per capita income levels. Two particular concerns have been (1) to identify whether total and individual tax revenues as a proportion of GDP rise as per capita income increases; and (2) to investigate how the shares of tax components in total revenue change with per capita income. For both cases, because of a paucity of time-series data, most studies have used cross-section data for samples of DCs and LDCs under the maintained hypothesis that this approximates long-run time-series changes. A few studies have, however, investigated changes over time for a number of countries.

Early studies by Hinrichs (1965, 1966) and Musgrave (1969) tested the hypotheses that total tax ratios and the share of direct taxes in total tax revenue rise with per capita income. Using regression analysis on samples of developed and less developed countries both studies found evidence in support of the hypo-theses, but only when both DCs and LDCs were included. When the two country groups were examined separately the relationships appeared to break down. However, even with an aggregate sample, Dosser (1965) found no clear evidence that increases in per capita income were associated with a declining importance of indirect taxes. Subsequent studies by Chelliah *et al.* (1975) and Tait *et al.* (1979) found that between 65 and 80 per cent of the countries in a sample of 47 LDCs experienced rising tax ratios during the 1966–75 period. For tax revenue shares, however, the evidence was less clear-cut, with only 52 per cent of the sample experiencing a rising share of direct taxes (1953–71). Using cross-section data for two periods, 1950–9 and 1960–72, Abizadeh and Wyckoff (1982) found that evidence on the direct tax share depended on whether DCs and LDCs were considered together or separately, and the decade chosen. Similarly Greenaway (1980, 1984), using cross-section data, found that the share of trade taxes in total revenue appeared to be related to per capita income and the size of the traded goods sector only for an aggregate sample of DCs and LDCs and for 'middle-income' countries, with no similar evidence for 'low' or 'high' income subsamples. However, some evidence of declining trade tax dependence as income rises was found from time-series data for a number of countries, 1962–78.

These results would seem to bear out the suggestions of Hinrichs and Musgrave that direct taxes are more likely to be prominent at very low income levels (when 'traditional' land and poll taxes can be most readily applied), and at high income levels when widespread use of personal and corporate income taxes becomes possible. Indirect taxes, initially on trade and then on internal transactions, could be expected to dominate middle income levels. Thus a U-shaped pattern for the direct tax share is more likely. Hinrichs (1966) also suggested that, partly as a result of this pattern, tax revenue growth is likely to be higher in the early and late stages of development, but slower in the middle. This is certainly consistent with the failure of several studies to identify a simple positive relationship between tax ratios and per capita income.

Effective tax rates

It has long been recognized that import tariffs can have widely different effects on the production costs of different domestic industries as a result of differing import tariff rates and different usages of intermediate imports across industries. Thus 'effective protection' to domestic industry may be quite different from 'nominal protection' as represented by the tariff. These issues were discussed in survey 1. In LDCs domestic indirect taxes – sales taxes, excises, etc. – typically apply to final consumer goods and hence differences in effective tax rates across sectors have not been thought to be a problem. However in India and Pakistan, for example, where taxes on intermediate goods are more common, effective tax rates estimated by Ahmad and Stern (1983), and Ahmad *et al.* (1984a) have revealed some interesting divergences between nominal and effective rates.

In India, for example, handloom and khadi manufactures of cotton faced an effective tax rate of 5 per cent though the nominal rate was zero; effective rates for tobacco were more than double the nominal 9 per cent rate; and in 'artificial silk and man-made fibres' the *difference* between effective and nominal rates amounted to 44 percentage points![3] For most intermediate goods and consumer durables the difference between rates was in the 15–25 percentage point range, and for non-durable consumer goods the range was 5–15 percentage points. A similar picture emerged for Pakistan with many goods facing effective tax rates 5–20 percentage points above nominal rates. These differences are clearly non-negligible, and highlight the possibility of unintended effects of tax policy in one area on another. It is clear that, where differences between nominal and effective tax rates are significant, the latter must be used in tax analysis if reliable results are to be obtained. It is possible, for instance, for a good which bears a nominal subsidy to face a positive *effective* tax rate.

8.2.2 Tax buoyancy and elasticity

Two important parameters of tax systems, and individual taxes, are 'buoyancy' and 'elasticity'. Tax buoyancy refers to the realized increase in tax revenues in association with increases in GDP (or some other income measure). The elasticity of a tax or tax system, on the other hand, measures the 'automatic' change in revenue for a given tax base, as GDP rises. Thus the elasticity measure excludes the effects of discretionary tax changes by the authorities, changes in compliance and collection rates and so on. In addition it is often of interest to decompose the tax elasticity into (1) the elasticity of tax revenue with respect to the relevant tax base, and (2) the elasticity of the tax base with respect to GDP. This can help to identify the extent to which the overall tax elasticity can be attributed to structural changes in the economy affecting the base-to-GDP elasticity, or to the properties of the tax schedule which affect the tax-to-base elasticity. It is common in the literature for elastic taxes to be identified as preferable to inelastic taxes because additional revenue can be raised more readily. However, it should be noted that while this may be true for the tax authority, its desirability from society's point of view will depend on preferred allocations of resources between private and public use. Nevertheless a knowledge of relevant tax elasticities can assist governments' decisions on discretionary tax and expenditure plans.

Unfortunately since most observed changes in tax revenue are a combination of automatic and discretionary effects, with only the combined change directly observable, it is difficult to calculate tax elasticities accurately. A number of approaches have been used including estimating discretionary revenue changes from treasury forecasts (for example, Byrne, 1983); using dummy variables for years when tax rate changes take place in a regression of revenues on GDP (for example Wilford and Wilford, 1978); and estimating 'tax functions' (for example, Choudhry, 1979; Creedy and Gemmell, 1982).

Given the acknowledged inaccuracies of the various methods, the elasticity estimates from several studies of LDC tax systems given in table 8.2 should be treated with caution, and can indicate only rough orders of magnitude (notwithstanding the precision with which some authors report results). The evidence in table 8.2, however, does tend to support (though not invariably) several generally held views regarding tax elasticities.

1 Tax buoyancies typically exceed elasticity estimates, indicating the prevalence of discretionary tax increases and/or improvements in collection, administration, etc.
2 Income and domestic consumption tax elasticities tend to be higher than trade tax elasticities.
3 Indirect tax elasticities can be highly variable across commodities, indicating opportunities to raise revenue by taxing 'elastic' commodities more.
4 Income tax elasticities tend to fall in association with income increases. This property of income tax systems has recently been demonstrated by Creedy and Gemmell (1982) and Hutton and Lambert (1982).
5 Particularly for indirect taxes, base-to-income elasticities may be high relative to tax-to-base elasticities, so that automatic revenue increases result mainly

Table 8.2 Estimates of tax buoyancy and elasticity

Study	Sample	Period covered	Total tax buoyancy	Total tax elasticity
Levin (1968)	Colombia	1925-65	—	—
Chelliah (1971)	Twenty-five LDCs	1953-5 to 1966-8	—	0.96-2.4 (ave. = 1.4)
Arrate and Geller (1971)	Six Latin American countries	1960-66	0.72-1.18[c]	—
Mansfield (1972)	Paraguay	1962-70	1.69	1.14
Wilford and Wilford (1978)	Central American Common Market (five countries)	1955-74 (1961-74)	1.03 (1.14)	1.03
Choudhry (1975)	Malaysia	1961-70	2.5 (personal income) 1.3 (business income)	
Choudhry (1979)	Malaysia	1961-73	1.70	1.57
	Kenya	1962-74	1.42	1.32
Ho (1979)	Hong Kong	1949/ 50 to 1975/ 6	1.12	1.02 (1947/ 8) 0.99 (1969/ 70)
Hutton (1980)	Malaysia	1960-76	—	—
Dwivedi (1981)	India	1955-6 to 1972-3	[d]	—
Purohit (1981)	India (State taxes only)	1960-1 to 1970-1	1.19 (0.79-1.64)[e]	1.07 (0.68-1.49)[e]
Bagchi and Rao (1982)	India	1965-6 to 1978-9	1.08 (income)	
Askari *et al.* (1982)	Nine oil exporters	1950-78	2.75 (1950-62) 1.29 (1973-8)	—
	Seven non-oil exporters (Middle East)		1.97 (1950-62) 1.19 (1973-8)	
Byrne (1983)	Zambia	1966-77	2.30	1.37

[a] Percentage of countries with elasticity ≥ 1.
[b] Buoyancies of individual taxes.
[c] Reported as 'elasticities' by Arrate and Geller (1971), but are actually buoyancies. These are greater than 1 for Brazil, Chile and Mexico, and less than 1 for Argentina, Guatemala and Venezuala.

Table 8.2 cont.

		Elasticity of			
Income taxes	Import taxes	Export taxes	Excise/ consumption taxes	Tax to base	Base to income
—	—	—	—	—	1.3 (sales)
0.5–5.1 (68)[a]	0.34–5.8 (76)[a]	0.21–5.6 (44)[a]	−0.7–11.7 (83)[a]		
—	—	—	—	—	—
1.08	1.21	0.06	0.39	0.70 0.17	1.56 (import) 1.05 (export)
1.01–1.83	0.12–0.16	0.01–1.32	0.98–1.53	—	—
1.72, 1.66 (1961,1969)	—	—	—	1.08,1.11	1.52
0.97 (both years)	—	—	—	1.00	0.97
1.84[b]	0.96[b]	0.83[b]	—	—	1.60 (income) 0.99 (import)
1.48[b]	0.88[b]		1.31[b]	—	0.80 (income) 1.18 (import) 0.90 (excise)
1.13	1.00			—	—
1.07	0.96 (all indirect taxes)			—	—
2.62 (1960–9)	—	—	—	—	—
1.73 (1970–6)					
—	Essential consumer goods Non-essential consumer goods Consumer/ commercial goods Intermediate goods		0.34–0.44 −1.16–2.4 0.8–2.4 0.3–1.6	—	—
—		Sales Excise	1.40 (1.1–2.1)[e] 1.28 (0.4–2.3)[e]	—	—
1.09–1.076[f]	—	—	—	—	—
1.32, 1.49	0.17	—	1.40	—	—

[d] Dwivedi (1981) reports buoyancies for commodity groups only. These are generally less than 2 for 'essential consumer goods' and most 'intermediate goods'; more than 2 for 'consumer/commercial goods' (such as vehicles); and variable for 'non-essential consumer goods'.

[e] Figures in parentheses are the range across Indian States.

[f] Estimate depends on the measure of discretionary change adopted.

from structural changes such as the changing composition of domestically produced goods and imports in consumption. Some studies (see Levin, 1968; Mansfield, 1972) suggest that low tax-to-base elasticities for imports result from shifts towards low-rated intermediate imports from high-rated consumer goods. Note that the tax-to-base elasticity of income taxes can be a function of their progressivity as measured by the difference between effective marginal and average tax rates.[4] Therefore policies aimed at redistribution via income taxation will affect tax elasticity.

8.2.3 Tax effort and capacity

Prominent among studies of taxation in LDCs have been attempts to identify the extent to which tax authorities have exploited available tax capacity, determined largely by the size and availability of tax bases. It has been argued by some IMF economists, with whom the approach is associated, that evidence on a country's tax 'effort' relative to its 'capacity' could be used, for example, to allocate foreign aid to LDCs, since tax effort indices would measure the extent to which governments were willing to use domestically available resources.

The essence of the approach is to use regression analysis on cross-section data to 'explain' tax ratios using a number of variables of tax capacity. This yields a set of predicted tax ratios for given tax capacity, and may be compared with countries' actual tax ratios, the difference between the two measuring tax effort (see Chelliah et al., 1975; Tait et al., 1979). Variables which have been used to proxy tax capacity include (a) the share of trade (exports plus imports) in GDP; (b) per capita income levels; (c) the relative size of the agricultural, mining or retail sectors; and (d) the literacy level.

Tax effort studies have been severely criticized on a number of grounds (see Bird, 1978; Bolnick, 1978a, b; Prest, 1978). Firstly, as can be seen from the discussion of tax structures above, a country's capacity to tax is determined by many factors, often highly specific to that country – such as the composition of domestic production and of imports, the efficiency of its civil service and so on. On the other hand, the variables listed above are such poor proxies for individual countries' actual tax bases that it seems likely that observed differences between actual and 'predicted' tax ratios are more a reflection of inaccurate measurement of capacity rather than a reflection of tax effort. Secondly the use of tax effort indices for *normative* judgments regarding desirable changes in countries' tax systems – for example to 'improve its effort' – is wholly inappropriate. At best the tax effort equations provide a description of the relationship between tax revenue and proxies for tax bases, and identify the extent of inter-country uniformity in the use of these tax bases. However they are likely to be highly misleading guides to tax improvement since they do not consider the characteristics of desirable tax systems – such as efficiency or equity. It is partly in response to these criticisms that Tait et al. (1979) appear to accept that the 'tax effort equations' are better thought of as descriptive devices, and they adopt the term 'international tax comparisons' to describe the approach.

8.2.4 Tax constraints

Evidence of lower tax ratios in LDCs compared to developed countries, coupled with the obvious pressures for government spending on such low revenue-yielding activities as infrastructure investment, health and education, has prompted the suggestion that public expenditure is constrained in LDCs more than in DCs by limited capacity to raise tax revenues. Alternatively where government expenditure is not restrained it can only expand with increasing deficits creating a potential 'fiscal crisis' (Fitzgerald, 1978). In an early study Thorn (1967) found that a relatively high income elasticity of central government expenditure of around 1.2–1.3 for a sample of developed and less developed countries was similar to estimates of tax elasticity. Fitzgerald, on the other hand, examining tax and expenditure growth in six Latin American countries, found that expenditure increases were associated with increasing fiscal deficits. More recent evidence from Goode (1984, pp. 56–9) is suggestive of strong pressures for increases in public expenditure in LDCs. Examining data on 75 LDCs during 1960–70 and 1970–80, Goode found that, for the countries where GDP was rising, government expenditure was increasing faster than GDP in 68 per cent of the sample. However, in the absence of *ex-ante* estimates of tax and expenditure growth none of these studies can test the tax constraint hypothesis. Rather what is required is information on the desired allocation of resources to publicly provided activities and the ability of governments to achieve that from tax sources. This is the approach followed by Bolnick (1982), who models the share of resources devoted to government activity as a function of a vector of 'demand-oriented characteristics' derived from social preferences and the marginal social cost of transferring resources to government, MCT. Bolnick hypothesizes the MCT to be a function of the tax ratio and a vector of 'supply-oriented characteristics' representing the capacity to raise taxes. He is thus able to derive a reduced form relationship between the tax ratio and the two vectors of 'supply' and 'demand' variables.

Variables expected to affect supply include per capita income, the relative size of the traded goods sector (exports plus imports/GDP), urbanization (which raises tax capacity) and literacy, 'as a proxy for the accessibility of a modern direct tax base' (Bolnick, 1982, p. 21). 'Demand' variables include per capita income, population size and density, urbanization and dependency rates, all of which may be expected to influence the desired provision of publicly provided goods. Using a sample of 'low'- and 'middle'-income countries, the tax constraint hypothesis would be supported if supply variables were relatively more important in an explanation of tax ratios in low-income countries, but demand variables were relatively more important for middle-income countries.

Unfortunately, since several variables enter both the demand and supply vectors it is likely to be difficult to identify the respective effects of supply and demand. Indeed Bolnick's results are ambiguous, with some regressions appearing to be consistent with, and others contrary to, the tax constraint hypothesis. One of the resaons for this ambiguity is undoubtedly the inability of some variables to proxy intended effects. Bolnick finds, for example, that youth dependency rates (proportion of the population below a given age) are negatively related to the tax ratio. This variable, however, via demand, was expected to increase the tax ratio, *ceteris paribus*. It seems likely that the variable also captures some supply effects, for example by encouraging increased food imports which may induce a reduction in the existing indirect tax base. Nevertheless Bolnick's approach is a useful one and improved data and variable specification may yet yield more reliable results.

8.3 Taxation and growth

A property commonly ascribed to the tax system, especially in LDCs, is its ability to accelerate the rate of economic growth. Particularly in the Keynesian tradition it has been argued that the generally lower utilization of resources in LDCs compared with DCs renders tax policy a potent instrument for expanding economic activity. It is important, however, to distinguish between the use of taxation and the use of 'deficit financing' to foster growth. Arguments for the former rely on the prospects of reallocating resources from the private to the public sector stimulating growth, as captured, for example, in the balanced budget multiplier. Deficit financing arguments, on the other hand, typically incorporate the notion that governments can create additional resources. Many of these latter arguments have lost their force in recent years with the recognition of the role played by the government budget constraint.

The ability of the tax system to generate growth hinges on three distinct steps:

1 the responsiveness of savings to tax incentives/policies;
2 the economy's ability to transform savings into investment resources, and
3 the effects of increased investment on income growth.

Where tax incentives are aimed directly at investment this process reduces to two steps. Tax incentives/ policies may of course also affect income growth directly via associated incentive effects. Each of the three steps will be considered in turn below.

8.3.1 Taxation and savings

The generation of additional savings through tax policy can take two main approaches – the creation of tax incentives to encourage increased *private* saving; and the use of tax instruments to reallocate investable resources to the public sector. An example incorporating both approaches would be differential taxation of savings and consumption which simultaneously encourages a substitution of private saving for consumption and provides revenues which, to the extent that it substitutes public investment for private consumption, raises savings. The choice between the two approaches – public saving or incentives to private saving – which are not of course mutually exclusive, depends on the relative magnitudes of the income and substitution effects associated with each tax instrument or incentive. For instruments such as a tax on wages it is desirable for income effects (presumed positive here) to outweigh negative substitution effects, while for tax incentives (for example tax concessions on retained profits) which usually represent implicit subsidies, large substitution effects relative to income effects are required.

It follows therefore that where producers, consumers, suppliers of labour and so on are responsive to price signals, substitution effects will tend to be relatively large, thus favouring tax policies which emphasize incentives to private savings, and those taxes with relatively low disincentive or substitution effects. For taxes on wages (where substitution effects are generally related to *marginal* tax rates but income effects depend mainly on *average* tax rates) this would suggest a tax structure with low marginal rates. Of course since this implies a *relatively* inelastic and regressive tax compared to one with a high ratio of marginal to average rates, this may conflict with other policy objectives.

In the opinion of Kaldor (1965) 'a great deal of the prevailing concern with incentives is misplaced' (p. 170), and indeed most empirical studies of the effects of tax policies on savings or investment have failed to find strong incentive effects. In a wide-ranging survey of studies on tax incentives to firms in LDCs, Shah and Toye (1978) found few instances where investment decisions by firms appeared to respond to tax incentive, though the technique most commonly used – of interviewing firms – is notoriously unreliable. Most studies using this technique found less than 5 per cent of firms apparently influenced to any significant extent by tax incentives. Lent (1975) quotes one study which found that tax incentives influenced firms' location choice but not the investment decision. An alternative technique estimates the critical minimum profit necessary for firms to invest (from information on discount rates and project lives) and compares this with investment projects' net present values both with and without the tax incentives. Where the value of the critical minimum profit lies between the two NPVs, the incentive may be said to have created or stimulated the investment (see Shah and Toye, 1978, pp. 282–3). While this method has produced apparently greater incentive effects (20 and 30 per cent of firms stimulated in Pakistan in two separate studies; 10 per cent of firms in Colombia) the results are of doubtful accuracy and are still not very high.

In another interview-based study of Jamaican tax incentives Chen-Young (1975) found only two of 55 firms reporting significant tax effects on investment decisions. More interestingly, Chen-Young attempted to evaluate the benefits and costs of the various incentive schemes (in terms of revenues foregone and investments created). He found a benefit–cost ratio of only 0.27 if businesses were assumed to set up regardless of incentives, rising to 0.66 under the most generous assumptions regarding incentives *necessary* for new investment and multiplier effects.

One policy often suggested to raise the savings rate is redistribution of income via taxation towards the relatively rich, and towards profits and away from wages. This is based on the view that within the wage distribution the rich save proportionately more, and that savings out of profit income exceed savings out of wage income. Unfortunately evidence in support of this view is ambiguous. Examining a number of Latin American countries, Griffin (1971, pp. 5–12), for example, found no correlation between income accruing to the top 10 per cent of earners and savings rates. King (1971), on the other hand, found some evidence to suggest a possible association between income distribution and savings in Latin America. He also suggests that savings out of profits *may* be higher than savings out of wages in some countries. Some recent evidence (see Ram, 1982, 1984) has also explored the effects of population dependency rates on savings but, perhaps surprisingly, failed to find any significant reductive effect of higher youth dependency rates on savings in LDCs.

Finally the interest sensitivity of savings represents an important variable to the tax authorities who can, via fiscal and monetary policy, alter this relative price. Unfortunately there appear to be no reliable studies of the interest elasticity of savings in LDCs. A few studies conducted for developed countries suffer from many estimation problems but tend to suggest generally low elasticities (see King, 1980).

8.3.2 Savings and growth

Savings and investment

For savings to contribute to growth they must be transformed into investable resources. There are, however, a number of reasons why this link in the chain of causation from taxation to growth may be unreliable. Three of these are discussed briefly here.

In 1966 Chenery and Strout suggested that a more important constraint on growth than shortages of savings or foreign exchange may be a constraint on absorptive capacity. Thus even if savings rates rise substantially these may not be able to be productively invested, not because of a lack of investment opportunities, but because these opportunities cannot be exploited. This may arise due to (1) a shortage of complementary inputs such as skilled labour or raw materials, (2) poorly developed financial institutions which prevent savings from being channelled smoothly and effectively where they are needed, and (3) where savings rise rapidly, an inability to achieve necessary reallocations of resources quickly enough (see Eshag, 1983).

Secondly, Please (1975) has suggested that where savings rates rise via increased *public* sector savings these may find their way into current rather than investment expenditures. Thus population, urbanization and poverty pressures lead to expenditure on food subsidies, housing, education and health. While some of these may have a substantial 'capital' element they may not represent the most efficient investments.[5] An important side issue here is that the type of expenditure undertaken by government may influence the effectiveness of its tax incentive policies. For example, the provision of housing or subsidized food may encourage the substitution of public provision for private purchases (see Goode, 1984, pp. 95–7).

Thirdly, the form in which savings are raised may be a determinant of the quantity of investment. Where savings accrue in the form of profits they may be used more for 'conspicuous consumption', or where they result from the activities of foreign-owned firms they may be channelled abroad instead of invested domestically. Alternatively savings out of profits may be transformed into investment more readily compared to household savings by avoiding the need to use the intermediary financial sector. It has also been observed that agricultural development banks set up to encourage agricultural investment can act as a mechanism for reducing rural investment when deposits by the agricultural sector exceed loans to that sector.

Do savings stimulate growth?

Clearly tax policies to expand savings and investment will have little effect on growth, at least directly, if increases in capital are incidental to growth. Space prevents a detailed review of the enormous literature on this subject, but it does seem to be the case that while many growth models have given a central role to capital accumulation, empirical evidence has generally not found increases in capital to be of primary importance, especially in LDCs. For a review of these studies see Thirlwall (1983, chapter 2).[6] Simon Kuznets, one of the most experienced researchers in this area, has concluded that improvements in the 'quality' of labour services – via shorter hours, education, etc., have been more important for growth in LDCs (see Kuznets, 1966, and his series of ten contributions on 'quantitative aspects of the economic growth of nations' in *Economic Development and Cultural Change*, 1956–67). This of course is quite consistent with evidence that capital per worker tends to be higher at higher income *levels* (see Stern and Lewis, 1980; Kravis *et al.*, 1982).

In fact the *a priori* arguments for the effects of savings (via investment) on growth are not universally accepted.[7] The model usually referred to in support of a positive effect of savings on growth is the Harrod–Domar (H–D) model (discussed in survey 7), but the savings result has been shown to be sensitive to a number of the model's assumptions, such as the fixity of factor proportions (see Solow, 1956). Finally it may be noted that evidence on the relationship between savings rates and income *levels* which has been used to support or deny the savings–growth relationship (see, for example, Griffin, 1971) is not an appropriate test of the model, though it can provide other insights into the role of savings. Various studies which have examined the effects of savings on *growth*, such as Hill (1964), Kuznets (1961), and Hamberg (1971), have typically failed to find any strong effects.[8]

Tax revenue instability

With governments in LDCs often heavily involved in planning development and providing a high proportion of investment funds, then, in so far as investment is important to growth, the availability of funds to governments may be an important determinant of growth rates. The effect that instability in government revenues might have, via government expenditures, on growth is analogous to the potential effects of export instability on growth, via unstable import purchases. The effects of expenditure instability on growth have not been investigated, but Lim (1983) has recently examined the impact of tax revenue fluctuations on expenditure instability. Using the period 1965–73, Lim employed time-series regressions for 45 LDCs to estimate instability indices for revenue and expenditure.[9] To the extent that governments can finance expenditures by non-tax revenues and borrowing, expenditure need not reflect revenue fluctuations. In fact Lim (1983) found the median value of revenue instability indices (for 45 LDCs) to be noticeably greater than that for expenditure instability (64 as against 48). The difference was greatest for African LDCs, less for Asian LDCs and non-existent for Latin American LDCs (on average). Considering the effects of tax revenue and other funding sources (borrowing, aid, etc.) on expenditure instability, Lim concluded that 'revenue instability was the main "cause" of spending instability' (p. 450), but alternative funding methods could slightly dampen the effects. However evidence on the most unstable *categories* of expenditure (defence, education and transport) suggested some of the instability may be due to inherent 'lumpiness' in the time profile of spending.

8.3.3 Taxation and employment generation

Doubt among many economists in recent years regarding the ability of faster growth in national income to generate enough new jobs in the 'modern' sector in LDCs, has prompted renewed interest in the use of tax incentives aimed specifically at employment generation.[10] These incentives may seek to encourage (a) the substitution of labour for capital, or (b) increases in capital which are complementary with labour. Broadly speaking, tax policies may be designed to affect either demand for, or supply of, *commodities and services*. Policies to affect the composition of demand towards more labour-intensive goods include (a) policies to redistribute income where, for example, low income earners consume the more labour-intensive products; and (b) changes in relative product prices by selective taxes and subsidies – for example by affecting the industry/agriculture terms of trade. Taxation to affect supply decisions may seek to alter (a) the *technical* substitution possibilities in production by encouraging the development of labour-using technologies; or (b) relative factor prices in favour of labour.

While the potential for using tax instruments in pursuit of these employment objectives is clearly large, empirical evidence does not lead to very optimistic conclusions. Progressive taxation which succeeds in redistributing income would seem to have employment effects in the right direction, but most studies conclude the relevant magnitudes are unlikely to be great (see survey 7). Secondly, changing the relative price of exports to import-competing goods may encourage increased labour intensity in so far as an export-oriented strategy is pursued, but evidence on the effectiveness of such a strategy to increase employment is limited. This is discussed in more detail in survey 2. Nevertheless it does seem that exports are often discriminated against in LDCs, both explicitly and by tariffs on intermediate imports. Changing the industry/agriculture terms of trade to favour the more labour-intensive agricultural sector may, according to Bird (1982), be counter-productive, since the responsiveness of each sector to price changes may differ. Thus decreased industrial employment may not be matched by increased employment in agriculture. Another important relative price is the exchange rate, which can alter the relative prices of (traded) capital and (non-traded) labour. This is often compounded by specially favourable exchange rates applicable to capital imports, though direct evidence on employment effects is difficult to obtain (see White, 1978).

Finally Prest (1971) has stressed the importance of identifying the incidence of taxes designed to promote employment. Where final incidence is not the same as initial incidence there is potential for unintended effects of tax policies, which may in some cases be in the opposite direction to those intended. The incidence of payroll taxes between wages, profits and commodity prices deserves particular attention. A payroll subsidy, for example, to producers in a labour-intensive sector, which is intended to increase employment there by raising profits, could be counter-productive if instead wages rise (and the tax is borne by producers), and may increase the consumption of relatively capital- or import-intensive commodities. It would seem, therefore, that carefully chosen taxes can assist employment creation in some sectors, but their widespread use is likely to create distortions which conflict with other policy objectives and their direct effects on employment are probably relatively small in any case.

8.4 Taxation and redistribution

General evidence of high levels of relative inequality and absolute poverty in LDCs (see survey 4) make the redistributive possibilities of the tax system a particularly important issue in these countries. In developed countries the major tax revenue source is frequently the income tax, and its distributional impact is usually an explicit consideration for governments. In LDCs, however, where trade taxes dominate, revenue and/ or protection issues have often been paramount when setting up taxes, and distributional questions may not have been addressed or were given a low priority. There is therefore greater potential in LDCs for *unintended* effects on income distribution resulting from tax policies, and careful study of tax incidence may help in tax reform.

As noted earlier, data problems and methodological difficulties bedevil many aspects of tax analysis in LDCs, but they are probably nowhere greater than in studies of tax incidence. In addition to the usual problems of defining and measuring incomes the use of *annual*, rather than *lifetime*, income data poses particular problems in LDCs where there tend to be greater numbers of young and part-time workers at the lower end of the (annual) income distribution than in DCs.

Secondly the inclusion or exclusion of social security contributions and various government transfers can make a difference to incidence results. The former are usually excluded, though they may effectively act as a tax, while the latter are often included with government expenditure, but may be seen as negative taxes. Thirdly, problems identifying the nature and extent of tax shifting have forced most studies to adopt blanket assumptions for groups of taxes, for which evidence is usually scanty. A few studies (such as Heller, 1981) have, however, attempted to test the sensitivity of their results to some shifting assumptions.

The shifting problem is especially acute in LDCs where there is greater scope for moving activities into or out of the market economy, and where there is greater selectivity in the application of individual taxes. Goode (1984) notes, for example, that large firms may be less able to shift taxes where they face competition from, frequently untaxed, small firms. This contradicts typical incidence assumptions.

Fourthly the reliability of income or expenditure distribution data is poor in most LDCs, further weakening the reliability of incidence results. Bird and De Wulf (1973) and Goode (1984) are particularly critical of tax incidence studies, but provided it is recognized that the apparently precise numbers commonly quoted have relatively large margins of error, the accumulated evidence of many studies can provide some guidance on the redistributive properties of taxes.

Finally most studies assume that the pre-tax income (or expenditure) distribution is unaffected by the taxes levied, an assumption which has proved impossible so far to test, but which is likely to vary in its accuracy according to the *types* of taxes used. Most studies also adopt a 'differential incidence' approach whereby the observed income distribution is compared to that resulting from an alternative, normally proportional tax, yielding the same revenue. Evidence on incidence is sometimes reported in summary distribution measures (for example, Hughes, 1985) but most often average effective tax rates are presented by income or expenditure class, as an estimate of the tax 'burden'.

8.4.1 Incidence of individual taxes

Income taxes

Personal income taxation is often thought to be progressive because of its rate structure – with marginal rates exceeding average rates and the former typically rising with income. However tax thresholds in LDCs are often very high, so excluding all but the highest income earners and the use of several 'schedular' income taxes can lead to complex sets of exemptions, as for example in Egypt, so that even high earners may pay little income tax. Goode (1984) suggests that corporate income taxes are likely to be progressive because share ownership is generally limited to those with high incomes. Both income taxes suffer, however, from the problem that inadequate indexation of thresholds during inflation, which may raise revenue in the short run, in the longer term encourages increased tax evasion. Evidence from Heller (1981) for Korea confirms that both schedular and global income taxes are progressive with corporate taxes either roughly proportional or progressive depending on incidence assumptions. Splitting his sample into farm and non-farm households, however, Heller found that for farm households the schedular income tax was mildly regressive and the corporate income tax may be regressive (depending on incidence assumptions). Ho (1979) also found income taxes to be progressive in Hong Kong, though exemptions tended to be high and some duties affect only the highest income groups. In both studies effective income tax burdens were low, however, reaching only 13 per cent in Korea and 16 per cent in Hong Kong, for the highest decile.

Property taxes

Many countries with property taxation use separate taxes for agricultural and non-agricultural sectors, and/ or different regional taxes or tax rates. This complicates the analysis of property tax incidence, which remains a theoretically unresolved issue (see De Wulf, 1983, pp. 355–8), but in general shifting of the tax is likely to be greater the more mobile is the property and the greater the differential in taxation between regions, sectors, etc. In practice some progressivity is created by the frequent exemption of low-value properties from taxation, but in several LDCs property taxes have fallen into disuse because of a failure to revalue properties during inflation. With negligible revenues their incidence becomes irrelevant. In Korea where the tax contributes significantly to revenue, Heller (1981) found it to be mildly progressive for farm households but either mildly regressive or progressive (depending on incidence assumptions) for non-farm households. In Hong Kong property taxes had little effect, since they affected only the top three deciles of the income distribution.

Domestic consumption and trade taxes

Since indirect taxation dominates the tax structures of so many LDCs it is not surprising that most incidence studies have concentrated on these taxes. They are often thought to be regressive because of limited variations in tax rates. However in LDCs excises at widely differing rates can be applied to a range of commodities, and subsidies/exemptions are frequently applied both to goods consumed mainly by the rich (such as education) and mainly by the poor (such as basic food items), so that determining incidence is not straightforward. Two important influences on indirect tax progressivity are (1) the progressivity of *income* taxation, and (2) the relationship of savings to income. *Ceteris paribus* an indirect tax will be less progressive the more progressive is the income tax and the more savings rise with income levels. These two effects serve to equalize the indirect tax base – expenditure – relative to the distribution of income.

Almost all incidence studies assume that indirect taxes are wholly shifted to consumers, although this implicitly assumes a vertical demand curve (Hughes, 1985, is a notable exception). Such an assumption clearly becomes less tenable when the incidence of sizeable changes in taxation is being examined. Also, the shifting of export and import taxes must be treated carefully, depending as it does on both domestic and foreign elasticities of demand and supply. (These issues are explored further in section 8.5.)

Evidence on the progressivity of indirect taxes is not uniform, which is perhaps hardly surprising given their diversity of rates, structures and enforcement. Indirect taxes have been found to be regressive as a whole for Egypt (Abdel-Fadil, 1980), and Colombia (Urrutia and De Sandoval, 1976); with some regressive elements in Hong Kong (Ho, 1979); roughly proportional or slightly progressive in Pakistan (Ahmad *et al.*, 1984b), and progressive in India (Ahmad and Stern, 1983; Chelliah and Lal, 1981).[11] Excises appeared to be regressive in Korea (Heller, 1981) and Lebanon (De Wulf, 1974) but in Egypt middle-income groups experienced highest tax burdens (Abdel-Fadil, 1980) while Indian State excises were found to be progressive (Chelliah and Lal, 1981). Customs duties show a similarly varied experience from progressive in India, and for all imports except tobacco in Egypt, to regressive in Korea. De Wulf (1983) reports a study by Ghandi of several LDCs which suggests negative income elasticities for alcohol and tobacco, so encouraging tax regressivity on these items.

It would seem from some studies that tax policies designed to be progressive need careful evaluation of their incidence. Katzman (1978) reports a progressive structure of public utility prices in several cities in LDCs designed to reflect ability to pay. However close examination of consumption patterns in Panang, Malaysia, revealed consumption to be much more closely correlated with family size than with income, so that large poor families may pay more than smaller, rich families. In fact Katzman suggests a flat rate plus a property tax would have been more progressive than the existing structure. A study of food subsidies by Davis (1977) also casts doubt on their redistributive effects. Davis argues that subsidies cannot affect those too poor to purchase the relevant commodity and they normally benefit *urban* rather than *rural* consumers, though the former are typically better off. Indeed many subsidy schemes explicitly or implicitly discriminate against rural consumers (for example, by using urban distribution centres for subsidized food). This appeared to be the case in Egypt, Pakistan, Bangladesh and Sri Lanka.

Finally, since subsidies are often excluded from incidence studies, evidence on the regressivity of indirect taxes may be unduly pessimistic. In Egypt, for example, the inclusion of subsidies counteracted regressive indirect taxes to produce a proportional system overall (see Abdel-Fadil, 1980).

8.4.2   Overall tax incidence

Evidence on overall tax incidence from a number of studies is given in figure 8.1, which shows effective average tax rates (for all taxes) by income group. By the nature of the data the distribution of effective tax burdens across income groups cannot be directly compared across countries, but they do reveal some features in common. In many cases (not just those shown) tax burdens seem to be roughly proportional for most income groups except the highest two or three, where burdens are almost always greater. However except where data are in percentile form (Korea and Hong Kong) there may be relatively few households in these higher income groups. It is also noticeable in a number of countries that tax rates can be higher at low income levels compared to the middle range of incomes. Bird and De Wulf (1973), after surveying 17 Latin American countries, conclude that most tax systems overall are either regressive or proportional. This conclusion is also shared for the region by Urrutia and De Sandoval (1976) and Furtado (1970). In a wider-ranging survey of 44 studies of 22 LDCs, however, De Wulf (1975) found evidence to support more optimistic conclusions. Of 32 studies whose results could be evaluated De Wulf suggests 22 'indicated some progressivity', though this was uneven across income groups. In only two studies (of Greece and The Philippines) could a 'regressive' conclusion be reached. It is

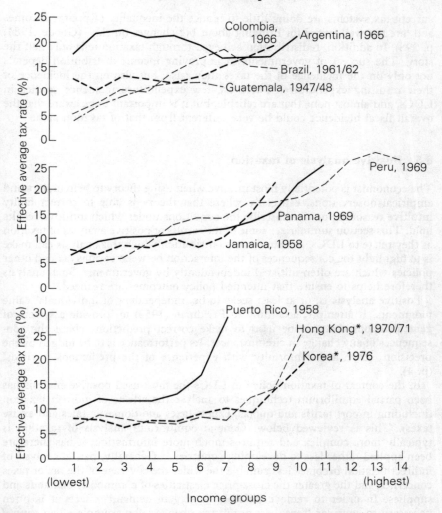

FIGURE 8.1 Total tax incidence by income group: selected countries.

Note: *Income groups equal deciles.
Source: Bird and De Wulf (1973) for Latin America; Ho (1979) for Hong Kong; Heller (1981) for Korea.

perhaps a little surprising then that De Wulf's (1983) conclusion is that 'it is difficult to analyse the pattern [of taxation] and not to conclude that the tax system in LDCs must be regressive' (p. 336).

However, what is clear from the data in figure 8.1, and from wider studies, is that effective tax rates, even where progressive, are typically low. As a result current tax systems are doing little to reduce the inequality of pre-tax incomes and 'are not well suited for bringing about big changes quickly' (Goode, 1984, p. 298). In addition, redistribution achieved through taxation tells only half the story. The success of governments in improving income distribution depends not only on the incidence of the taxes they raise, but also on the incidence of their resulting expenditure. There are few expenditure incidence studies in LDCs, and almost none that are reliable, but it is important to be aware that the overall fiscal incidence could be very different from that of taxation alone.

8.5 Positive analysis of taxation

The economist is potentially most incisive when using theory to help understand empirical observations, especially where that theory is able to correct faulty intuitive reasoning or circumscribe the conditions under which intuitive results hold. This section summarizes some of the results of positive analyses of taxation as they relate to LDCs. An important contribution which this analysis can make is to highlight the consequences of the interaction between various tax and other policies which are often initiated independently by governments. Such analysis therefore helps to ensure that intended policy outcomes are realized.

Positive analysis is, or at least seeks to be, independent of individuals' value judgments. It attempts, according to Friedman (1953) to 'provide a system of generalizations that can be used to make correct predictions about the consequences of any change in circumstances. Its performance is to be judged by the precision, scope and conformity with experience of the predictions it yields' (p. 4).

In the context of taxation policy in LDCs the most-used positive analysis has been partial equilibrium techniques to analyse the effects of indirect taxation (including import tariffs and quotas, export taxes and domestic sales and excise taxes). This is reviewed below. General equilibrium analysis of taxation is typically more complex and requires much more information; it has therefore been applied rather less to developing countries.[12] Generally, partial analysis of indirect taxation becomes less suitable the wider the coverage of the tax or taxes concerned and the greater the cross-price elasticities of commodity demands and supplies. In order to remove possible 'aggregate demand' effects it is often necessary to consider 'revenue-neutral' tax changes; for example when *general* sales or trade taxes are being considered.

This section reviews some general results of indirect tax analysis but cannot always identify the full set of conditions necessary for them to hold, nor all the underlying analysis. An excellent comprehensive treatment can be found in Lewis (1984, part IV).

8.5.1 Import and export taxes

The outcome of imposing taxes on imports and exports, in terms of effects on domestic producers and consumers and tax revenues, can be expected to vary, depending on the answers to the following questions.

1 Is there domestic production of import-competing goods? (That is, does the domestic supply curve lie wholly above the price of available imports?).
2 Is there a domestic market for exports?
3 Are the country's exports or imports small or large fractions of world trade in the relevant commodities? Where they are both 'small' – the most usual case – then the supply curve of imports and the demand curve for exports may be assumed to be perfectly elastic (that is, 'world' prices are given).
4 Will the taxes considered involve more than small changes in net foreign exchange earnings? Where the answer is yes, a change in the exchange rate (or pressure for such a change) must be allowed for.

Using the 'small country assumption' in (3) above, the following results will generally hold:

(a) An import tax will be borne wholly by domestic consumers.
(b) An export tax will be borne wholly by domestic producers.
(c) The domestic price of imports (or the price received by exporters) will rise (fall) by the full amount of the tax.
(d) The 'deadweight loss' as a result of the tax will be less the less elastic is demand for imports (or the supply of exports).[13]
(e) Import taxes (export taxes) yield less revenue when there is import-competing production (domestic demand for exportables) compared to a situation of no domestic production (demand).
(f) Import taxes (export taxes) encourage domestic production (consumption) of the commodities concerned.
(g) Foreign exchange earnings may rise or fall depending on the elasticities of *domestic* demand and supply.

These results, for the import tax case, can be seen in figure 8.2. This shows the *domestic* demand (DD) and supply (SS), for a commodity which may be imported at a price, OP_1, the import supply curve being given by P_1M_1. A tax of P_1P_2 on the import shifts P_1M_1 to P_2M_2 (the amount of the tax) so reducing consumption from OQ_4 to OQ_3 but increasing domestic production (where applicable) from OQ_1 to OQ_2. Government revenue is given by the area CDEF and the deadweight loss is the sum of triangles CBF and ADE. In the absence of domestic supply, government revenue would be P_2CFP_1 (and the deadweight loss is now simply CBF). Notice that the tax has introduced two distortions into the economy by (1) raising the marginal valuation of consumption (marginal revenue) at C above the true opportunity cost (the price of imports, OP_1) at B; and (2) enabling domestic production at marginal costs in excess of opportunity cost (on the line segment, AD). Of course in the absence of information on the prevailing economic environment (such as the magnitude of any externalities) no *normative* conclusions can be drawn on the appropriateness of these distortions.

Where it is more appropriate to assume that domestic supply or demand conditions can affect the 'world' price of the country's exports or imports then (1) some of the 'burden' of the tax can be shifted to foreigners and (2) the extent

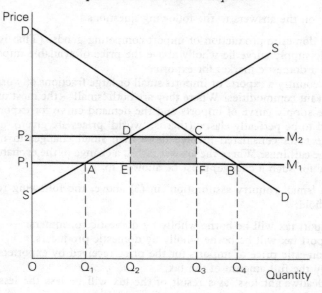

FIGURE 8.2   Effects of an import tax

of this also depends on the relevant foreign demand and supply elasticities (see Lewis, 1984, pp. 186–91). It is also possible in this case for the domestic price to vary from the world price.

Where *general import or export taxes* are used the assumption of an exchange rate unaffected by tax changes (implicit in the above analysis) becomes less tenable. When exchange rate changes are allowed for a number of other effects of the tax changes must be considered. From an initial balance of payments position the imposition of a general import tax which reduces imports will create pressure for an exchange rate appreciation. This raises the foreign currency price of exports (or reduces the domestic currency price) resulting in decreased exports which may be shifted to the domestic market where one exists. In addition an export industry using intermediate imports may also find imports dearer because of the new import tax. Therefore part of the import tax incidence lies with exporters – 'since the purpose of exporting is to purchase imports, the real output of the export industry is imports' (Lewis, 1984, p. 199); thus import taxes do not protect domestic industry at the expense of foreign industry but protect import-competing industry at the expense of exporters. The converse argument applies to export taxes which affect exchange rates. The resulting depreciation benefits exporters at the expense of domestic import-using industry. The effect must again be a fall in the country's net foreign exchange earnings. In the case of import taxes foreign exchange is reduced because of a fall in demand for imports, while with export taxes they are reduced because of a decline in supply via exports. This point is important for LDCs which often use import taxes to 'save' foreign exchange. In fact, where the exchange rate alters in consequence, the new equilibrium involves a lower (foreign exchange) value of imports *and* exports. Of course there may be little change in the *volume* of exports depending on elasticities of demand. This latter variable would be the relevant one when considering employment effects for example.

8.5.2 Domestic indirect taxes

Sales taxes and excises in LDCs may be applied to domestic production only, or may include exports and/ or imports. This distinction is clearly important since the exemption of some traded goods has the effect of changing relative prices which the more comprehensive taxation does not. Where exports are included in the domestic tax regime but imports are exempt, or vice-versa, there will also be the opportunity for the effects described in the previous subsection to operate.

Where sales or excise taxes apply to *domestic production/ consumption only* then, again with the 'small country assumption':

1 For import-competing goods, price will be unaffected (being fixed at world levels), and *producers* bear the full cost of the tax (at least initially), with imports substituting for domestic production.
2 For exportables, the tax will be borne by consumers with producers able to pass on the full amount of the tax to domestic consumers and switch surplus domestic production to export markets (assuming no foreign demand constraint for this 'small' producer).

Where the sales or excise taxes apply to *all production/ consumption* then:

1 For import-competing goods the tax can now be passed on to consumers, and therefore they now bear the cost of the tax. Obviously government revenue will now also be higher than when imports are exempt, both due to higher revenue from domestic producers and import revenues.
2 For exportables, the tax is now borne by domestic producers (who cannot switch to export markets in this case). Price therefore remains fixed for domestic consumers at world levels and they are unaffected by the tax. Only if foreign demand is less than perfectly elastic can domestic producers pass some of the tax incidence on to foreigners.

It can be seen therefore that for domestic taxes, including imports and/ or exports, a critical condition is the degree of substitution between foreign and domestic markets; in particular the extent to which domestic market prices are set by world levels.[14]

Finally it is common in LDCs to find one set of taxes on domestic production and an array of import tariffs and export subsidies. It is therefore important to examine the extent to which the effects of domestic excises may be offset by import or export taxes, and vice-versa. Thus, for example, an import tariff on motor vehicles designed to encourage import substitution will be undermined if subsequently a domestic excise or sales tax applies to motor vehicles. Such a situation can easily arise when tax systems develop in a piecemeal fashion as governments seek new revenue-raising opportunities, and it is evidenced in some of the wide disparities between nominal and effective tax rates discussed in section 8.2. Another frequently adopted policy, alongside various taxes, is the use of import quotas or other 'quantity-controlling' devices. By affecting the demand or supply of some commodities they can obviously affect the results described above. In general, where these controls are effective in the sense that imports are less than they would be in their absence, then the unit of the good consumed *at the margin* will be *domestically* supplied, and domestic producers may therefore be able to pass on part of any tax to consumers. Where there is no domestic production then *importers* will gain from import quotas, which restrict supply and therefore raise prices. Governments in this case can, and sometimes do, auction import licences to transfer some of the 'windfall' profits from importers to the tax authorities.

8.6   Normative analysis of taxation

It is clear from the results discussed in section 8.5.1 that alternative tax policies can have varying effects on the economy and may affect different groups in society to differing extents. This of course raises the normative question of which taxes should be preferred, which not only requires knowledge of the positive effects of taxation but also clearly specified objectives of tax policy. Having identified the objectives of public policy (which in LDCs usually include the promotion of economic growth, a fairer distribution of resources and stabilization), the means by which governments intend to meet these objectives determines the amount of tax revenue required.

Normative tax analysis has generally been concerned with the best way of raising a given amount of tax revenue and has concentrated on two main aspects – the efficiency and the equity of the tax system. A tax system should be (a) efficient, in the sense of minimizing the resource costs to the economy, and (b) equitable, since social welfare is a function both of the amount and *distribution* of resources. In LDCs particularly, administrative feasibility is another important principle governing tax design. In most developed countries this can be captured within the efficiency aspects where different administrative costs between taxes can be included by defining tax revenues net of administration costs. However, for many LDCs some taxes may be infeasible in the sense that administration costs for these taxes may be so high that a given net revenue target may not be achievable.[15]

These three principles of tax design of course may conflict, so that improvements in equity, for example, may entail efficiency losses or increased administration costs. In addition as the theory of the 'second-best' makes clear, a tax which satisfies two of the three principles is not necessarily preferable to a tax which achieves only one, since the magnitudes of the various costs or distortions involved must also be considered. The theory of optimal taxation attempts to identify 'second-best' solutions to the tax design problem.

8.6.1 Optimal taxation

The theory of optimal taxation is based on the principle of Pareto optimality and uses the tools of welfare economics to identify the allocation of resources which maximizes social welfare. Within this framework it is known that, given initial endowments of resources and competitive markets with no externalities, a Pareto optimum can be achieved with a set of lump-sum taxes and transfers which can be varied according to individuals' characteristics. However where these conditions are not met – where markets fail, externalities exist or lump-sum transfers are not possible – the optimal combination of taxes depends on where the distortions from a competitive equilibrium exist, whether both efficiency and equity considerations are relevant for policy, and the range of tax instruments available.

Not surprisingly the mathematics of optimal tax theory is complex; results are often not intuitively obvious and require many restrictive conditions to yield unambiguous policy prescriptions. Some examples will serve to illustrate this here, but a more detailed description of optimal tax theory results may be found in Atkinson and Stiglitz (1980, lectures 11–14).

A straightforward result of optimal commodity taxation (the 'Ramsey rule') states that where consumers are identical (and lump-sum transfers are ruled out) a given amount of tax revenue can be raised at minimum cost if taxes as a proportion of commodity prices vary inversely with the elasticity of demand.[16] This tends to support higher tax rates for necessities and lower rates for luxuries, but of course by specifying identical individuals it 'avoids' distributional issues. The result is also modified if externalities exist or if profits are above competitive levels, and depends on the nature of labour taxation and the relationship between leisure and consumption.

It is, however, possible to show, again under certain very restrictive conditions including the nature of individuals' utility functions, that if a linear or non-linear income tax is available it may be preferable to use direct taxation both on efficiency and equity grounds (where individuals differ only in terms of their wage rates but have identical preferences). Where positive indirect taxes rates are used they should be uniform.

It should be clear even from the limited discussion above that 'it is not easy to come to a judgement as to how the obvious fact of the divergence of the world from these special conditions should influence views on the balance between direct and indirect taxation' (Stern, 1984, p. 362). Nevertheless Stern suggests that some general lessons for tax policy can be learned from the optimal taxation literature, and he offers three 'general principles' which might form a useful basis for tax policy (Stern, 1984, pp. 368–9). These are not specific to developed or less developed countries but may be especially useful in the context of LDCs which have not yet developed a large array of *ad hoc* tax structures. The three general principles are:

1 'Tax revenue is raised most efficiently by taxing goods and factors with inelastic demand or supply.' Broadly speaking this follows from the earlier

analysis of deadweight losses and because effects external to the good/factor being taxed are minimized. For this latter reason 'care should be taken with the pattern of complements and substitutes'.

2 'Taxation concerned with distribution and with externalities or market failures should go as far as possible to the root of the problem.' This enables better targeting of tax policies and the avoidance of distortions via unintended relative price changes. Thus taxation of externalities, for example, should aim to affect only the goods producing the externality.

3 It is frequently impossible to tax the source of distortions or inequities directly. Hence taxes which seek to counteract these problems should be examined carefully for possible effects on other policy objectives 'since the optimum policy for any one tax is often very sensitive to assumptions concerning the existence and levels of other taxes'.

From principle (1) Stern argues against the argument (frequently used in the context of LDCs) for uniform commodity tax rates. In LDCs where income taxation may be ineffective, where distributional considerations are particularly important and where market distortions are commonplace, different rates may be necessary. However the most pressing argument for differing tax rates in LDCs is often on the basis of *distribution* rather than efficiency, as a 'second-best' solution in the absence of other effective redistributional devices. Indirect taxes should also, where possible, avoid intermediate goods because of the issues identified under principle (3).

Finally various authors have pointed to the fact that a rising structure of marginal income tax rates is not necessary for redistribution. The income tax will be progressive so long as marginal rates exceed average rates and rising *average* rates will assist redistribution while falling marginal rates may be more efficient. Indeed in some circumstances optimal income taxation involves rising then falling marginal income tax rates.

8.6.2 Tax reform

When a tax system is being introduced where none previously existed the optimal taxation literature now offers some guidance on how best to design such a system. However, unfortunately such a situation rarely arises in practice, with even the least developed countries already having a variety of tax regimes, while more developed LDCs such as India often have complex and entrenched tax systems. Political and administrative factors therefore rule out radical change. This has given rise to the *theory of tax reform*, associated mainly with the work of Ahmad and Stern (initially on the Indian tax system), which used the optimal taxation framework to consider beneficial reforms to an *existing* tax system.[17]

The basic approach of the theory of reform is based in Paretian welfare economics, generally taking a competitive equilibrium as optimal. The model considers an economy in which households seek to maximize utility from consumption of a bundle of commodities. The government requires a given amount of tax revenue, R, to undertake a set of predetermined activities which it raises by *indirect* commodity taxation. Factor incomes and producer prices are fixed, and competitive conditions ensure that indirect taxes are fully passed on in market prices.[18]

This then allows the construction of a fairly simple social welfare function, V, which is a function of households' utilities which are themselves functions (indirectly) of commodity prices. Thus.

$$V(q) = W(v^1(q), v^2(q) \ldots v^h(q)) \tag{8.1}$$

where there are h households and q is a vector of tax-inclusive prices. Government revenue is simply given by

$$R = \sum_i t_i X_i \tag{8.2}$$

where t_i is the tax on good i and X_i is the aggregate demand (by all households) for good i. The problem for tax reform is therefore to find tax changes which will raise social welfare for a given (or greater) tax revenue, or vice-versa. If present taxes are non-optimal there must be at least one, and possibly several, welfare-improving tax changes. This is illustrated in figure 8.3, which considers two taxes i and j on the vertical and horizontal axes respectively. The line AA' represents combinations of the two tax rates yielding constant revenue, while BB' shows combinations of t_i and t_j yielding constant social welfare. Clearly increases in both rates raise revenue and lower social welfare. From an initial position at O, the shaded area AOB shows desirable tax rate changes ($\partial V \geqslant 0, \partial R \geqslant 0$).

To identify desirable tax changes Ahmad and Stern use the marginal cost, λ_i, in terms of social welfare, of one additional unit of revenue raised by the ith tax. This may be compared with λ_j, the marginal cost of raising an additional unit of revenue via the jth tax, and if $\lambda_i < \lambda_j$ social welfare can be improved by increasing t_i and reducing t_j.

Thus λ_i may be defined as

$$\lambda_i = \frac{\partial V}{\partial t_i} \bigg/ \frac{\partial R}{\partial t_i} \tag{8.3}$$

It can be shown that $\partial R / \partial t_i$ is a function of the vector of tax rates and the response of aggregate demand to a change in t_i (see Ahmad and Stern, 1984, pp. 264-6). *Aggregate* demand changes must be considered so long as cross-price effects are significant since changes in the demand for complements to, or substitutes for, good i when t_i changes will affect total revenue through their associated tax rates. Having defined a social welfare function, $\partial V / \partial t_i$ may be estimated from information on households' consumption patterns and the 'welfare weights' attached to each household's utility in the social welfare function. $\partial V / \partial t_i$ will therefore be sensitive to differences in the pattern of goods consumed by 'rich' and 'poor' households, and value judgments relating to preferences for equality.[19] Without information on a given society's 'inequality aversion' it is necessary to examine the λs for alternative weighting schemes.

Using data on household consumption patterns (for nine household 'groups') and taxes for India in 1979/80, Ahmad and Stern (1984) estimated the λ_is for

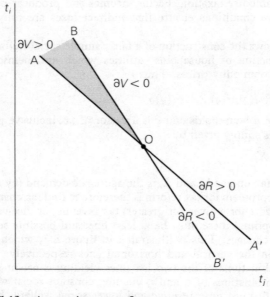

FIGURE 8.3 Welfare-improving tax reforms.
Source: Ahmad and Stern (1984, p. 264)

nine commodity groups of mainly food and clothing products. They found that the ranking of λ_is was very sensitive to assumed inequality aversion. For example, with no aversion to inequality the λ_i for 'cereals' was lower than the λ_is for seven of the other eight commodity groups. However moderate aversion to inequality led the λ_i for cereals to be ranked second-*highest*. Nevertheless it was found that the existing tax rate structure was optimal for *no* assumed inequality aversion, and for each inequality aversion there was always at least one welfare-improving tax change.

Another useful application of the tax reform model is that it can be used to assess the merits of some proposed tax reform in terms of its effects on the λ_is. This exercise was undertaken by Ahmad and Stern (1983), again for India, to consider a possible replacement of a wide range of existing excises with a proportional VAT system. They found that, except with extreme (Rawlsian) aversion to inequality, the range of λ_is produced by the VAT system was very wide and not dissimilar to that of the existing excises. In addition, the VAT appeared to be inegalitarian in that it reduced expenditure by the poorest households and increased it for the rich. These results appeared to hold even when such 'basic' commodities such as cereals were zero-rated and higher rates imposed on other items.[20]

Assessing the contribution of the theory of tax reform is perhaps premature at this stage because it can probably be developed further to allow relaxation of some of its more restrictive assumptions such as the 100 per cent shifting of taxes to consumers and the absence of monopoly profits. One problem with the analysis is that it requires detailed and accurate data on tax rates, cross-price elasticities, consumer demand matrices and so on, and these data when available in LDCs are of dubious quality. The resulting need to aggregate across household or commodity groups raises further problems of sensitivity of the results, and this problem must be carefully assessed in each application of the model. One consequence of these data deficiencies is that it is probably only when *substantial* differences in λ_is are observed that tax advisors might reasonably advocate some reform to tax administrators (bearing in mind the likely costs of any changes). However it is also likely to be those taxes with atypical λ_is that are most readily identifiable as worthy of reform, *without* the use of a tax reform model! Nevertheless the theory of tax reform provides a useful theoretical underpinning for approaches to tax reform which have hitherto been *ad hoc* and have often concentrated on revenue or administrative aspects without considering the consequences for social welfare.

8.7 Conclusions

One conclusion that may be drawn from the above review is that much has been learned about the operation of tax systems in developing and developed countries over the past 30 years or so. The tools used by economists have also developed over the years, enabling the results of early research to be confirmed, amended or rejected as appropriate. What is also clear, however, is that many aspects of how tax systems do, and should, affect an economy remain unresolved in some cases because we do not yet have the necessary analytical tools.

However existing knowledge does permit a number of general conclusions.

1 Tax systems in LDCs put a greater reliance on indirect (domestic and trade) taxes relative to income taxes than is typically the case in developed countries. Simple relationships between tax structure and per capita income, however, are not generally confirmed.

2 LDCs can be expected to continue to rely on indirect taxes in the near future, but a tendency for development to cause shifts towards domestic production and intermediate imports and away from consumer imports may require increased use of *domestic* taxes to maintain revenue.

3 The relationship between taxation, savings and growth is complex, and early views that taxation could significantly influence the growth rate now seen unwarranted. Price signals can be important in LDCs but the impact of taxation on these signals is generally too small to have large effects on incentives for growth.

4 There may be a tendency among LDCs for tax systems to be mildly progressive (especially if government transfers are included) but the impact of taxation on income redistribution is, and is likely to remain, small.

5 Various tax and expenditure policies are often introduced independently and in an *ad hoc* manner to meet a variety of objectives. As a result unforeseen

interactions between tax and expenditure policies can easily occur, causing unintended consequences; for example, in the form of effective protection, distorted incentives, or differing incidences from those presumed. There would seem to be substantial agreement that explicit and implicit taxes on agriculture and exports and subsidies to capital have produced unwarranted distortions in several LDCs.

6 The dominant use of indirect taxation, and especially a variety of excise rates in LDCs, may not be so much at variance with optimal taxation prescriptions as is often supposed, *given the constraints which LDCs face*. Indirect taxation needs to assist both efficiency and equity in many LDCs and uniform commodity taxation will typically inhibit this. This is not to suggest, however, that the existing set of excises and duties could not be beneficially reformed.

7 Finally, many tax parameters and variables important for policy, such as tax elasticity, vary considerably across countries for similar types of taxes. Advice on tax policy must therefore be based soundly on the results of individual country studies, and cannot rely on the 'average' performance identified in cross-section studies.

NOTES

1. In some countries schedules for the taxation of profits may be firm-specific, such as those applied to multinational corporations in extractive industries.
2. One should, however, be wary of these results since in no case do the differences in group averages appear to have been subjected to the usual tests of significance. Earlier studies of tax ratio differences and tax revenue share differences between DCs and LDCs include Martin and Lewis (1956), Oshima (1957) and Williamson (1961).
3. That is, a nominal rate of 60 per cent, but an effective rate of 104 per cent.
4. Tax elasticity may be defined as the effective marginal tax rate, $\partial R/\partial Y$, divided by the effective average tax rate, R/Y. Note that because the bases for income and indirect taxes are related, changes in the income tax elasticity can affect indirect tax elasticities. See Gemmell (1985; 1986, chapter 5).
5. Many of these arguments have been pursued in the debate on the relationship between 'basic needs' provision and growth – see survey 4.
6. For an introduction to growth models see Hacche (1979), Hamberg (1971) or Jones (1975).
7. Goode (1984, chapter 10) provides an excellent review of alternative strategies for development resulting from different theoretical views on the growth process.
8. Though most of these studies include mainly developed countries, a number have included several LDCs. For a review of results see Hamberg (1971, pp. 168–73).
9. Lim's instability index is obtained as the standard error of a regression of revenue (or expenditure) on time.
10. This 'employment problem' is discussed in detail by Morawetz (1974).
11. Unlike Chelliah and Lal, Ahmad and Stern (1983) estimate *effective* tax rates and include subsidies. Their results indicate Indian indirect taxes are slightly less progressive than the Chelliah and Lal study suggested.
12. For a review of general equilibrium models for LDCs, some of which are suitable for tax analyses, see Taylor (1979).

13. A deadweight loss in this case implies that the net change in producers' surplus, consumers' surplus and government revenue is negative.
14. The extent of foreign competition is also important when the domestic market has elements of monopoly power. The effects on price, output, etc. of monopolistic domestic suppliers need careful treatment, but in general a monopolist's ability to exploit market power is less the more readily available are imports and foreign substitutes for exports (see Lewis, 1984, chapter 9).
15. Note that, by this definition, the requirement to raise a *large* amount of (gross) tax revenue may render some taxes infeasible because extracting the marginal unit of tax revenue may be very costly (due, for example, to disincentive effects). For other taxes, however, economies of scale in collection may render them infeasible for *small* amounts of (gross) revenue. On problems of tax administration and evasion see Ahmad and Stern (forthcoming, section 4), Cowell (1985), Goode (1984, pp. 306–10) and Srinivasan (1973).
16. This has the effect of minimizing the 'deadweight loss' or excess burden of the tax, identified (in a partial equilibrium context) by triangle BCF in figure 8.2.
17. The theory of tax reform is now articulated in a number of places including Ahmad and Stern (1981, 1983, 1984, forthcoming) but the most readable source is probably the 1984 paper.
18. In more complex extensions of the model, shadow prices are introduced to allow for 'distortions' in market prices. See Ahmad *et al.* (1984a) and Drèze and Stern (1985).
19. Rawlsian preferences, for example, would lead to a welfare weight of unity being associated with $V^1(q)$ – the poorest household's utility – in equation (8.1), with zero weights attached to $V^2(q) \ldots V^h(q)$.
20. The use of the marginal social cost (λ) concept for taxes has recently been extended to evaluate the alternatives of tax and loan finance; see Ahmad and Stern (forthcoming). Two recent surveys of the role of loan finance in LDCs are Glick and Kharas (1986) and McDonald (1982).

REFERENCES

Abdel-Fadil, M. 1980. *The Political Economy of Nasserism. A Study in Employment and Income Distribution Policies in Urban Egypt 1952–72.* Cambridge: Cambridge University Press.

Abizadeh, S. and Wyckoff, J. B. 1982. Tax system components and economic development. An international perspective. *Bulletin for International Fiscal Documentation*, 34, 483–91.

Ahmad, S. E. and Stern, N. H. 1981. *On the Evaluation of Indirect Tax Systems: An Application to India.* University of Warwick, Development Economics Research Centre, Discussion Paper No. 1.

Ahmad, S. E. and Stern, N. H. 1983. *Effective Taxes and Tax Reform in India.* University of Warwick, Development Economics Research Centre, Discussion paper No. 25.

Ahmad, S. E. and Stern, N. H. 1984. The theory of reform and Indian indirect taxes. *Journal of Public Economics*, 25, 259–98.

Ahmad, S. E. and Stern, N. H. Forthcoming. Public economics for developing countries. In H. B. Chenery and T. N. Srinivasan (eds), *Handbook of Development Economics.* Amsterdam: North-Holland.

Ahmad, S. E., Coady, D. and Stern, N. H. 1984a. *Tax Reform, Shadow Prices and Effective Taxes: Illustrations for Pakistan for 1975/76.* University of Warwick, Development Economics Research Centre, Discussion Paper No. 48.

Ahmad, S. E., Leung, H.-M., and Stern, N. H. 1984b. *Demand Response and the Reform of Indirect Taxes in Pakistan*. University of Warwick, Development Economics Research Centre, Discussion Paper No. 50.

Arrate, J. and Geller, L. 1971. Economic surplus and the budget. In K. Griffin (ed.), *Financing Development in Latin America*. London: Macmillan, pp. 51–72.

Askari, H., Cummings, J. T. and Glover, M. 1982. *Taxation and Tax Policies in the Middle East*. London: Butterworths.

Atkinson, A. B. and Stiglitz, J. E. 1980. *Lectures in Public Economics*. Maidenhead: McGraw-Hill.

Bagchi, A. and Rao, M. G. 1982. Elasticity of non-corporate income tax in India. *Economic and Political Weekly*, 17 (4 September), 1452–8.

Bedrossian, A. and Hitiris, T. 1985. Trade taxes as a source of government revenue: a re-estimation. *Scottish Journal of Political Economy*, 32, 199–204.

Bird, R. M. 1978. Assessing tax performance in developing countries. A critical review of the literature. In J. F. J. Toye (ed.), *Taxation and Economic Development*. London: Frank Cass, pp. 33–61.

Bird, R.M. 1982. Taxation and employment in developing countries. *Finanzarchiv*, 40, 211–39.

Bird, R. M. and De Wulf, L. 1973. Taxation and income distribution in Latin America: a critical review of empirical studies. *IMF Staff Papers*, 20, 639–82.

Bird, R. M. and Oldman, O. (eds). 1975. *Readings on Taxation in Developing Countries*, 3rd edn. Baltimore: Johns Hopkins University Press.

Bolnick, B. R. 1978a. Tax effort in developing countries: what do regression measures really measure. In J. F. J. Toye (ed.), *Taxation and Economic Development*. London: Frank Cass, pp. 62–80.

Bolnick, B. R. 1978b. Demographic effects on tax ratios in developing countries. *Journal of Development Economics*, 5, 283–306.

Bolnick, B. R. 1982. A test of tax constraints on fiscal development. *Public Finance*, 37, 18–35.

Brown, C. V. and Jackson, P. M. 1986. *Public Sector Economics*, 3rd edn. Oxford: Basil Blackwell.

Byrne, W. J. 1983. The elasticity of the tax system of Zambia, 1966–1977. *World Development*, 11, 153–62.

Chelliah, R. J. 1960. *Fiscal Policy in Underdeveloped Countries. With Special Reference to India*. London: George Allen and Unwin.

Chelliah, R. J. 1971. Trends in taxation in developing countries. *IMF Staff Papers*, 18, 254–331.

Chelliah, R. J. and Lal, R. N. 1981. The incidence of indirect taxation in India (1973–74). In D. N. Dwivedi (ed.), *Readings in Indian Public Finance*. Delhi: Chanakya Publications, pp. 71–95.

Chelliah, R. J., Bass, H. J. and Kelly, M. R. 1975. Tax ratios and tax effort in developing countries, 1969–71. *IMF Staff Papers*, 22, 187–205.

Chen-Young, P. 1975. Evaluating tax incentives: the case of Jamaica. In R. M. Bird and O. Oldman (eds), *Readings on Taxation in Developing Countries*, 3rd edn. Baltimore: Johns Hopkins University Press, pp. 378–86.

Chenery, H. B. and Strout, A. M. 1966. Foreign assistance and economic development. *American Economic Review*, 56, 679–733.

Choudhry, N. N. 1975. A study of the elasticity of the West Malaysian income tax system, 1961–70. *IMF Staff Papers*, 22, 494–509.

Choudhry, N. N. 1979. Measuring the elasticity of tax revenue: a divisia index approach. *IMF Staff Papers*, 26, 87–122.

Cline, W. R. and Weintraub, S. (eds). 1981. *Economic Stabilization in Developing Countries*. Washington, DC: The Brookings Institution.

Cnossen, S. 1983. *Comparative Tax Studies. Essays in Honor of Richard Goode.* Amsterdam: North-Holland.

Cowell, F. A. 1985. *The Economics of Tax Evasion. A Survey.* ESRC Programme on Taxation, Incentives and the Distribution of Income, LSE, Discussion Paper No. 80.

Creedy, J. and Gemmell, N. 1982. The built-in flexibility of progressive income taxes: a simple model. *Public Finance*, 37, 361-71.

Davis, J. M. 1977. The fiscal role of food subsidy programs. *IMF Staff Papers*, 24, 100-27.

De Wulf, L. 1974. Taxation and income distribution in Lebanon. *Bulletin for International Fiscal Documentation*, 28, 151-9.

De Wulf, L. 1975. Fiscal incidence studies in developing countries: survey and critique. *IMF Staff Papers*, 22, 61-131.

De Wulf, L. 1983. Taxation and income distribution. In S. Cnossen (ed.), *Comparative Tax Studies. Essays in Honor of Richard Goode*. Amsterdam: North-Holland, pp. 345-70.

Dosser, D. 1965. Indirect taxation and economic development. In A. T. Peacock and G. Hauser (eds), *Government Finance and Economic Development*. Paris: OECD, pp. 127-142.

Dreze, J. and Stern, N. H. 1985. *The Theory of Cost-Benefit Analysis*. University of Warwick, Development Economics Research Centre, Discussion Paper No. 59. Forthcoming in A. Auerbach and M. Feldstein (eds), *Handbook of Public Economics*. Amsterdam: North-Holland.

Dwivedi, D. N. 1981. A buoyancy approach to evaluation of excise taxation. In D. N. Dwivedi (ed.), *Readings in Indian Public Finance*. Delhi: Chanakya Publications, pp. 96-111.

Eshag, E. 1983. *Fiscal and Monetary Policies and Problems in Developing Countries*. Cambridge: Cambridge University Press.

Fitzgerald, E. V. K. 1976. *The State and Economic Development: Peru Since 1968*. Cambridge: Cambridge University Press.

Fitzgerald, E. V. K. 1978. The fiscal crisis of the Latin Amerian State. In J. F. J. Toye (ed.), *Taxation and Economic Development*. London: Frank Cass, pp. 125-58.

Friedman, M. 1953. *Essays in Positive Economics*. Chicago: University of Chicago Press.

Furtado, C. 1970. *Economic Development of Latin America*. Cambridge: Cambridge University Press.

Gemmell, N. 1985. Tax revenue shares and income growth: a note. *Public Finance*, 40, 137-45.

Gemmell, N. 1986. *Economic Development and Structural Change*. London: Macmillan.

Ghatak, S. and Ingersent, K. 1984. *Agriculture and Economic Development*. Baltimore: Johns Hopkins University Press and London: Wheatsheaf.

Glick, R. and Kharas, H. J. 1986. The costs and benefits of foreign borrowing: a survey of multi-period models. *Journal of Development Studies*, 22, 279-99.

Goode, R. 1981. Some economic aspects of tax administration. *IMF Staff Papers*, 28, 249-74.

Goode, R. 1984. *Government Finance in Developing Countries*. Washington, DC: The Brookings Institution.

Greenaway, D. 1980. Trade taxes as a source of government revenue: an international comparison. *Scottish Journal of Political Economy*, 27, 175-82.

Greenaway, D. 1984. A statistical analysis of fiscal dependence on trade taxes and economic development. *Public Finance*, 39, 70-89.

Greenaway, D. 1985. Trade taxes as a source of government revenue: a comment on the Bedrossian–Hitiris re-estimation. *Scottish Journal of Political Economy*, 32, 205–8.

Griffin, K. (ed.). 1971. *Financing Development in Latin America*. London: Macmillan.

Hacche, G. 1979. *The Theory of Economic Growth. An Introduction*. London: Macmillan.

Hamberg, D. 1971. *Models of Economic Growth*. New York: Harper and Row.

Hansen, B. and Marzouk, G. A. 1965. *Development and Economic Policy in the UAR (Egypt)*. Amsterdam: North-Holland.

Heller, P. S. 1975. A model of public fiscal behaviour in developing countries: aid, investment and taxation. *American Economic Review*, 65, 429–45.

Heller, P. S. 1981. Testing the impact of value added and global income tax reforms on Korean tax incidence in 1976. An input–output and sensitivity analysis. *IMF Staff Papers*, 28, 375–410.

Hill, T. P. 1964. Growth and investment according to international comparisons. *Economic Journal*, 74, 287–304.

Hinrichs, H. H. 1965. Determinants of government revenue shares among less developed countries. *Economic Journal*, 75, 546–57.

Hinrichs, H. H. 1966. *A General Theory of Tax Structure Change During Economic Development*. Cambridge, Mass.: The Law School of Harvard University.

Ho, H. C. Y. 1979. *The Fiscal System of Hong Kong*. London: Croom Helm.

Hughes, G. A. 1985. 'The incidence of fuel taxes: a comparative study of three countries'. Mimeo. Forthcoming in D. M. G. Newbery and N. H. Stern (eds), *The Theory of Taxation in Developing Countries*. New York: Oxford University Press, for World Bank.

Hutton, J. P. 1980. Income tax elasticity and the distribution of income, with an application to Peninsular Malaysia. *South East Asian Economic Review*, 1, 13–34.

Hutton, J. P. and Lambert, P. J. 1980. Evaluating income tax revenue elasticities. *Economic Journal*, 90, 901–6.

Hutton, J. P. and Lambert, P. J. 1982. Simulating the revenue elasticity of an individual income tax. *Economics Letters* ,9, 175–9.

Jones, H. G. 1975. *An Introduction to Modern Theories of Economic Growth*. London: Nelson.

Kakwani, N. C. 1976. Measurement of tax progressivity: an international perspective. *Economic Journal*, 87, 71–80.

Kaldor, N. 1964. Will underdeveloped countries learn to tax? In *Essays in Economic Policy*, Vol. 1. London: Duckworth.

Kaldor, N. 1965. The role of taxation in economic development. In E. A. G. Robinson (ed.), *Problems in Economic Development*. London: Macmillan, pp. 170–89.

Katzman, M. T. 1978. Progressive public utility rates as an income redistribution device in developing countries: the case of municipal water. In J. F. J. Toye (ed.), *Taxation and Economic Development*. London: Frank Cass, pp. 174–92.

King, M. A. 1980. Savings and taxation. In G. M. Heal and G. A. Hughes (eds), *Public Policy and the Tax System*. London: Allen and Unwin, pp. 1–35.

King, T. 1971. Private savings. In K. Griffin (ed.), *Financing Development in Latin America*. London: Macmillan, pp. 152–81.

Kravis, I. B., Heston, A. and Summers, R. 1982. The share of services in economic growth. In F. G. Adams and B. G. Hickman (eds), *Global Econometrics. Essays in Honor of Lawrence R. Klein*. Cambridge, Mass.: MIT Press, pp. 188–218.

Krishnaswamy, K. S. 1965. The evolution of tax structure in a development policy. In A. T. Peacock and G. Hauser (eds), *Government Finance and Economic Development*. Paris: OECD, pp. 75–88.

Kuznets, S. 1961. Quantitative aspects of the economic growth of nations. VI: Long-term trends in capital formation proportions. *Economic Development and Cultural Change*, 9,4(*II*), 3-124.

Kuznets, S. 1966. *Modern Economic Growth. Rate, Structure and Spread*. New Haven: Yale University Press.

Lam, N. V. 1978. Domestic price stabilization of a staple export crop: an evaluation of the rice premium tax in Thailand. In J. F. J. Toye (ed.), *Taxation and Economic Development*. London: Frank Cass, pp. 249-68.

Lent, G. E. 1975. Tax incentives in developing countries. In R. M. Bird and O. Oldman (eds), *Readings on Taxation in Developing Countries*, 3rd edn. Baltimore: Johns Hopkins University Press, pp. 363-77.

Levin, J. 1968. The effects of economic development on the base of a sales tax: a case study of Colombia. *IMF Staff Papers*, 15, 30-99.

Lewis, S. R. Jr. 1984. *Taxation for Development. Principles and Applications*. New York: Oxford University Press.

Lim, D. 1983. Instability of government revenue and expenditure in less developed countries. *World Development*, 11, 447-50.

Lotz, J. R. 1966. Taxation in the United Arab Republic (Egypt). *IMF Staff Papers*, 13, 121-51.

Mansfield, C. Y. 1972. Elasticity and buoyancy of a tax system. A method applied to Paraguay. *IMF Staff Papers*, 19, 425-43.

Martin, A. and Lewis, W. A. 1956. Patterns of public revenue and expenditure. *Manchester School*, 24, 203-44.

McDonald, D. C. 1982. Debt capacity and developing country borrowing: survey of the literature. *IMF Staff Papers*, 29, 603-46.

Morawetz, D. 1974. Employment implications of industrialization in developing countries: a survey. *Economic Journal*, 84, 491-542.

Musgrave, R. A. 1969. *Fiscal Systems*. New Haven: Yale University Press.

Oshima, H. T. 1957. Share of government in Gross National Product for various countries. *American Economic Review*, 47(3), 381-90.

Please, S. 1971. Mobilising internal resources through taxation. In R. E. Robinson (ed.), *Developing the Third World: Experience of the 1960s*. Cambridge: Cambridge University Press, pp. 160-71.

Please, S. 1975. Saving through taxation – reality or mirage? In R. M. Bird and O. Oldman (eds), *Readings on Taxation in Developing Countries*. Baltimore: Johns Hopkins University Press, pp. 38-47.

Prest, A. R. 1971. The role of labour taxes and subsidies in promoting employment in developing countries. *International Labour Review*, 103, 315-32.

Prest, A. R. 1972. *Public Finance in Developing Countries*, 2nd edn. London: Weidenfeld and Nicolson.

Prest, A. R. 1978. The taxable capacity of a country. In J. F. J. Toye (ed.), *Taxation and Economic Development*. London: Frank Cass, pp. 13-32.

Purohit, M. C. 1981. Buoyancy and income-elasticity of State taxes. In D. N. Dwivedi (ed.), *Readings in Indian Public Finance*. Delhi: Chanakya Publications, pp. 112-41.

Ram, R. 1982. Dependency rates and aggregate savings: a new international cross-section study. *American Economic Review*, 72, 537-44.

Ram, R. 1984. Dependency rates and savings: reply. *American Economic Review*, 74, 284-7.

Shah, S. M. S. and Toye, J. F. J. 1978. Fiscal incentives for firms in some developing countries: survey and critique. In J. F. J. Toye (ed.), *Taxation and Economic Development*. London: Frank Cass, pp. 269-96.

Solow, R. M. 1956. A contribution to the theory of economic growth. *Quarterly Journal of Economics*, 70, 65–94.

Srinivasan, T. N. 1973. Tax evasion: a model. *Journal of Public Economics*, 14, 526–36.

Stern, J. J. and Lewis, J. D. 1980. *Employment Patterns and Income Growth*. World Bank Staff Working Paper No. 419. Washington, DC: World Bank.

Stern, N. H. 1984. Optimum taxation and tax policy. *IMF Staff Papers*, 31, 339–78.

Tait, A. A., Gratz, W. L. M. and Eichengreen, B. J. 1979. International comparisons of taxation for selected developing countries, 1972–76. *IMF Staff Papers*, 26, 123–56.

Tanzi, V. 1978. Inflation, real tax revenue and the case for inflationary finance: theory with an application to Argentina. *IMF Staff Papers*, 25, 417–51.

Tanzi, V. 1983. Taxation and price stabilization. In S. Cnossen (ed.), *Comparative Tax Studies. Essays in Honor of Richard Goode*. Amsterdam: North-Holland, pp. 409–30.

Taylor, L. 1979. *Macro Models for Developing Countries*. New York: McGraw-Hill.

Taylor, M. C. (ed.). 1970. *Taxation for African Economic Development*. London: Hutchinson.

Thirlwall, A. P. 1983. *Growth and Development*, 3rd edn. London: Macmillan.

Thorn, R. S. 1967. The evolution of public finances during economic development. *Manchester School*, 35, 19–53.

Thurow, L. D. 1971. Development finance in Latin America: basic principles. In K. Griffin (ed.), *Financing Development in Latin America*. London: Macmillan, pp. 26–50.

Toye, J. F. J. (ed.). 1978. *Taxation and Economic Development*. London: Frank Cass.

Urrutia, M. and De Sandoval, C. E. 1976. Fiscal policy and income distribution in Colombia. In A. Foxley (ed.), *Income Distribution in Latin America*. Cambridge: Cambridge University Press, pp. 223–41.

Webb, R. C. 1977. *Government Policy and the Distribution of Income in Peru, 1963–73*. Cambridge, Mass.: Harvard University Press.

White, L. J. 1978. The evidence on appropriate factor proportions for manufacturing in less developed countries: a survey. *Economic Development and Cultural Change*, 26, 27–59.

Wilford, D. S. and Wilford, W. T. 1978. Estimates of revenue elasticity and buoyancy in Central America, 1955–1974. In J. F. J. Toye (ed.), *Taxation and Economic Development*. London: Frank Cass, pp. 83–101.

Williamson, J. G. 1961. Public expenditure and revenue: an international comparison. *Manchester School*, 29, 34–56.

9

Techniques of project appraisal

Ivy Papps

9.1 Introduction

Because the implementation of an investment project uses scarce resources it is necessary to be able to evaluate whether such an undertaking is worthwhile compared to the alternative uses of such resources. Other things being equal, therefore, it could be argued that policy-makers should try to ensure that resources are used where their social value is highest.

Various techniques have been developed to enable such an evaluation to be made. Amongst these many techniques, two approaches stand out in terms of their generality and their integration with economic theory. These approaches are macroeconomic planning and cost-benefit analysis.

The planning approach – sometimes described as a 'top-down' approach – considers the economic system as a whole and derives the investment requirements of each sector. By focusing on the system as a whole this approach identifies explicitly the interrelationships between sectors and, therefore, the indirect effects of investment in one sector on the output of another. Consistency of investment plans is, theoretically, ensured. The complexity of planning models varies a great deal both in terms of the number of sectors considered (the level of aggregation) and in terms of assumptions about utility and production functions. However, they all share the general feature that their development owes more to the tradition of general equilibrium and/or macroeconomic models than it does to conventional microeconomic partial equilibrium models.

An important sub-group of macroeconomic plans are those concerned with manpower planning. This area is, perhaps, the one in which the planning approach has had the most widespread application to project appraisal. In manpower planning, educational investments are judged with respect to their ability to fulfill manpower requirements which are determined by the overall plan. Again, there is no single model used for manpower planning, but a variety of models of different degrees of sophistication applicable to different situations. They all, however, operate in a similar fashion by forecasting manpower needs using forecasts of output for each sector derived from the national plan and then applying a suitable incremental labour–output ratio derived from either cross-section or time-series data. The sets of educational investments which can produce the forecast requirements most cheaply would be the investment which makes the best use of resources.

Cost–benefit analysis (CBA), on the other hand, concentrates on assessing the desirability of individual projects, and is sometimes described as a 'bottom-up' approach. This technique considers investment on a project-by-project basis by attempting to evaluate the costs and benefits of each project. A project is worth undertaking if the benefits are greater than the costs. There are, of course, a number of problems connected with the identification and evaluation of costs and benefits, and with the basis on which they are to be compared, and a variety of approaches have been developed in order to deal with these problems. All approaches have the common feature that they are based on the theoretical underpinnings of conventional welfare economics. The principal analytical tools are, therefore, derived from microeconomic theory.

The rest of this survey will concentrate on the development of the basic framework of CBA, and will discuss the special problems raised by the use of this approach in developing countries, together with their proposed solutions. While recognizing that the planning approach has some influence on investment decisions in developing countries, this survey will not consider it in any detail, for two reasons. First, the planning approach encompasses issues much wider than that of project appraisal and cannot be adequately considered in a single chapter. Secondly, many of the recent developments in CBA have been made in the context of developing countries, and are therefore particularly appropriate for our consideration. An introduction to the planning approach may be found in Lewis (1966), and Healey (1972) provides a critical view, while manpower planning is discussed in Blaug (1970, chapter 5) and Sinclair (1977).

9.2 The theoretical basis of CBA

9.2.1 CBA and welfare economics

Cost–benefit analysis takes as its starting point the assumption that the objective of policy is the maximization of social welfare. Thus a project is worth undertaking if it results in a net addition to social welfare. In this way, investment projects are treated analogously to other policies within the framework of welfare economics. In itself, of course, this criterion for policy analysis is not very helpful. There are serious problems connected with the definition and evaluation of social welfare.

Paretian welfare economics has tried to solve the problem of definition by considering changes in *individual* welfare to assess changes in *social* welfare. However, the well-known Pareto criterion is so restrictive that it is possible to apply it only to a very narrow range of policies. It cannot, for example, be used to evaluate a policy which benefits some people at the expense of others. Thus, for example, the Pareto criterion cannot evaluate an irrigation project which by building a dam yields benefits to those farmers downstream by providing increased control over their water supply but which, at the same time, harms the rural population living above the dam by increasing the incidence of bilharzia – a debilitating, and ultimately fatal, disease. Moreover, the Pareto criterion does not solve the problem of interpersonal comparisons of utility. Although it does not require us to compare explicitly the welfare of different individuals, it is still necessary to be able to identify whether individuals' own welfare has increased or decreased and the Pareto criterion provides us with no way of measuring such changes.

The development of compensation tests provides a solution to both the evaluation of changes in individuals' welfare and to the analysis of policies which benefit some individuals at the expense of others. The Hicks–Kaldor compensation test – sometimes known as the potential Pareto improvement criterion – asserts that the policy would represent an improvement in social welfare if the gainers could compensate the losers. In other words, if the gainers were willing to pay more to obtain the change than the losers were willing to pay to avoid it, a potential Pareto improvement exists since, if compensation were paid, the gainers would be better off while the 'losers' would have their welfare unchanged. If the compensation were, in fact, paid, there would be no problem since the Pareto criterion itself would be satisfied. Thus the potential Pareto improvement criterion is required only when compensation is not intended to be paid.

A major advantage of the compensation test is that it provides a measure of social welfare in money terms based on current market prices, which is comparable to the measure of national income. Thus, maximizing social welfare by using a compensation test would be equivalent to maximizing national income if all activities were correctly evaluated and each policy can be judged in terms of its impact on national income. The disadvantages of using the Hicks–Kaldor compensation test are therefore the same as those of using national income as a measure of social welfare, and will not be pursued here.[1]

The use of the compensation test depends on acceptance of the Pareto criterion for an increase in social welfare. However, the Pareto criterion itself is not uncontroversial because it ignores distributional considerations. Suppose the policy in question provides for increases in welfare to those in society who are already very well off, while leaving the welfare of the very poor unchanged. Society as a whole may not feel that social welfare has been increased by such a change, since it might be felt that the rich already had 'enough'. Such distributional issues cause severe problems for the use of CBA for project appraisal in developing countries where the distribution of income is often very unequal and where the changing of this distribution is a major policy objective. The way in which distributional objectives may be taken into account in CBA is considered in section 9.6.

However, while recognizing the theoretical and practical problems attached to the use of compensation tests to evaluate policy, CBA – in common with other economic analyses of policy – has accepted the use of such tests as a basis. Thus a project is considered worthwhile if the money value of the benefits to gainers is greater than the money value of costs to the losers.

9.2.2 Comparing costs and benefits over time

The compensation test provides us with a way of comparing the costs and benefits accruing from a project in each year with the national income of the same year. However, since the essence of investment projects is that there is a stream of costs and benefits over a number of years, we require some method of comparing costs and benefits accruing in different years. If one were simply to aggregate all costs and benefits irrespective of when they occurred, one is implying that society is indifferent between £1 of benefits occurring this year and £1 of benefits occurring in, say, 20 years' time. Under the potential Pareto improvement criterion this could be the case if not only were all individuals indifferent between £1 of present and future consumption, but also if there were no ways of using present resources yielding a positive rate of return. However, if, for whatever reason, the social value of £1 this year is r per cent higher than £1 received next year then the value this year of £1 next year – its present value – is $£1/(1+r)$. The present value of £1 received in 2 years' time is $£1/(1+r)^2$. Thus, by the process of discounting, pounds received or paid in different years may be compared by converting them into their present value. The net present value (NPV) of a project is the difference between the present value of the costs and benefits of a project and is defined as:

$$\text{NPV} = \sum_{t=0}^{n} \frac{(B_t - C_t)}{(1+r)^t}$$

where B_t and C_t are the value of benefits and costs respectively accruing in year t, n is the length of life of the project, and r is the discount rate – that is, the rate at which society prefers this year's pound to next year's pound. By the potential Pareto improvement criterion the project is worth doing if the present value of benefits is greater than the present value of costs – that is, if the NPV is positive.

It is clear that, in general, there is a negative relationship between NPV and r, as shown in figure 9.1. For all discount rates below r^* the NPV is positive, and therefore that project is worthwhile, while for all discount rates above r^* the NPV is negative, and the project is not worthwhile. r^* is known as the internal rate of return (IRR) of the project. For some investment appraisals the IRR is calculated by finding the discount rate for which the NPV is equal to zero and then comparing the IRR with the social discount rate. Using this criterion the project is worth undertaking if, and only if, the IRR is greater than the social discount rate. It should be clear from figure 9.1 that in many cases the IRR criterion will result in the same decision as that given by the NPV.[2]

Most CBAs follow the route discussed in this section, and compare costs and benefits accruing in different years in terms of their value relative to consumption in the initial year. In other words, current consumption is the usual numeraire. However, the important and influential manual prepared for the OECD by Little and Mirrlees (L–M) (1968) focuses on the importance of investible resources and the numeraire used by L–M is investment.[3] While this

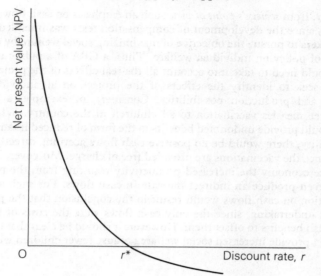

FIGURE 9.1 The relationship between NPV and the discount rate

difference in the numeraire reflects a difference in emphasis, and initially attracted a great deal of attention, it can be shown that such a change in the numeraire affects only the scaling of projects. It affects neither their ranking nor their profitability. Although the L–M approach can produce a different number for the NPV than the conventional approach – as typified, for example, in UNIDO (1972) – worthwhile projects will, *ceteris paribus*, be acceptable using either numeraire, and both approaches will rank them identically.[4]

The NPV approach provides an investment criterion for *any* individual or institution facing an investment decision. It is relevant for an individual considering a university education, a farmer purchasing a tractor, a large firm purchasing capital equipment or a government undertaking an irrigation project. These decisions differ only in the nature of the costs and benefits to be included, the way in which they are to be valued, and the discount rate used to compare costs and benefits at different times. The important issues in CBA revolve around these three aspects of the NPV calculations. These are considered in turn below.

9.3 Identification and evaluation of costs and benefits

9.3.1 The nature of costs and benefits

In the case of a firm considering an investment project the identification of the costs and benefits of the project is relatively straightforward. From *the firm's point of view* the costs and benefits are measured by the reductions in, and additions to, the cash flow of the firm resulting from the project.

However, from *society's point of view* such an emphasis on cash flows would be misplaced, since the development of compensation tests was intended to enable policy-makers to pursue the objective of maximizing social welfare by examining the effect of policy on individual welfare. Thus, a CBA of a public investment project would need to take into account all the real effects of the project; that is, it should seek to identify the effects of the project on all individuals' consumption and production possibilities. Consider, for example, a project to provide free measles vaccination to all children in the country. While such a project would provide undoubted benefits in the form of reduced infant mortality and disability, there would be no positive cash flows accruing directly from the project, since the vaccinations are provided free of charge. Moreover, in a largely subsistence economy the increased productivity resulting from the programme may not even produce an indirect increase in cash flows. For such a project, a concentration on cash flows would result in the conclusion that the project was not worth undertaking, since the only cash flows were the costs of the project with no cash benefits to offset them. However, it should be clear that this project does in fact provide increased social welfare because fewer children will die or be disabled.

Real and pecuniary effects

Since CBA of a public project is interested in the real effects – it follows that the analysis should include *all* real effects, both direct and indirect. This implies that in the case of the irrigation project mentioned earlier, for example, the costs should include not only the direct cost of the labour, land, machinery and raw materials used to construct the project but also the indirect costs imposed on people living above the new dam because of the increased incidence of bilharzia.[5] If such indirect effects are ignored the CBA will not reflect the project's impact on social welfare.[6]

Some analysts (for example, Prest and Turvey, 1965) would argue that an appraisal of public projects requires only an analysis of the real effects, and that pecuniary effects and changes in cash flows may be ignored. Such an approach assumes that the maximization of the present value of national income – as a proxy for social welfare – is the only policy objective. Much CBA in developed countries follows this philosophy, and in this context such an approach has commanded a wide measure of agreement.

However, there is less agreement on such a procedure in developing countries. Indeed, the influential UNIDO (1972) recommends that all appraisals should include both a financial appraisal showing the cash flows generated by the project and also an analysis of the distributional effects of the project, as well as a social CBA.

Financial appraisal

There are two main justifications for carrying out a financial appraisal of a development project. First, many projects considered by planning bureaus in

LDCs are, in fact, projects to be carried out by the private sector – a situation seldom met in developed countries. These projects are of interest to the public sector sometimes as part of the overall development strategy and sometimes because of their claim on a constrained resource – for example, foreign exchange. Thus, a social CBA would determine whether the project is socially valuable while the financial appraisal would indicate whether the private sector would be willing to undertake it. If the results of these analyses are not consistent the public sector may then take action to adjust the cash flows – for example, by means of a subsidy to socially valuable projects – in order to bring private decisions into line with social requirements.

Second, if the financial resources of the country are constrained in some way – because of a shortage of foreign exchange, for example, or because of a limited capacity to raise tax revenue – it may be useful to know the financial implications of the project.[7]

Distributional objectives

If the public sector has distributional objectives it is unlikely to be satisfied with the use of the compensation test alone to determine its investment policy. It will be interested in the impact of the project on different socioeconomic groups. Most discussions of the use of CBA in developing countries accept that these distributional issues are important. The UNIDO *guidelines* advocate supplying the greatest amount of information to the policy-maker by providing an explicit distributional appraisal. L–M suggest that such an analysis should be implicit in the CBA itself (see section 9.6).

Uncertain outcomes

The preceding discussion assumes that all outcomes of the project could be forecast with certainty. This is, of course, unlikely to be the case, particularly in LDCs. If the probability distribution of outcomes is known, the uncertainty inherent in the project can be dealt with by calculating the expected value of the outcomes. In many cases, however, there will be no way of obtaining such a probability distribution, and the project analyst will have no choice but to test the sensitivity of the NPV for different assumptions about likely outcomes. L–M (1974, chapters 8 and 15), Sugden and Williams (1978, chapters 5 and 12) and UNIDO (1972, chapter 10) all discuss various ways in which risk and uncertainty may be taken into account.

9.3.2 Measurement of costs and benefits

If markets are functioning efficiently, demand curves reflect the marginal social value and supply curves reflect the marginal social cost of providing commodities, so that the equilibrium market price is equal to both marginal social value and marginal social cost. In this case the equilibrium price of an *input* is equal to the compensation which would be required either by other users (where the input is withdrawn from other uses) or by producers (where the production of the input is increased), in order to leave them in the same position after the introduction of the project as they were before. Similarly, the price of an *output* is both the amount which the beneficiaries of the project would be willing to pay rather than not have the benefits (where the project produces a net increase in the output) and also the amount which would have had to be paid to encourage existing producers to supply it (where the project replaces output from other sources). Thus, where markets are operating efficiently, it does not matter whether the project's inputs are withdrawn from other uses or whether they are a result of increased production. Nor does it matter whether the project's outputs constitute a net addition to supply or whether they replace existing sources of supply. In either case the market price equals the required compensation. In such cases inputs and outputs of the project may be valued at market prices for the purposes of CBA. There are, unfortunately, four major problems which inhibit the application of this simple rule.

1 Markets may not exist for some commodities. If there is no market for measles vaccination, one cannot apply a market price per vaccination to measure the value of output of a vaccination programme. If all university education is provided free by the public sector there is no market price which may be used directly to measure the value of additional university places.
2 The project may be large enough to affect relative prices so that the set of prices facing the economy without the project is different from that with the project. One then faces the question of which set of prices one uses to value the costs and benefits of the project.
3 Markets – particularly in LDCs – may not operate efficiently. There are likely to be distortions which prevent an equilibrium at which marginal social benefit is equal to marginal social cost. Such distortions may arise from taxes, subsidies, price controls, lack of competition, or externalities.[8]
4 Any set of supply and demand curves is the outcome of a given distribution of income, and a change in the distribution would imply a different set of prices. This point constitutes no real problem if one is concerned only with the impact of the project on national income since the measurement of national income itself is the outcome of the same set of prices. However, if one is concerned with distributional objectives as well as with the objective of maximizing national income, then some adjustment to market prices may be desirable.

9.3.3 Non-marketed goods

Much of the output of projects to improve the social and economic infrastructure is not directly marketed. Investments in education, medical care and roads produce output which is not sold directly to consumers. Similarly, many projects impose costs which have no direct counterpart in a market transaction. The irrigation project increasing the incidence of bilharzia is an example of this, since there is no market for bilharzia (or for avoiding the disease).

Although the issue is of importance for many projects in LDCs, it receives little explicit discussion in the three important manuals prepared for international agencies.[9] In contrast, practical applications of CBA in LDCs have had to grapple with the problem. Blaug (1976), Harberger (1965) and Krueger (1972), for example, have applied CBA to investment in education in Thailand, India and Turkey respectively, while Enke (1966), Leibenstein (1969) and Simon (1977) all discuss problems of applying CBA to family planning programmes in LDCs.

In general, the way in which such studies solve the problem of non-marketed output is to recognize that the demand for the project's output is a derived demand so that education, for example, is demanded not for its own sake but because it improves the quality of the labour force. Thus the present value of a given level of education of an average individual can be estimated by comparing the present value of the average income of individuals who have that level of education with the present value of the average income of those who have the level of education below it. In this way market prices are used to value the output of the project by valuing the impact of the project on individuals' productivity. The difficulties inherent in this procedure are mainly due to the problems involved in identifying education's contribution to earnings, since the higher earnings of more educated people may be due to intelligence, social class or custom as well as to education.[10]

9.3.4 Large projects

If the project is large relative to the relevant markets, then the introduction of the project may affect market prices. In the case of the irrigation project, for example, the increase in agricultural output will reduce significantly the price of this output if the increase is a significant proportion of existing output and if the demand for output is less than totally elastic.

In figure 9.2 the increase in output from Q_1 to Q_2 generated by the project reduces the market price of output from P_1 to P_2. In this case it is clear that neither price may be used to value output even if P_1 and P_2 are equal to the marginal social value of output before and after the project. Without the project the marginal social value of output is P_1 while with the project it is P_2. Thus the marginal social value of an amount between Q_1 and Q_2 lies between P_1 and P_2. In other words, the total social value of the increased output is measured by the area under the demand curve between Q_1 and Q_2 – that is, the area Q_1ABQ_2. Similarly, in the case of an input for which the project raises the market price, the total social cost of the input used by the project is the relevant area below the marginal social cost curve.

While recognizing that there may be problems in interpreting the area under demand curves as the value for the social benefit of consumption,[11] there is widespread agreement that this procedure provides the best measure of costs and benefits for large projects.

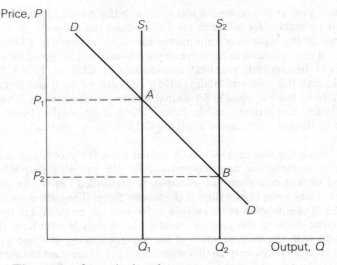

FIGURE 9.2   The market for agricultural output

9.4   Determination of shadow prices

9.4.1   Shadow prices for inputs and outputs

Where markets are distorted, so that marginal social cost is not equal to marginal social benefit, market prices may not provide an accurate guide to the value of costs and benefits generated by the project. In such cases one needs to estimate shadow prices (sometimes called accounting prices) which will reflect social values. There are various approaches suggested in the literature.

The Little–Mirrlees Approach[12]

Little and Mirrlees (1968 and 1974) take as their numeraire 'uncommitted social income measured at border prices' – that is, resources available for investment valued at international prices.[13] This numeraire implies that, in general, shadow prices of inputs and outputs should be the relevant border prices. In order to calculate these, L–M classify all commodities as traded or non-traded. 'In general . . . if some of the demand for a commodity will be satisfied from imports, or some of the supply exported, it is a *traded good*. Other goods and services are referred to as *non-traded*' (L–M, 1974). They recognize that there may well be difficulties in assigning goods to particular categories but argue that, where world markets exist, the commodity should be treated as traded since it would be optimal for the country to engage in such trade.[14]

The shadow prices of traded goods should represent the terms on which the country can trade. In the case of imported goods the shadow price should equal the *marginal import cost*, which will be equal to the world price (net of taxes and tariffs) where the country faces an infinite elasticity of supply. Where the country's own purchases affect the world price of the import, use of the commodity by the project will increase the amount of foreign exchange necessary to acquire existing imports, and this increase should be treated as a cost of the project. In the case of exported goods the shadow price should equal the *marginal export revenue* which will be the world price (net of taxes and tariffs) where the country faces an infinitely elastic world demand for its exports.

In the case of non-traded commodities the L–M approach places great emphasis on the use of the marginal social cost of production. Indeed, they argue that, for many non-traded commodities, the shadow price *is equal to* the marginal social cost of production. There are two aspects of their argument. First they believe that 'the MSC is constant over the relevant range of output' (L–M, 1974). In such cases the project will not affect the amount of the commodity available to consumers, and therefore MSB is irrelevant. Consider, for example, the market for a project input which is subject to a tax, as shown in figure 9.3, so that the market price, P_1, lies above the constant MSC, P_0. An increase in the demand for this good as a result of the project will shift the market demand curve from D *to* D^1 with a resultant increase in equilibrium quantity from Q_1 to Q_2, and Q_1Q_2 is equal to the project's use of the commodity. All of the project's use of the commodity is satisfied by increased production, which should therefore be valued at the MSC of production. Second, optimal government policy will equate MSC and MSB and, since they see CBA as part of an optimal planning strategy, the shadow price can be calculated as the MSC at the optimal output of

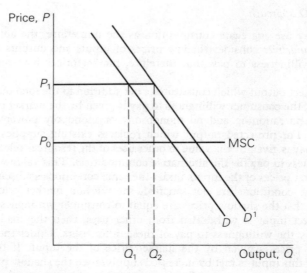

FIGURE 9.3 Shadow pricing with constant MSC

that commodity. Either of these assumptions would be sufficient justification for using a shadow price equal to the MSC of production. If neither of these conditions can be assumed to hold, they advise that the project analyst should estimate both the amount of production affected by the project (valuing this quantity at a shadow price equal to the MSC) and the amount of consumption affected by the project (valuing this quantity at a shadow price equal to the MSB). They give no advice on how these estimates should be made.

The marginal social cost of the commodity is found by valuing all inputs used for the production of that commodity at their shadow prices. In the case of inputs which are traded goods there is no problem. The shadow price is simply the marginal import cost or marginal export revenue as discussed above.[15] However, there is one non-traded input which may not be dealt with quite so easily. The shadow price of labour raises some particular problems, which will be dealt with in section 9.4.2.

A great deal of work has been devoted to calculating shadow prices using the L–M approach. For example, Little and Scott (1976), Powers (1981), Scott *et al.* (1976) and Stern (1972) all contain examples of shadow prices calculated in this way. Scott *et al.* (1976) provide a long list of shadow prices for Kenya which suggests that the shadow price may be as much as 57 per cent less than the market price (for motor spirit and tobacco) or 87 per cent higher than the market price (for imported maize), while the estimates for Ghana constructed by Page (1976) show all shadow prices but one to be less than market prices – one shadow price (rail transport) being only 26 per cent of the market price. These adjustments are typical of those obtained under the L–M method and are clearly not insignificant. They are quite likely to affect the investment decision.

The UNIDO approach

Because they use aggregate consumption as the numeraire, the authors of the UNIDO *Guidelines* consider shadow prices of inputs and outputs in terms of consumer willingness to pay and, therefore, market prices have an important part to play.

For a project output which constitutes a net addition to the total output of that commodity, the consumer willingness to pay is given by the market price as long as there is no rationing and no monopsony or monopoly power enjoyed by purchasers. For projected output which replaces existing supplies, then willingness to pay is given by the value in other uses of the resources released (that is, the willingness to pay for the alternative commodities). This value will be given by the market prices of the inputs under the same conditions as discussed above. Where these conditions are not satisfied, the relevant market prices must be adjusted so that the shadow prices are equal to consumer willingness to pay.

If a project input is withdrawn from other uses, then the shadow price is measured by the willingness to pay of these other users. Under the conditions above, this price is given by the market price of the input. If the project's demand for this input is met by increased supply, then the shadow price is given by consumer willingness to pay for the resources used in the input's production.

Again, under the appropriate conditions these prices are market prices. Where these conditions are not met, appropriate adjustment must be made.

Although the UNIDO *Guidelines* start from an apparently different basis, the end-result is the same prescription as that of L–M. For outputs, MSB is used to value the output which constitutes a net addition to supply, while MSC is used to value that which replaces existing supplies. For inputs, MSB is used to value those inputs withdrawn from other uses, and MSC is used to value those which are available as a result of new production. The two sets of authors differ in the extent to which they believe that market prices will be a useful guide to shadow prices, but this is really only a matter of judgment. The analytical procedures are essentially identical. Neither provides any mechanism for the estimation of the proportion of the output (input) which is to be measured at MSB and that which is to be measured at MSC.

Since the methods are essentially identical, one would expect them to have the same effects on the measurement of shadow prices. The UNIDO *Guidelines* have not been used as widely as the OECD *Manual*, but the examples given in the *Guidelines* give some idea of the extent to which the authors expect adjustments to be important. As one would expect, the examples reflect their belief that market prices will generally reflect shadow prices, but this does not change the conclusion that the analytical procedures are the same.

A weighted average of MSC and MSB

This approach extends the analytical framework used by UNIDO and L–M. Consider the example, shown in figure 9.4, of the market for an input which is distorted by a tax, so that at the market equilibrium output Q_1, MSB (P_1) is not equal to MSC (P_2) where $P_1 - P_2$ is equal to the tax. The project is assumed to shift the demand for the input to MSB¹ parallel to MSB by an amount (ΔQ) equal to the use of the input by the project. The new equilibrium output is Q_2. It is clear, therefore, that the increased demand for the project is met partly by increased production ($Q_1 Q_2$) and partly by reduction in the amount available to other uses ($Q_1 Q_3$) and this is recognized by both UNIDO and L–M as being the case when either supply or demand is less than perfectly elastic.

The cost to society of using this input, $P^\star \Delta Q$, is given by:

$$P^\star \Delta Q = \text{MSB (amount withdrawn from other uses)}$$
$$+ \text{MSC (amount of new production)}$$
$$= P_1(Q_1 Q_3) + P_2 (Q_1 Q_2) \qquad (9.1)$$

where $P^\star$ is the shadow price of the input.[16] It can be shown[17] that this gives:

$$P^\star = \frac{\eta P_1}{\eta + \epsilon} + \frac{\epsilon P_2}{\eta + \epsilon} \qquad (9.2)$$

where η and ϵ are the price elasticities of market demand and supply curves respectively at the market equilibrium. Thus, the shadow price, $P^\star$, may be

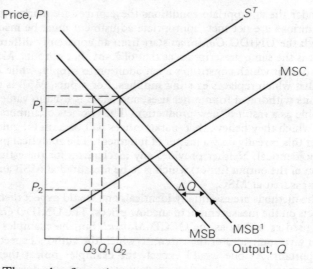

FIGURE 9.4   The market for an input

calculated as a weighted average of MSB and MSC where the weights depend on the elasticities of supply and demand.[18] It is worth noting that extreme values of the elasticities (either zero or infinity) result in a shadow price equal to either MSB or MSC.[19] Thus to some extent the different emphases of L–M and UNIDO reflect different judgments about the likely values of the elasticities. Indeed L–M (1974) recognize this and, as we have seen, provide some discussion and justification for their own judgments.

It should be clear that the three approaches to shadow pricing discussed in this section are complements rather than substitutes. Both L–M and UNIDO concentrate on different aspects of the deviation of market prices from MSB and MSC, and recognize that either the MSB or the MSC represent the appropriate valuation under certain conditions. However, while both approaches recognize the importance of determining whether the input (output) is subject to a net increase in supply or is withdrawn from other uses (replaces existing sources of supply) they provide no analytical procedure for determining the relevant proportions. The weighted average approach takes and MSB and MSC as determined, and uses information about the relevant curves in order to form a shadow price taking into account the different proportions determined by the observed elasticities.

9.4.2   The shadow wage

If labour markets functioned perfectly so that all labour was allocated to its highest valued use, the shadow wage would generally equal the market wage.[20] However, as for other commodities, distortions in the labour market usually prohibit, particularly in LDCs, such an easy interpretation of the market wage. Moreover, the estimation of the shadow wage may be sensitive to distortions in the capital market, because since labour and capital are the principal basic factors of production[21] any estimation of the shadow price of one factor has implications for the shadow price of the other. Finally, many LDCs appear to face a situation of chronic and persistent aggregate excess supply typified by sustained high levels of unemployment and underemployment.

Labour market distortions

Distortions in the labour market result in divergence between the value of the marginal product (VMP) of labour and its marginal cost of supply (which may be either the value of its marginal product in other areas of production or the marginal value placed on leisure time). Such distortions may occur, for example, because of the imposition of minimum wage legislation, trade union restrictions or the widespread operation of family enterprises in which each member receives a wage equal to the value of the average product.[22]

Figure 9.5 shows the case of a minimum wage for homogeneous unskilled industrial labour in competitive labour and product markets. With a minimum real wage of W_1 there will be an excess supply of labour, L_1L_2. More importantly for our purposes, there is a divergence between the value of the marginal product (W_1) and the marginal cost of supply (W_2). Formulated in these terms it is clear that the problem is essentially no different from that already considered above (section 9.4.1). The shadow wage may be calculated as the weighted average of W_1 and W_2 where the weights depend on the elasticities of supply of, and

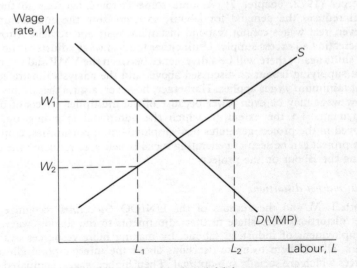

FIGURE 9.5 The market for unskilled industrial labour

demand for, labour. Most of the analyses assume that there is a perfectly elastic supply of labour to the industrial sector (because the marginal product of labour in agriculture is thought to be constant over the relevant range) so that the shadow wage is equal to W_2.

However, there are special features of the labour market which make it more difficult to determine the shadow wage and much of the literature on this point has been concerned with such features. In the case of unskilled industrial labour it is common to interpret the supply curve as the value of the marginal product of labour in agriculture. Thus, W_2 may be measured by the agricultural wage. Unfortunately, however, there are various circumstances under which such an interpretation would lead to a serious under-estimate of the shadow wage.

First, as the UNIDO *Guidelines* point out, the social costs of using a worker in the industrial sector may be higher than the value of the output forgone by withdrawing that same worker from the agricultural sector. The work in the industrial sector may be harder than that in the agricultural sector, so that he requires more food, while housing and travel costs may be higher. The value of W_2 should include the value of these costs as well as the value of the worker's marginal product in agriculture.

Second, the operation of family farms may result in the supply curve of labour reflecting the *average* rather than the *marginal* product of labour. Where the marginal product is constant this distinction is of no importance, since the marginal and average products will be equal. However, with a declining marginal product of labour the supply curve of labour to the industrial sector will be less than perfectly elastic, and it is important to discover whether the agricultural wage reflects the value of average or marginal product.

Third, wage stickiness can result in cyclical unemployment as discussed by Harberger (1972, chapter 7). Assume some factor exogenous to the labour market reduces the demand for labour, so decreasing the equilibrium wage. However, real wages cannot respond instantaneously and remain at too high a level, creating an excess supply. Until either the real wage adjusts or the demand curve shifts again, there will be a divergence between the VMP and the marginal cost of supplying labour as discussed above, and the analysis illustrated by the case of minimum wages applies. Harberger, however, argues that in this case the shadow wage may be even lower because of the multiplier effects of increased employment. To the extent to which the additional spending by workers employed in the project generates new employment opportunities, employment on the project can be seen as generating social benefits, so reducing the net costs of using the labour on the project.

Capital market distortions

As both L–M and the authors of the UNIDO *Guidelines* recognize, capital market distortions necessitate further adjustments to the shadow wage because the employment of industrial labour, by making more resources available to workers, allows them to make decisions about the intertemporal allocation of resources which are socially sub-optimal. Their higher wages, compared to those in agriculture, allow them to consume more than is socially optimal.

Both the *Manual* and the *Guidelines* respond to this problem by discounting[23] the value of industrial workers' additional consumption so that the shadow wage, W^*, is given by:

$$W^* = W_1 - \frac{1}{s}(W_1 - W_2) \tag{9.3}$$

where s is the social value of investment relative to consumption and W_1 and W_2 are, as before, the industrial wage (therefore industrial workers' consumption) and the marginal opportunity cost of supply of industrial workers respectively.

9.4.3 The shadow exchange rate

Since most projects in LDCs have a mixture of tradeables and non-tradeables in their inputs and outputs, one needs some way to bring domestic and world prices to a common unit of measurement. The obvious way of carrying out such a conversion is by the use of the exchange rate, measuring all prices either in terms of domestic currency or in terms of a common foreign currency – for example, dollars.

Unfortunately, foreign exchange markets are themselves distorted so that the existing exchange rate may not be the appropriate shadow price of foreign exchange. There are two main sources of distortion. (1) The widespread existence of import taxes and export subsidies results in a divergence between the marginal value which society places on foreign exchange and the marginal cost of earning it. An import tax, for example, causes the domestic price of the import to be higher than its world price, thus raising the marginal value of the foreign exchange used to purchase it above the marginal cost of earning this foreign exchange through exports. (2) National exchange rate policy may prevent the exchange rate from reaching its equilibrium level, thus resulting in a shortage – sometimes acute – of foreign exchange. Both types of distortion are common in foreign exchange markets of LDCs and frequently occur together. Various approaches have been suggested to deal with the distortions and these approaches can be classified into two groups: (a) attempts to estimate the equilibrium exchange rate and (b) attempts to estimate the 'second-best' exchange rate. L–M claim that their approach does not require the use of a shadow exchange rate.

The equilibrium exchange rate

This approach is typified by the work of Bacha and Taylor (1973).[24] The equilibrium exchange rate is that rate 'which prevails in a floating foreign exchange market when all import restrictions and export subsidies are removed'. They show that under the simplifying assumption of constant elasticities of supply and demand for exports and imports, the shadow exchange rate, R^*, is a function of the official exchange rate, the rate of protection against imports, the elasticities of demand for exports and imports, and the corresponding elasticities of supply.

Bacha and Taylor argue that such an exchange rate[25] is the appropriate rate to use for project appraisal, since if it is used consistently throughout the economy for all public and private investment decisions it will allow large efficiency gains to be made because investment policy will counteract the inefficiencies caused by the distortion of trade. In the long run, when all the existing capital stock has been subjected to this test, the allocation of resources throughout the economy will be the same as that which would occur if optimal trade policies were followed. In other words, the use of the equilibrium exchange rate in project evaluation would lead to an efficient allocation of resources in the sense that there would be no potential gains to be made by trade liberalization. Thus this approach looks further than the evaluation of the project in hand, and sees it as part of an exercise aimed at improving the allocation of resources in the economy as a whole.

The 'second-best' exchange rate

The proponents of a second-best exchange rate, such as Fontaine (1969), Harberger (1969), and Schydlowsky (1968) accept that distortions in the foreign exchange market will persist, and that private sector decisions will be made in the presence of such distortions. Under these conditions efficient resource allocation requires that decisions in the private and public sector should be consistent in the sense that there should be no potential gains to be made, given the constraints imposed by the existence of the distortions, by shifting the resources from one use to another. The allocation of resources under this regime will not be globally efficient, since the economy would still be able to make gains by, for example, adopting a policy of trade liberalization, but public investment policy will be efficient in the sense that no gains could be made by any further switching of investment funds to other uses.

Under these conditions the shadow exchange rate may be calculated as a weighted average of the marginal social cost and marginal social value of foreign exchange, where the weights depend on the elasticities of supply and demand for exports and imports and the shares of each commodity in the nation's trade. The calculation of the shadow exchange rate following this method is identical to that of the shadow price of an input or output given in equation (9.2), is derived in much the same way and may be given the same interpretation.[26]

The Little–Mirrlees method

At first sight the L–M method may seem a radical departure from either of the two preceding approaches. L–M argue that their methodology does not require the calculation of a shadow exchange rate. Traded goods are measured in world prices while non-traded goods are given shadow prices[27] which measure the foreign exchange cost or earnings they represent. In this way all goods are measured in world-price equivalents and the effects of tariffs and subsidies are taken into account.[28] Moreover, they argue that appropriate shadow pricing of non-traded goods – notably labour – will take into account any shortages of foreign exchange generated by the government's exchange rate policy. If the exchange rate is overvalued such that a devaluation would restore balance of payments equilibrium, they argue that the process of project selection should anticipate such a devaluation. While the use of a shadow exchange rate less than the current rate would achieve this aim, the same result may be achieved by applying an appropriate conversion factor, since when the devaluation takes place it will reduce the price of domestic goods vis-à-vis foreign goods and, in particular, will reduce the real wage. A further advantage of this procedure, it is claimed, is that it will allow for the effects of distortions on a sector-by-sector basis rather than averaging the effects of distortions over all sectors as with the use of a single shadow exchange rate.[29]

Choice of procedure

To a great extent the choice of the methodology to deal with distortions in the foreign exchange market depends on one's view of the environment in which the project analyst is operating. The use of the equilibrium exchange rate to achieve a first-best allocation of resources may be appropriate in a situation where the planning authority has a great deal of control over all sectors of the economy. Where the planning authority can control not only all areas of public investment but also all private sector investment – perhaps by means of investment licences – then a first-best allocation of resources may be achieved even in the face of large distortions in the foreign exchange market. On the other hand, the approach using a second-best shadow exchange rate may be preferred in situations where individual public agencies evaluate their own investments on a project-by-project basis. Finally, the simplicity of the L–M method using standard conversion factors has much to recommend it in cases where the extreme assumptions about elasticies are thought to be approximately justified over the relevant range.

9.5 The discount rate

In section 9.2 we argued that discounting was necessary because, in general, a pound received some time in the future is not considered as valuable as a pound received immediately.

If capital markets functioned perfectly with no distortions, all individuals and institutions would face the same interest rate. They would borrow or lend until the rate at which they preferred present over future consumption (the individual marginal time preference rate) were just equal to the single rate of interest.[30] With no externalities in consumption the unique *private* marginal time preference rate (PMTPR) would equal the *social* marginal time preference rate (SMTPR). Similarly, investors would use funds for capital projects as long as the rate of return they could obtain from the project was greater than the single market rate of interest. Thus the marginal product of capital (MPK) would equal the rate of interest, and as long as there were no externalities in investment the private and social marginal products would be equal. Therefore, in a perfectly functioning capital market with no externalities and no distortions, the interest rate will equal both the SMTPR and the social MPK, and this interest rate can be used to measure the relative value of receipts over time.

Unfortunately, however, as discussed in section 9.4.2, capital markets – particularly in developing countries – seldom exhibit these convenient features. It is argued that it is unlikely that private preferences will reflect social preferences, and that externalities exist particularly with respect to the time preference rate. Moreover, capital markets tend to be distorted so that the PMTPR diverges from the MPK. Under these conditions the question arises of the extent to which the market interest rate can be used as an indication of the discount rate to be used for CBA.

9.5.1   Divergence between social and private valuations

The difference between social and private valuations may be manifested in the capital market either on the demand or the supply side. On the demand side, externalities (either positive or negative) which occur as a result of private investment may result in a divergence between the private and social rate of return. The supply curve reflects the MTPR of individuals supplying funds to the capital market, who will equate this rate to the market rate of interest, and it may be argued that this rate does not equate the *social* MTPR. Two major reasons for such a divergence have been advanced. (1) It is argued that by its very nature the capital market takes into account the preferences only of the current generation. Society, however, has a dynamic nature and should be seen as a combination of both current *and future* generations. The discount rate should therefore take into account the preferences of the future as well as the current generation. (2) Even if we were to consider only the preferences of the present generation, the existence of externalities prevents individuals from registering their true preferences. All individuals of the current generation may feel better off if society contributed more resources to future generations, but each individual alone would not be willing to do so.

The first problem is essentially of a philosophical nature. Whether the current choices of society should or should not take account of the preferences of future generations is a value judgment about which economic analysis has little to say. The second issue, on the other hand, is a technical problem which implies that observations of the capital market will overstate the true SMTPR. However, it is not easy to see how one might adjust the market rate to take the externalities into account.[31]

Although the divergence between the social and private MTPR has been an important component of the debate about the social discount rate in general, the literature on the use of CBA in developing countries has paid it little attention. Indeed, L–M ignore it completely, while the UNIDO *Guidelines* afford the issue only a few lines.

9.5.2   Distortions in the capital market

In contrast, distortions in the capital market *per se* which cause a divergence between PMTPR and the MPK have received a great deal of attention in the context of developing countries. Such distortions are usually analysed in terms of the effect of a tax on income from capital, although they may have other sources such as company taxation, or interest rate controls.[32] Figure 9.6 shows the effects of such a tax. The demand (*DD*) for loanable funds is determined by the MPK, while the supply (*SS*) of loanable funds is determined by the PMTPR. With a tax on the income from capital, therefore, *SS* shows the net-of-tax rate of interest required by savers, while *S'S'* shows the gross-of-tax supply curve faced by borrowers where the vertical difference between *SS* and *S'S'* is the amount of tax. Equilibrium occurs at L_1 with an MPK equal to ϱ and an PMTPR equal to r.[33] In a sense it is clear that both the TPR and the MPK reflect the opportunity cost of public investment, since if this investment is not undertaken the funds could be used either for private investment or private consumption. In a long and complicated debate on the subject, one can identify two strands of opinion. The first argues that the appropriate social discount rate is the SMTPR accompanied by an adjustment to the cost of investment to take into account the rate of return which the funds could have earned in the private sector. The second argues that the appropriate discount rate may be found more directly as a weighted average of the SMTPR and the MPK.

Discounting by the social time preference rate

Since the SMTPR (or the consumption rate of interest – CRI – as L–M call it) is the relative value to society of consumption at different times, this is the discount rate which should be used to evaluate the present value of society's consumption stream. Thus the net consumption stream of a public investment should be

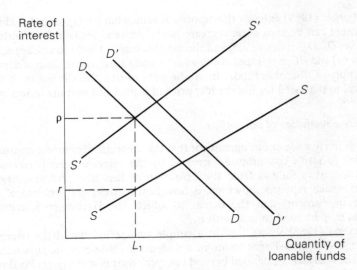

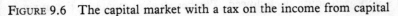

FIGURE 9.6   The capital market with a tax on the income from capital

discounted by the SMTPR. This net consumption stream includes both the stream of net benefits obtained directly and indirectly from the project itself and the impact of society's consumption stream occurring as a result of the private investment forgone. If we define α as the opportunity cost of public investment, it can be shown that:

$$\alpha = \frac{\theta\varrho}{r} + (1 - \theta) \tag{9.4}$$

where θ is the proportion of public investment obtained by forgoing private investment.[34] It may be seen that α is the present value of the consumption stream forgone as a result of public investment.[35]

This approach, developed in Marglin (1963a, b) and extended by Diamond (1968), is that used by both L–M and the UNIDO *Guidelines*.

Discounting by a weighted average

By contrast, Harberger (1969) and Sandmo and Drèze (1971) have argued that the effects on private investment should be taken into account directly by means of the discount rate. They argue that the proportion of the investment under-taken at the expense of private investment should be discounted at the MPK, while that undertaken at the expense of consumption should be discounted at the time preference rate. More generally, the social rate of discount, $r^\star$, can be evaluated as:

$$r^\star = \theta\varrho + (1 - \theta)r \tag{9.5}$$

Harberger (1969) extends this approach somewhat by arguing that the public investment can be seen as an increase in the demand for loanable funds (to, for example, $D'D'$ in figure 9.6) and the weights θ and $(1 - \theta)$ can be approximated by $\eta/(\eta + \epsilon)$ and $\epsilon/(\eta + \epsilon)$ respectively, where η and ϵ are the elasticities of demand for, and supply of, loanable funds. It will be noticed that this derivation is formally identical to that used for the shadow price of inputs and outputs in section 9.4.1.

Towards a resolution of the conflict

There is fairly widespread agreement that the theoretically correct approach is to discount society's consumption streams by the relevant time preference rate. This conclusion follows from the definition of the time preference rate. The conflict which remains, however, is how best to treat the problem of forgone private investment, and the extent to which the Harberger–Sandmo–Drèze formula may be used to deal with it.

Diamond (1968) shows that in a simple two-period world the Marglin and Harberger–Sandmo–Drèze solutions are identical. However, he goes on to argue that if the analysis is extended beyond two periods this identity breaks down, and Marglin's approach must be followed. Further developments of the analysis suggest that Diamond's conclusion is somewhat too hasty, and that the difference between the two appraoches in the multi-period case rests on differing assumptions about the impact of public investment on the capital market.

The Harberger–Sandmo–Drèze approach depends on the assumption that public investment manifests itself by an equivalent shift in the demand for loanable funds. The Marglin approach depends on the assumption that public investment is financed by taxation and affects the capital market only by means of an income effect. Drèze (1974) argues that his approach is identical to that of Marglin, even in the multi-period case, as long as one makes the assumption that public investment has a direct effect on the capital market. In a development of this argument, Sjaastad and Wisecarver (1977) show that the two approaches are identical under a wide range of conditions as long as the effects on the capital market are taken into account. They show further that the major conflict between the two approaches occurs as a result of different assumptions about the way in which individuals view the depreciation of public sector projects. They argue that the Marglin approach implies that individuals are unable to distinguish between gross and net output from public sector projects, although they are able to do so for private sector projects. However, on the other hand they argue that the Harberger–Sandmo–Drèze solution ignores the possibility of the reinvestment of part of the surplus of the public sector project.

The importance of the analysis of Sjaastad and Wisecarver is not in the resolution of the conflict between the two approaches, but in the clarification of the assumptions underlying them. The choice between them will therefore depend on which assumptions one believes to be applicable to any particular case.

9.6 Distributional objectives

The Hicks–Kaldor compensation test which underpins most modern welfare economies essentially assumes that the value to society of a given cost or benefit is independent of the characteristics of the individual who incurs or receives it. Moreover, transfers of benefits or costs between individuals leave social welfare unchanged.

While such an assumption may be justified where the existing distribution of income is socially acceptable, it appears less plausible when there is public concern about the existence of considerable inequalities. In many LDCs, for example, policy-makers may be concerned not only with increasing the present value of national income but also with increasing the standard of living of its poorest members. In such circumstances, it is argued, the income flows of disadvantaged groups are considered more important than those of others.

9.6.1 Distributional weights

To attach distributional weights to the flows of costs and benefits, it is necessary to divide society into relevant groups on the basis of income or other characteristics. One can then determine the importance which society attaches to the income flows of each group, and their costs and benefits can be weighted accordingly. Suppose, for example, that the incomes of people living below the poverty line in this society were considered to be four times as important as the incomes of the average member. Each £1 of costs and benefits accruing to this group would then be worth £4 to society.

Although the idea of distributional weights is simple enough, it is not obvious how they should be determined. By their very nature there is no market information which could be helpful. The weights refer to a political objective, and can only be determined in some way from the political process. Weisbrod (1968) suggests that they may be inferred from decisions taken on earlier projects, while Mera (1969) attempts to infer them from income tax schedules. In the development field, while L–M assume that the weights are known,[36] the UNIDO *Guidelines* discuss their derivation in some detail. The authors suggest that the weights should not be imposed at the start of the project, but that one should treat them as '*unknowns* of the planning problem. Values of weights that make significant differences in the design and operation of projects will be identified, and a set of project variants will be elaborated that are optimal in different ranges of parameter values' (UNIDO, 1972, p. 139). The implication of this approach is that the policy-maker's choice of one project rather than another will determine the set of distributional weights. If the policy-maker approves of this set of weights, they can be used for this project and those in the immediate future. If he does not, the process may then be repeated. Although the UNIDO approach is very similar to that of Weisbrod, in that it infers weights from policy choices, it differs crucially in that it makes the policy-maker part of the process of determining the weights. Weisbrod implicitly assumes that the policy-makers have, in the past, made informed choices, and that their implied weights are those desired. The UNIDO approach allows for the possibility that policy-makers may not have full information about the distributional implications of various projects, and makes the provision of this information an integral part of the process of determining the weights.

A further advantage of the UNIDO approach is that it is likely to lead to a consistent set of weights to be used in all projects. There is nothing in Weisbrod's approach which ensures that the weights used in previous projects will be consistent.

A major advantage of the use of consistent distributional weights is that it allows distributional value judgments to be included explicitly in the CBA, and ensures that the same value judgments are used for all projects.

9.6.2 Appropriate weights

It is clear that this argument is more important the greater is the range of weights which policy-makers think are appropriate. L–M (1974) argue that weights in the range 0.001 to 64 are not implausible, though they argue that for simplicity a more restricted range of 0 to 2 may be used. Weisbrod derives implicit weights for US government projects in the range −2 to 9.

Harberger (1978) cautions against an insufficiently critical use of a wide range of weights. He argues that the derivation of weights simply on the basis of social preferences may result in the acceptance of a set of projects involving an unnecessary cost in terms of lost efficiency. Since the principal argument for the use of distributional weights is that it is impossible to transfer the costs and benefits of the project at zero cost,[37] he argues that the cost of the best alternative methods of transfer must be taken into account. Thus, the weight given to person A's consumption vis-à-vis that of person B should not exceed the cost of transferring resources from B to A by the best alternative – however poor A is relative to B.[38]

9.7 *Ex-post* evaluation

For most of this survey, CBA has been considered as part of the planning strategy and has therefore been discussed in an *ex-ante* context. In other words, we have considered CBA as a technique intended to inform policy decisions so that policy-makers can make choices between various uses of the nation's resources. Increasingly, however, CBA has begun to be used to evaluate the success of investments after they have been undertaken. Such evaluations may be carried out during the construction of the project, or soon after, as is commonly done by the UK Overseas Development Administration, in order to monitor the capital costs of the project. On the other hand, the evaluation may be carried out some time after the completion of the project, as the World Bank does, in order to assess the total impact of the project.

An obvious difference between *ex-ante* and *ex-post* evaluations is that the latter will be able to use more certain information. By the very nature of *ex-post* evaluation, out of the many possible *ex-ante* states of the world, only one will have actually occurred. Thus we should not be surprised that, *ex-post*, some projects will have 'failed' in the sense that the NPV actually achieved was less than that expected – or in some cases even negative – since the state of the world *ex-post* could be that most unfavourable to the project. However, if the *ex-ante* appraisals have been carried out correctly, such failed projects should on average be countered by successful projects with results which were better than expected.

Although *ex-post* evaluations can be carried out under conditions of greater certainty than those existing *ex-ante*, there are some considerable difficulties encountered in their implementation and interpretation. In particular, the impact of a project may be difficult to assess since such an assessment would require the development of a counterfactual analysis of the state of the world which would have existed had the project not been undertaken.[39] In addition, it may be difficult to identify whether a project failed because of (a) poor administration, (b) an unfortunate *ex-post* state of the world, or (c) an incompetent *ex-ante* evaluation which ignored the existence of risk, or failed to assess it correctly.[40] Clearly, the identification of the reasons for failure has implications not simply for the apportioning of blame but for adjustments to future planning procedures.

9.8   Conclusions

This survey started with a distinction between the macroeconomic planning approach to project appraisal and that of CBA. The subsequent development of the CBA approach will have made it clear that this distinction is, to some extent, artificial. To undertake a satisfactory CBA some account must be taken of other projects, possible methods of income redistribution and interrelationships among markets. Thus, distributional weights cannot be determined without information about other projects and alternative methods of transferring income and, once determined, they have implications not only for the social discount rate but also for the shadow wage, while a faithful adherence to L-M's methodology for determining accounting prices requires knowledge of the full input–output matrix for the economy.

However, the convergence between the two approaches should not be overstated. Although CBA should take these interrelationships into account, in practice there still remains a considerable difference in emphasis and methodology. CBA concentrates on the desirability of a particular project and any general strategy for, say, industrialization or redistribution will be manifested through the use of particular weights or shadow prices rather than by favouring – or prejudicing – any project directly. Because of large distortions in the economies of LDCs the estimation of shadow prices is crucial to the CBA approach, and most of the literature has centred on the question of the determination of shadow prices in general and of the shadow wage, the social discount rate and the shadow price of foreign exchange in particular. Although the approaches of various authors may seem to differ on these issues, it was shown that many of the differences are a result of different assumptions about the state of the world. Thus, as in many areas of economics, the differences often reduce to differences in empirical assumptions (which can, in principle, be tested) rather than the theoretical differences which they at first appear.

NOTES

1. See, for example, Begg *et al* .(1984) and Creedy *et al.* (1984) for basic discussions of the problems of using national income as an indicator of social welfare. For a spirited defence of the use of compensation tests to evaluate policy changes see Harberger (1971), and for a defence of its use in CBA see Sugden and Williams (1978).
2. The use of the IRR criterion raises certain problems, as discussed in Harberger (1972, chapter 2), and it can be shown that the NPV criterion is to be preferred on theoretical grounds. Hirshleifer (1958) provides a formal proof of this proposition. A discussion of other investment criteria may be found in Herrick and Kindleberger (1983).
3. L-M (1974) define their numeraire as 'uncommitted social income' – that is, income available for use by the public sector. However, since 'government income counts for one . . . and that of workers unity or less depending on the value the government puts on savings versus immediate consumption' (L-M, 1972) this is equivalent to using savings (investible resources) as the numeraire. Dasgupta (1972) interprets their numeraire in this way and L-M (1972) do not disagree.

4. See, for example, Dasgupta (1972), Lal (1974), and L–M (1974) for proof of this point.
5. See Mabro (1974) and Shibl (1971) for discussions of the building of the High Dam at Aswan, which produced similar effects.
6. However, care must be taken to avoid double-counting. If the increased output generated by a project is evaluated at appropriate prices, there is no need to consider separately income gains which may be obtained by market intermediaries. See Prest and Turvey (1965) and Sugden and Williams (1978) for a more detailed discussion.
7. A purist would argue that this argument implies that certain resources have not been allocated their correct shadow price (see section 9.4). If all resources used and generated by the project are given their correct social value, then information about cash flows provides no additional useful information. For example, if foreign exchange is constrained by balance of payments problems it may be argued that it would be useful to have a financial appraisal which allowed identification of the effects of the project on the availability of foreign exchange so that, *ceteris paribus*, projects could be chosen which either economized on the use of foreign exchange or generated foreign exchange earnings. However, this example is simply a situation where the social value of foreign exchange is higher than its nominal value. Once this is allowed for in the CBA, there is no further need of a separate financial appraisal.
8. See, for example, Begg *et al.* (1984, chapters 14–16) or Layard and Walters (1978, chapters 3 and 6) for discussions of the effects of such distortions.
9. The authors of the UNIDO *Guidelines*, for example, argue that they need not concern themselves with this problem since they are primarily concerned with the analysis of industrial projects. This argument is not entirely convincing in the light of large projects such as the High Dam at Aswan in Egypt, which had a large industrial component – the construction of additional electricity-generating plant. This dam created the problem of increased incidence of bilharzia, as discussed in the examples above. See Shibl (1971) for further details.
10. Blaug (1970) provides a more detailed discussion of these problems and the way in which they may be solved. See also survey 6.
11. See, for example, Blaug (1978) or Laidler (1981) for a discussion of the problems associated with using the area under the demand curve as a measure of the value of consumers' surplus, and Harberger (1971) for a defence of this procedure. Squire and van der Tak (1975) and UNIDO (1972) both discuss some of the problems in relation to CBA. In a similar vein Mishan (1981) discusses the often-ignored question of the extent to which the area below the market supply curve can be interpreted as total social costs.
12. The approach used by Squire and van der Tak (1975) is essentially the same.
13. Prices are measured in terms of domestic currency converted from the foreign currency prices at the official exchange rate. See L–M (1972) for further details. The use of the official exchange rate in this case is considered further in section 9.4.3.
14. This advice is consistent with L–M's general philosophy of attempting to use project analysis as part of an overall planning strategy in which the government is assumed to be trying to achieve an optimal allocation of resources. See L–M (1972 and 1974) for an elucidation of this point.
15. Some non-traded goods may be used as an input in their own production. The shadow prices of such goods are the solutions to a set of equations relating the shadow price of each non-traded good to the shadow prices of all other goods (including its own price).
16. This formula is, of course, only an approximation, assuming that price changes are small enough to be ignored.

17. Sugden and Williams (1978) provide a textbook treatment of this analysis which is formally identical to that used by Harberger (1969) for the shadow discount rate and Balassa (1974) for the shadow exchange rate.

18. The shadow price for an output may be derived in the same way (by an appropriate shift of the supply curve). The formula will be identical.

19. $\eta = 0$ implies that $P^\star = P_2 = \text{MSC}$
    $\eta = \infty$ implies that $P^\star = P_1 = \text{MSB}$
    $\epsilon = 0$ implies that $P^\star = P_1 = \text{MSB}$
    $\epsilon = \infty$ implies that $P^\star = P_2 = \text{MSC}$

20. Even under these ideal conditions there may be some labour whose shadow wage is higher than their market wage. The most common example is that of full-time housewives. For women who spend all their time in household work we know that their shadow wage must be at least equal to their market wage at the margin, or they would spend some of their time in paid employment. However, their shadow wage may be higher – sometimes considerably higher – than the market wage in the sense that the market wages have to rise a great deal before they would be attracted into paid employment. See Becker (1981) for a more detailed discussion of the problems of estimating the shadow wage in the context of such corner solutions.

21. It may be argued that 'land' should be seen as a third basic factor of production, and should therefore be considered in this context. While conceding the theoretical point, it is generally argued that its inclusion in the calculations would not have much impact because of its relatively small role in the production function and that, therefore, the additional complexity of the model would not be worthwhile. This is, of course, an empirical matter.

22. See, for example, Nurkse (1957).

23. The actual formula allows for workers' consumption to be valued at a premium, but it is more usual to consider the case where it is discounted since it is generally considered that capital markets in LDCs allocate a less than optimal amount of funds to investment. Warr (1985) shows that this procedure may not be valid for some types of capital market distortions.

24. It may also be argued that L–M's methodology implies this approach. See, for example, Balassa (1974).

25. An alternative approach to the equilibrium exchange rate is to derive the rate which achieves purchasing power parity. However, as Bacha and Taylor (1973) argue, such a rate is useful only for international welfare comparisons. It is devoid of allocational implications because of the existence of the price of non-tradeable goods in its calculation.

26. An alternative method of calculating the second-best exchange rate is to use the domestic resource cost method exemplified by Bruno (1967) and Krueger (1969). See survey 1.

27. The extent to which this shadow price differs from the domestic price is known as the standard conversion factor.

28. This method has clear analogies to the domestic resource cost method.

29. Balassa (1974) shows that L–M's argument depends on their assumption that all primary inputs are in perfectly elastic supply and exports face a perfectly elastic demand. If these assumptions are not satisfied, then the calculation of the appropriate conversion factors requires the same information as that necessary to calculate the equilibrium exchange rate.

30. See, for example, Laidler (1981, pp. 71–9).

31. See Feldstein (1964), Marglin (1963a) and Sen (1967) for further discussion about the problem and possible solutions. Warr and Wright (1981) present a dissenting view.

32. Interest rate controls may be of particular importance in LDCs with a predominantly Muslim culture, where the Islamic prohibition of interest inhibits the operation of capital markets.
33. A further complication is introduced by the fact that savers may face different marginal tax rates so that a single market interest rate may result in a multiplicity of PMTPRs. One would then need to form some weighted average of the private rates in order to obtain a single social rate. See Harberger (1969) and Sugden and Williams (1978) for discussions of how such an average might be derived. In what follows we shall follow the usual convention in this area and assume that a single SMTPR may be observed or derived.
34. A simplifying assumption underlying many of these arguments is that the public investment is financed by current taxation. One may, therefore, interpret θ as the marginal propensity to save.
35. This is the simplest possible derivation of the opportunity cost of public investment. A more sophisticated derivation would take into account the possibility of reinvestment. It should be noted that α and s (the social value of investment in equation (9.3)) are related by the formula:

$$\alpha = (2s - 1)/s.$$

α is derived using present consumption as the numeraire while s uses investment as the numeraire. See L–M (1974, p. 359) for more details.
36. L–M (1968) provide no discussion of how the weights are derived, but L–M (1974) calculate values for weights based on plausible (as they see it) assumptions about social preferences.
37. If transfers were costless, there is no reason why policy-makers should not achieve the desired distribution of income. In this case a simple application of the Hicks-Kaldor compensation test would be sufficient for the appraisal of investment projects.
38. See Harberger (1980), Layard (1980) and Sugden and Williams (1978) for further discussion of this point.
39. See World Bank (1979) and Overseas Development Administration (1981) for a more detailed discussion of methods of evaluation.
40. See Tribe (1984) for an example of these problems.

REFERENCES

Bacha, E. and Taylor, L. 1973. Foreign exchange shadow prices. A critical review of the current theories. In R. S. Eckaus and P. N. Rosenstein-Rodan (eds), *Analysis of Development Problems*. Contributions to Economic Analysis, No. 83. Amsterdam: North-Holland.
Balassa, B. 1974. Estimating the shadow price of foreign exchange in project appraisal. *Oxford Economic Papers*, 26, 147–68.
Becker, G. S. 1981. *A Treatise on the Family*. Cambridge, Mass.: Harvard University Press.
Begg, D., Fischer, D. and Dornbusch, R. 1984. *Economics*, British edition. London: McGraw-Hill.
Blaug, M. 1970. *An Introduction to the Economics of Education*. Harmondsworth: Penguin.
Blaug, M. 1976. The rate of return on investment in education in Thailand. *Journal of Development Studies*, 12, 270–83.

Blaug, M. 1978. *Economic Theory in Retrospect*, 3rd edn. Cambridge: Cambridge University Press.

Bruno, M. 1967. The optimal selection of export-promoting and import-substituting projects, In *Planning the External Sector: Techniques, Problems and Policies*. New York: UN, pp. 88–136.

Creedy, J., Evans, L., Thomas, B., Johnson, P. and Wilson, R. 1984. *Economics: an Integrated Approach*. London: Prentice-Hall.

Dasgupta, P. 1972. A comparative analysis of the UNIDO Guidelines and the OECD Manual. *Bulletin of the Oxford University Institute of Economics and Statistics*, 34, 33–51.

Diamond, P. 1968. The opportunity costs of public investment: Comment. *Quarterly Journal of Economics*, 82, 682–8.

Drèze, J. H. 1974. Discount rates and public investment: a post-scriptum. *Economica*, 41, 52–61.

Enke, S. 1966. The economic aspects of slowing population growth. *Economic Journal*, 76, 44–56.

Feldstein, M. S. 1964. The social time preference discount rate in cost–benefit analysis. *Economic Journal*, 74, 360–79.

Fontaine, E. R. 1969. *El Precio Sombra de la Divisas in la Evaluacion Social de Progectos*. Santiago: Universidad Catolica de Chile.

Harberger, A. C. 1965. Investment in men versus investment in machines: The case of India. In C. A. Anderson and M. J. Bowman (eds), *Education and Economic Development*. Chicago: Aldine Publishing Company.

Harberger, A. C. 1969. Professor Arrow on the social discount rate. In G. G. Somers and W. D. Woods (eds), *Cost–Benefit Analysis of Manpower Policies*. Industrial Relations Centre, Queen's University, Kingston, Ontario.

Harberger, A. C. 1971. Three basic postulates for applied welfare economics. *Journal of Economic Literature*, 9, 785–97.

Harberger, A. C. 1972. *Project Evaluation*. London: Macmillan.

Harberger, A. C. 1978. On the use of distributional weights in social cost-benefit analysis. *Journal of Political Economy.*, 86, Supplement S87–S120.

Harberger, A. C. 1980. Reply to Layard and Squire. *Journal of Political Economy*, 88, 1050–2.

Healey, D. T. 1972. Development policy: new thinking about an interpretation. *Journal of Economic Literature*, 10, 757–97.

Herrick, R. and Kindleberger, C. 1983. *Economic Development*, 4th edn. New York: McGraw-Hill.

Hirshleifer, J. 1958. On the theory of optimal investment decisions. *Journal of Political Economy*, 66, 329–51.

Krueger, A. O. 1969. *The Role of Home Goods and Money in Exchange Rate Adjustments*. Minneapolis: University of Minnesota.

Krueger, A. O. 1972. Rates of return to Turkish higher education. *Journal of Human Resources*, 7, 482–99.

Laidler, D. 1981. *Introduction to Microeconomics*, 2nd edn. Oxford: Philip Allan.

Lal, D. 1974. *Methods of Project Analysis: A Review*. World Bank Staff Occasional Papers, No. 16. Baltimore: Johns Hopkins University Press.

Layard, P. R. G. and Walters, A. A. 1978. *Microeconomic Theory*. New York: McGraw-Hill.

Layard, R. 1980. On the use of distributional weights in social cost–benefit analysis. *Journal of Political Economy*, 88, 1041–7.

Leibenstein, H. 1969. Pitfalls in benefit–cost analysis of birth prevention. *Population Studies*, 23, 161–70.

Lewis, W. A. 1966. *Development Planning*. London: Allen and Unwin.

Little, I. M. D. and Mirrlees, J. A. 1968. *Manual of Industrial Project Analysis in Developing Countries*, vol. II. Paris: OECD.

Little, I. M. D. and Mirrlees, J. A. 1972. A reply to some criticisms of the OECD Manual. *Bulletin of the Oxford University Institute of Economics and Statistics*, 34, 153-68.

Little, I. M. D. and Mirrlees, J. A. 1974. *Project Appraisal and Planning for Developing Countries*. London: Heinemann.

Little, I. M. D. and Scott, M. F. G. 1976. *Using Shadow Prices*. London: Heinemann.

Mabro, R. 1974. *The Egyptian Economy, 1952-1972*. Oxford: Clarendon Press.

Marglin, S. A. 1963a. The social rate of discount and the optimal rate of investment. *Quarterly Journal of Economics*, 77, 95-111.

Marglin, S. 1963b. The opportunity costs of public investment. *Quarterly Journal of Economics*, 77, 274-89.

Mera, K. 1969. Experimental determination of relative marginal utilities. *Quarterly Journal of Economics*, 83, 464-77.

Mishan, E. J. 1981. *Introduction to Normative Economics*. Oxford: Oxford University Press.

Nurkse, R. 1957. Excess population and capital construction. *Malayan Economic Review*, 2, 1-11.

Overseas Development Administration. 1981. *Guidelines for the Preparation of Evaluation Studies*. London: HMSO.

Page, J. M. 1976. The social efficiency of the timber industries in Ghana. In Scott *et al.* (1976).

Powers, T. A. (ed.) 1981. *Estimating Accounting Prices for Project Appraisal*. Washington DC: Inter-American Development Bank.

Prest, A. R., and Turvey, R. 1965. Cost-benefit analysis: a survey. *Economic Journal*, 75, 683-735.

Sandmo, A. and Drèze, J. H. 1971. Discount rates for public investment in closed and open economies. *Economica*, 38, 395-412.

Schydlowsky, D. M. 1968. *On the Choice of a Shadow Price for Foreign Exchange*. Economic Development Report No. 108. Cambridge, Mass.: Development Advisory Service.

Scott, M. F. G., MacArthur, J. D. and Newbery, D. M. G. 1976. *Project Appraisal in Practice*. London: Heinemann.

Sen, A. K. 1967. Isolation, assurance and the social rate of discount. *Quarterly Journal of Economics*, 81, 112-24.

Shibl, Y. 1971. *The Aswan High Dam*. Beirut: Arab Institute for Research and Publishing.

Simon, J. L. 1977. *Economics of Population Growth*. Princeton, NJ: Princeton University Press.

Sinclair, C. A. 1977. A review of alternative techniques of planning manpower development. In ILO, *Manpower Assessment and Planning Projects in Asia*. Geneva: International Labour Office.

Sjaastad, L. A. and Wisecarver, D. C. 1977. The social cost of public finance. *Journal of Political Economy*. 85, 513-47.

Squire, L. and van der Tak, H. G. 1975. *Economic Analysis of Projects*. Baltimore: Johns Hopkins University Press.

Stern, N. H. 1972. Experience with the use of the Little/Mirrlees method for an appraisal of small-holder tea in Kenya. *Bulletin of the Oxford University Institute of Economics and Statistics*, 34, 93-124.

Sugden, R. and Williams, A. 1978. *Principles of Practical Cost-Benefit Analysis*. Oxford: Oxford University Press.

Tribe, M. A. 1984. *Komenda Sugar Factory and Estate: a Case Study in Technology Selection and Performance*. Discussion Paper, Centre for Development Studies, University of Cape Coast/David Livingstone Institute, University of Strathclyde.

United Nations Industrial Development Organisation (UNIDO). 1972. *Guidelines for Project Evaluation*. New York: UN.

Warr, P. G. 1985. Sub-optimal saving and the shadow price of labor. The public good argument. *Journal of Development Economics*, 17, 239–57.

Warr, P. G. and Wright, B. D. 1981. The isolation paradox and the discount rate for benefit–cost analysis. *Quarterly Journal of Economics*. 96, 129–45.

Weisbrod, D. 1968. Income redistribution effects and benefit–cost analysis. In S. B. Chase, Jr (ed.), *Problems in Public Expenditure Analysis*. Washington, DC: The Brookings Institution.

World Bank. 1979. *Operations Evaluation: World Bank Standards and Procedures*. Washington, DC: World Bank.

PART V

The Rural Sector

10

Agriculture and economic development

Subrata Ghatak

10.1 Introduction

In this survey I shall first discuss the contribution of agriculture to economic development. Particular attention will be paid to the special role of agriculture in the capital formation of less developed countries (LDCs) by generating 'surplus' within a dual economy. Next, I will examine different methods to generate surplus, and the role of incentives in mobilizing resources and increasing production and supply will be investigated. Third, problems of the transformation of backward agriculture will be reviewed. Fourth, constraints on transforming poor agriculture will be identified and the role of institutions such as land reform, marketing, credit and insurance agencies will be analysed. Fifth, the major causes and consequences of the introduction of technical progress in underdeveloped agriculture will be reviewed and specific problems of employment generation and income distribution due to the Green Revolution (GR) will be highlighted. Finally, some measures will be suggested to alleviate poverty and famine in the agricultural sector of LDCs.

10.2 The contribution of agriculture to economic development

It is now well accepted that agriculture can make a major contribution to the economic development of an LDC for the following reasons:

1 Agriculture is generally the dominant sector of most LDCs, measured either in terms of the proportion of GDP originating in this sector or in terms of its contribution to total employment, or both. In LDCs the share of agricultural output in total real GDP generally varies from 35 to 90 per cent. Clearly, because of its vast size and contribution to GDP, the performance of the agricultural sector can be an overwhelming help or hindrance to overall economic development.

2 The growth of the non-agricultural sector in LDCs is crucially dependent on the steady rise in food supply as it keeps inflation and wage costs down. In addition, many manufacturing industries in LDCs depend upon agriculture for the supply of raw materials (for example, textiles).

3 It is well known that agriculture provides *labour* for the growth of the non-agricultural sector of the economy. Such a labour transfer is of mutual benefit to both sectors in labour-surplus economies when the marginal productivity of labour is low. The process of labour transfer from agriculture to industry will reduce the pressure of population on the land. At the same time it will shift factors from lower productivity to higher productivity areas.

4 The rate of capital accumulation in LDCs can be substantially increased by an improvement of the agricultural sector. Such a process of accumulation hinges crucially upon the elasticity of food supply. An efficient agriculture is necessary to make the food supply more elastic, reduce the rate of increase in wages and costs and enhance the profit margins necessary for accumulation of capital. Also, as farm incomes rise, a higher proportion can be taxed away for capital formation.

5 Agriculture can make useful contributions to the balance of payments either by raising a country's earnings from exports or by producing agricultural import substitutes. Exports of agricultural goods can also help to earn valuable foreign exchange to pay for imports of machinery or other capital goods for the industrialization of the economy.

6 Since agriculture plays a dominant role in LDCs its growth and expansion is critically related to the growth of the home market. A growing agrarian economy, coupled with a fair distribution of farm income, will raise aggregate demand, stimulating the demand for industrial products and thus aiding the process of industrialization.

In summary, following Kuznets (1961) we can say that agriculture can make the following types of contribution:

1 a 'product' contribution, for example food and raw materials;
2 a 'factor' contribution, for example labour;
3 a 'market' contribution by stimulating home demand; and
4 a 'foreign exchange' contribution.

10.2.1 Major features of underdeveloped agriculture

This section examines some special features of backward agriculture in order to understand the problems of, and prospects for, resource mobilization in agrarian economies. Agriculture is said to be backward if the yield is poor due to the limited use of modern inputs.

Small family farms

One of the main features of underdeveloped agriculture is the small family farm. The chief inputs of production are land and family labour, and production sometimes takes place merely for subsistence. However, in the case of cash crops, production is largely geared to the needs of the market. In many instances the relationship between farm size and family size is inverse. This leads to considerable fragmentation of land, and accounts for a substantial degree of inequality in the distribution of rurual income and wealth.

Average crop yields

The average crop yield per acre of land in underdeveloped agriculture is generally very low in comparison with developed agriculture. Such a low yield underlies the problem of generally low productivity of resources utilized in agriculture. This occurs for a number of reasons: poor land quality; lack of fertilizer and capital machinery; food shortage and malnutrition. In many LDCs scarcity of rainfall and water constitute severe constraints on raising yields and total production. Further, allocation of resources to agriculture can be relatively low due to public or private apathy towards the sector. Given poor productivity of labour real wages in the agricultural sector are generally low.

In the case of land-abundant, *labour-scarce* underdeveloped economies (as in many parts of Africa), the objective may be to raise output per unit of labour rather than land, and the cultivated area may be altered in line with the variation in labour supply. In this situation agricultural real wages can be relatively high and land rent relatively low. These types of situations are at variance with the more usual system of factor income distribution in underdeveloped agriculture – low real wages and high rent in the face of high man–land ratios.

Given the presence of family labour, wages are not always determined by the marginal product of labour. In a large number of cases, wages are given by average productivity as labourers working within a farm 'share' output. In the case of very poor agriculture, real wages are generally at the subsistence level.

Use of technology

Use of modern technology in underdeveloped agriculture is often low. Although, in some parts of LDCs, machinery and fertilizer have been used in larger quantities, the typical intensity of modern input use is not high. Thus the rate of adoption of new technology in backward agriculture remains low. Several factors account for such technological backwardness.

1 Farmers' ignorance of alternative and modern farming methods due to illiteracy and inadequate spread of information.
2 The absence of an alternative method of production which is 'appropriate' for local conditions.
3 The relative risk and returns from the adoption of new technology. If farmers regard these risks as high, and returns as low, then the incentive to use the new technology will be limited. This point underlines the need to develop a suitable price/cost policy.
4 The poor system of transportation and communication in rural areas of many LDCs usually makes both product and factor markets inaccessible to many farmers.

5 The poverty and low income of many farmers in rural areas, combined with a lack of proper credit, marketing and insurance facilities. Even when farmers may be well informed about the availability of better seeds and fertilizer, the lack of borrowing facilities from the organized credit market can act as a serious constraint. An absence of marketing facilities implies that farmers are obliged to sell crops at a time when harvest prices are usually at their lowest. Sometimes, organized credit agencies discriminate against borrowing by small farmers simply because their creditworthiness is supposed to be lower and the rate of default higher. These small farmers are then forced to borrow from private money lenders at high rates of interest which inevitably raises the cost of credit. Thus, market imperfections and credit restrictions prevent the adoption of new technology.

6 A number of important political and institutional factors can perpetuate agricultural stagnation. For instance, poor farmers do not have much political power in LDCs. The tenancy laws usually provide little incentive for tenants to raise production. Property rights are ill-defined and sometimes share-croppers are at the mercy of big landlords. In some cases landlords act as creditors to their tenants, and consumption loans are usually advanced by these landlords at high rates of interest. Hence, the tenant leases his land from the same man to whom he is indebted. This is supposed to reduce him to the state of a traditional 'serf' (Bhaduri, 1973, 1977). The semi-feudal landlord, then, exploits the tenant both through usury and through his 'property rights on land'. Where the tenant has little access to the commodity market he cannot always sell at the highest price. As noted above, he usually has to sell when harvest prices are at their lowest, and in this situation tenants frequently need consumption loans just to survive. When they fail to repay loans, their position to re-contract, negotiate and bargain with the landlords is considerably weakened.

Clearly, ill-defined property rights, inaccessibility to the product and factor markets, lack of infrastructural facilities and absence of strong political organization to improve the bargaining positions combine to weaken incentives for adoption of new technology.

10.2.2 The role of agriculture in capital formation

It has already been indicated that agriculture can play an important role in the capital formation of developing countries. The mechanism of capital accumulation may be explained as follows.

Consider a backward economy where corn is the main product and it is produced using inputs of labour, capital and a fixed amount of land. It is assumed that the most productive land is used first, so that as the labour force (assumed equal to population here) grows, less productive land is brought into production. Thus the average and marginal product of labour falls as the labour input rises. This is shown in figure 10.1: the curve OQ shows the relationship between total product of corn, Q, and the labour force, N. Wages are equal to the level of

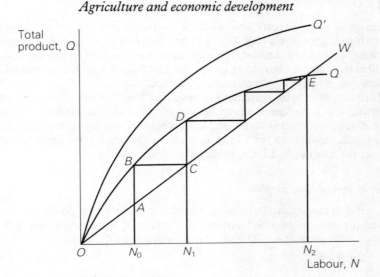

FIGURE 10.1   Agricultural surplus

subsistance in the long run but may vary in the short run. The constant slope of the line OW indicates the fixed long-run wage rate at the subsistence level, with the difference between OQ and OW indicating the level of surplus or profit.

The size of the 'surplus' is of crucial importance as it determines the size of capital formation. In figure 10.1, when employment rises from ON_0 to ON_1, the surplus falls ($DC < AB$). At employment ON_2 the surplus disappears completely and production is exactly equal to the wage bill.

Why does this happen? The answer lies in the interaction between the growth of population and the level of wages. It is assumed that the Malthusian theory of population prevails in LDCs. Thus, whenever wages are above the level of subsistence, population tends to rise as people enlarge their family sizes due to a rise in their standard of living. For instance, at ON_0 production is N_0B but wages are N_0A. The surplus, AB, is available for capital formation. A rise in accumulation raises the demand for labour. With a given population (at ON_0) and a rise in demand for labour, wages exceed the level of subsistence in the short run (at N_0B) and population growth is encouraged. Hence population rises to ON_1 in the next period. This rise, however, raises the supply of labour (population increases) and wages drop to the level of subsistence (N_1C). But as production is N_1D at ON_1 a 'surplus' of CD arises, which is now available for further accumulation. The economy advances until it reaches a point such as E where it grinds to a halt as the whole of production is equal to the level of subsistence wages (N_2E) and nothing is available for accumulation and growth. The point can be compared with the 'stationary state' in classical economic analysis (for details, see Ghatak, 1986).

The role of 'surplus' in capital formation and growth is now easy to understand. The question then arises: what should happen at the stationary state when the economy simply reproduces itself? The answer is: a shift in the production function to higher levels (e.g. OQ') by the *introduction* of technical progress in backward agriculture. Indeed, the introduction of modern technology has been regarded by many as essential to escape the Malthusian trap. Simultaneously this reduces the pressure of population on the land.

There are, of course, reasons to believe that the Malthusian assumptions for validating the 'subsistence theory of wages' are rather dubious. For instance, it is not at all convincing to assume that, whenever wages are above the level of subsistence, population will tend to rise. In the choice between babies and bicycles for couples in LDCs, frequently babies lose!

Types of agricultural surplus

It is useful to distinguish between different forms of surplus. So far we have considered the case of '*physical*' surplus, S. Usually, it is defined as the difference between total production, Q and total consumption, C. Thus,

$$S = Q - C \qquad (10.1)$$

Apart from the physical surplus, it is possible to envisage two other types of surplus: labour surplus and financial surplus. *Labour surplus* arises when the marginal productivity of labour in agriculture is close to, or equal to, zero. Labour is surplus because further addition of labour to a productive activity is unlikely to raise production. This implies that the cost of transferring labour from agriculture to industry for stimulating the growth of industrialization in LDCs is not large. A number of economic models have been developed to explain the process of labour transfer and economic growth in LDCs. (See for example, Dixit, 1968; Fei and Ranis, 1964; Jorgenson, 1967; Kanbur and McIntosh, 1984; Lewis, 1954; see Ghatak, 1986, for a summary.)

Financial surplus can be defined as the difference between the payments received by the agricultural sector and its expenditure on the non-agricultural sector. With a rise in farm income over expenditure, a financial saving or surplus clearly emerges, which can be siphoned off by taxes or other means. Such revenue can then be utilized for reinvestment in agriculture and industry. More formally, financial surplus, S_F, can be defined as follows:

$$S_F \equiv Y_a^m - E_a^m \qquad (10.2)$$

where:

Y_a^m = total money income received by the agricultural sector;
E_a^m = total money expenditure of the agricultural sector.

Among a number of factors that can affect Y_a^m, the following stand out as important: (a) the level of production; (b) the price that the farmer receives for his product; (c) the crop-yield; (d) the level of subsistence consumption. Any changes in any one of these factors will change the level of farm income. Similarly, farm money expenditure, E_a^m, can be influenced by factors such as (a) farm demand for non-farm products such as fertilizer, water, pesticides, farm machinery, textiles and other industrial goods; (b) payments of rents and taxes in cash; (c) subsidies paid by the government on the purchase of inputs from the non-farm sector; (d) purchase of social services such as education and medicare.

Economists have been primarily concerned for a long time with the different methods to generate both the physical and the financial surplus from the agricultural sector. The main interest centres around the use of the 'price mechanism' to generate surplus. This will be discussed in section 10.3.

10.3 The role of price incentives to generate surplus

10.3.1 The price mechanism and the supply response

A government can try to generate 'surplus' agricultural output by *persuading* farmers to save more. Alternatively, saving can be promoted by the imposition of taxes or levies in a centralized command economy, and this transfer of saving (by taxes) from the private to the public sector can then be invested. Sometimes farmers can be compelled to give up a part of their production, as happened to peasants in Russia after the 1917 Revolution. This is therefore generally known as the 'Soviet method' to extract surplus. Needless to say, the enforcement of such a policy requires the existence of a totalitarian state and a centrally planned economy. The economic history of Soviet Russia also tells us that the cost of mobilizing surplus from agriculture, in terms of loss of human lives and livestock, has been rather heavy (Dobb, 1966).

An interesting method for removing surplus from agriculture was suggested by Preobrazhensky (1965). In its simplest form the idea is to turn the terms of trade against agriculture. Let P_a be the price of agricultural goods and P_i the price of industrial goods. Terms of trade can then be defined as P_a/P_i. Any fall in the terms of trade will imply that farmers, with a given demand for money to buy non-farm goods (for example fertilizer, or to pay taxes and rents in cash) will be forced to sell more of their crops on the open market as farm income decreases. A fall in the terms of trade can be achieved in a number of ways:

1 industrial goods entering into farmers' consumption can be taxed;
2 state trading and price controls can allow prices of industrial goods to rise faster than those of agricultural goods;
3 while prices of agricultural goods can be kept fixed through price controls, prices of industrial goods can be allowed to rise because of imposition of tariffs or other forms of levies.

In a centrally planned economy it is possible to use some compulsion under which farmers will sell a part of their production even when the terms of trade are unfavourable to the agricultural sector. But in a more decentralized and democratic society, farmers may retaliate by not selling much in the open market (thereby reducing the marketable surplus) whenever they face adverse terms of trade.

We can show the validity of this argument with a diagram such as figure 10.2. Let the vertical axis measure agricultural goods and the horizontal axis measure industrial goods. Let there be 'surplus' labour in the agricultural sector whose marginal productivity is zero. Now the farmer's budget constraint in terms of agricultural goods is given by OA and OB, respectively *prior to* and *after* the transfer of the 'surplus' labour. The initial equilibrium is at E where AC (whose slope shows the original terms of trade) is tangential to the indifference curve I_1. When the terms of trade move against the agricultural sector we obtain a new price line BK which must pass through E to mop up total available savings when the required amount of marketed surplus is available. Since the slope of BK is greater than that of AC and BK passes through E the new equilibrium at E' must lie above E. This implies a *fall* in marketed surplus since the farmer's consumption of agricultural goods has risen. It follows that, as long as the income and the substitution effects operate normally, an adverse movement in the terms of trade against agriculture will lead to a fall in marketed surplus.

The above analysis does not preclude the fact that a very drastic fall in the terms of trade will lead to a rise in marketed surplus. Such a situation is shown by the line BT with equilibrium at a point such as E''. It is clear from the very steep slope of the line BT that the decline in the terms of trade must be very severe indeed (as farmers can now trade OB amount of agricultural goods for only OT amount of industrial goods). Further, if it is assumed that farmers' demand for money is fixed, as they wish to enjoy the same level of money income, then again, as price falls marketed surplus can rise. However, this assumption implies a very low income elasticity of demand for non-foodgrains by

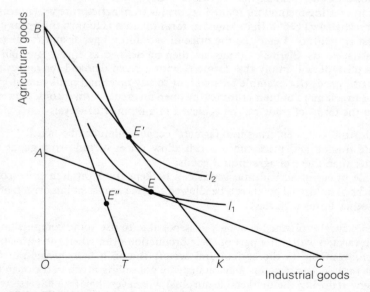

FIGURE 10.2   The Agricultural terms of trade

farmers, as well as the complete absence of substitution effects (see Mathur and Ezekiel, 1961).

Clearly, such cases are rather unrealistic. In the following I will argue, on the basis of empirical evidence, that farmers in LDCs *do* respond to price signals and other incentives, and hence it is useful to know the workings of the price mechanism for the generation of marketed surplus.

The mechanism by which marketed surplus increases when the terms of trade move in *favour* of the agricultural sector can be shown with the help of figure 10.3. The vertical axis measures agricultural goods and the horizontal axis measures industrial goods. The diagram shows the effects of the change of terms of trade (P_i/P_a) on marketed surplus. Without 'trade', the farmer consumes all he produces at OA, but initial equilibrium involves a 'surplus' of AB. After a fall in P_i/P_a, a surplus of AC results, and clearly $AC > AB$. However, this result depends on farmers' assumed preferences.

An indefinite rise in the terms of trade in favour of agriculture may not raise surplus any more, because after a point farmers may like to consume more leisure and the supply curve of labour may turn backwards with respect to the level of real wages (see Ghatak, 1975b, 1986; Ghatak and Ingersent, 1984), causing the price–consumption curve, PP, in figure 10.3 to become upward-sloping at some point.

Empirical evidence tends to suggest that the income elasticity of demand for food is usually less than unity; but the elasticity for industrial goods in the rural sector is quite high, and greater than unity in almost all cases. The price elasticity of industrial goods in the rural sector is also observed to be high. Thus it is conceivable that a relative *decline* in the price of industrial goods (for example by 10 per cent) will increase farmers' demand for industrial goods by more than 10 per cent and hence they will sell more crops in the market.

It has already been mentioned that payments of rents and taxes can explain the correlation between marketed surplus and the terms of trade. If farmers' consumption of agricultural products is fixed, then in a bad year, if a farmer is required to pay his rent *in kind*, marketed surplus will fall. Similarly, if farmers *repay* their *debt* in kind, then such repayment will affect the size of the surplus. Conversely, greater use of currency and increasing monetization of the agrarian economy will raise farmers' demand for money and hence increase the surplus.

10.3.2 Empirical evidence

Empirical evidence available so far confirms the hypothesis that farmers in almost all LDCs tend to respond positively to price signals and economic incentives. (For an excellent survey of the literature, see Askari and Cummings, 1976; also Ghatak and Ingersent, 1984.) Researchers tend to use acreage rather than output to test the price sensitivity. Since an increase in acreage under cultivation usually implies a rise in farm production, this method of investigation is well accepted. In this sense it is more correct to say that *acreage* tends to respond directly to price movements. However there is evidence to confirm a direct relationship between farm output and price (see Askari and Cummings, 1976;

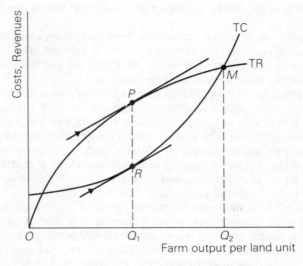

FIGURE 10.3   Farmers' preferences and the terms of trade

Ghatak and Ghatak, 1985). It is, of course, possible to observe negative price elasticities of supply due to the production of inferior feed crop (Krishna, 1967) where a price rise leads to a fall in production.

10.3.3   Limits to price policies

While governments can manipulate the terms of trade, there are some major limitations on the use of price policy for mobilizing marketed surplus. These include:

1   Surplus may be influenced by a number of *non-price* factors, such as the size and type of land holdings. In India the proportion of marketed output has been found to *fall* as the size-holding rises to about 10–15 acres and thereafter it rises (Narain, 1961). The implication of this finding is that a land ceiling up to 15 acres should not affect the flow of marketed surplus adversely, and a policy of land reform can be designed accordingly.
2   Most studies confirm the view that the relationship between the growth of output and marketed surplus is direct. Hence any increase in output due to a rise in acreage, more fertilizer, better seeds, or an increase in yield, should be helpful to generate greater surplus. The use of more inputs can be promoted by the extension of government subsidies for purchasing such inputs.
3   Natural factors such as rainfall, temperature, and quality of soil, can significantly affect the level of production and marketed surplus. The impact of soil erosion and desertification on crop-yield is now receiving increasing attention in the context of famine in the Sahel regions of Africa. The study of environmental effects on agricultural production is worthy of serious con-

sideration – future research and development may well be directed at innovations in agricultural technology which will be useful in the semi-arid regions.

4　Fiscal and monetary policies can be judiciously used to mobilize savings. With a rise in farm incomes, farmers can be given a number of incentives to save more. For instance, deposit rates of interest on savings, which are quite low in a large number of countries, can be raised. Indeed, real rates of interest in many LDCs are negative and hence the d∼sire to save can be very low. In many countries agricultural income is taxed at low rates and land tax forms a very small proportion (usually less than 5 per cent) of total tax revenue. There is considerable scope to increase taxes on agricultural income, particularly in those regions of LDCs where the agricultural sector has been successfully modernized and agricultural income has substantially increased. Reasons for *not* taxing expanding farm incomes have largely been political; but where the political will exists the case for taxing such incomes is strong.

10.4　Transformation of backward agriculture

The transformation of traditional agriculture in developing countries follows a number of phases. In the first phase we usually observe *subsistence farming*, where farmers generally produce for their own consumption. The main objective of production is to increase the chances of survival. In the second phase the growth of *mixed* farming is generally witnessed where farmers produce partly for 'home' consumption and partly for the market.

When production takes place mainly for the market, agriculture is said to be fully commercialized. Here the main objective of production is to 'maximize' profit, and farming becomes similar to industry.

Despite the presence of *subsistence* farming in many LDCs, a number of factors have contributed to its transformation into more developed agriculture. Where the process of transformation has been quite rapid, it has been labelled the *Green Revolution*. This is examined in section 10.5. First, however, it is worth examining the major causes of change in backward agriculture.

10.4.1　The major causes of agricultural transformation

New seed varieties

The invention of new, high-yielding varieties, HYVs, of seed (generally known as the 'miracle' seeds), for the production of a number of major food crops such as wheat and rice, opened up the possibility of increasing foodgrain production substantially in many developing countries. This type of seed was first used in Mexico, and hence it is sometimes called 'Mexican seed', or IR8. Its yield per acre is much higher than that of traditional varieties and it has been successfully adopted in different LDCs with different weather conditions. In South-East Asia, for example, it has vastly improved foodgrain production (see for example Lipton, 1985).

Due to the success of the miracle seeds, the proportion of total wheat area planted to the new HYVs of wheat in Indian Punjab rose from 3.6 per cent in 1966 to 65.6 per cent in 1970. In the major wheat-producing areas of Pakistan about 73 per cent of wheat acreage was sown with Mexican wheat, while the proportion of agriculturists adopting the HYV seeds in The Philippines was 15 per cent in 1970.

Population pressure

The pressure of population on land in many LDCs began to increase considerably after the end of the Second World War. One reason has been the decline in the mortality rate due to progress in medical science, and its impact on life expectancy and infant mortality. While the death rate in LDCs fell sharply, the birth rate remained fairly stable. This difference between a static birth rate and a falling death rate accounted for a sharp rise in the population growth rates, particularly in rural areas, and the pressure on agricultural land began to rise considerably in large parts of Asia. Countries such as India, Pakistan, Bangladesh and The Philippines began to look for ways to raise agricultural production. The severe drought and the subsequent famine condition in the middle-1960s made governments of South and South-East Asian countries aware of the urgent need to take action to alleviate famine, mass poverty and serious malnutrition. Hence more resources were devoted to agriculture to raise food production. In many cases, public policy played a vital role in creating a proper environment for the introduction of new technology in agriculture. For instance, public irrigation systems have been developed considerably, to facilitate the availability of water. The price of basic inputs such as fertilizer has been subsidized. Credit facilities have been extended to farmers with government support for the growth of credit co-operatives and commercial banks. In a number of LDCs, farmers' marketing problems have been mitigated with the introduction of public procurement systems. Finally, appropriate price incentive schemes have been adopted (for example, in India and Pakistan) to raise farm production and income, which has provided farmers with the necessary means to buy modern inputs.

In short it can be said that necessity, once again, became the mother of invention. Governments in many LDCs, faced with the urgent need to feed a large number of extra mouths, had to create a favourable climate for the introduction of new technology in agriculture.

Production shocks

Some LDCs (for example India, Pakistan) wished to achieve rapid industrialization during the 1950s and 1960s through planning, and massive public sector industrial investment. A large part of scarce foreign exchange was spent on imports of capital goods, and reserves were inadequate to pay for food imports. When food production – barely keeping abreast with the rise in population – received sudden huge 'shocks' (due to severe droughts or floods), the entire economy went out of gear. Food had to be imported and less foreign exchange was available to pay for the imports of capital goods. Thus the industrial growth rate was adversely affected. With the agricultural sector dominating the economy growth rates of GDP fell sharply. Once again, the need to inject more resources into agriculture was acknowledged and public policies (for example, expenditure and revenue policies) were manipulated to raise the flow of investment to agriculture.

Cropping intensity

The increase in cropping intensity due to the adoption of double- or multiple-cropping transformed the nature of traditional agriculture. Cropping intensity was low in most LDCs because the growing seasons of the traditional varieties of wheat and rice were quite long. But the availability of the new dwarf varieties of seed opened up the possibility of multiple-cropping in many areas.

Use of fertilizers and water

In most areas of backward agriculture the increasing use of fertilizer has played a crucial role in raising crop-yield and the level of foodgrain production substantially. Once again, public policies have significantly influenced this. Apart from a rise in physical production, the monetary returns from increased use of fertilizer for an individual farmer increased considerably. As governments in many LDCs subsidized the price of fertilizer to stimulate its demand, the real marginal rate of return from its use rose. The value/cost ratios (that is, the value of yield increases to the cost of fertilizer) in the use of fertilizer for many LDCs strongly indicate the need to provide such incentives to poor farmers (UNIDO, 1969). In fact, the impact of the use of new seeds and more fertilizers has been so significant that many regard the change in backward agriculture as a 'seed–fertilizer revolution' (Johnston and Cownie, 1969). It needs to be emphasized, however, that a greater use of fertilizer without a *timely and assured water supply* (via a well-developed system of irrigation) is unlikely to increase yield in the long run. Most empirical studies confirm that to sustain an increase in crop-yields over a long period it is imperative to provide *timely* water supply and the right quantities of fertilizer to agriculture (see, for example, Ishikawa, 1967). More recent evidence concludes that 'irrigation has made the largest contribution to increased agricultural production in much of Asia, North Africa, and the Middle East. In many areas it can double or treble yields during the main growing season, can make a second or even a third crop possible, and can sharply reduce the risk of crop failure' (World Bank, 1983).

10.4.2 Production and efficiency in underdeveloped agriculture

A number of writers have investigated problems of production and efficiency in traditional agriculture. T. W. Schultz, for example, argues that backward agriculture may be poor but 'efficient' (Schultz, 1964). Farmers in LDCs are regarded as efficient when they seek to maximize a certain objective function (for example, profit) subject to some constraints (for example, land and labour) and try to equalize benefits to costs at the margin. One of the tests of efficiency that Schultz suggests is for the existence of a positive or zero marginal productivity of labour. The 'dual-economy' models, developed by Lewis (1954), Fei and Ranis (1961), Jorgenson (1967) and others, assume the existence of some 'surplus labour' in underdeveloped agriculture because the marginal productivity of some labour (MPL) is zero or negligible. Despite zero marginal productivity, labourers remain employed in agriculture and receive positive wages. If we use the standard neoclassical theory, it is clear that this production process is 'inefficient' (since farmers will lose some potential profit by employing such labourers). Schultz, however, demonstrates that the MPL in backward agriculture is positive, and the employment of a labourer yielding a positive MP is justified and efficient as long as wages are approximately equal to the MPL. Schultz does observe the 'niggardliness' of traditional agriculture, but it 'is not a function of a unique set of preferences related to work and thrift' (p. vii). Indeed, on the basis of his empirical work in India and Africa, Schultz concludes that the view that 'a part of the labour working in agriculture in poor countries has a marginal productivity of zero . . . is a false doctrine' (p. 70). Farmers are poor but efficient because they do the best they can in a given environment.

Thrift and work are not enough to overcome the niggardliness of this type of agriculture. To produce an abundance of farm products requires that the farmer has access to, and has the skill and knowledge to use, what science knows about soils, plants, animals, and machines. To command farmers to increase production is doomed to failure even though they have access to knowledge. Instead, an approach that provides incentives and rewards to farmers is required (Schultz, 1964, p. 206).

Several criticisms have been levelled at Schultz's findings. First, it has been argued that 'disguised' unemployment (due to zero MPL) may be present in one region but not in others. Empirically it is important to know not only whether the MPL is equal to zero but also the amount of surplus labour and the effect of its withdrawal on output (see Sen, 1964, 1967, 1975). Second, Schultz failed to distinguish between the summer and the winter seasons of the production cycle. Mehra, on the basis of her study, has shown that the *summer* agricultural crop in India, following the influenza epidemic examined by Schultz, did not decline at all as a result of the epidemic (which reduced the size of the labour force). The observed decline was due to bad weather (Mehra, 1966). Note that if output remains constant after the withdrawal of labour, then this labour must be 'surplus'. Subsequently a more disaggregated analysis of farm-level data has shown that in India the MPL can be positive or zero, depending on the *type* of agriculture and the season (Desai and Mazumdar, 1970).

In summary, the evidence on zero MPL is rather inconclusive: the MPL can be positive in one country but not in others. Even within a country, the MPL in agriculture can differ significantly; thus any judgement on the nature of efficiency in underdeveloped agriculture needs to be stated carefully.

10.4.3   Efficiency and farm size

An interesting aspect of the analysis of efficiency in underdeveloped agriculture is related to the *scale of farm holding*, production levels and the proportion of marketed surplus. Empirical studies in the 1960s confirmed that farm size and output per acre are *inversely* correlated in Indian agriculture. In other words, output per *acre* falls as the size of the farm increases, from which it may be inferred that, *ceteris paribus*, small farms are more efficient than large farms. The main reasons for such an inverse relationship are as follows:

1   Poor farmers, when they are in distress, due to a sudden fall in production or bad debt obligations, sell *inferior-quality* land to large landowners. If this is true, then for an owner of a large farm the proportionate increase in output will be less than the increase in land. The small farmer may own a small plot of land, but since it is more fertile, productivity per acre will be higher.
2   Small farmers tend to use inputs such as labour more intensively and efficiently because they operate close to the level of their survival. Large farms, on the other hand, earn more income and they are therefore better able to absorb the 'supply shock' when the harvest fails. Small farmers do not have such a cushion and hence may maximize their total income rather than profit. Figure 10.4 illustrates this situation, showing the total costs, TC, and total revenue, TR, associated with a given size unit of land. It can be seen that as each unit of land is farmed more intensively, costs rise more steeply, while revenues rise at a declining rate. The large farmer produces OQ_1 output (per land unit) and the difference between total revenue and total cost is maximized and marginal revenue equals marginal cost (as shown by the tangents at P and R). The small farmer, however, follows a different objective function and wishes to maximize output. Hence, he produces OQ_2 where total revenue is equal to total cost (at M). Production is not carried out beyond Q_2 because this implies a loss for producers. Since the small farmer is following the 'survival algorithm' (stay alive as long as possible), he wants to maximize production per unit of land used by cultivating it as extensively as possible. Such a compulsion does not occur in the case of the larger farmer. (Technically, the small farmer is not maximizing output unless TR is horizontal. In figure 10.4 the small farmer is maximizing output subject to the constraint that he does not make a loss).
3   Following (2), it can be argued that large farmers produce on the basis of *capitalistic farming*, and as such employ labour up to the point where the marginal productivity is equal to the wage level. Hence, they produce only that output which maximizes profit. The small farmer, on the other hand, employs *family labour*, who can be used up to the point where MP = 0.
4   Large farmers use tenants and share croppers for production, but given a large number of *tenural disincentives* in LDCs, the use of inputs can become very inefficient. In many cases tenancy rights are vaguely defined, and few institutions exist to enforce such rights. As a result, tenants and sharecroppers seldom enjoy adequate protection by law. Poor tenants and sharecroppers are

at a further disadvantage as they cannot afford to buy legal services. Under such circumstances it is hardly surprising to observe inefficiency in the use of hired inputs. This problem is further aggravated due to land fragmentation and poor managerial and innovative abilities of large farmers, particularly when we distinguish the small *owner* from the large tenant/landlord. Many well-off farmers spend more in conspicuous consumption than in efficient investment. Mostly they live in towns rather than in the villages, and hence are regarded as '*absentee landlords*'. Given such a poor attitude towards improvement of agriculture it is not surprising that large farmers can use land inefficiently.

Farm size and 'surplus'

The size of land holdings can influence the amount of surplus. Evidence, albeit scant, tends to suggest that the *size* of land holding is not a very serious problem in constraining the supply (as long as it is not too low) if only the proportions of output marketed are considered. In India, land holdings of less than 5 acres supplied about 21 per cent of the value of their output. It is also reported that the proportion of marketed surplus to total output *falls* as farm size increases until size-holdings of 10–15 acres are reached, but increases thereafter (Narain, 1961, Krishna, 1967). If this holds in general, then a reduction of large size-holdings may actually *increase* total marketed surplus as long as small farms are viable.

Effects of technology

With the advent of new technology in underdeveloped agriculture, it is possible to envisage a change in the inverse correlations between farm size and output per acre, and between farm size and marketed surplus. Most literature on the Green Revolution (GR) suggests that resources (such as the new seeds, credit, water supply and fertilizer) tend to gravitate towards the large farms. The reasons for such unequal distribution of inputs in favour of large farms are easy to understand. Big landlords can use their wealth as the collateral to borrow from the organized financial agencies to buy modern inputs. Since banks tend to advance credit on the basis of orthodox principles of security and liquidity, the credit-worthiness of the large farmers is usually rated as higher than that of the small farmers. If farmers are responsive to economic incentives, and if they follow the principle of profit maximization (as many studies tend to confirm: see for example Askari and Cummings, 1976; Behrman, 1968; Ghatak, 1975b; Lipton, 1977) then large farmers should use their inputs efficiently. This should encourage a positive correlation between the size-holding and the output per acre. Some studies, however, still validate the inverse correlation hypothesis between farm size and output per acre due to the superior *technical* efficiency of the small farms, even when all farms, independent of size, seem to be price-efficient (Yotopoulos and Nugent, 1976). A more comprehensive survey for many LDCs also confirms the inverse relationship, and the difference in output per acre between large and small farms is mainly explained by differences in

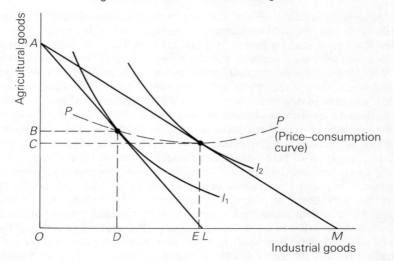

FIGURE 10.4   Farm size and profitability

cropping intensity and *product mix* rather than by crop-yield disparities (for details see Berry and Cline, 1979).

10.4.4   The role of institutions in agricultural transformation

The relationship between agricultural output, surplus, and size-holding and the analysis of the efficiency of different sizes of farms in LDCs prompts us to make some points regarding the role of institutions in traditional agriculture. This section considers first the effects of land reform, and then we examine the role of financial and marketing institutions.

Land reform

It seems that land reform can play a very important role in backward agriculture to provide incentives for increasing production. Land is the major form of wealth-holding in the rural economies of LDCs, and therefore a policy of redistribution of land should be welcomed for providing incentives to small farmers. It has also been demonstrated above that, both theoretically and empirically, small farms can be more efficient than large farms in LDCs. In addition it has been shown that the rate of adoption of new technology, *ceteris paribus*, has been *scale-neutral* in many LDCs. That is, the relative differences in the introduction of new technology to different size-holdings has been negligible (see Hayami and Ruttan, 1984). From the standpoint of equity, such a policy has the obvious merit of providing more resources to greater numbers of the rural population. If labour utilization and employment creation are major aims of public policy then, again, the case for land reform deserves special attention.

A programme of land reform with the twin objectives of equity and higher productivity can entail considerable economic *and* social costs. First, any redistribution of land in favour of small farms is likely to create *uncertainty*. Unless the government is stable, and the policy is enforced firmly, small farmers are unlikely to invest substantially as the stakes can be too high. The greater the period of uncertainty, the slower will be the rate of growth of investment and the rate of adoption of new technology. Second, a redistribution of land in favour of small farmers, by itself is unlikely to raise productivity unless such farmers are also provided with ancillary services such as marketing and crop insurance facilities, agricultural credit, education and extension services. Third, a more egalitarian system of land reform can actually generate 'spite-effects' whereby farmers who have lost land due to the reform programme may lose incentives to produce. They may even reduce investment in agriculture and transfer funds from the agricultural to the non-agricultural sector. Fourth, sometimes the political costs due to social conflicts generated by the land reform policy can be considerable. Finally, in some densely populated countries in South and South-East Asia, land alone is unlikely to solve the problem of massive rural poverty. Usually, *landless* labourers comprise a high proportion of rural households in these countries. A policy of land reform in such cases may be inadequate to provide viable farms for all households. Also in such countries, given the large population size, the compensation costs can be very high. Here a policy of tenancy reform can be much less expensive. The major disadvantage of this policy, however, is that it does not alter the balance of political power within the country (Mellor, 1966; World Bank, 1975).

The empirical evidence available so far from LDCs suggest mixed results. If success is defined in terms of higher production *and* productivity and greater equity, then the 'successful' group of countries should include Taiwan, Egypt and South Korea. The 'unsuccessful' group includes Mexico, Peru, Bolivia and Iraq. Inconclusive results are obtained in the case of India, chiefly due to large-scale evasion and incomplete implementation (World Bank, 1975; see also, Southworth and Johnston, 1967).

Financial institutions, rural credit policy and marketing efficiency

It is useful to analyse the nature and composition of the rural financial institutions in LDCs to formulate appropriate credit policies for promoting agricultural development. Rural money markets usually comprise moneylenders, merchants, landlords, cooperative credit societies, rural banks, and even friends and relatives. The demand for credit results both from consumption needs and from investment expenditure, but interest rates in rural areas are usually high. The reasons for such high rates are fairly complex. Some argue that interest rates are high because farmers' repayment capacity is low (due to low income) and hence they incur a high risk premium. High rates of interest therefore reflect a high probability of default. If real income goes up, then farmers' ability to repay will rise, the risk premium falls and the interest rate falls. (For details, see

Bottomley, 1971; Ghatak, 1975a, 1976, 1983.) It is thus necessary to raise agricultural income to reduce rural interest rates.

Others argue that in 'semi-feudal' agriculture landlords frequently act as creditors to their tenants and *consumption loans* are generally advanced by the landlords at high interest rates. As a result tenants remain heavily indebted to their landlords. Substantial debt and interest payments *in kind* by tenants usually imply a significant fall in the marketable surplus, and the poor tenant is forced to borrow at high rates for consumption. Thus the landlord 'exploits' the tenant both through usury and through his property rights on land. The situation for tenants worsens considerably when they have no access to the organized credit or goods market. They are compelled to sell to the landlord who pays a very low price for the crops just after the harvest. Hence the landlord assumes monopoly power and exploits it to gain maximum profit. He also underprices the value of loan repayment and interest by buying crops from his tenants when prices are very low (due to the seasonality of price movements). The landlord, however, charges a very high rate of interest against the future harvest and thus 'overprices' capital. In this way the landlord realises 'monopoly' and 'exploitative' profit (see Bhaduri, 1973, 1977).

If this argument is correct, it follows that farmers in LDCs are prevented by their landlords from adopting new technology which might raise their income and repayments, reduce indebtedness and thus release them from the clutches of landlord moneylenders. To maximize the income from usury, however, it is in the landlords' interests to keep farmers heavily indebted for as long as possible. Thus the introduction of technical progress in 'semi-feudal' agriculture will be prevented by landlords as long as the gains from usury are more than those from increased productivity.

Several criticisms can be levelled at this type of analysis of farmers' behaviour. First, given the complete dominance of landlords over poor farmers, and given the principle of profit/income maximization, a landlord can always maximize his income by 'appropriating' the gains from increased productivity due to the adoption of new technology, instead of resorting to usury. If landlords have enough control to prevent innovation, they should also have sufficient power to obtain from tenants the additional gains from the adoption of new technology. Second, usury as a 'mode of exploitation' can be unnecessary in 'labour-surplus' agriculture where the bargaining strength of the poor farmers is, in any case, very weak. Third, the empirical evidence available so far does not validate the strong linkages assumed between moneylenders, merchants and landlords (Bardhan, 1980; Bliss and Stern, 1982; Ghatak, 1983). Nor does it support the theory that gains from usury are always greater than those from rising productivity (for a theoretical analysis, see Srinivasan, 1979).

To assist small farmers it is therefore necessary to formulate an appropriate financial policy to raise the rate of growth of agricultural real incomes, increase repayment capacity, reduce the risk premium and usurious rural interest rates. However, it is also necessary to change the socioeconomic and legal frameworks which help to perpetuate the age-old system of land tenure which generates an unequal access to resources, including credit. A more egalitarian system of land reform can improve the creditworthiness of poor farmers, and organized credit institutions will be more willing to extend the necessary credit facilities. Another policy option is to raise the deposit interest rates offered by rural financial institutions. If farmers in LDCs respond to price signals, then there are good reasons to believe that such a policy can be useful to mobilize financial surpluses or savings (see Ghatak, 1981; Ghatak and Ingersent, 1984; McKinnon, 1973; Shaw, 1973).

As regards the problems of *marketing* in underdeveloped agriculture, we can identify three major constraints: (a) the weak bargaining power of producers, (b) infrastructural deficiencies, and (c) producers' lack of information. Removal of infrastructure deficiences (for example development of rural transport and communications) is likely to develop rural markets considerably, reduce costs and aid the process of general development.

It is well known that in LDCs small farmers are generally unorganized, and their bargaining position in the market place is rather weak. Their position is further undermined by lack of information on current market prices, crop prospects and expected changes in demand. Any policy to improve the flow of information to farmers and improve their bargaining power will enhance their economic standing.

10.5 Technical change in agriculture

10.5.1 Institutions and technical change

The role of institutions in inducing technical progress has been a matter of considerable interest to economists. We have already discussed the Malthusian theory of interaction between economic growth and population. The economy reaches a state of stagnation unless technical progress shifts the production function upwards (see figure 10.1). However, such a shift is assumed to be 'manna from heaven'. Technical progress is, thus, completely exogenous and no economic theory is advanced to explain it.

Boserup, on the other hand, argues that a stock of unused inventions always remains at the disposal of farmers. Hence, even in LDCs, the elasticity of food supply *with respect to population growth* should be high. In backward agriculture, farmers will adopt improved technology only when population pressure forces them to do so (Boserup, 1965). Many, however, consider the underlying assumption of Boserup's 'contra-Malthusian' theory rather dubious.

Hayami and Ruttan provide an interesting alternative theory of technical change in backward agriculture (Hayami and Ruttan, 1971). This is now labelled as the theory of induced technical and institutional change. In short, the theory states that research and development which precedes inventions and innovations is generally induced by market forces. Relative scarcities in factor supplies (for example, land and capital in underdeveloped agriculture) will result in relative changes in factor prices. This will induce a derived demand for technical improvement to carry out the necessary factor substitution of cheap inputs for more scarce ones. For instance, in a *land-scarce* economy such as India, we should expect a technological improvement in agriculture which will be land-saving and yield-increasing (per acre of land) as improved irrigation, more fertilizer and better seeds are substituted for land to increased food production.

Hayami and Ruttan then demonstrate with a 'meta-production function' how induced technical progress enlarges the elasticity of response to a change in factor prices. A drop in the fertilizer to product price ratio will lead to a greater use of fertilizer. But increases in the amount of fertilizer used and crop-yield will be comparatively small unless new crop varieties are developed which are more responsive than traditional varieties to fertilizer use. The model stresses the link between the technological input and the discovery of innovations which widen the scope for factor substitution due to changes in price.

Figure 10.5 explains: the horizontal axis measures units of fertilizer and the vertical axis measures units of land. However, below the origin (O), the vertical axis measures R and D activities in the search for more fertilizer-responsive crops. In the top half of the figure the short-run iso-product curves show the same level of output but different varieties of crop. Thus the curve U_1 is more fertilizer-responsive than U_0. With an initial fertilizer–land price ratio P_0, the optimal (least-cost) use of land and fertilizer is OL_1 and OF_1 respectively, and the corresponding R and D activity is OT_1. A decline in the fertilizer–land price

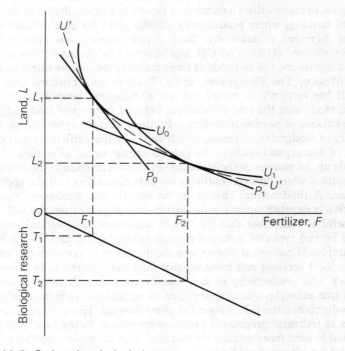

FIGURE 10.5 Induced technical change

ratio will give us the line P_1, which is matched by a greater research input, OT_2. The level of fertilizer use at OF_2 is matched with the discovery of crop type U_1. The optimal use of factors is now given by OL_2 land and OF_2 fertilizer. Note that there has been a considerable rise in the use of the cheaper input and a fall in the use of the scarce input. This substitution is taking place along the long-run isoquant U', which is the envelope of the short-run isoquants. The 'meta-production function' is really a family of such short-run isoquants.

10.5.2 The impact of technical progress: the Green Revolution

The theory of induced factor substitution can be extended to all factors and from biological to mechanical technology. If the price of labour increases relative to that of capital, then farmers will be induced to substitute machinery for labour and technical progress will be labour-saving. This has been witnessed in the case of agricultural development in the USA, where agriculture has been substantially mechanized. In the case of Japanese agricultural development, given relative land scarcity, improvements in yield-increasing biological technology were dominant. Elasticities of factor substitution can be estimated and used as indicative of the influence of induced innovations on the rate of growth of output. *A priori*, a *fixed* technology can afford only a little scope for factor substitution.

While in some areas of LDCs we still observe subsistence farming with old technologies, in many others a number of factors have contributed to the growth of modern farming, where productivity (chiefly yield per acre of land) of some crops has increased substantially. Such a phenomenon has been called the 'Green Revolution' (GR). The GR was observed in the late 1960s and early 1970s in a significant rise in yields of some major crops such as wheat and rice in parts of Mexico, The Philippines, India, Pakistan and Thailand (see section 10.4.1). It has certainly increased the overall economic growth rates of these countries, moderated the rate of inflation, reduced imports of food and thereby eased the balance of payments problem. Further, with the spread of the GR the availability of foodgrains increases, which aids nutrition, efficiency and the pro-ductivity of labour, and leads to the general improvement of welfare. The GR also speeds up the process of social change and modernization as the extension of rural education alters farmers' outlooks towards risk-taking and the appropriate family size. A fundamental change in outlook for the maximum number of farmers clearly depends upon a wide distribution of gains from the GR.

It is useful to remember that the GR in underdeveloped agriculture can be explained by two types of technical change: (a) biological; and (b) mechanical. Good examples of biological innovations are the use of better seeds (for example, IR8 or its local version) and more organic fertilizers (in the right doses at the right time). The productivity of *land* usually rises in such cases. When more machines (for example, tractors) are used in agriculture (which usually raises *labour* productivity), the GR is regarded as mechanical. Here, the capital–labour ratio rises as technical progress is capital-augmenting. In the case of biological GR, as land is used more intensively (via double or multiple-cropping systems), the demand for labour should rise.

Major features of the GR

On the basis of considerable evidence available so far, the following features of the GR deserve special emphasis:

1 Although different rates of adoption of new technology by tenure and farm size have been observed, neither tenure nor farm size has been a very significant constraint on the adoption of these new techniques.

2 In a large number of cases, neither tenure nor farm size has been considered as an important source of differential rates of growth in agricultural productivity (see Azam, 1973; Managhas, 1974; Soejono, 1976). However, it is likely that in the case of poor farmers (with little land) and agricultural labourers, these constraints will be binding.

3 In some LDCs the introduction of the new technology has increased the demand for farm labour and induced a rise in real wages (Johl, 1975; Sidhu, 1974a). However, within a country, evidence of declines in rural real wages and employment due to mechanization is also available for some regions.

4 The onset of the GR has increased the existing disparity of income distribution in many cases. Large-scale landlords have benefited *relatively* more than the tenants and agricultural labourers (Mellor, 1976). However, it is important to note that in absolute terms there has generally been a significant increase in employment and rural wages for small farmers in areas which experienced the GR.

Distribution of GR benefits

Several factors are responsible for the differential growth rates of agriculture in different regions of the same country. These include:

1 differences in the availability of water, fertilizer, better seeds, pesticides and credit facilities;

2 differences in the flow of information about the availability of inputs, their prices, and marketing facilities;

3 differences in the attidue of farmers towards risks, as well as difference in entrepreneurship.

However, if farmers in LDCs (and elsewhere) are found to be risk-neutral or risk-averse, then they should not be regarded as 'irrational'. Farmers in poor countries may seem to be unresponsive to proposed technical change due to *perceived* high risks and low returns (Griffin, 1979). In these circumstances public policy can play a very useful role in creating a proper environment (by providing education, marketing and extension services, insurance schemes, etc.) for the modernization of agriculture.

What initiated the GR?

The main reasons for the emergence of the GR can be summarised briefly:

1 The population explosion of many LDCs due to a substantial fall in the death

rate without much decline in the birth rate sometimes led to an absolute *fall* in the availability of foodgrain per head. The urgent need to feed extra populations left governments in LDCs no choice but to raise food production.

2 A policy of rapid industrialization and 'urban bias' adopted in some LDCs led to the relative neglect of agriculture. A large part of valuable foreign exchange was spent for importing capital goods. When food production suffered badly due to natural causes (for example drought and flood), little foreign exchange was available to import food and other agricultural inputs. An inadequate growth of food production, coupled with rising population growth rates, led to massive poverty and near-famine conditions in parts of South Asia and Africa. Governments of these countries were obliged to take urgent action to raise food production. Fortunately, by the middle of the 1960s the new varieties of seed were invented and results of the use of the new seed variety showed dramatic success in Mexico and a number of other LDCs in South and South-East Asia. *Total* production began to rise substantially as more land was taken under HYV cultivation.

3 Increases in cropping intensity has been a significant factor in the rise in yield and production in areas affected by the GR. Previously the growing seasons used to be longer due to the use of traditional varieties of seeds. With the increasing use of HYV seeds the growing seasons became shorter, and double- and sometimes multiple-cropping systems led to more intensive use of land and higher food production. In some cases, use of farm machinery also helped to raise farm output.

4 Agricultural price policy, taxes and subsidies also helped to create a favourable condition for the introduction of the new technology. The favourable internal terms of trade (that is, the ratio between agricultural and industrial prices) provided farmers with the necessary *incentives* to adopt the new technology. Similarly, the necessary adjustments in taxes and subsidies for the purchase of vital inputs such as fertilizer induced farmers to use more inputs and raise production, (see, for example, Brown, 1971; Nulty, 1972; Ranadhawa, 1974, Sidhu, 1974 a,b).

The use of public policy has not always been an unmixed blessing, however. Sometimes highly overvalued exchange rates, discriminatory rates of tariff favouring imports of tractors, and the provision of agricultural credit at a very low rate of interest, have resulted in the use of *capital-intensive* techniques in labour-surplus agriculture. In a large number of cases resources have tended to gravitate towards the better-off farmers. They could provide satisfactory collateral (for example, their large plots of land) to obtain a large proportion of the total credit to buy crucial inputs. Hence, many argue that the GR had led to increasing concentration of wealth and power. The rich landlord has been made richer, and the poor, poorer. Thus, although the GR has increased production it has also worsened the existing inequalities in the distribution of income and wealth in the rural sector (Junankar, 1978). It is thus useful to analyse the impact of the GR on factor shares and income distribution.

10.5.3 The GR and income distribution: a simple model

We assume that the GR can be *both* technological and biological. Thus it can be both capital-augmenting and labour-using. To understand the effect on cost, it is useful to know whether cost increases due to biological innovations are greater or less than the reduction of cost because of mechanical innovations (Srivastava *et al.*, 1971). Biological innovations increase cost, while mechanical innovations reduce costs because the former require complementary labour. It is generally acknowledged that the adoption of new technology lowers the *unit* cost of production and increases the profit or net income of farmers. As more factors are used to raise production, the *absolute* income of all factors should increase. The *relative* changes in factor income depend, *inter alia*, upon the following:

1 the nature of technical progress (is it neutral or non-neutral?);
2 changes in the capital–labour ratios after the introduction of new technology;
3 changes in the sum of production elasticities under technical progress.

To illustrate changes in factor shares, let us assume a Cobb–Douglas production function of the following type:

$$Q = aL^{\alpha}B_1^{\beta}B_2^{\gamma}C_1^{\delta}C_2^{\varrho}$$

where:

Q = crop production;
L = land;
B_1 = human labour;
B_2 = bullock labour;
C_1 = machinery and equipment;
C_2 = non-mechanical inputs (better seeds, fertilizer, etc.);
$\alpha, \beta, \gamma, \delta$ and ϱ are therefore the relevant partial elasticities.

We know that the ratios of partial elasticities show the relative factor shares and the use of a Cobb–Douglas production function implies that the value of the elasticity of substitution (the ratio of a percentage change of factors to a percentage change in relative factor prices) is unity. In addition, it is assumed that factor shares change only when a new input, which may be either a substitute or a complement to existing inputs, embodies technical progress (see Brown, 1971; Ghatak, 1986; Srivastava *et al.*, 1971).

Assume now (realistically) increased use of C_1 and C_2, embodying technical progress. A new production function can be written as

$$Q' = a'\ L^{\alpha'}\ B_1^{\beta'}\ B_2^{\gamma'}\ C_1^{\delta'}\ C_2^{\varrho'}$$

where 'primed' parameters are the new partial elasticities. Clearly C_1 is capital-augmenting (labour-saving) and C_2 is labour-augmenting (capital-saving). Empirical evidence suggests that adoption of these different types of technical progress in underdeveloped agriculture have had different impacts on employment i.e. C_1

is becoming more labour-saving but C_2 more capital-saving (Billings and Singh, 1970; Hayami and Ruttan, 1984; Khan, 1975; Nulty, 1972; Ruttan, 1977; Sen, 1975). The overall effect on employment can be shown by estimating the values of β, β', δ, δ', ϱ, ϱ'. Thus, when $\beta'/\delta' < \beta/\delta$, a fall in the share of labour should be expected with respect to C_1. When C_2 is a complementary input to labour (for example, new seeds and fertilizer) we can expect $\beta'/\varrho' > \beta/\varrho$.

Generally, the GR will lower labour's share (wages) in national income if the following condition holds:

$$\left[\frac{\beta}{\delta + \varrho} \right] > \left[\frac{\beta'}{\delta' + \varrho'} \right]$$

Empirical evidence does not help to draw any unequivocal conclusion regarding movements of real wages in areas affected by the GR. Within the same country, real wages in rural households have gone up in some areas but not in others. In a few they have actually gone down. On balance, it seems that in most cases average rural real wages and farmers' incomes have increased. Large-scale farmers seem to have benefited relatively more than medium- and small-scale farmers. Some argue that the GR has increased inequality, and that farmers do not always follow the principle of profit maximization in LDCs (Junankar, 1978, 1980). In some cases the effect of the *mechanical* GR has been a reduction of employment and lower real wages for an increasing number of tenants, sharecroppers and landless labourers (see for example, Byres, 1972, 1981; Falcon, 1970; Lipton, 1977; Palmer, 1974; Wharton, 1969; for a debate on the impact of GR on income distribution in Pakistan, see for example Chaudhury, 1982, 1983; Khan, 1975, 1983). However, a review of the literature suggests that the adoption of new technology into traditional wheat and rice production systems in Asia has resulted in significant increases of annual employment per unit of cropped area, and in some cases in higher cropping intensity (Bartsch, 1977; see also Barker and Cordova, 1978; Ranade and Herdt, 1978; Sidhu, 1974a,b). Nevertheless, in a number of villages the use of inappropriate technology has reduced rural income of a certain *class* of agricultural labour such as tenants, sharecroppers and landless labourers (see for example, Gaiha, 1985).

Thus it would seem that any long-term solution for the alleviation of poverty should include a number of *economic and institutional reforms*: (a) a better minimum rural wage for landless labourers and tenants; (b) a fairer system of land reform to provide incentives and endowments to a large class of peasants; (c) a simplification of the present complex system of implicit and explicit tenancy laws and contracts and their alteration to improve the bargaining position of the weakest and economically most vulnerable sections of the population; (d) more investment in agriculture in particular and the rural sector in general for the simultaneous growth of *both* agriculture and industry; and (e) the *political* will to implement a programme of reform. (On tenancy reform, see Bardhan, 1977; Bardhan and Rudra, 1978; Cheung, 1969).

10.6 Famine and agriculture

It is ironical to reflect that, even in the midst of plenty, people perish due to hunger, malnutrition, poverty and famine. Famine may occur due to a shortfall in the availability of food. Sen uses the term 'food availability decline' (FAD) to signify the most obvious explanation (see Sen, 1981 for an illuminating analysis). However, after examining certain major famines in India, Bangladesh and Ethiopia, Sen argues that the FAD explanation of famine is either incomplete or unconvincing. Conversely, Sen contends that famine occurs when those who starve lack the means to obtain enough food to remain alive. This is Sen's explanation of 'entitlement failure'. In cases of *direct* entitlement failures, a farmer fails to feed himself and his family by self-supply or trade because of crop failure. *Trade* entitlement failures are, however, related to those who can usually afford to purchase enough food, but are priced out of the market by a sudden rise in demand. Sen calls the latter a 'boom famine', which may arise due to a massive rise in military expenditure, whereas famines due to direct entitlement failures are labelled as 'slump famine'. The interesting implication of Sen's theory is that famines can occur without an overall FAD.

The FAD and the entitlement failure explanations of famine are not, of course, always mutually exclusive. Sometimes FAD may be the dominant cause of famine. However, Sen shows that in the Bengal famine of 1943 (when about 5 million people died) per capita food availability was not very low. Rather, the real incomes of the major victims of the famine (for example, landless labourers, tenants, etc.) fell drastically due to a steep rise in food prices, increased unemployment, adverse weather conditions and dislocation of the Indian economy due to the war with Japan (Sen, 1981).

10.6.1 Policies for alleviating poverty and famine

Several important policies can be formulated to prevent the occurrence of poverty and famine in underdeveloped agriculture in the light of the analysis of their causes.

1 Increasing food supplies (domestic and/or imported) by shifting more resources into food production. Sometimes a more rational allocation of resources within the agricultural sector can increase food production. Food aid can help in the short run but a long-run solution lies in raising domestic food production by the provision of appropriate incentives and proper institutional and topographical reform (for example aforestation).
2 Redistribution of food supplies from the 'over-fed' to the 'under-fed', though such a policy can only be used occasionally.
3 A package of economic and social reforms to reduce population growth rates in the rural sector. A fall in fertility can be brought about by increasing literacy, particularly among females. A better system of social welfare, which includes old-age pensions and an improved family planning service in rural areas, can reduce infant mortality and produce a sustained rise in real per capita incomes (see, for example, Birdsall, 1980; World Bank, 1981).

10.7 Conclusions

This survey has shown the important role that agriculture can play in LDCs. Two major reasons for agricultural impoverishment are inadequate access to land and capital for the majority of farmers, and technological backwardness. It follows that, to raise farm income and output, it is imperative to relax constraints on the availability *and* use of resources, introduce technical progress in agriculture and alter attitudes among (understandably) risk-averse farmers. A system of proper incentives coupled with necessary institutional reform can improve backward agriculture considerably. A more equal system of income distribution can be achieved after raising production and income by a careful use of public policy to promote biological rather than mechanical innovation.

REFERENCES

Askari, H. and Cummings, J. T. 1976. *Agricultural Supply Response: A Survey of the Econometric Evidence*. New York: Praeger.

Azam, K. M. 1973. The future of the green revolution in West Pakistan: a choice of strategy. *International Journal of Agrarian Affairs*, 5, 404–29.

Bandyopadhyay, K. 1976. *Agricultural Development in China and India*. Delhi: Allied Publishers.

Bardhan, P. K. 1970. Green revolution and agricultural labourers. *Economic and Political Weekly*, 5, 1239–46.

Bardhan, P. K. 1977. Variations in forms of tenancy in a peasant economy. *Journal of Development Economics*, 4, 105–18.

Bardhan, P. K. 1980. Interlocking factor markets and agrarian development: a review of issues. *Oxford Economic Papers*, 32, 82–98.

Bardhan, P. K. and Rudra, A. 1978. Interlinkage of land, labour and credit relations: an analysis of village survey data in East Asia. *Economic and Political Weekly*, 13, 367–84.

Barker, R. W. and Cordova, V. 1978. Labour utilization in rice production. In R. Barker and Y. Hayami (eds), *Economic Consequences of the New Rice Technology*. Manila, Philippines: International Rice Research Institute (IRRI), pp. 113–36.

Barker, R. W., Meyers, C., Cristostomo, C. and Duff, M. 1972. Employment and technological change in Philippine agriculture. *International Labour Review*, 106, 111–39.

Bartsch, W. H. 1977. *Employment and Technology Choice in Asian Agriculture*. New York: Praeger.

Behrman, J. A. 1968. *Supply Response in Underdeveloped Agriculture: A Case Study of Four Major Annual Crops in Thailand, 1937–1963*. Amsterdam: North-Holland.

Berry, R. A. and Cline, W. R. 1979. *Agrarian Structure and Productivity in Developing Countries*, Baltimore: Johns Hopkins University Press.

Bhaduri, A. 1973. A study of agricultural backwardness in semi-feudalism. *Economic Journal*, 83, 120–37.

Bhaduri, A. 1977. On the formation of usurious interest rates in backward agriculture. *Cambridge Journal of Economics*, 1, 341–52.

Bhalla, S. 1979. Real wages of agricultural labourers in the Punjab. *Economic and Political Weekly*, 14 (June), A.57–A.68.

Billings, M. H. and Singh, A. 1970. Mechanization and rural employment with some implications for income distribution. *Economic and Political Weekly*, 5 (June), A.61–A.72.

Binswanger, H. P. and Ruttan, V. W. (eds). 1978. *Induced Innovation: Technology, Institutions and Development*. Baltimore: Johns Hopkins University Press.

Birdsall, N. 1980. *Population and Poverty in the Developing World*. World Bank, Staff Working Paper No. 404. Washington, DC: World Bank.

Bliss, C. and Stern, N. 1982. *Palanpur: A Study of an Indian Village*. Oxford: Basil Blackwell.

Blyn, G. 1983. The green revolution revisited. *Economic Development and Cultural Change*, 31, 705–25.

Boserup, E. 1965. *The Conditions of Agricultural Growth*. London: George Allen and Unwin.

Bottomley, A. 1971. *Factor Pricing and Economic Growth in Underdeveloped Rural Areas*. London: Crosby Lockwood.

Brown, D. 1971. *Agricultural Development in India's Districts*. Cambridge, Mass.: Harvard University Press.

Brown, L. 1970. *Seeds of Change: The Green Revolution and Development in the 1970s*. London: Praeger.

Byres, T. J. 1972. The dialectic of India's green revolution. *South Asian Review*, 5, 99–116.

Byres, T. J. 1981. The new technology, class formation and class action in the Indian countryside. *Journal of Peasant Studies*, 8, 405–54.

Chaudhury, M. G. 1982. Green revolution and redistribution of rural incomes: Pakistan's experience. *Pakistan Development Review*, 21, 173–205.

Chaudhury, M. G. 1983. Green revolution: a reply. *Pakistan Development Review*, 22, 117–24.

Cheung, S. 1969. *The Theory of Share Tenancy*. Chicago: Chicago University Press.

Desai, M. and Mazumdar, D. 1970. A test of the hypothesis of disguised unemployment. *Economica*, 37, 39–53.

Dixit, A. 1968. The optimal development in the labour surplus economy. *Review of Economic Studies*, 35, 23–34.

Dobb, M. 1966. *Soviet Economic Development Since 1917*, 6th edn. London: Routledge and Kegan Paul.

Falcon, W. P. 1970. The green revolution: generations of problems. *American Journal of Agricultural Economics*, 52, 698–710.

Farmer, B. (ed.) 1977. *Green Revolution*. London: Macmillan.

Fei, J. C. H. and Ranis, G. 1964. *Development of the Labour Surplus Economy: Theory and Policy*, Homewood, Ill.: Irwin.

Gaiha, R. 1985. Poverty, technology and infrastructure in rural India. *Cambridge Journal of Economics*, 9, 221–43.

Ghatak, S. 1975a. Rural interest rates in the Indian economy. *Journal of Development Studies*, 11, 190–201.

Ghatak, S. 1975b. Marketed surplus in Indian agriculture: theory and practice. *Oxford Bulletin of Economics and Statistics*, 37, 143–53.

Ghatak, S. 1976. *Rural Money Markets in India*. Delhi: Macmillan.

Ghatak, S. 1981. *Technology Transfer to Developing Countries: The Case of the Fertilizer Industry*. Greenwich, Conn.: JAI Press.

Ghatak, S. 1983. On interregional variations in rural interest rates in India. *Journal of Developing Areas*, 18, 21–34.

Ghatak, S. 1986. *An Introduction to Development Economics*. London: George Allen and Unwin.

Ghatak, A. and Ghatak, S. 1985. Output response in underdeveloped agriculture: a case study in West-Bengal districts. *Indian Journal of Economics*, 66, 115-23.

Ghatak, S. and Ingersent, K. 1984. *Agriculture and Economic Development*. Baltimore: Johns Hopkins University Press, and London: Wheatsheaf.

Griffin, K. 1979. *The Political Economy of Agrarian Change: An Essay on the Green Revolution*, (2nd edn.). London: Macmillan.

Hayami, Y. 1971. Elements of induced innovation: a historical perspective for the green revolution. *Explorations in Economic History*, 8, 445-72.

Hayami, Y. 1981. Induced innovation, green revolution and income distribution: comment. *Economic Development and Cultural Change*, 30, 169-76.

Hayami, Y. and Ruttan, V. W. 1971. *Agricultural Development: An International Perspective*. Baltimore: Johns Hopkins University Press.

Hayami, Y. and Ruttan, V. W. 1984. The green revolution: inducement and distribution. *Pakistan Development Review*, 23, 37-63.

Ishikawa, S. 1967. *Economic Development in Asian Perspective*. Tokyo: Kunokuniya Publishing.

Johl, S. S. 1975. Gains from the Green Revolution. How have they been shared in the Punjab? *Journal of Development Studies*, 11, 178-89.

Johnston, B. F. and Cownie, J. 1969. The seed-fertilizer revolution and labour force absorption. *American Economic Review*, 59, 569-82.

Johnston, B. F. and Mellor, J. 1961. The role of agriculture in economic development. *American Economic Review*, 51, 566-93.

Jorgenson, D. W. 1967. Surplus agricultural labour and the development of a dual economy. *Oxford Economic Papers*, 19, 288-312.

Junankar, P. N. 1978. Has the green revolution increased inequality? *Development Research Digest*, 16-17.

Junankar, P. N. 1980. Do Indian farmers maximise profits? *Journal of Development Studies*, 17, 48-61.

Kanbur, R. and McIntosh, J. 1984. *Dual Economy Models: A Survey*. Paper presented to the ESRC Development Economics Study Group Annual Conference, University of Warwick.

Khan, M. H. 1975. *The Economics of the Green Revolution in Pakistan*. New York: Praeger.

Khan, M. H. 1983. Green revolution and redistribution of rural incomes: Pakistan's experience – a comment. *Pakistan Development Review*, 22, 47-56.

Krishna, R. 1967. Agricultural price policy and economic development. In H. M. Southworth and B. F. Johnston (eds), *Agricultural Development and Economic Growth*. Ithaca: Cornell University Press, pp. 497-540.

Kuznets, S. 1961. Economic growth and the contribution of agriculture: Notes on measurement. *International Journal of Agrarian Affairs*, 3, 56-75.

Lewis, W. A. 1954. Economic development with unlimited supplies of labour. *Manchester School*, 22, 139-91.

Lipton, M. 1977. *Why Poor People Stay Poor: Urban Bias in World Development*. London: Temple Smith.

Lipton, M. 1985. *Modern Varieties, International Agricultural Research and the Poor*. Paper presented to the Development Studies Association. Annual Conference, University of Bath.

Managhas, M. 1974. Economic aspects of agrarian reform under the new society. *Philippine Review of Business and Economics*, 11, 175-87.

Mathur, P. N. and Ezekiel, H. 1961. Marketed surplus of food and price fluctuations in a developing economy. *Kyklos*, 14, 396–408.

McKinnon, R. I. 1973. *Money and Capital in Economic Development*. Washington, DC: The Brookings Institution.

Mehra, S. 1966. Surplus labour in Indian agriculture. *Indian Economic Review*, 1, 111–29. Reprinted in P. K. Chaudhury (ed.) 1972. *Readings in Indian Agricultural Development*. London: George Allen and Unwin, pp. 34–49.

Mehra, S. 1981. *Instability in Indian Agriculture in the Context of New Technology*. Manila, Philippines: IRRI. RR. 25.

Mellor, J. W. 1966. *Economics of Agricultural Development*. Ithaca: Cornell University Press.

Mellor, J. 1976. *The New Economics of Growth: A Strategy for India and the Developing World*. Ithaca: Cornell University Press.

Narain, D. 1961. *Distribution of the Marketed Surplus of Agricultural Produce by Size-Level of Holding in India: 1950–51*. Bombay: Asia Publishers.

Nulty, L. 1972. *The Green Revolution in West Pakistan*, New York: Praeger.

Palmer, I. 1974. *The New Rice in Asia: Conclusions from Four Country Studies*. Geneva: UN Research Institute for Social Development.

Parikh, A. 1971. Farm supply response. A distributed lag analysis. *Oxford Bulletin of Economics and Statistics*, 33, 57–72.

Parikh, A. and Shah, C. H. 1984. Poverty, growth and policy options. *Canadian Journal of Development Studies*, 5, 257–72.

Preobrazhenski, E. A. 1965. *The New Economics*. Oxford: Oxford University Press.

Ranade, G. G. and Herdt, R. W. 1978. Shares of farm earnings from rice production. In R. Barker and Y. Hayami (eds), *Economic Consequences of the New Rice Technology*. Los Banos, Philippines: IRRI.

Ranadhawa, N. S. 1974. *Green Revolution: Case Study in Punjab*. Bombay: Allied Publishing.

Rao, C. H. H. 1975. *Technological Change and Distribution of the Gains in Indian Agriculture*. Delhi: Macmillan.

Ruttan, V. W. 1977. The green revolution: seven generalizations. *International Development Review*, 19, 16–23.

Schultz, T. W. 1964. *Transforming Traditional Agriculture*. New Haven: Yale University Press.

Sen, A. K. 1966. Peasants and dualism with or without surplus labour. *Journal of Political Economy*, 74, 425–50.

Sen, A. K. 1967. Surplus labour in India: a critique of Schultz's statistical tests. *Economic Journal*, 77, 154–61.

Sen, A. K. 1975. *Employment, Technology and Development*. Oxford: Oxford University Press.

Sen, A. K. 1981. *Poverty and Famines. An Essay on Entitlements and Deprivation*. Oxford: Basil Blackwell.

Sen, S. 1975. *Reaping the Green Revolution*. Delhi/New York: Tata–McGraw-Hill.

Shaw, E. S. 1973. *Financial Deepening in Economic Development*. New York: Oxford University Press.

Sidhu, S. S. 1974a. Economics of technical change in wheat production in the Indian Punjab. *American Journal of Agricultural Economics*, 56, 217–26.

Sidhu, S. S. 1974b. Relative efficiency in wheat production in the Indian Punjab. *American Economic Review*, 64, 742–51.

Soejono, I. 1976. Growth and distributional changes in paddy farm income in Central Java. *Indonesian Journal of Social and Economic Affairs*, 3, 26–32.

Southworth, H. M. and Johnston, B. F. (eds). 1967. *Agricultural Development and Economic Growth*. Ithaca: Cornell University Press.

Srinivasan, T. N. 1979. Agricultural backwardness under semi-feudalism. *Economic Journal*, 89, 416–19.

Srinivasan, T. N. and Bardhan, P. K. (eds). 1975. *Poverty and Income Distribution in India*. Calcutta: Statistical Publishing House.

Srivastava, U., Crown, R. and Heady, E. 1971. Green revolution and farm income distribution. *Economic and Political Weekly*, 6 (December), A.163–A.170.

UNIDO. 1969. *Fertilizer Industry*, E69 (vol. 6). Vienna: UN.

Verghese, M. 1977. *Issues Facing the World Fertilizer Industry*. Vienna: UN.

Wharton, C. R. 1969. The green revolution: cornucopia or Pandora's box? *Foreign Affairs*, 47, 464–76.

World Bank. *World Development Report*. 1975, 1981, 1982, 1983, 1984, Washington, DC: World Bank.

Yotopoulos, P. A. and Nugent, J. B. 1976. *Economics of Development*. New York: Harper and Row.

Bibliography of surveys/reviews in development economics, 1970–86

Norman Gemmell

Anderson, D. 1982. Small industries in developing countries: a discussion of issues. *World Development*, 10, 913–48.

Arndt, H. W. 1981. Economic development: a semantic history. *Economic Development and Cultural Change*, 29, 457–66.

Askari, H. and Cummings, J. T. 1976. *Agricultural Supply Response: a Survey of the Econometric Evidence*. New York: Praeger.

Bacha, E. and Taylor, L. 1973. Foreign exchange shadow prices. A critical review of the current theories. In R. S. Eckaus and P. N. Rosenstein-Rodan (eds), *Analysis of Development Problems*. Amsterdam: North-Holland, pp. 3–29.

Baer, W. 1972. Import-substitution and industrialization in Latin America: experiences and interpretations. *Latin American Research Review*, 7, 95–122.

Balassa, B. 1982. Disequilibrium analysis in developing countries: an overview. *World Development*, 10, 1027–38.

Bardhan, P. K. 1980. Interlocking factor markets and agrarian development: a review of issues. *Oxford Economic Papers*, 32, 82–98.

Baron, C. 1978. Appropriate technology comes of age: a review of some recent literature and aid policy statements. *International Labour Review*, 117, 625–34.

Berry, R. A. and Sabot, R. H. 1978. Labour market performance in developing countries: a survey. *World Development*, 6, 1199–1242.

Bird, R. M. 1978. Assessing tax performance in developing countries: a critical review of the literature. In J. F. J. Toye (ed.), *Taxation and Economic Development*. London: Frank Cass, pp. 33–61.

Bird, R. M. and De Wulf, L. 1973. Taxation and income distribution in Latin America: a critical review of empirical studies. *IMF Staff Papers*, 20, 639–82.

Birdsall, N. 1977. Analytical approaches to the relationship of population growth and development. *Population and Development Review*, 3, 63–92.

Bruton, H. J. 1970. The import-substitution strategy of economic development. *Pakistan Development Review*, 10, 123–46.

Bruton, H. J. 1973. Economic development and labour use: a review. *World Development*, 1. Reprinted in E. O. Edwards (ed.). 1974. *Employment in Developing Nations*. New York: Columbia University Press, pp. 49–82.

Cassen, R. H. 1976. Population and development: a survey. *World Development*, 4, 785-830.

Cline, W. R. 1975. Distribution and development: a survey of literature. *Journal of Development Economics*, 1, 359-400.

Corden, W. M. 1975. The costs and consequences of protection: a survey of empirical work. In P. B. Kenen (ed.), *International Trade and Finance: Frontiers for Research*. Cambridge: Cambridge University Press, pp. 51-91.

Cutler, P. 1984. The measurement of poverty: a review of attempts to quantify the poor, with special reference to India. *World Development*, 12, 1119-30.

Dahlman, C. and Westphal, L. 1982. Technological effort in industrial development – an interpretative survey of recent research. In F. Stewart and J. James (eds), *The Economics of New Technology in Developing Countries*. London: Frances Pinter, pp. 105-37.

De Wulf, L. 1975. Fiscal incidence studies in developing countries: survey and critique. *IMF Staff Papers*, 22, 61-131.

Dixit, A. K. 1973. Models of dual economies. In J. A. Mirrlees and N. H. Stern (eds), *Models of Economic Growth*. London: Macmillan, pp. 325-57.

Donges, J. B. 1976. A comparative survey of industrialization policies in fifteen semi-industrial countries. *Weltwitschaftliches Archiv*, 112, 626-59.

Dornbusch, R. 1983. Stabilization policies in developing countries: what have we learned? *World Development*, 11, 701-8.

Fields, G. S. 1980. Education and income distribution in developing countries: a review of literature. In T. King (ed.), *Education and Income*. World Bank Staff Working Paper No. 402. Washington, DC: World Bank, pp. 231-315.

Fransman, M. 1985. Conceptualizing technical change in the Third World in the 1980s: An interpretative survey. *Journal of Development Studies*, 21, 572-652.

Gaude, J. 1975. Capital-labour substitution possibilities: a review of empirical evidence. In A. S. Bhalla (ed.), *Technology and Employment in Industry*. Geneva: ILO, pp. 41-64.

Glick, R. and Kharas, H. J. 1986. The costs and benefits of foreign borrowing: a survey of multi-period models. *Journal of Development Studies*, 22, 279-99.

Hammer, J. S. 1986. Population growth and savings in LDCs: a survey article. *World Development*, 14, 579-92.

James, J. 1978. Growth, technology and the environment in less developed countries: a survey. *World Development*, 6, 937-65.

Johnston, B. F. 1970. Agriculture and structural transformation in developing countries: a survey of research. *Journal of Economic Literature*, 8, 369-404.

Johnston, B. F. 1977. Food, health and population in development. *Journal of Economic Literature*, 15, 879-907.

Kanbur, R. and McIntosh, J. 1984. *Dual Economy Models: A Survey*. Paper presented to the ESRC Development Economics Study Group Annual Conference, University of Warwick.

Killick, T. 1981. Inflation in developing countries: an interpretative survey. *ODI Review*, 1, 1-17.

Krueger, A. O. 1983. *Alternative Trade Strategies and Employment, vol. 3: Synthesis and Conclusions*. Chicago: Chicago University Press, for NBER.

Kuznets, S. 1973. Modern economic growth: findings and reflections. *American Economic Review*, 63, 247-58.

Lal, D. 1974. *Methods of Project Analysis: A Review*. Baltimore: Johns Hopkins University Press.

Lal, D. 1976. Distribution and development: a review article. *World Development*, 4, 713-24.

Lall, S. 1974. Less developed countries and private foreign direct investment. A review article. *World Development*, 2, 43–8.

Lall, S. 1978. Transnationals, domestic enterprises and industrial structure in host LDCs: a survey. *Oxford Economic Papers*, 30, 217–48.

Lecaillon, J., Paukert, F., Morrison, C. and Germidis, C. 1983. *Income Distribution and Economic Development: an Analytical Survey*. Geneva: ILO.

Leeson, P. F. 1979. The Lewis model and development theory. *The Manchester School*, 47, 196–200.

Machlup, F. 1977. *A History of Thought on Economic Integration*. New York: Columbia University Press.

Manne, A. S. 1974. Multi-sector models for development planning: a survey. *Journal of Development Economics*, 1, 43–69.

Maxwell, S. J. and Singer, H. W. 1979. Food-aid to developing countries: a survey. *World Development*, 7, 225–47.

Maynard, G. and Bird, G. 1975. International monetary issues and the developing countries: a survey. *World Development*, 3, 609–31.

McDonald, D. C. 1982. Debt capacity and developing country borrowing: a survey of the literature. *IMF Staff Papers*, 29, 603–46.

Mikesell, R. and Zinser, J. 1973. The nature of the savings function in developing countries: a survey of the theoretical and empirical literature. *Journal of Economic Literature*, 11, 1–26.

Morawetz, D. 1974. Employment implications of industrialization in developing countries: a survey. *Economic Journal*, 84, 491–552.

Morawetz, D. 1977. *Twenty-Five Years of Economic Development: 1950–1975*. Washington, DC: World Bank.

Paukert, F. 1973. Income distribution at different levels of development: a survey of evidence. *International Labour Review*, 108, 97–125.

Reynolds, L. G. 1983. The spread of economic growth to the Third World: 1850–1980. *Journal of Economic Literature*, 21, 941–80.

Roemer, M. 1979. Resource-based industrialization in developing countries: a survey. *Journal of Development Economics*, 6, 163–202.

Ruttan, V. W. 1977. The green revolution: seven generalizations. *International Development Review*, 19, 16–23.

Sahota, G. S. 1978. Theories of personal income distribution: a survey. *Journal of Economic Literature*, 16, 1–55.

Schmitz, H. 1982. Growth constraints on small scale manufacturing in developing countries: a critical review. *World Development*, 10, 429–50.

Seers, D. (ed.) 1981. *Dependency Theory: A Critical Reassessment*. London: Frances Pinter.

Sethuraman, S. V. 1980. *The Urban Informal Sector in Developing Countries: Employment, Poverty and Environment*. Geneva: ILO.

Sharif, M. 1986. The concept and measurement of subsistence: a survey of the literature. *World Development*, 14, 555–78.

Smith, S. and Toye, J. F. J. 1979. Three stories about trade and poor countries. *Journal of Development Studies*, 15, 1–18.

Snyder, D. W. 1974. Econometric studies of household saving behaviour in developing countries: a survey. *Journal of Development Studies*, 10, 139–53.

Spraos, J. 1980. The statistical debate on the net barter terms of trade between primary commodities and manufactures. *Economic Journal*, 90, 107–28.

Squire, L. 1981. *Employment Policy in Developing Countries: a survey of Issues and Evidence*. New York: Oxford University Press, for World Bank.

Thirlwall, A. P. 1971. The valuation of labour in surplus labour economies. *Scottish Journal of Political Economy*, 18, 299–314.

Todaro, M. P. 1976. *Internal Migration in Developing Countries: a Review of Theory, Evidence, Methodology and Research Priorities*. Geneva: ILO.

Turnham, D. 1971. *The Employment Problem in Less Developed Countries: a Review of Evidence*. Paris: OECD.

Udall, A. and Sinclair, S. 1982. The 'luxury unemployment' hypothesis: a review of recent evidence. *World Development*, 10, 49–62.

Yap, L. Y. L. 1977. The attraction of the cities: a review of the migration literature. *Journal of Development Economics*, 4, 239–64.

White, L. J. 1978. The evidence on appropriate factor proportions for manufacturing in less developed countries: a survey. *Economic Development and Cultural Change*, 27, 27–59.

Index

Note: The following abbreviations are used in the index: CBA cost–benefit analysis, DRC domestic resource cost, EOI export-oriented industrialization, EP effective protection, IC industrialized country, ISI import-substituting industrialization, LDC less developed country, MNE multinational enterprise, NIC newly industrializing country.

Index

Index compiled by Meg Davies